OPTICAL NETWORK COMMUNICATIONS

AN ENGINEER'S PERSPECTIVE

By Sanjay Yadav

PRACTICAL INSIGHTS FOR YOUR
PROFESSIONAL GROWTH

This book is dedicated to ***You*** *(the readers) with deep gratitude to my parents, my wife , my siblings and to all the people who have helped me at any point of time.*

Introduction

Welcome to "Optical Network Communications: An Engineer's Perspective." There are many books available on optical fiber communication, but most are written by professors, scientists, or academics. These books provide deep theoretical knowledge, lab results, and insights that have revolutionized the industry. If you seek in-depth theoretical understanding, I recommend reading those works, many of which I've studied myself to enhance my career.

However, there are relatively few books that focus on the practical aspects of optical fiber communication. These aspects include the information needed to run, operate, maintain, innovate, and develop new technologies for telecom networks, data centers, and submarine communications. I have added some useful tables, graphs, and charts that can help readers understand the concepts. These were created using available tools and may have some deviations from ideal images. Certain information may look repetitive but has been added to provide a seamless experience to the reader.

This book aims to fill that gap. I believe in sharing practical knowledge that can benefit both new and experienced professionals. Whether you are considering a career in optical fiber communication, looking to enhance your skills, or wanting to explore different roles in the industry, this book is for you.

Through my website, and professional connections, I have interacted with many engineers who need guidance. I remember feeling the same way early in my career. I've been fortunate to work with talented engineers and managers who openly shared their knowledge. My proactive approach to learning has helped me gain both theoretical and practical expertise.

In this book, I share the most valuable insights from my industry experience. My goal is to provide practical knowledge, industry insights, and exercises to help you grow professionally and innovate. I hope this book inspires and empowers you to make meaningful contributions to the field of optical fiber communication.
Wishing you great success and happy reading!

Regards,
Sanjay Yadav
Sydney, Australia
www.mapyourtech.com

This page is intentionally left blank

Table of Content

Part I

Fundamentals

Chapter 1

Overview of Optical Networks

Chapter 1
Overview of Optical Networks

"Light brings us the news of the Universe." - C.V. Raman

Optical network communications have become a cornerstone of modern telecommunication systems, enabling high-speed data transfer over vast distances with minimal loss. These networks leverage the properties of light, transmitted through optical fibers, to carry information. This chapter provides a comprehensive introduction to the principles, importance, and applications of optical network communications.

Basic Principles of Optical Communication

Optical communication involves transmitting data as light pulses through optical fibers. Key principles include:

- **Light Propagation**: Light travels through the core of the optical fiber by total internal reflection.
- **Modulation**: Data is encoded onto light waves using various modulation techniques.
- **Multiplexing**: Multiple data streams are combined onto a single optical fiber using techniques like Wavelength Division Multiplexing (WDM). For example, modern WDM systems can support up to 96 channels, each carrying 100 Gbps.
- **Amplification**: Optical signals are amplified using devices like Erbium-Doped Fiber Amplifiers (EDFAs) to maintain signal strength over long distances.
- **Detection**: At the receiving end, light signals are converted back into electrical signals for further processing.

Advantages of Optical Networks

Optical networks offer several advantages over traditional copper-based networks, including:

- **High Bandwidth**: Optical fibers can carry much more data than copper cables. For instance, a single mode fiber can support up to 100 Tbps.

- **Low Latency**: Light travels faster than electrical signals, resulting in lower latency.
- **Long Distance**: Optical signals can travel long distances without significant loss, thanks to low-loss fibers and amplifiers. Modern systems can transmit signals over distances exceeding 1000 kilometers without significant degradation.
- **Interference Immunity**: Optical fibers are immune to electromagnetic interference, ensuring signal integrity.
- **Scalability**: Optical networks can be easily scaled by adding more wavelengths or fibers.

Applications of Optical Networks

1. Telecommunications

- **Current Infrastructure**: Major telecom providers have deployed over 500,000 kilometers of fiber optic cables globally as of 2024
- **Case Study**: Verizon's 2023 fiber expansion project connected over 400,000 additional homes, supporting both 5G backhaul and FTTH services
- **Impact**: Enables speeds up to 100 Gbps for residential users and 400 Gbps for business customers

2. Internet Infrastructure

- **Global Traffic**: Internet traffic reached 7.4 zettabytes per year in 2023, projected to exceed 12 zettabytes by 2025
- **Case Study**: Google's "Dunant" subsea cable (2023) achieves 250 Tbps capacity using space-division multiplexing
- **Cloud Computing**: Major providers (AWS, Azure, Google Cloud) utilize dense optical networks supporting sub-millisecond latency

3. Enterprise Networks

- **Data Center Interconnect**: Modern data centers utilize 400G and 800G optical connections
- **Case Study**: Meta's 2024 data center deployment using co-packaged optics for improved energy efficiency
- **Enterprise Applications**: 78% of Fortune 500 companies now use optical networks for their core infrastructure

4. Healthcare

- **Market Growth**: Telemedicine market reached $70 billion in 2023
- **Case Study**: Mayo Clinic's implementation of 100G optical networks for real-time surgical video streaming.
- **Applications**: Remote surgery, medical imaging transfer (8K resolution), and real-time patient monitoring.

5. Education

- **Research Networks**: Internet2 network upgraded to 400G in 2023
- **Case Study**: CERN's optical network handling 1 petabyte per day of LHC data
- **Distance Learning**: Supporting 4K/8K video streams for multiple simultaneous virtual classrooms

Historical Development

1840s – Early Theories of Light Transmission

- **1841**: **Jean-Daniel Colladon**, a Swiss physicist, and **Jacques Babinet** demonstrated light guiding through a water stream, showing how light could be directed along a transparent medium, marking the early understanding of guided light transmission.
- **1854**: British physicist **John Tyndall** demonstrated **total internal reflection**, the principle behind fiber optics, by showing that light could be guided through a stream of water. His work was one of the earliest demonstrations of guiding light along a curved path.

1920s – Contributions of C.V. Raman

- **1928**: Indian physicist **Sir Chandrasekhara Venkata Raman (C.V. Raman)** discovered the **Raman Effect**, which describes how light scatters when it passes through different media. While not directly related to optical fibers at the time, this discovery later became important for **Raman amplification** in optical fibers, which is used to boost light signals over long distances. For this groundbreaking work, Raman received the **Nobel Prize in Physics in 1930**, marking a significant contribution to the study of light and its interaction with matter.

1950s – The Birth of Fiber Optics and Narendra Kapany

- **1953**: Indian-born physicist **Narendra Singh Kapany**, often referred to as the **Father of Fiber Optics**, conducted experiments demonstrating that light could be transmitted through bent glass fibers. His research showed that light could travel through a thin fiber, even when the fiber was curved or twisted. In **1954**, Kapany coined the term "**fiber optics**" to describe this technology in a scientific paper published in *Nature*. This discovery laid the groundwork for modern optical fiber communication.
- **1954**: **Narendra Kapany** and his colleague **Harold Hopkins** developed the first **optical fiber bundle**, successfully transmitting images using a coherent array of fibers. This marked a major step toward the development of modern optical fiber systems used in telecommunications and medical imaging.

1960s – Development of Lasers and Theoretical Foundation of Fiber Optics

- **1960**: The invention of the **laser** by **Theodore Maiman** was a monumental breakthrough, providing a coherent, monochromatic light source crucial for optical fiber communication. Lasers would later become the primary light sources for fiber-optic communication systems.
- **1966**: **Charles K. Kao**, often regarded as the **Father of Fiber Optic Communications**, and his colleague **George Hockham** at **Standard Telecommunication Laboratories** in the UK, proposed that optical fibers could be used for long-distance communication if the attenuation (signal loss) could be reduced. Kao's work demonstrated that high-purity glass fibers could allow light signals to travel long distances with minimal loss, making fiber-optic communication practical. This was a pivotal moment in optical communications. Kao's contributions earned him the **Nobel Prize in Physics** in 2009.
- **1966**: **Narendra Kapany** further expanded on his earlier work and contributed extensively to the development of **fiber-optic bundles** for various applications, including medical endoscopy and imaging, in addition to his contributions to communication technology.

1970 – Breakthrough in Low-Loss Optical Fibers

- **1970**: A significant breakthrough came when **Corning Glass Works** (now Corning Incorporated) developed the first practical **low-loss optical fiber**. Researchers **Robert Maurer**, **Donald Keck**, and **Peter Schultz** successfully produced silica-based fibers with a signal attenuation of less than 20 dB/km, a requirement set by **Charles K. Kao** for fiber communication to be feasible. Their fiber, which had an attenuation of 16 dB/km, allowed optical signals to travel long distances without significant signal degradation.

1977 – First Commercial Fiber-Optic Communication Systems

- **1977**: The first commercial fiber-optic communication system was installed by **General Telephone and Electronics (GTE)** in Chicago and by **Bell Labs** in Atlanta. These early systems operated at a wavelength of 0.8 μm (micrometers) and achieved data rates of up to 45 Mbps (megabits per second) over distances of about 10 kilometers.

1980s – Advancements in Optical Fiber Technology

- **1980**: **Single-mode fibers** were developed, allowing for higher bandwidth and lower attenuation. These fibers became the standard for long-distance, high-capacity telecommunications.
- **1987**: The invention of the **Erbium-Doped Fiber Amplifier (EDFA)** by researchers at **Bell Labs** was a major milestone. The EDFA could amplify optical signals directly without converting them into electrical signals, allowing for long-distance communication without signal degradation. This enabled optical fibers to transmit data over thousands of kilometers with minimal loss, revolutionizing long-haul communication networks.
- **Late 1980s**: The development of **Dense Wavelength Division Multiplexing (DWDM)** allowed for multiple wavelengths (or channels) to be transmitted simultaneously over a single optical fiber, significantly increasing the bandwidth capacity of fiber-optic communication systems.

1990s – Global Expansion and Undersea Cables

- **1990s**: Optical fiber networks expanded globally during the **dot-com boom**, with significant investments in laying fiber-optic cables both terrestrially and under the sea. Undersea cables, such as **TAT-8**, the first transatlantic fiber-optic cable, and **FLAG (Fiber-optic Link Around the Globe)**, revolutionized global telecommunications, enabling high-speed, high-capacity international communication.

- **1997**: The **TAT-12/13** fiber-optic cable was deployed, carrying data at rates up to 5 Gbps (gigabits per second). These advancements made the global internet and telecommunications infrastructure faster and more reliable.

2000s – Broadband Expansion and FTTH (Fiber to the Home)

- **2000s**: The proliferation of high-speed internet and video streaming services created an increased demand for **Fiber-to-the-Home (FTTH)** deployments. Optical fibers were now being installed directly into homes, enabling consumers to access ultra-fast internet and broadband services.
- **2005**: The introduction of **Gigabit Passive Optical Networks (GPON)** and **Ethernet Passive Optical Networks (EPON)** enabled the delivery of gigabit-speed internet to consumers, further enhancing FTTH technology.

2010s – Data Centers, Cloud Computing, and 5G

- **2010s**: The rise of **cloud computing** and **data centers** drove the need for ultra-fast, low-latency communication between data centers, both within a facility and across regions. Optical fiber became the backbone of cloud infrastructure, connecting data centers and enabling real-time data processing.
- **2010s**: With the development of **5G technology**, optical fibers became crucial for connecting 5G base stations (cell towers) to the network core. The low latency and high capacity of optical fibers enabled the ultra-fast, high-bandwidth communication required for 5G applications, such as the Internet of Things (IoT) and autonomous vehicles.
- **2020s**: Researchers are now working on next-generation optical fiber technologies such as **space-division multiplexing** (SDM), which involves using multiple spatial channels within the same fiber to increase capacity.

- Hollow-core fibers are also being developed, which can carry light signals with less latency and signal degradation, making them ideal for real-time applications like financial trading and remote surgery.
- Quantum communication is another frontier for optical fiber technology. Using quantum states of light, optical fibers may soon enable quantum cryptography and quantum teleportation, offering unprecedented levels of security and communication speed.
- 2020: 800G systems commercially available
- 2022: Demonstration of 1.2 Tbps transmission
- 2023: Co-packaged optics deployment begins and practical fiber capacity reached ~80Tbps
- 2024: Research pushing toward 1.6T per wavelength
- 2025 Future: Research pushing toward 2.4/3.2 T per wavelength

The future of optical network communications looks promising, with ongoing research and development aimed at overcoming current limitations and expanding capabilities. Emerging technologies, such as photonic integrated circuits and quantum communication, hold the potential to revolutionize the field. For instance, the global optical networking market is projected to reach $37.7 billion by 2027, driven by advancements in technology and increasing data demands.

Challenges and Limitations

Despite their advantages, optical networks face certain challenges:

- **Cost**: High initial deployment costs due to the expense of optical fibers and related equipment. For example, the cost of deploying fiber optic cables in urban areas can exceed $10,000 per mile.
- **Fragility**: Optical fibers are more fragile than copper cables, requiring careful handling and installation.
- **Complexity**: Designing and maintaining optical networks requires specialized knowledge and skills.

Major Companies in Optical Network Evolution

The development of optical fiber communication and the evolution of optical networks have been driven by numerous companies that specialize in various aspects of the technology, from manufacturing optical fibers to developing advanced networking equipment and solutions. Below is a comprehensive list of major companies that have significantly contributed to the evolution of optical networks and optical technologies:

1. Corning Incorporated

- **Key Contribution**: Corning developed the first practical **low-loss optical fiber** in 1970, a breakthrough that made long-distance optical communication feasible. Today, Corning remains a global leader in the manufacture of optical fiber and cable.
- **Specialization**: Optical fibers, photonic components, fiber optic cable solutions.
- **Notable Innovations:**
    - Ultra-low-loss fibers.
    - Bend-insensitive fibers.
    - Ribbon cable designs for high-density data centers.

2. Ciena Corporation

- **Key Contribution**: Ciena is a pioneer in the development of **Dense Wavelength Division Multiplexing (DWDM)** technology, which significantly increased the bandwidth capacity of optical networks.
- **Specialization**: Optical networking equipment, SDN (Software-Defined Networking), coherent optics, and automation platforms.
- **Notable Innovations:**
    - Coherent optical technology.
    - Optical transport solutions for submarine networks.
    - Blue Planet automation platform.

3. Nokia (Formerly Alcatel-Lucent)

- **Key Contribution**: Nokia, through its acquisition of **Alcatel-Lucent**, became one of the key players in **optical transmission systems**, providing comprehensive optical networking solutions for both backbone and metro networks.
- **Specialization**: Optical networking hardware, IP routing, mobile networking, and broadband solutions.
- **Notable Innovations:**
    - Photonic Service Engines (PSE) for high-speed data transmission.
    - Submarine cable systems.
    - GPON (Gigabit Passive Optical Networks) for FTTH (Fiber-to-the-Home).

4. Huawei Technologies

- **Key Contribution**: Huawei has been a leading provider of **optical transport networks (OTN)** and passive optical network (PON) solutions globally, helping telecom companies build high-speed broadband networks.

- **Specialization**: Optical networking, SDN/NFV, GPON, DWDM/OTN solutions.
- **Notable Innovations:**
    - Optical line terminals (OLTs) for broadband networks.
    - DWDM systems for high-capacity data transmission.
    - Integrated OTNs for telecom carriers.

5. Cisco Systems

- **Key Contribution**: Cisco has played a major role in **IP over DWDM (IPoDWDM)** and packet-optical transport technologies. Its solutions integrate IP routing with optical transport to deliver scalable, high-performance networks.
- **Specialization**: Optical routers, switches, coherent optics, and networking systems.
- **Notable Innovations:**
    - Packet-optical transport solutions.
    - Converged SDN and optical networking platforms.
    - DWDM optical transceivers and interfaces.

6. Juniper Networks

- **Key Contribution**: Juniper provides **packet-optical convergence** solutions that integrate IP, MPLS, and optical networks. Their innovations help service providers scale and automate network infrastructure.
- **Specialization**: Routers, coherent optics, and SDN solutions.
- **Notable Innovations:**
    - High-performance optical networking platforms.
    - MX Series routers with integrated optical transport.

7. Fujitsu Network Communications

- **Key Contribution**: Fujitsu is a leader in **optical transport networks (OTN)**, particularly in providing equipment for metro and long-haul networks. They focus on high-capacity, scalable optical solutions.
- **Specialization**: Optical networking systems, packet-optical transport, and coherent optical technologies.
- **Notable Innovations:**
    - 1FINITY series of open optical transport solutions.
    - Advanced OTN switching for dynamic optical networks.

8. ADVA Optical Networking

- **Key Contribution**: ADVA specializes in developing **innovative packet-optical transport** solutions for data centers, enterprises, and service providers. They focus on scalability, high capacity, and low latency.
- **Specialization**: Optical transport, timing synchronization, Ethernet services.
- **Notable Innovations:**
    - FSP 3000 CloudConnect platform.
    - Coherent optical transport for metro and long-haul networks.

9. Infinera Corporation

- **Key Contribution**: Infinera is known for pioneering **digital optical networks** and developing **photonic integrated circuits (PICs)**, which are crucial for scaling optical network capacity.
- **Specialization**: Optical transport solutions, coherent optics, and long-haul networks.
- **Notable Innovations:**
    - Infinite Capacity Engine (ICE) for terabit-scale networking.
    - Photonic integrated circuits for DWDM systems.
    - Submarine optical networking solutions.

10. NEC Corporation

- **Key Contribution**: NEC provides **submarine and terrestrial optical networking solutions** with a strong focus on high-performance DWDM systems for long-haul data transmission.
- **Specialization**: Optical networking, submarine cables, and SDN solutions.
- **Notable Innovations:**
    - Advanced submarine cable systems.
    - Large-capacity optical cross-connect (OXC) systems.

11. Lumentum (Formerly JDS Uniphase)

- **Key Contribution**: Lumentum is a key supplier of **optical transceivers, amplifiers**, and **photonic components** used in high-capacity optical networks.
- **Specialization**: Optical transceivers, photonic components, coherent optical modules.
- **Notable Innovations:**
    - Tunable transceivers for DWDM systems.
    - High-power erbium-doped fiber amplifiers (EDFAs).

12. ZTE Corporation

$$n_1 \cdot \sin(\theta_1) = n_2 \cdot \sin(\theta_2)$$

- **Key Contribution**: ZTE offers **optical networking** solutions across multiple areas, including DWDM, OTN, and passive optical networks (PON), especially in emerging markets.
- **Specialization**: Optical networking equipment, SDN/NFV, GPON/EPON.
- Notable Innovations:
    - 5G optical transport solutions.
    - Integrated packet-optical platforms for telecom operators.

13. Prysmian Group

- **Key Contribution**: Prysmian is one of the world's largest manufacturers of **optical fiber** and **cable solutions**, playing a crucial role in the deployment of fiber-optic networks globally.
- **Specialization**: Optical fibers, fiber optic cables, submarine cables.
- **Notable Innovations:**
    - Bend-insensitive fibers for high-density installations.
    - Fiber optic cables for harsh environments, including submarine cables.

14. Sumitomo Electric Industries

- **Key Contribution**: Sumitomo is a leading manufacturer of **optical fiber** and **optical fusion splicing equipment**. Their innovations have contributed to more efficient fiber installation and maintenance.
- **Specialization**: Optical fibers, fiber fusion splicers, photonics products.
- **Notable Innovations:**
    - World-class fusion splicers for optical network installations.
    - High-performance optical fibers for telecommunications.

15. OFS (Formerly Lucent Technologies)

- **Key Contribution**: OFS is a pioneer in optical fiber technology, providing high-quality optical fiber and cable solutions that are widely used in telecommunications and data networks.
- **Specialization**: Optical fibers, fiber optic cables, fusion splicing solutions.
- **Notable Innovations:**
    - Low-loss, bend-optimized optical fibers.

    - Specialty fibers for high-density data centers and long-haul networks.

16. Viavi Solutions (Formerly JDSU)

- **Key Contribution**: Viavi Solutions provides **test and measurement equipment** for optical networks. Their tools are widely used by network operators to ensure the performance and reliability of optical infrastructure.
- **Specialization**: Optical test solutions, network performance monitoring.
- **Notable Innovations:**
    - Network test and validation tools for DWDM and coherent systems.
    - Optical time-domain reflectometers (OTDRs).

17. Tejas Networks

- **Key Contribution**: Tejas Networks offers advanced **optical transmission** and **access solutions** tailored to telecom operators, focusing on scalable network architecture.
- **Specialization**: Optical transport, OTN, SDH, and packet-optical solutions.
- **Notable Innovations:**
    - T1000 series for flexible optical transport.
    - Converged packet-optical platforms for telecom and enterprise networks.

18. Sterlite Technologies (STL)

- **Key Contribution**: STL is a global leader in developing and deploying **optical fiber cables** and **network solutions** for telecom and data center environments.
- **Specialization**: Optical fibers, fiber cables, and network design solutions.
- **Notable Innovations:**
    - High-density optical fiber cables.
    - End-to-end network management solutions.

19. ECI Telecom (Now Ribbon Communications)

- **Key Contribution**: ECI Telecom, now part of **Ribbon Communications**, has been a long-standing player in the **optical transport** market, offering packet-optical transport systems for service providers.
- **Specialization**: Packet-optical transport, OTN, and broadband solutions.

- **Notable Innovations:**
    - Apollo optical transport solutions for metro and long-haul networks.
    - Optical packet switching for carrier networks.

20. Ribbon Communications

- **Key Contribution**: Ribbon provides advanced optical networking solutions with a focus on integrating packet and optical networks for service providers and enterprises.
- **Specialization**: Optical transport, network analytics, packet-optical convergence.
- **Notable Innovations:**
    - Advanced DWDM platforms for metro and regional networks.
    - Optical analytics for network optimization.

Chapter 2

Optical Theory and Design

Chapter 2
Optical Theory and Design

"Light is the fastest thing in the universe, and fiber optics puts that speed to work." - Gerd Keiser

---

Optical communication systems rely on the principles of light propagation, fiber characteristics, and various design parameters to ensure efficient data transmission over long distances. In this chapter, we will explore the key aspects of optical theory and their role in the design of optical networks. This includes fundamental concepts such as light propagation, reflection, refraction, and more complex factors such as chromatic dispersion, optical nonlinearity, link budget calculations, and optical power balancing. We will also provide detailed explanations of the formulas used to design these systems and their importance in practical applications.

Fundamental Principles of Optics

Refraction and Reflection

Snell's Law: When light passes from one medium to another, its direction changes due to the difference in refractive indices. This phenomenon is described by Snell's Law:

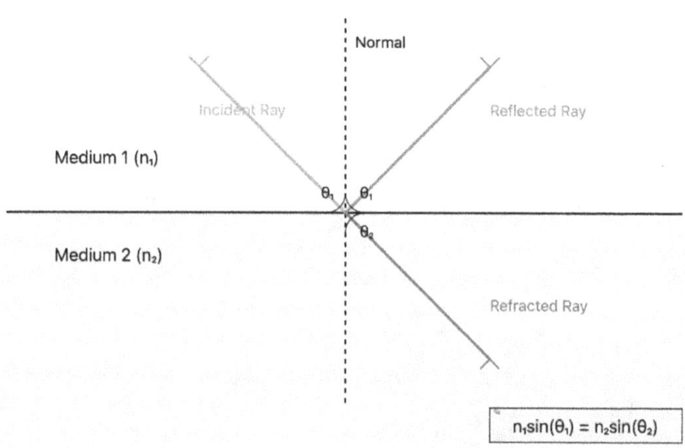

Where:

- n_1 and n_2 are the refractive indices of the two media,
- θ_1 is the angle of incidence,
- θ_2 is the angle of refraction.

This law governs the behaviour of light at the interface between two materials and is critical in understanding how light enters and propagates through optical fibers.

Importance: This principle helps in the design of optical fibers, where light must be guided within the core with minimal loss. The refractive index difference between the core and cladding ensures total internal reflection, allowing the signal to travel over long distances.

Total Internal Reflection (TIR)

Critical Angle: Total internal reflection occurs when light traveling within a medium (e.g., the core of an optical fiber) strikes the interface with a less dense medium (e.g., the cladding) at an angle greater than the critical angle. The critical angle is defined by:

Total Internal Reflection in Fiber

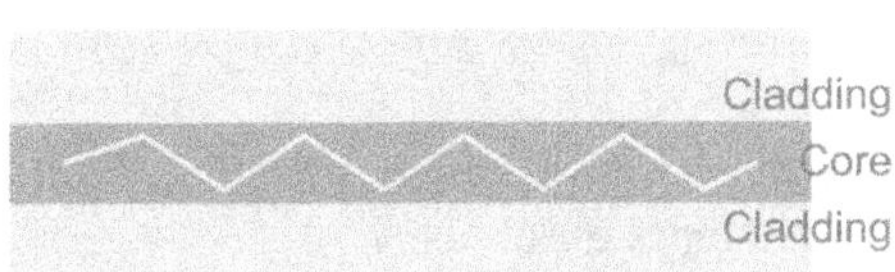

$$\theta_c = \sin^{-1}\left(\frac{n_2}{n_1}\right)$$

Where:

- θ_c is the critical angle,
- n_1 is the refractive index of the core,
- n_2 is the refractive index of the cladding.

Significance: This principle ensures that light remains confined within the core of the optical fiber, reducing transmission loss. The design of an optical fiber must consider the refractive indices of the core and cladding to maintain efficient light propagation through total internal reflection.

Diffraction

Diffraction occurs when light waves encounter obstacles or apertures comparable to their wavelength. The Huygens-Fresnel principle describes how each point on a wavefront acts as a source of secondary wavelets, which combine to form new wavefronts.

The diffraction limit determines the minimum spot size achievable in optical systems:

$$d = \frac{1.22\lambda}{NA}$$

where:

- d is the minimum spot diameter
- λ is the wavelength
- NA is the numerical aperture

This principle affects various aspects of optical system design:

- Minimum bend radius in fibers
- Coupling efficiency between components
- Core size limitations in single-mode fibers

Dispersion

Dispersion in optical fibers causes pulse spreading, limiting the data transmission rate. Three main types exist:

1. **Material Dispersion**: Results from wavelength-dependent refractive index variations:

$$D_m = -\frac{\lambda}{c} \cdot \frac{d^2 n}{d\lambda^2}$$

where:

- λ is wavelength
- c is speed of light
- n is refractive index

2. **Waveguide Dispersion**: Caused by fiber geometry:

$$D_w = -\frac{\Delta}{\lambda} \cdot \frac{d^2(Vb)}{dV^2}$$

where:

- Δ is relative refractive index difference
- V is normalized frequency

3. **Modal Dispersion** (multimode fibers only): Due to different path lengths:

$$\Delta t = \frac{L \cdot NA^2}{2cn_1}$$

where:

- L is fiber length
- NA is numerical aperture

Total chromatic dispersion is the sum of material and waveguide dispersion. Standard single-mode fiber at 1550nm typically exhibits dispersion of 17 ps/(nm·km).

Attenuation (Losses in Optical Fiber)

Definition: Attenuation refers to the gradual reduction in the power of the optical signal as it propagates through the fiber. This loss is measured in decibels per kilometer (dB/km) and is caused by factors such as absorption, scattering, and bending losses.

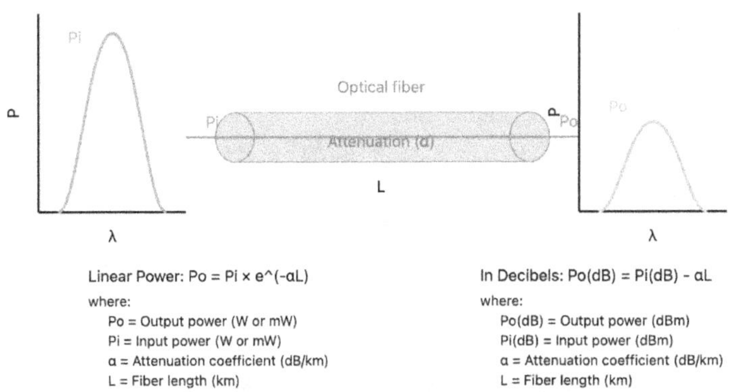

Major sources of Attenuation:

1. Rayleigh scattering (proportional to λ^{-4})

2. Material absorption
3. Waveguide imperfections
4. Bending losses

Importance: When designing optical networks, engineers must account for attenuation to ensure that the optical signal reaches the receiver with sufficient power. This affects the placement of amplifiers or repeaters in long-haul networks.

Shannon's Limit

Shannon's channel capacity theorem defines the theoretical maximum data rate:

This fundamental limit drives development of advanced modulation schemes and coherent detection systems.

$$C = B \cdot \log_2(1 + \frac{S}{N})$$

where:

- C is channel capacity (bits/s)
- B is bandwidth (Hz)
- S/N is signal-to-noise ratio

e.g

Consider 100G DWDM System

Given parameters:

- Bandwidth per channel (B) = 50 GHz
- Signal to Noise Ratio (SNR) = 25 dB = 316.23 (linear)

Calculate maximum theoretical capacity:

$$C = (50 \times 10^9) \cdot \log_2(1 + 316.23)$$

$$C = (50 \times 10^9) \cdot \log_2(317.23)$$

$$C = (50 \times 10^9) \cdot 8.31$$

$$C \approx 415.5 \text{ Gbps}$$

This shows 400G per channel is achievable with advanced modulation formats if used.

For a coherent system:

- Dual Polarization (2×)

- Bandwidth = 75 GHz
- SNR = 20 dB = 100 (linear)

Theoretical capacity with dual polarization:

$$C = 2 \cdot (75 \times 10^9) \cdot \log_2(1 + 100)$$

$$C = 150 \times 10^9 \cdot 6.658$$

$$C \approx 998.7 \text{ Gbps}$$

Practical Implementation:

- Actual achievable rate ≈ 70-80% of Shannon limit
- Using 64-QAM modulation: 6 bits/symbol
- Forward Error Correction (FEC) overhead ≈ 20%
- Practical data rate ≈ 800 Gbps

> **Spectral Efficiency:**
>
> $$\eta = \frac{C}{B} = \log_2(1 + \frac{S}{N}) \text{ bits/s/Hz}$$
>
> For the above example:
>
> $$\eta = \frac{998.7 \times 10^9}{75 \times 10^9} \approx 13.32 \text{ bits/s/Hz}$$

Key Optical Components

Optical Fibers

The optical fiber serves as the essential link between the transmitter and receiver, comprising three primary components:

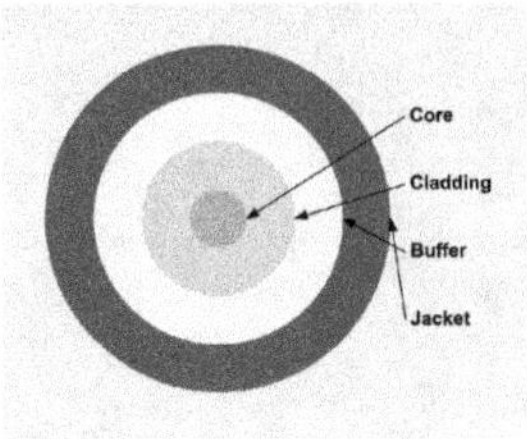

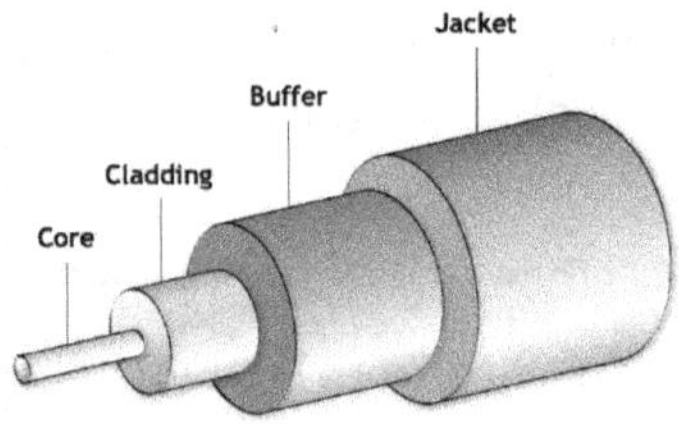

1. **Core**: The central region of the fiber where light signals are transmitted and it glass.
2. **Cladding**: A surrounding layer made of glass with a refractive index different from that of the core. This ensures light remains confined within the core through total internal reflection.
3. **Coating (or Buffer)**: A protective layer, typically made of plastic, applied directly to the fiber to provide strength and safeguard it from physical damage.

Encasing the fiber is the **jacket** or **cable sheath**, an outer protective covering that shields the optical fiber cable from external environmental and mechanical stresses.

Optical fibers consist of a core surrounded by cladding with lower refractive index. Two main types exist:

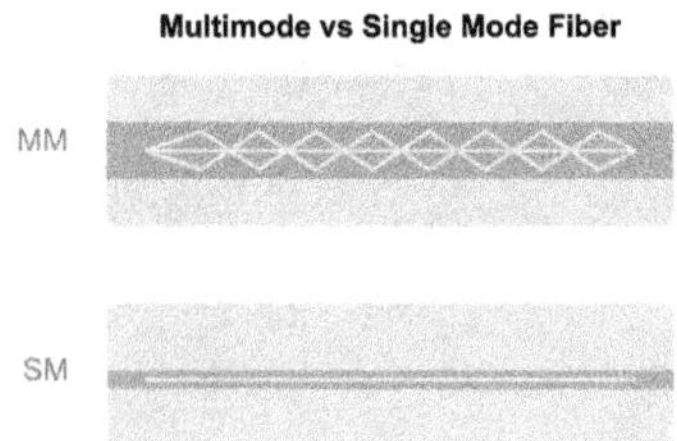

Single-mode Fiber:

- Core diameter: 8-10 μm
- One propagation mode
- Higher bandwidth, longer distance
- Used in long-haul communications

Multimode Fiber:

- Core diameter: 50-62.5 μm

- Multiple propagation modes
- Lower cost, shorter distance
- Used in local networks

Key parameters:

Numerical Aperture:

$$NA = \sqrt{n_1^2 - n_2^2}$$

V-number:

$$V = \frac{2\pi a}{\lambda} \cdot NA$$

where a is core radius

Lasers

Semiconductor lasers provide coherent light sources for optical communications. Key types:

1. **Fabry-Perot Lasers:**
    - Multiple longitudinal modes
    - Simpler design
    - Used in short-distance links
2. **Distributed Feedback (DFB) Lasers:**
    - Single longitudinal mode
    - Narrow linewidth
    - Essential for high-speed, long-distance transmission

Important parameters:

- Threshold current
- Slope efficiency
- Spectral width
- Modulation bandwidth
- Relative intensity noise (RIN)

Photodetectors

Photodetectors convert optical signals to electrical current. Common types:

1. PIN Photodiodes:

- Simple structure
- Linear response
- Lower sensitivity

2. Avalanche Photodiodes (APD):

- Internal gain mechanism
- Higher sensitivity
- More complex biasing

Important parameters:

- Responsivity (A/W)
- Quantum efficiency
- Dark current
- Bandwidth
- Noise equivalent power (NEP)

Splitters and Couplers

These components distribute optical power between multiple paths. Types include:

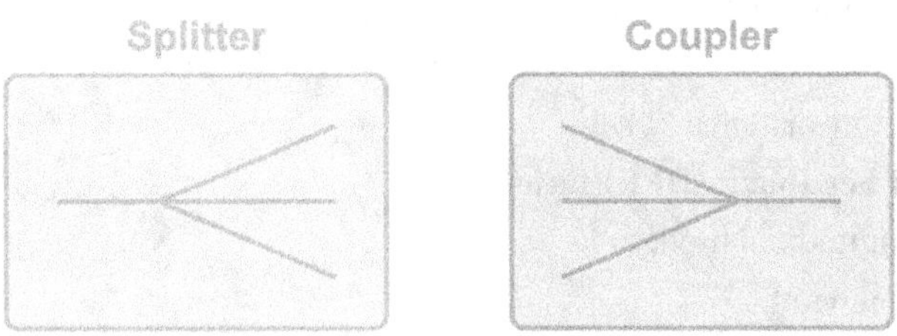

1. **Y-Branch Splitters:**
   - Fixed splitting ratio
   - Low return loss
   - Simple structure
2. **Directional Couplers:**
   - Variable coupling ratio
   - Wavelength dependent
   - Used in WDM systems

Important parameters:

- Insertion loss

- Splitting ratio
- Directivity
- Return loss
- Wavelength dependence

Isolators and Connectors

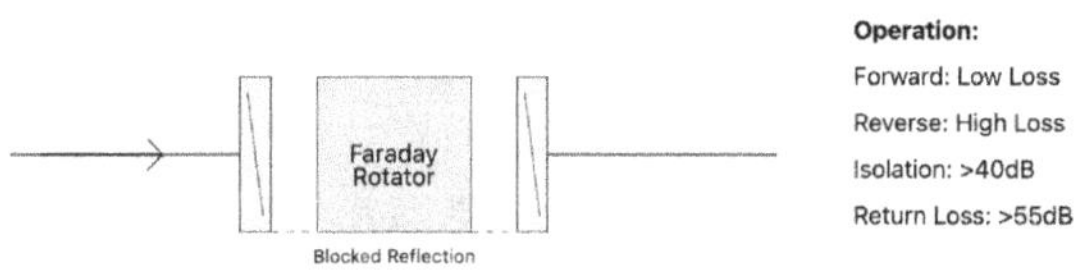

Isolators prevent reflected light from affecting sources:

- Based on Faraday rotation
- Typical isolation >40 dB
- Essential for laser protection

Connectors provide detachable joints:

1. Physical Contact (PC):
   - Standard polish
   - Return loss ~40 dB
2. Angled Physical Contact (APC):
   - 8° angle polish
   - Return loss >60 dB

Important parameters:

- Insertion loss
- Return loss
- Repeatability
- Temperature stability
- Mechanical durability

Connector Performance Metrics:

- Return Loss (RL):

$$RL = -10\log_{10}(\frac{P_{reflected}}{P_{incident}})$$

- Insertion Loss (IL):

$$IL = -10\log_{10}(\frac{P_{out}}{P_{in}})$$

Typical Values:

- PC Connector: RL > 40 dB
- APC Connector: RL > 60 dB
- Typical IL: 0.2-0.5 dB
- Isolator: >40 dB isolation

Performance Comparison

Component	Insertion Loss	Return Loss	Key Parameters	Applications
Isolator	0.3-0.6 dB	>55 dB	- Isolation >40 dB - PDL <0.1 dB	- Laser protection - Amplifier stability - Reflection suppression
Coupler	3-3.5 dB	>50 dB	- Coupling ratio - Directivity >55 dB	- Power monitoring - Signal splitting - Bidirectional transmission
Splitter	3n dB	>55 dB	- Split ratio - Uniformity <0.5 dB	- PON networks - Signal distribution - Test access points
Combiner	≥3n dB	>50 dB	- Channel spacing - Crosstalk <-50 dB	- DWDM systems - PON upstream - Signal aggregation

Chapter 3

Types of Optical Fibers and Modules

Chapter 3
Types of Optical Fibers and Modules

"The future of communication lies in a thread of glass thinner than a human hair." - Narinder Singh Kapany

---

Optical fibers are the backbone of modern communication networks, transmitting data over long distances with minimal loss. This chapter explores the different types of optical fibers, their characteristics, and guidelines on when to use each type in various network applications, including the latest advancements in fiber technology.

Types of Optical Fibers

Single-Mode Fiber (SMF)

- **Core Diameter**: Approximately 8-10 microns.
- **Wavelength**: Optimized for 1310 nm and 1550 nm.
- **Characteristics**:
  - Low attenuation and dispersion, making it suitable for long-distance transmission.
  - Supports higher bandwidth compared to multimode fibers.
- **Applications**: Long-haul networks, metropolitan area networks (MANs), data center interconnects (DCIs), and high-speed internet.
- **Example**: Single-mode fiber is commonly used in transcontinental and submarine cable systems to transmit data over thousands of kilometers with minimal signal degradation.

Multimode Fiber (MMF)

- **Core Diameter**: Typically 50 or 62.5 microns.
- **Wavelength**: Optimized for 850 nm and 1300 nm.
- **Characteristics**:
  - Higher attenuation and dispersion compared to single-mode fibers.
  - Suitable for shorter distances due to modal dispersion.

- **Types**: OM1, OM2, OM3, OM4, OM5.
    - **OM1**: 62.5/125 microns, supports up to 1 Gb/s over 300 meters.
    - **OM2**: 50/125 microns, supports up to 1 Gb/s over 600 meters.
    - **OM3**: 50/125 microns, laser-optimized, supports 10 Gb/s over 300 meters.
    - **OM4**: 50/125 microns, enhanced version of OM3, supports 10 Gb/s over 550 meters.
    - **OM5**: 50/125 microns, wideband multimode fiber, supports multiple wavelengths and higher data rates.
- **Applications**: Local area networks (LANs), data centers, and short-distance communication.
- **Example**: OM4 multimode fiber is widely used within data centers to connect servers, switches, and storage systems, supporting high-speed data transfer over short distances.

Plastic Optical Fiber (POF)

- **Core Diameter**: Typically 1 mm.
- **Characteristics**:
    - Easy to install and handle due to larger core diameter and flexibility.
    - Higher attenuation compared to glass optical fibers.
    - Limited to short distances and lower data rates.
- **Applications**: Home networking, consumer electronics, automotive applications.
- **Example**: POF is used in home entertainment systems to connect audio and video equipment, providing an easy and cost-effective solution for short-range communication.

Bend-Insensitive Fiber

- Characteristics:
    - Designed to maintain performance even when bent or twisted.
    - Reduced macro-bending losses, making it suitable for tight installation spaces.
- **Types**: Available in both single-mode and multimode variants.
- **Applications**: Data centers, office buildings, and FTTH (Fiber to the Home) deployments.
- **Example**: Bend-insensitive fiber is used in FTTH installations, where fibers need to be routed through tight spaces and around corners without compromising signal quality.

Low Water Peak Fiber

- Characteristics:
    - Minimized water absorption in the 1400 nm region, reducing attenuation.
    - Enhanced performance across a wider wavelength range.
- **Applications**: DWDM systems, where multiple wavelengths are transmitted over a single fiber.
- **Example**: Low water peak fiber is used in metropolitan and long-haul networks to support DWDM systems, enabling high-capacity data transmission across various wavelengths.

Armored Fiber

- Characteristics:
    - Enhanced protection against physical damage due to an outer protective layer.
    - Suitable for harsh environments and outdoor installations.
- **Applications**: Industrial environments, outdoor deployments, and areas with a high risk of physical damage.
- **Example**: Armored fiber is deployed in industrial settings and outdoor environments, providing robust protection against physical damage and ensuring reliable data transmission.

Hollow Core Fiber

- Characteristics:
    - Light travels through a hollow core, significantly reducing latency.
    - Lower non-linear effects and attenuation compared to traditional solid-core fibers.
- **Applications**: High-speed data transmission, long-haul networks, and latency-sensitive applications.
- **Example**: Hollow core fiber is used in financial trading networks where ultra-low latency is critical for high-frequency trading applications.

Pure Silica Core Fiber (PSCF)

- Characteristics:
    - Made entirely of silica, offering very low attenuation and high resistance to radiation.

- Ideal for harsh environments and long-distance transmission.

- **Applications**: Submarine cables, space applications, and high-reliability networks.
- **Example**: PSCF is used in submarine cable systems to provide high-capacity and reliable communication across oceanic distances.

Fiber Selection Criteria

Choosing the right fiber for a network requires balancing performance with cost. Fiber selection for optical communication networks depends on the following key factors:

1. Attenuation

- **Definition:** Attenuation refers to the loss of signal power over the length of the optical fiber.
- **Importance:** Lower attenuation allows signals to travel longer distances without needing amplification.
- **Typical Values:**
    - G.652 fibers: 0.18 dB/Km
    - G.654 fibers: 0.20 dB/Km
    - G.655 fibers: 0.35 dB/Km

2. Dispersion

- **Definition:** Dispersion refers to the spreading of the optical pulse as it travels through the fiber, causing different wavelength components to travel at different speeds.
- **Types**:
    - **Chromatic Dispersion (CD):** The wavelength-dependent delay that broadens pulses.
    - **Waveguide Dispersion:** The speed difference between light propagating in the fiber core and cladding.
- **Typical Values:**
    - G.652 fibers: 18 ps/nm-Km
    - G.654 fibers: 20 ps/nm-Km
    - G.655 fibers: 9 ps/nm-Km

3. Polarization Mode Dispersion (PMD)

- **Definition:** PMD occurs when light traveling in different polarization states moves at different velocities, causing pulse distortion.
- **Importance:** PMD can limit high-speed communication, making it essential to minimize.
- **Typical Values:**
    - G.652 fibers: 0.1 ps/√Km
    - G.654 and G.655 fibers: 0.2 ps/√Km

4. Effective Area (Aeff)

- **Definition:** The effective area of a fiber influences its capacity to carry power and handle nonlinear effects.
- **Importance:** A larger effective area minimizes nonlinear impairments, such as self-phase modulation (SPM).
- **Example**:
    - **G.654 fiber** has a larger core size, making it suitable for long-haul applications.

Effect of Fiber Parameters

Optical fiber parameters play a significant role in determining the performance and efficiency of communication networks. Here are the main parameters to consider:

1. Attenuation

- **Effect:** Higher attenuation means more signal loss per kilometer, which reduces the distance signals can travel without amplification. Attenuation can be caused by fiber impurities, absorption, and scattering.
- **Impact:** Networks with higher attenuation require more amplifiers, raising the cost and complexity of the system.

2. Dispersion

- **Chromatic Dispersion (CD):** Pulse broadening due to different wavelengths traveling at different speeds leads to inter-symbol interference (ISI), reducing the maximum achievable data rate.
- **Zero Dispersion Wavelength:** The wavelength at which chromatic dispersion is zero is typically around 1300 nm for single-mode fibers. Minimizing dispersion improves signal clarity, especially in high-capacity systems.

3. Polarization Mode Dispersion (PMD)

- **Effect:** PMD causes pulse distortion over long distances, making it critical to minimize in high-speed networks. High PMD can reduce the transmission capacity.
- **Solution:** Fibers with low PMD (like **G.652** and **G.655**) are typically chosen for long-distance and high-speed communication.

4. **Core Diameter and Mode Field Diameter (MFD)**
    - **MFD** refers to the distribution of light across the fiber core. A larger MFD improves coupling efficiency but may increase bending loss.
    - **Core Concentricity:** Core alignment affects splicing and signal loss. Misalignment can increase attenuation.
5. **Bending Loss**
    - **Micro-bending Loss:** Caused by small distortions in the fiber, increasing attenuation.
    - **Macro-bending Loss:** Larger bends in the fiber can cause significant signal loss, which is more prevalent in standard fibers compared to bend-insensitive fibers.
6. **Nonlinear Effects**

    In optical fibers, high power levels can induce **nonlinear effects**, which significantly affect system performance.

    Nonlinear Effects:

    - **Self-Phase Modulation (SPM):** Occurs when high-power signals change the refractive index of the fiber, altering the phase of the signal.
    - **Cross-Phase Modulation (XPM):** Arises in systems with multiple channels, where one channel's intensity affects the phase of another channel.
    - **Four-Wave Mixing (FWM):** A process in dense wavelength division multiplexing (DWDM) where three wavelengths combine to generate a new fourth wavelength, interfering with the original signals.

    Impact on System Performance:

    Nonlinear effects, such as FWM, can degrade system performance by creating noise and interference between channels. **G.654 fibers**, with their larger effective area, help minimize these effects, making them suitable for long-haul, high-capacity networks.

Fiber Selection Based on Application

Fiber optic technology is critical in modern communications, serving diverse applications across long-haul networks, data centers, and local area networks

(LANs). Each use case has distinct requirements for performance, bandwidth, and durability, necessitating specific fiber types and configurations.

Long-Haul Communication

Long-haul communication refers to the transmission of data over significant distances, often spanning hundreds or thousands of kilometers. This application is foundational for intercontinental and national networks, requiring fibers optimized for minimal signal degradation and high capacity.

Fiber Type:

Single-mode fiber is preferred for long-haul applications due to its minimal attenuation and high data-carrying capacity over long distances. Specific types like G.652, G.653, and G.655 are often employed, each offering unique properties in terms of dispersion and wavelength compatibility. Dispersion-shifted (G.653) and non-zero dispersion-shifted fibers (G.655) are particularly advantageous for Dense Wavelength Division Multiplexing (DWDM), which is essential for maximizing capacity in long-haul networks.

Key Characteristics:

- **Low Attenuation**: Essential for reducing signal loss over extensive distances, especially in the 1550 nm wavelength range where fiber has the lowest loss.
- **High Capacity through DWDM**: DWDM allows multiple wavelengths to transmit on a single fiber, significantly enhancing data throughput. This technique relies on precise wavelength control and low dispersion characteristics to prevent signal overlap and distortion.
- **Use of Optical Amplifiers**: Erbium-Doped Fiber Amplifiers (EDFAs) are strategically placed along the route to amplify signals, compensating for attenuation without requiring conversion to electrical signals. Amplifiers in the C-band (1530-1565 nm) and L-band (1565-1625 nm) support the high capacities demanded in long-haul networks.

Challenges and Solutions:

- **Dispersion Management**: Over long distances, chromatic dispersion can broaden light pulses, causing data errors. Dispersion compensation modules (DCMs) and advanced modulation techniques like coherent detection are employed to address this issue.
- **Non-linear Effects**: High-power signals and dense channel spacing in DWDM systems can lead to non-linear effects such as four-wave mixing and self-phase modulation. Fiber selection and proper system de-

sign, including power management and channel spacing, are crucial to mitigate these effects.

In long-haul systems, fibers are deployed in various physical forms, such as buried cables, ducts, and aerial installations, each requiring robust protection against environmental factors like temperature fluctuations, mechanical stress, and physical obstructions.

Data Centers

Data centers house vast amounts of critical data and require high-performance networks to support rapid data exchange between servers and storage systems. Fiber optics plays a crucial role in ensuring data integrity and high-speed connections within data centers.

Fiber Type:

Data centers typically use both single-mode and multimode fibers. However, multimode fibers like OM3 and OM4 are common within short-distance data center interconnects due to their high bandwidth over short ranges and cost efficiency.

Key Characteristics:

- **High Bandwidth**: To support high-speed data transfer (often 10 Gbps or higher), multimode fiber is preferred within a data center due to its capability to handle high data rates over short distances (up to 300 meters with OM4). For connections exceeding these ranges, single-mode fiber provides a scalable solution.
- **Low Latency**: Minimizing latency is essential in data centers to ensure fast data access and processing. Fiber optics inherently offers low latency compared to copper connections, making it suitable for high-performance computing and storage networks.
- **Compatibility with Modern Transceivers**: Fiber types in data centers must align with the transceivers used, such as SFP, QSFP, and CFP modules, which support Ethernet speeds up to 400 Gbps and beyond. Compatibility with these modules ensures efficient data transfer and minimal signal degradation.

Network Architecture and Design:

- **Structured Cabling**: Data centers use structured cabling with centralized or zone-based architectures to optimize the organization and management of fiber connections. Proper planning helps reduce clutter, enhance airflow, and simplify future upgrades.

- **Redundancy and Failover**: To maintain uninterrupted service, data centers incorporate redundant paths and automatic failover mechanisms. These networks are often designed with ring or mesh topologies, allowing alternate pathways for data transmission in case of link failure.

Data centers also benefit from innovations like optical circuit switches and advanced cabling techniques, allowing the seamless management of data flows across servers and network devices.

Metro Networks

Metro networks serve as intermediaries between long-haul backbones and access networks, typically spanning cities or regions. These networks focus on providing high-capacity connectivity with low latency for enterprise, residential, and mobile users.

Fiber Type:

Metro networks primarily use **single-mode fibers** like G.652.D or G.657, which offer low attenuation and good bending performance. G.657 fibers are especially suited for metro environments with frequent bends due to dense urban deployments.

Key Characteristics:

- **Medium Distance Optimization:** Metro networks require fibers that balance cost-effectiveness with excellent performance over distances of tens to hundreds of kilometers.
- **High Bandwidth and Scalability:** With increasing data demands from 5G, IoT, and cloud services, metro networks often rely on Dense Wavelength Division Multiplexing (DWDM) to maximize capacity.
- **Resilience and Redundancy:** Metro networks are critical for maintaining service continuity, necessitating fibers with robust physical properties and redundancy mechanisms.

Technologies and Enhancements:

- **DWDM and CWDM Support:** Metro networks commonly employ CWDM for cost-sensitive applications and DWDM for high-capacity demands, ensuring seamless connectivity between long-haul and access networks.

- **Advanced Modulation Formats:** Modulation techniques like QAM and coherent optics optimize data rates and spectrum efficiency for metro applications.
- **Low Bending Loss:** G.657 fibers are ideal for installations in urban conduits and tight spaces, where bending loss could otherwise degrade performance.

Challenges and Solutions:

- **Urban Deployment Constraints:** Metro fibers face challenges such as limited space, high interference potential, and physical damage risks. Armored cables and micro-duct solutions provide enhanced protection in these environments.
- **Latency and Congestion:** To reduce latency and manage congestion, traffic engineering techniques like optical switching and dynamic routing are employed.
- **Cost Efficiency:** Operators balance performance and affordability by adopting hybrid architectures with passive and active components.

Access Networks

Access networks connect the last mile to end-users, supporting residential, enterprise, and mobile broadband services. These networks prioritize flexibility, cost-effectiveness, and scalability to accommodate diverse customer needs.

Fiber Type:

Single-mode fibers (e.g., G.657.A and G.657.B) are widely used due to their low bending loss and suitability for Fiber-to-the-Home (FTTH) and Fiber-to-the-Building (FTTB) applications.

Key Characteristics:

- **Short Distance Focus:** Access networks typically span shorter distances (a few kilometers), requiring fibers optimized for minimal bending loss and easy installation.
- **High Density and Flexibility:** Deployment in densely populated areas demands fibers that can withstand tight bends and confined spaces while maintaining performance.
- **Compatibility with Passive Optical Networks (PONs):** PON technologies like GPON and XGS-PON are standard in access networks, enabling efficient data distribution to multiple endpoints.

Technologies and Enhancements:

- **Splitters and Connectors:** Passive splitters enable cost-effective signal distribution to multiple users from a single fiber.
- **Pre-terminated Fiber Solutions:** Pre-connectorized cables reduce installation time and costs in FTTH and FTTB deployments.
- **Low Bend Insensitivity:** G.657 fibers are critical in access networks where frequent bends occur in ducts, walls, and customer premises.

Challenges and Solutions:

- **Deployment Complexity:** Access networks often require installations in challenging environments such as multi-dwelling units (MDUs) or overhead poles. Solutions like drop cables and aerial installations ensure efficient deployment.
- **Service Scalability:** As user demand grows, scalable architectures with higher split ratios and upgraded PON technologies (e.g., 10G PON) ensure future-readiness.
- **Cost Management:** Operators adopt hybrid approaches combining fiber and wireless solutions (e.g., Fiber to the Node with 5G) to minimize costs while maximizing coverage.

Combined Table of Optical Fiber Properties.

Fiber Type	Core Diameter	Wavelength	Characteristics	Applications
Single-Mode Fiber (SMF)	8-10 microns	1310 nm, 1550 nm	Low attenuation and dispersion, high bandwidth	Long-haul networks, MANs, DCIs, high-speed internet
Multimode Fiber (MMF)	50/62.5 microns	850 nm, 1300 nm	Higher attenuation and dispersion, cost-effective for short distances	LANs, data centers, short-distance communication
Plastic Optical Fiber (POF)	1 mm	Varies	Easy installation, high attenuation, short distances	Home networking, consumer electronics, automotive applications
Bend-Insensitive Fiber	Varies	1310 nm, 1550 nm	Maintains performance when bent, reduced macrobending losses	Data centers, office buildings, FTTH deployments
Low Water Peak Fiber	Varies	1400 nm region minimized	Reduced attenuation across wider wavelengths	DWDM systems, metro, long-haul networks

Armored Fiber	Varies	Varies	Enhanced protection against physical damage	Industrial environments, outdoor installations
Hollow Core Fiber	Varies	Varies	Ultra-low latency, low non-linear effects	High-speed data transmission, latency-sensitive applications
Pure Silica Core Fiber (PSCF)	Varies	Varies	Very low attenuation, high resistance to radiation	Submarine cables, space applications, high-reliability networks

ITU-T Fiber Category

Fiber Category	Subcategory	Cable Cutoff Wavelength	Mode Field Diameter (MFD)	Attenuation (@1310/1550 /1625 nm)	Chromatic Dispersion (CD)	PMD
G.652 (SMF)	G.652.B	≤1260 nm	8.6-9.5 µm @1310nm	≤0.40/0.35/0.40 dB/Km	≤20 ps/(nm-km) @1550nm	≤0.2 ps/
	G.652.D (SMF-28)	≤1260 nm	8.6-9.2 µm @1310nm	≤0.40/0.30/0.40 dB/Km	≤18 ps/(nm-km) @1550nm	≤0.2 ps/
	SMF-28E+	≤1260 nm	8.6-9.2 µm @1310nm	≤0.32/0.18/0.20 dB/Km	≤18 ps/(nm-km) @1550nm	≤0.1 ps/
	SMF-28 ULL	≤1260 nm	8.6-9.2 µm @1310nm	≤0.31/0.17/0.20 dB/Km	≤18 ps/(nm-km) @1550nm	≤0.1 ps/
G.653 (DSF)	G.653.A	≤1270 nm	-	≤0.40/0.35/0.40 dB/Km	≤3.5 ps/(nm-km) (1525-1575nm)	≤0.5 ps/
	G.653.B	≤1270 nm	-	≤0.40/0.35/0.40 dB/Km	≤0.01 ps/(nm-km) @1550nm	≤0.2 ps/
G.654 (CSF)	G.654.A	≤1530 nm	9.5-10.5 µm @1550nm	-/≤0.22/0.30 dB/Km	≤20 ps/(nm-km) @1550nm	≤0.5 ps/

	G.654.B	≤1530 nm	9.5-13 µm @1550nm	-/≤0.22/0.30 dB/Km	≤22 ps/(nm-km) @1550nm	≤0.2 ps/
G.655 (NZDSF)	-	≤1450 nm	8-11 µm @1550nm	-/≤0.35/0.40 dB/Km	≤9 ps/(nm-km) (1525-1575nm)	≤0.2 ps/
G.657 (BIF)	A1	≤1260 nm	8.6-9.5 µm @1310nm	≤0.30/0.30/0.40 dB/Km	≤20 ps/(nm-km) @1550nm	≤0.20 ps/ (A)
	A2/B2	≤1260 nm	8.6-9.5 µm @1310nm	≤0.30/0.30/0.40 dB/Km	≤20 ps/(nm-km) @1550nm	≤0.50 ps/ (B)
	B3	≤1260 nm	8.6-9.5 µm @1310nm	≤0.30/0.30/0.40 dB/Km	≤20 ps/(nm-km) @1550nm	≤0.50 ps/ (B)

Pluggables in Optical Networks

Modules and pluggables are critical components in optical networks, providing the necessary interfaces for data transmission and reception. This section explores the various types of optical modules and pluggables, including ZR, ZR+, FR, and ZR-lite, their functions, specifications, and applications in modern optical networks.

Importance of Modules and Pluggables

Modules and pluggables enable the flexibility and scalability of optical networks by allowing easy upgrades and maintenance. They support different data rates, distances, and applications, making them essential for the efficient operation of optical networks.

Types of Optical Modules and Pluggables

Small Form-Factor Pluggable (SFP)

- **Definition**: A compact, hot-swappable transceiver used for both telecommunication and data communication applications.
- **Variants**: SFP (1G), SFP+ (10G), and SFP28 (25G).
- **Applications**: Ethernet, Fibre Channel, SONET/SDH, and more.

- **Example**: SFP+ modules are widely used in data centers for 10G Ethernet connectivity, providing high-speed links between servers and switches.

Quad Small Form-Factor Pluggable (QSFP)

- **Definition**: A compact, hot-swappable transceiver capable of supporting higher data rates and multiple channels.
- **Variants**: QSFP+ (40G), QSFP28 (100G), QSFP-DD (400G).
- **Applications**: Data centers, high-performance computing, and telecommunication networks.
- **Example**: QSFP28 modules are commonly used for 100G Ethernet connections in data center interconnects, offering high-density and high-bandwidth solutions.

XFP (10 Gigabit Small Form-Factor Pluggable)

- **Definition**: A standard for 10G optical transceivers that are protocol-independent and used for high-speed network applications.
- **Applications**: 10G Ethernet, SONET/SDH, Fibre Channel.
- **Example**: XFP modules are utilized in enterprise networks and data centers to provide 10G connectivity for various network devices.

CFP (C Form-Factor Pluggable)

- **Definition**: A large, multi-channel pluggable transceiver designed for 40G and 100G applications.
- **Variants**: CFP, CFP2, CFP4.
- **Applications**: High-speed data transmission in metro and long-haul networks.
- **Example**: CFP2 modules are used in service provider networks to support 100G DWDM applications, offering long-distance transmission capabilities.

CPAK

- **Definition**: A Cisco proprietary pluggable transceiver supporting high-density and high-speed data rates.
- **Applications**: Data centers, enterprise networks, service provider networks.

- **Example**: CPAK modules are used in Cisco network equipment to provide high-density 100G Ethernet connectivity with lower power consumption and increased port density.

OSFP (Octal Small Form-Factor Pluggable)

- **Definition**: A new standard for 400G optical transceivers, designed to be larger than QSFP-DD but offering better thermal management.
- **Applications**: Data centers and high-capacity networks requiring 400G links.
- **Example**: OSFP modules are deployed in next-generation data centers to provide 400G connectivity, supporting the growing demand for higher bandwidth and faster data rates.

Active Optical Cables (AOC) and Direct Attach Cables (DAC)

- **AOC**: Integrated optical transceivers with fiber optic cable, used for short-range, high-speed connections.
- **DAC**: Integrated copper cabling with transceivers, used for very short-range connections with lower power consumption.
- **Example**: AOC and DAC cables are commonly used within data centers to connect servers, switches, and storage devices, offering cost-effective and low-latency solutions for high-speed links.

ZR, ZR+, FR, and ZR-lite Modules

ZR (Ze Best Reach) Modules:

- **Definition**: Designed for 80 km point-to-point DWDM links, supporting 400G data rates over a single wavelength.
- **Applications**: Data center interconnects (DCI), metro networks.
- **Specifications:**
  - Data Rate: 400G.
  - Distance: Up to 80 km.
  - Form Factor: QSFP-DD and OSFP.
  - Modulation: 16QAM.
- **Example**: ZR modules enable high-capacity DCI over relatively short distances, providing efficient and cost-effective solutions for linking data centers in a metro area.

ZR+ Modules:

- **Definition**: Enhanced version of ZR modules with extended reach and flexibility.
- **Applications**: Long-haul DCI, metro and regional networks.
- **Specifications**:
    - Data Rate: 100G/200G/400G.
    - Distance: Up to 1000 km.
    - Form Factor: QSFP-DD and OSFP.
    - Modulation: QPSK, 8QAM, 16QAM (adaptive modulation).
- **Example**: ZR+ modules provide versatile, high-capacity links for various network segments, supporting adaptive modulation to optimize performance over longer distances.

FR Modules:

- **Definition**: Designed for 2 km optical links, primarily for data center and campus environments.
- **Applications**: Data centers, enterprise networks.
- **Specifications:**
    - Data Rate: 100G.
    - Distance: Up to 2 km.
    - Form Factor: QSFP28.
    - Modulation: PAM4.
- **Example**: FR modules offer a cost-effective solution for medium-distance connections within data centers and campuses, providing 100G links for server and switch interconnects.

ZR-lite Modules:

- **Definition**: Simplified and lower-cost version of ZR modules, targeting shorter distances with reduced power consumption.
- **Applications**: DCI, metro access networks.
- **Specifications:**
    - Data Rate: 100G/200G/400G.
    - Distance: Up to 40 km.
    - Form Factor: QSFP-DD and OSFP.
    - Modulation: PAM4.
- **Example**: ZR-lite modules provide an economical option for shorter DCI links, offering flexibility and lower power consumption while maintaining high data rates.

Note: *ZR doesn't hold all properties of OTN.*

Specifications and Standards

Form Factors

- **SFP/SFP+**: Compact size, supporting data rates up to 10G.
- **QSFP/QSFP28**: High-density, supporting data rates up to 100G and beyond.
- **CFP/CFP2/CFP4**: Larger size, supporting high-speed and long-distance transmission.
- **QSFP-DD/OSFP**: Advanced form factors for 400G and beyond, with enhanced thermal management and high density.

Data Rates

- **1G**: SFP modules for standard Ethernet connections.
- **10G**: SFP+, XFP, and CFP modules for higher-speed connections.
- **25G**: SFP28 modules for emerging high-speed applications.
- **40G**: QSFP+ modules for data center and backbone networks.
- **100G**: QSFP28, CFP, and CFP2 modules for high-capacity links.
- **400G**: QSFP-DD, OSFP, ZR, ZR+, and ZR-lite modules for next-generation networks.
- 800G: yet to deploy in market and maybe QSFP-DD.

Distance and Reach

- **Short Range (SR)**: Typically used within data centers, supporting distances up to 300 meters.
- **Medium Range (FR)**: Supporting distances up to 2 km, suitable for data center and campus environments.
- **Long Range (LR)**: Used for metro and long-haul networks, supporting distances up to 10 km or more.
- **Extended Range (ER)**: Designed for even longer distances, often exceeding 40 km.
- **Ultra Long Range (ZR, ZR+, ZR-lite)**: Supporting distances from 40 km up to 1000 km, for DCI and long-haul applications.

Wavelengths

- **850 nm**: Used in multimode fiber for short-distance applications.

- **1310 nm**: Used in single-mode fiber for medium-distance applications.
- **1550 nm**: Used in single-mode fiber for long-distance and DWDM applications.

Practical Examples and Case Studies

Data Center Upgrade

- **Scenario**: A data center needs to upgrade its network to support higher data rates and increased traffic.
- **Implementation**:
- **Technology**: Deploy QSFP28 and ZR modules to upgrade from 10G to 100G and 400G Ethernet connections.
- **Outcome**: Enhanced network capacity and performance, supporting higher data rates and reducing congestion.

Metro Network Expansion

- **Scenario**: A service provider is expanding its metro network to accommodate growing demand for high-speed internet services.
- **Implementation:**
- **Technology**: Use CFP2 and ZR+ modules for 100G and 400G DWDM links, enabling long-distance transmission and high capacity.
- **Outcome**: Improved network scalability and reliability, meeting customer demands for faster internet speeds and higher data volumes.

High-Performance Computing (HPC) Network

- **Scenario**: An HPC facility requires high-speed, low-latency connectivity for data-intensive applications.
- **Implementation**:
- **Technology**: Deploy AOC cables and FR modules to connect servers and switches within the HPC network.
- **Outcome**: Achieved low-latency, high-bandwidth connections, enhancing the performance of data-intensive applications and reducing bottlenecks.

Pluggables Summary Table

Module Type	Form Factor	Data Rate	Distance	Wave-length	Modula-tion	Ap-plications

SFP	SFP	1G	Up to 80 km	850 nm (MMF), 1310 nm (SMF), 1550 nm (SMF)	NRZ	Ethernet, Fibre Channel, SONET/ SDH
SFP+	SFP	10G	Up to 80 km	850 nm (MMF), 1310 nm (SMF), 1550 nm (SMF)	NRZ	Ethernet, Fibre Channel
SFP28	SFP	25G	Up to 40 km	850 nm (MMF), 1310 nm (SMF)	NRZ	Ethernet
QSFP+	QSFP	40G	Up to 10 km	850 nm (MMF), 1310 nm (SMF)	NRZ	Data Centers, High-Perfor-mance Computing
QSFP28	QSFP	100G	Up to 10 km	850 nm (MMF), 1310 nm (SMF)	NRZ, PAM4	Data Centers, Metro Networks
QSFP-DD	QSFP	400G	Up to 80 km	1310 nm (SMF), 1550 nm (SMF)	PAM4, 16QAM	Data Centers, DCI
XFP	XFP	10G	Up to 80 km	850 nm (MMF), 1310 nm (SMF), 1550 nm (SMF)	NRZ	Ethernet, SONET/ SDH, Fibre Channel
CFP	CFP	40G/ 100G	Up to 40 km	850 nm (MMF), 1310 nm (SMF), 1550 nm (SMF)	NRZ	High-Speed Data Transmis-sion
CFP 2	CFP	100G	Up to 80 km	1310 nm (SMF), 1550 nm (SMF)	NRZ, PAM4	Metro, Long-Haul Networks
CFP 4	CFP	100G	Up to 40 km	1310 nm (SMF)	NRZ	High-Speed Data Transmis-sion
CPAK	Propri-etary	100G	Up to 40 km	1310 nm (SMF)	NRZ	Data Centers, Enterprise Networks
OSFP	OSFP	400G	Up to 80 km	1310 nm (SMF), 1550 nm (SMF)	PAM4, 16QAM	Data Centers, High-Capacity Networks

AOC	Varies	10G/ 25G/ 40G/ 100G	Up to 100 meters	N/A	Varies	Short-Range High-Speed Connections
DAC	Varies	10G/ 25G/ 40G/ 100G	Up to 10 meters	N/A	Varies	Very Short-Range Connections
ZR	QSFP-DD, OSFP	400G	Up to 80 km	1550 nm (DWDM)	16QAM	DCI, Metro Networks
ZR+	QSFP-DD, OSFP	100G/ 200G/ 400G	Up to 1000 km	1550 nm (DWDM)	QPSK, 8QAM, 16QAM	Long-Haul DCI, Metro, Regional Networks
FR	QSFP28	100G	Up to 2 km	1310 nm (SMF)	PAM4	Data Centers, Enterprise Networks
ZR-lite	QSFP-DD, OSFP	100G/ 200G/ 400G	Up to 40 km	1550 nm (DWDM)	PAM4	DCI, Metro Access Network

Optical Transceivers Categorized by Application

1. Intra-Data Center (Short Reach, <500m)

Transceiver	Speed	Reach	Wavelength	Form Factor	Power (W)	Cost Level
SR2	50G	100m	850nm	SFP56	1.5	$
SR4	100G	100m	850nm	QSFP28	3.5	$
SR8	400G	100m	850nm	QSFP-DD/ OSFP	12.0	$$
VSR4	100G	300m	850nm	QSFP28	3.5	$
SR4.2	200G	100m	850nm	QSFP56	4.5	$$

AOC	100/400G	100m	850nm	Various	3.0-12.0	$

2. Inter-Data Center (Medium Reach, 500m-2km)

Transceiver	Speed	Reach	Wavelength	Form Factor	Power (W)	Cost Level
PSM4	100G	500m	1310nm	QSFP28	3.5	$$
CWDM4	100G	2km	1271-1331nm	QSFP28	3.5	$$
DR4	400G	500m	1310nm	QSFP-DD/ OSFP	12.0	$$$
FR4	400G	2km	1310nm	QSFP-DD/ OSFP	14.0	$$$
PSM8	400G	500m	1310nm	QSFP-DD	14.0	$$$
DR8	800G	500m	1310nm	QSFP-DD800	20.0	$$$$

3. Metro Access (Long Reach, 2km-40km)

Transceiver	Speed	Reach	Wavelength	Form Factor	Power (W)	Cost Level
LR4	100G	10km	1295-1310nm	QSFP28	4.5	$$$
LR8	400G	10km	1310nm	QSFP-DD	14.0	$$$$
ER4	100G	40km	1295-1310nm	QSFP28	4.5	$$$$
ER8	400G	40km	1310nm	QSFP-DD	15.0	$$$$$

4WDM-40	100G	40km	C-band	QSFP28	4.5	$$$$
LR4-40	100G	40km	1295-1310nm	QSFP28	4.5	$$$$

4. Metro/Regional (Extended Reach, 40km-120km)

Transceiver	Speed	Reach	Wavelength	Form Factor	Power (W)	Cost Level
ZR	400G	120km	C-band	QSFP-DD/ OSFP	15-20	$$$$$
ZRP	400G	120km	C-band	QSFP-DD/ OSFP	15-20	$$$$$
ZR400	400G	120km	C-band	CFP 2	16-20	$$$$$
ER4-40	100G	40km	1295-1310nm	QSFP28	4.5	$$$$
4WDM-80	100G	80km	C-band	QSFP28	4.5	$$$$$

5. Long Haul/DCI (Ultra Long Reach, >120km)

Transceiver	Speed	Reach	Wavelength	Form Factor	Power (W)	Cost Level
ZR+	400G	1000km	C+L band	QSFP-DD/ OSFP	15-22	$$$$$
800ZR	800G	80km	C+L band	QSFP-DD800	20-25	$$$$$
800ZR+	800G	1000km	C+L band	QSFP-DD800	20-25	$$$$$
DCO-T	400G	2000km	C+L band	CFP 2	20-25	$$$$$

Coherent	100-800G	2000km+	C+L band	Various	20-30	$$$$$

6. Enterprise/Campus (Cost-Optimized)

Transceiver	Speed	Reach	Wavelength	Form Factor	Power (W)	Cost Level
1000BASE-SX	1G	550m	850nm	SFP	1.0	$
10GBASE-SR	10G	300m	850nm	SFP+	1.0	$
25G-SR	25G	100m	850nm	SFP28	1.5	$$
40GBASE-SR4	40G	100m	850nm	QSFP+	2.5	$$
BiDi	40G	150m	832/918nm	QSFP+	2.5	$$
100G-SR4	100G	100m	850nm	QSFP28	3.5	$$$

7. Special Applications

7.1 Industrial/Extended Temperature

Transceiver	Speed	Temp Range	Wavelength	Form Factor	Power (W)	Cost Level
I-temp SR4	100G	-40/85°C	850nm	QSFP28	4.0	$$$$
I-temp LR4	100G	-40/85°C	1310nm	QSFP28	5.0	$$$$$
I-temp BiDi	40G	-40/85°C	Dual	QSFP+	3.0	$$$$

7.2 Military/Aerospace

Transceiver	Speed	Features	Wavelength	Form Factor	Power (W)	Cost Level
MIL-SR4	100G	Ruggedized	850nm	QSFP28	4.0	$$$$$
MIL-LR4	100G	Ruggedized	1310nm	QSFP28	5.0	$$$$$
Aero-Opti-caL	10G	DO-254	1310nm	SFP+	2.0	$$$$$

7.3 DWDM Applications

Transceiver	Speed	Channel Spacing	Wavelength	Form Factor	Power (W)	Cost Level
DWDM-ZR	400G	75GHz	C-band	QSFP-DD	15-20	$$$$$
DWDM-lite	100G	100GHz	C-band	QSFP28	4.5	$$$$
Tunable	400G	50/75/100GHz	C+L band	QSFP-DD	15-22	$$$$$

8. Hyperscale Data Center / Cloud Service Providers

Type	Speed	Reach	Lanes	Format	Power (W)	Cost	Common Applications
DR4	400G	500m	4×100G	PAM4	12.0	$$$	Server connectivity
FR4	400G	2km	4×100G	PAM4	14.0	$$$	Inter-building
800G-SR8	800G	100m	8×100G	PAM4	20.0	$$$$	Top-of-rack
400G-SR8	400G	100m	8×50G	PAM4	12.0	$$$	Rack-to-rack

QSFP-DD800	800G	500m	8×100G	PAM4	20.0	$$$$	Spine-leaf
ZR	400G	120km	1×400G	Coherent	15-20	$$$$$	DCI

9. Enterprise Networks

Type	Speed	Reach	Lanes	Format	Power (W)	Cost	Common Applications
SR4	100G	100m	4×25G	NRZ	3.5	$$	Campus backbone
LR4	100G	10km	4×25G	NRZ	4.5	$$$	Branch connectivity
BiDi	40G	150m	2×20G	NRZ	2.5	$$	Building uplinks
10G-SR	10G	300m	1×10G	NRZ	1.0	$	Access switches
25G-LR	25G	10km	1×25G	NRZ	1.5	$$	Metro connectivity
SFP28	25G	100m	1×25G	NRZ	1.5	$$	Server connections

10. Telecom / Service Provider

Type	Speed	Reach	Lanes	Format	Power (W)	Cost	Common Applications
ZR+	400G	1000km	1×400G	Coherent	15-22	$$$$$	Long-haul
ER4	100G	40km	4×25G	NRZ	4.5	$$$$	Metro access
DWDM	100G	80km	1×100G	DP-QPSK	6.0	$$$$$	Metro core

800G-ZR	800G	80km	1×800G	DP-32QAM	20-25	$$$$$	DCI
CFP2-DCO	400G	2000km	1×400G	Coherent	20-25	$$$$$	Submarine
400G-FR8	400G	2km	8×50G	PAM4	14.0	$$$$	Central office

11. 5G / Mobile Infrastructure

Type	Speed	Reach	Lanes	Format	Power (W)	Cost	Common Applications
25G-LR	25G	10km	1×25G	NRZ	1.5	$$	Cell backhaul
SFP28	25G	300m	1×25G	NRZ	1.5	$$	RRU connectivity
CWDM4	100G	2km	4×25G	NRZ	3.5	$$$	Fronthaul
BiDi	50G	10km	1×50G	PAM4	2.5	$$$	Midhaul
LR4	100G	10km	4×25G	NRZ	4.5	$$$	Core transport
ER4	100G	40km	4×25G	NRZ	4.5	$$$$	Regional backhaul

12. Cable / MSO Networks

Type	Speed	Reach	Lanes	Format	Power (W)	Cost	Common Applications
CWDM4	100G	2km	4×25G	NRZ	3.5	$$$	Hub interconnect
LR4	100G	10km	4×25G	NRZ	4.5	$$$	Regional hubs

BiDi	10G	10km	1×10G	NRZ	1.0	$	Node access
DWDM	200G	80km	1×200G	DP-16QAM	15.0	$$$$$	Core transport
400G-FR4	400G	2km	4×100G	PAM4	14.0	$$$$	Head-end
ER4	100G	40km	4×25G	NRZ	4.5	$$$$	Regional transport

13. Industrial / Special Applications

Type	Speed	Reach	Lanes	Format	Power (W)	Cost	Common Applications
I-temp LR4	100G	10km	4×25G	NRZ	5.0	$$$$$	Factory automation
MIL-SR4	100G	100m	4×25G	NRZ	4.0	$$$$$	Military
Aero-Optical	10G	5km	1×10G	NRZ	2.0	$$$$$	Aerospace
Mining	25G	10km	1×25G	NRZ	2.0	$$$$	Underground
Marine	100G	40km	4×25G	NRZ	5.0	$$$$$	Maritime
Rail	10G	40km	1×10G	NRZ	2.5	$$$$	Railway

14. Edge Computing / IoT

Type	Speed	Reach	Lanes	Format	Power (W)	Cost	Common Applications
SFP+	10G	300m	1×10G	NRZ	1.0	$	Edge nodes

25G-SR	25G	100m	1×25G	NRZ	1.5	$$	Local processing
CWDM4	100G	2km	4×25G	NRZ	3.5	$$$	Edge aggregation
BiDi	25G	10km	1×25G	NRZ	1.5	$$	IoT gateways
LR4-Lite	100G	2km	4×25G	NRZ	4.0	$$$	Edge data centers
400G-DR4	400G	500m	4×100G	PAM4	12.0	$$$$	Edge core

Key Specifications:

- Power consumption is typical operational value
- Reach assumes SMF/MMF as appropriate
- Costs are approximate market averages
- Industrial temps: -40°C to +85°C
- Commercial temps: 0°C to +70°C
- Extended temps: -5°C to +85°C

Emerging Trends:

- 800G/1.6T development for data centers
- Coherent optics moving to pluggable form factors
- Silicon photonics integration
- Power optimization for edge applications
- Increased density requirements
- Enhanced diagnostic capabilities

Cost Level Legend:

- $: <$100
- $$: $100-$500
- $$$: $500-$1000
- $$$$: $1000-$5000
- $$$$$: >$5000

Notes:

1. Prices are approximate and can vary significantly based on volume and market conditions
2. Power consumption values are typical and may vary by implementation
3. Reach distances assume high-quality fiber and proper installation
4. Temperature ranges for standard versions are typically 0°C to 70°C

5. Form factor availability may vary by vendor
6. Some transceivers may fit multiple application categories

15. Comparison of OTN, ZR, and ZR+

Characteristic	OTN	ZR	ZR+
Protocol Purpose	Digital wrapper for multiple client signals	400G Ethernet transport	Enhanced 400G with flexible rates
Standards Body	ITU-T	OpenZR+ MSA	OpenZR+ MSA
Reach	Variable based on implementation	80-100 km	120+ km
Supported Rates	Multiple (OTU1/2/3/4)	Fixed 400G	100/200/300/400G
Modulation	Various	16QAM	QPSK, 8QAM, 16QAM
Network Application	Carrier/Telecom networks	Data Center Interconnect	Metro/Regional networks
Form Factor	Various	QSFP-DD, OSFP	QSFP-DD, OSFP
Management Features	Full OAM&P capabilities	Basic	Enhanced
ROADM Support	Yes	No	Yes
Overhead	~4%	Minimal	Minimal
Power Consumption	Higher	Lower	Moderate

Client Protocols	Multiple (Ethernet, FC, SONET/SDH)	Ethernet only	Ethernet only
Performance Monitoring	Comprehensive	Basic	Enhanced
Network Integration	Complex networks	Point-to-point	Flexible deployment
Cost	Higher	Lower	Moderate
Interoperability	High (ITU-T standardized)	High (MSA standardized)	Moderate (some vendor-specific)
FEC Type	GFEC/EFEC	oFEC	oFEC and proprietary options
Baud Rate	Variable	Fixed 59.84 GBd	Flexible
Wavelength Band	C-band, L-band	C-band	C-band
Chromatic Dispersion Tolerance	High	Moderate	Enhanced
OSNR Performance	High	Good	Better
Future Evolution	FlexO, B100G	800G ZR in development	Enhanced reach/capacity versions
Typical Applications	Long-haul, submarine, metro	Point-to-point DCI, campus	Metro-regional, multi-span
DSP Architecture	Vendor-specific	Standardized	Semi-standardized

Network Management Requirements	Complex	Simple	Moderate
Multiplexing Capability	ODU multiplexing supported	None	Limited
TCM Support	Yes	No	Limited
GCC Support	Yes	No	Optional

Optical and Power Parameters Comparison for OTN, ZR, and ZR+

Parameter	OTN	ZR	ZR+
Power Specifications			
Typical Power Consumption	20-30W	14-15W	15-20W
Maximum Power	30W+	16W	22W
Power Class	Various	Class 8	Class 8
Operating Temperature	-5 to 70°C	0 to 70°C	0 to 70°C
Transmitter Parameters			
Launch Power	-10 to +1 dBm	-10 to 0 dBm	-10 to +1 dBm
Tx OMA (Optical Modulation Amplitude)	Variable	-6 dBm (typical)	-5 dBm (typical)
Side Mode Suppression Ratio (SMSR)	> 30 dB	> 30 dB	> 30 dB
Maximum Input Power	+3 dBm	+2.5 dBm	+3 dBm
Tx Wavelength Range	C-band/L-band	C-band	C-band
Center Wavelength Accuracy	±20 pm	±20 pm	±20 pm

Receiver Parameters			
Receiver Sensitivity	-20 dBm (typical)	-18 dBm (typical)	-20 dBm (typical)
Maximum Input Power	0 dBm	0 dBm	+2 dBm
LOS Assert	-25 dBm	-20 dBm	-22 dBm
LOS De-assert	-23 dBm	-18 dBm	-20 dBm
OSNR Parameters			
Required OSNR (@BER 10^-12)	13-18 dB	20-22 dB	18-20 dB
Tx OSNR	> 35 dB	> 35 dB	> 35 dB
Min Rx OSNR	12 dB	16 dB	14 dB
OSNR Margin (typical)	3-5 dB	2-3 dB	2-4 dB
Link Budget			
Maximum Link Loss	30 dB	18 dB	24 dB
Dispersion Tolerance	±2000 ps/nm	±800 ps/nm	±1000 ps/nm
PDL Tolerance	3 dB	2 dB	2.5 dB
Performance Metrics			
Pre-FEC BER Target	2.0E-02	2.4E-02	2.4E-02
Post-FEC BER	1E-15	1E-15	1E-15
Latency (typical)	10-50 µs	< 10 µs	< 15 µs

Note: *Values are typical/approximate and may vary by vendor implementation*

Chapter 4

Fiber Characterization and Testing

Chapter 4
Fiber Characterization and Testing

"The true character of a fiber reveals itself under test." - Donald Keck

---

Fiber characterization is a crucial process for ensuring optimal performance and reliability in optical networks. This chapter will cover advanced fiber characterization techniques, explore the impact of fiber imperfections on high-speed and long-distance communications, and provide detailed methodologies for accurately characterizing fiber properties both before and after deployment.

Importance of Fiber Characterization

1. **Why Fiber Characterization is Essential**
   - In high-speed optical networks, fiber characterization ensures that the physical infrastructure can support the desired data rates (e.g., 100G, 400G, and beyond). It helps operators understand the health of the fiber, detect any imperfections, and optimize the network for performance.
   - Without proper characterization, factors such as chromatic dispersion, polarization mode dispersion (PMD), and fiber nonlinearities can severely impact signal quality, leading to degraded service and increased bit errors.
2. **When Fiber Characterization is Performed**
   - **Pre-Deployment**: Characterization is conducted before fiber installation to assess its suitability for high-speed transmission.
   - **Post-Deployment**: After the network is up and running, routine characterization is needed to monitor fiber aging, detect faults, and ensure ongoing performance.

Key Parameters in Fiber Characterization

1. **Attenuation**

- **Definition**: Attenuation is the loss of signal power as light travels through the fiber.
- **Measurement**: Measured in dB/km using an optical power meter and light source.
- **Significance**: Low attenuation is essential for long-distance transmission.
- **Thresholds**: Single-mode fibers typically have attenuation rates of 0.2-0.35 dB/km at 1550 nm.
- **Example**: A single-mode fiber with an attenuation of 0.25 dB/km over a 100 km link results in a total attenuation of: Total Attenuation=0.25 dB/km×100 km=25 dB

2. **Dispersion**

- **Definition**: Dispersion causes the spreading of light pulses as they travel through the fiber, leading to signal distortion.
- **Types**:
  - **Chromatic Dispersion (CD)**: Wavelength-dependent spreading of pulses.
  - **Polarization Mode Dispersion (PMD)**: Spreading due to polarization effects.
- **Measurement**: Measured using an OTDR or dedicated dispersion test equipment.
- **Significance**: Managing dispersion is critical for high-speed data transmission.
- **Thresholds**:
  - CD: Typically around 16-20 ps/nm/km at 1550 nm.
  - PMD: Should be less than 0.5 ps/√km for high-speed networks.
- **Example**: A fiber with a chromatic dispersion of 17 ps/nm/km over a 100 km link results in a total dispersion of: Total Dispersion=17 ps/nm/km×100 km=1700 ps/nm

3. **Optical Return Loss (ORL)**

- **Definition**: ORL is the amount of light reflected back towards the source in an optical fiber.
- **Measurement**: Measured using an OTDR or optical return loss meter.
- **Significance**: High ORL can cause interference and affect signal quality.

- **Thresholds**: ORL values should typically be greater than 30 dB for good performance.
- **Example**: An ORL value of 35 dB indicates good performance, with minimal reflection affecting the signal.

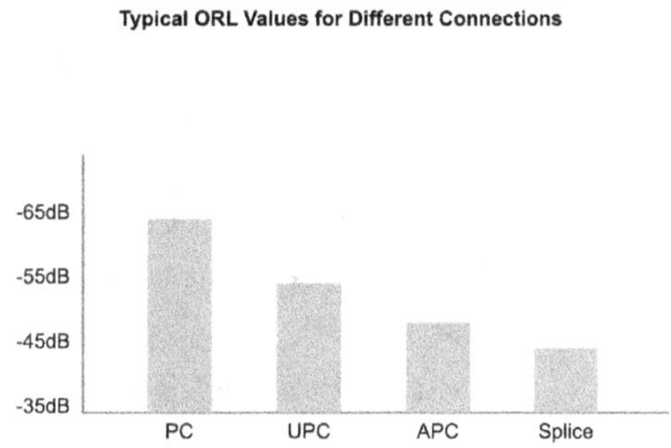

4. Non-Linear Effects

- **Definition**: Non-linear effects such as self-phase modulation (SPM), cross-phase modulation (XPM), and four-wave mixing (FWM) can distort signals in high-power and dense wavelength division multiplexing (DWDM) systems.
- **Measurement**: Specialized test equipment is used to measure non-linear effects.
- **Significance**: Mitigating non-linear effects is essential for maintaining signal integrity in high-capacity networks.
- **Thresholds**: Non-linear effects should be minimized; for DWDM systems, managing input power levels to stay below 15 dBm per channel can help.
- **Example**: In a DWDM system, reducing input power levels and optimizing channel spacing helps mitigate non-linear effects such as FWM.

Advanced Fiber Characterization Techniques

Optical Time-Domain Reflectometer (OTDR) Testing

- **Principle**: OTDR works by injecting a pulse of light into the fiber and measuring the backscattered and reflected light to identify the fiber's length, attenuation, splice losses, and connector reflections.
- **Use Cases**:

- Detecting fiber breaks, bends, and other discontinuities.
- Measuring splice and connector losses.

- **Practical Example**: A network operator uses OTDR to test a 120 km fiber link during deployment. The OTDR trace identifies a high splice loss at 40 km, which is then repaired to ensure minimal signal degradation in a 100G system.
- **Key Metrics from OTDR:**
  - **Reflectance**: Reflective events such as connectors and mechanical splices.
  - **Splice Loss**: Loss at fusion splices, typically measured in dB.
  - **Attenuation Coefficient**: Total fiber loss measured in dB/km, used to ensure that fiber meets the design specifications for long-haul networks.

Chromatic Dispersion (CD) Testing

- **Chromatic Dispersion Overview**: CD occurs when different wavelengths travel at different speeds through the fiber, causing signal distortion. As data rates increase, CD becomes a more critical factor, especially for coherent 100G and 400G systems.
- **Testing Methodology**: CD can be measured by sending a series of test signals through the fiber and analyzing the relative delay between different wavelengths. Dispersion compensation can then be applied based on the results.
- **Example**: In a 400G long-haul system, CD tests show that the fiber exhibits 17 ps/nm/km of dispersion. Dispersion compensation modules (DCMs) are installed at various points along the route to reduce CD and maintain signal integrity.

Polarization Mode Dispersion (PMD) Testing

- **Overview of PMD**: PMD arises from slight imperfections in the fiber's geometry that cause different polarization states to travel at different speeds. This effect is more pronounced in long-distance, high-speed optical systems, where it can cause pulse broadening and degradation.
- **Testing PMD**: PMD is measured by sending polarized light through the fiber and analyzing the differential group delay (DGD) between the two polarization modes.

- **Practical Case Study**: A transatlantic fiber link is tested for PMD before upgrading to 100G channels. The test reveals that certain sections of the link exhibit high DGD, which could impair high-speed transmission. The operator uses PMD compensation to mitigate these effects.

Impact of Fiber Imperfections on High-Speed Communications

1. **Bend Loss and Splice Quality**
    - **Bend Loss**: Even minor bends in the fiber can result in significant attenuation, especially in long-haul systems operating at high data rates. Bend-insensitive fibers are often used to minimize losses, but even these fibers require careful installation.
    - **Splice Quality**: Poor splicing results in higher splice losses, which can degrade signal quality in systems using dense wavelength division multiplexing (DWDM). Ensuring good fusion splicing is essential to maintaining low-loss connections.
    - **Example**: An optical network using 400G channels experiences significant attenuation due to fiber bends at junction points. OTDR testing identifies the exact locations, and the fiber is reinstalled with a wider bend radius, reducing attenuation and improving signal performance.
2. **Nonlinear Effects in Long-Distance Transmission**
    - **Nonlinearities**: In high-power optical systems, fiber nonlinearities such as self-phase modulation (SPM) and four-wave mixing (FWM) can become more pronounced. These effects are particularly problematic in DWDM systems where multiple closely spaced channels are transmitted through the same fiber.
    - **Mitigation**: Nonlinear effects can be mitigated by optimizing the launch power of optical signals and using advanced DSP algorithms at the receiver.
    - **Example**: In a long-haul network carrying 40 channels of 100G, SPM is observed to cause distortion on several channels. The operator reduces the launch power slightly, balancing the trade-off between OSNR and nonlinear impairments.

Tools and Methodologies for Accurate Fiber Characterization

1. **OTDR and Chromatic Dispersion Analyzers**
   - **Advanced OTDR Tools**: Modern OTDR devices can pinpoint precise locations of faults, allowing network engineers to diagnose and resolve issues quickly. OTDR testing is also used during routine maintenance to monitor fiber degradation over time.
   - **Chromatic Dispersion Tools**: Specialized CD analyzers measure dispersion in both legacy and newly installed fibers. This ensures that high-speed coherent systems operate without significant signal distortion.
   - **Practical Application**: A telecom operator uses a CD analyzer to test a newly installed metro fiber. The results show that the fiber meets the required dispersion tolerance for 100G services, allowing for immediate service activation.

2. **Automated Fiber Characterization Systems**
   - **Overview**: Automated tools for fiber characterization can continuously monitor fiber health and trigger alarms when attenuation, dispersion, or PMD exceed predefined thresholds. This is particularly useful in networks that require high uptime, such as financial institutions and government networks.
   - **Benefits**: Automated systems reduce the need for manual testing and help operators maintain high network availability through proactive maintenance.
   - **Example**: In a mission-critical network supporting 400G data centers, automated OTDR systems are deployed to monitor fiber health. When a degradation in splice quality is detected, technicians are automatically alerted, allowing for preventive maintenance before service degradation occurs.

Real-World Use Cases of Fiber Characterization

1. **Long-Haul Network Deployment**
   - **Scenario**: A national telecom operator is deploying a new 1,000 km fiber link to support 100G and 400G services. Before turning up the network, the operator conducts

OTDR, CD, and PMD tests to ensure that the fiber is within specification for high-speed transmission.

- **Results**: OTDR testing reveals two high-loss splices, which are re-spliced to reduce the loss to acceptable levels. CD tests indicate the need for dispersion compensation at several points along the route, and PMD tests confirm that the fiber is suitable for coherent transmission at 100G and 400G.

2. **Upgrading Legacy Fiber to Support 100G**
   - **Scenario**: A service provider plans to upgrade its legacy 10G network to 100G. Before the upgrade, the operator conducts comprehensive fiber characterization tests to ensure that the existing infrastructure can support higher data rates.
   - **Results**: Testing reveals that some sections of the fiber exhibit high chromatic dispersion, which would impair 100G signals. The operator installs tunable dispersion compensators (TDCs) to mitigate the effects and ensure the fiber can support 100G without the need for replacement.

Below is a comprehensive table summarizing threshold values for key parameters used in fiber characterization:

Parameter	Unit	Typical Threshold Value	Description
Attenuation (Loss)	dB/km	≤ 0.35 dB/km @ 1310 nm, ≤ 0.22 dB/km @ 1550 nm	Measures the loss of signal power as it travels through the fiber. Lower values are preferable.
Chromatic Dispersion	ps/(nm·km)	≤ 3.5 ps/(nm·km) @ 1310 nm, ≤ 18 ps/(nm·km) @ 1550 nm	Describes pulse broadening due to different wavelengths traveling at different speeds.
Polarization Mode Dispersion (PMD)	ps/km^(1/2)	≤ 0.2 ps/km^(1/2)	Measures pulse broadening caused by polarization effects.
Optical Return Loss (ORL)	dB	≥ 26 dB	Reflects the amount of signal reflected back toward the source. Higher values are preferable.

Splice Loss	dB	≤ 0.1 dB	Loss introduced at a splice point between two fibers.
Connector Loss	dB	≤ 0.5 dB per mated connector	Loss introduced at a fiber connection point.
Fiber Bend Radius	mm	≥ 30 mm (for standard fibers), ≥ 10 mm (for bend-insensitive fibers, e.g., G.657)	Minimum radius to avoid excessive bending loss.
Backscatter Coefficient	dB	-70 dB (typical value)	Relative level of light scattered back in the fiber, used in OTDR testing.
Mode Field Diameter (MFD)	µm	8.6–9.5 µm @ 1310 nm, 9.0–10.5 µm @ 1550 nm	Describes the effective area through which light propagates in the fiber.
Effective Area (Aeff)	μm^2	≥ 80 μm^2	Area where light propagates, important for non-linear effects.
Insertion Loss (IL)	dB	≤ 1.0 dB	Loss of signal power due to an optical component (connector, splice, or filter).
Wavelength Range	nm	1260–1625 nm	Operating wavelength range for standard single-mode fibers.
Non-linear Coefficient (n2)	W^(-1)·km^(-1)	≤ 2.6 × 10^(-20) m^2/W @ 1550 nm	Describes non-linear effects such as self-phase modulation and four-wave mixing.
Refraction Index Difference (Δn)	Dimensionless	≤ 0.36%	Difference in refractive index between the core and cladding.

These thresholds may vary slightly based on fiber type (e.g., G.652, G.655, G.657) and specific application requirements. Ensuring fiber characterization parameters remain within acceptable thresholds is crucial for high-performance optical networks.

Part II

Core Technologies

Chapter 5

Dense Wavelength Division Multiplexing (DWDM)

Chapter 5
Dense Wavelength Division Multiplexing (DWDM)

"DWDM doesn't just multiply capacity; it transforms the economics of optical networks." - Paul Green Jr.

Dense Wavelength Division Multiplexing (DWDM) is an advanced optical fiber technology that multiplexes multiple optical carrier signals on a single optical fiber by using different wavelengths (colors) of laser light. This technology has revolutionized telecommunications by dramatically increasing the capacity of optical fiber networks.

Core Principles

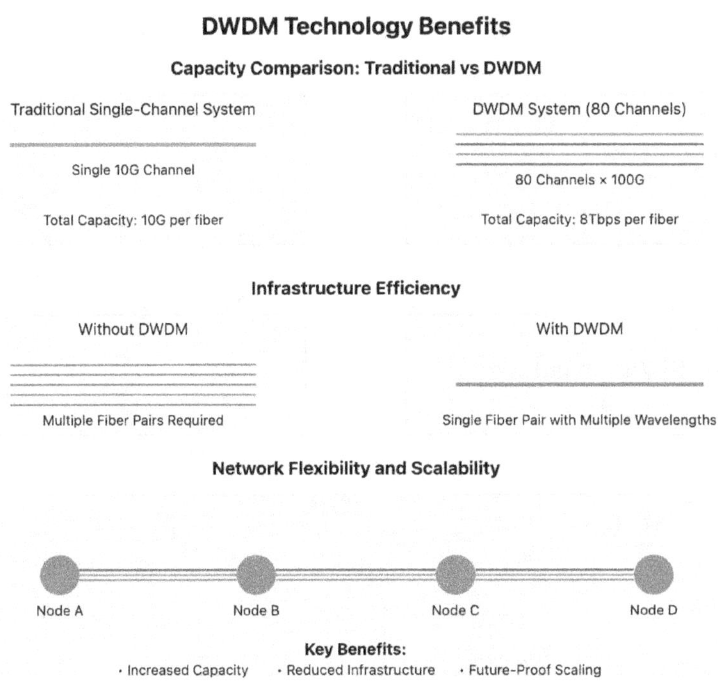

The fundamental principle of DWDM is based on the fact that multiple wavelengths of light can travel through a fiber simultaneously without interfering with each other. The relationship between wavelength (λ) and frequency (f) is given by:

$$c = \lambda f$$

where:

- c is the speed of light (approximately 3×10^8 m/s)

- λ is the wavelength in meters

- f is the frequency in Hertz

DWDM systems typically operate in the C-band (conventional band) of the optical spectrum, ranging from approximately 1530nm to 1565nm. The channel spacing in DWDM systems can be as narrow as 0.8nm or 100GHz, allowing for up to 40 channels in a single fiber.

Channel Spacing Calculation

The frequency spacing (Δf) between adjacent channels can be calculated using:

$$\Delta f = c(1/\lambda_1 - 1/\lambda_2)$$

where:

- λ_1 and λ_2 are the wavelengths of adjacent channels

- Δf is typically 100GHz or 50GHz in modern DWDM systems

Transmission windows

Band	Range (nm)	Loss (dB/km)	Dispersion (ps/nm·km)	Applications
O	1260-1360	0.32-0.34	0 at 1310nm	Short-reach
E	1360-1460	0.32-0.35	3.5 to 8	Reserved

S	1460-1530	0.21-0.24	8 to 12	Extended reach
C	1530-1565	0.19-0.22	15 to 18	Primary DWDM
L	1565-1625	0.20-0.24	18 to 22	Expanded DWDM
U	1625-1675	0.21-0.27	22 to 26	Ultra-long haul

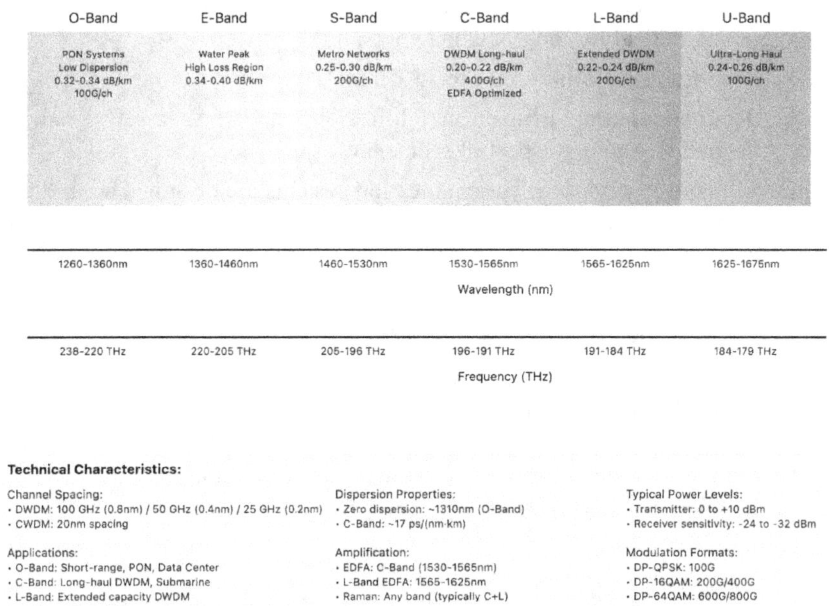

Wavelength Bands in Optical Fiber Networks

Optical fiber communications are typically divided into multiple wavelength bands, each suited for different purposes. The most common bands used in Dense Wavelength Division Multiplexing (DWDM) systems are:

1. **O-Band (1260 – 1360 nm):** Used for legacy systems and Passive Optical Networks (PON).
2. **E-Band (1360 – 1460 nm):** Known for water peak attenuation.
3. **S-Band (1460 – 1530 nm):** Rarely used in modern systems.

4. **C-Band (1530 – 1565 nm):** The most widely used band for DWDM systems.
5. **L-Band (1565 – 1625 nm):** The "long" band, considered the second choice when C-band capacity is exhausted.

Why C-Band is the First Choice?

C-Band Overview:

The C-band (Conventional band) has historically been the go-to for DWDM systems due to its optimal balance of low attenuation and high transmission capacity. The erbium-doped fiber amplifier (EDFA), which operates in the C-band, allows for signal amplification without the need for electrical regeneration, making it ideal for long-haul networks.

- **Wavelength Range**: 1530 to 1565 nm.
- **Key Advantage:** Efficient amplification via EDFA, lower signal attenuation, and high spectral efficiency.

The vast majority of optical communication systems are designed around the C-band, making it the most cost-effective and reliable option for network operators.

When is L-Band the Second Choice?

When the capacity of the C-band is fully utilized, network operators look to the L-band as the next option. The L-band, or Long Band, operates between **1565 nm and 1625 nm**. While its operational characteristics are similar to those of the C-band, the L-band offers more room for expansion by utilizing a different portion of the optical spectrum.

Advantages of L-Band:

1. **Increased Capacity:**
    - The primary reason to turn to the L-band is the need for additional bandwidth. By utilizing the L-band, operators can essentially double the available spectrum, adding another layer of capacity on top of the C-band network.
2. **Reduced Nonlinear Effects:**
    - Due to lower signal power requirements in the L-band, nonlinear effects such as **four-wave mixing (FWM)** and **stimulated Brillouin scattering (SBS)** are less severe compared to the C-band. This allows for cleaner signal transmission, particularly in long-distance networks.
3. **Complementary Amplification with EDFA:**

- Similar to the C-band, L-band systems can also benefit from **erbium-doped fiber amplifiers (EDFAs)** designed specifically for this wavelength range. While L-band amplifiers tend to be less efficient than their C-band counterparts, they offer a practical solution for extending network reach and capacity.

Challenges of L-Band Implementation:

Despite its advantages, the L-band is not without its challenges, which is why it remains a "second choice" rather than a primary option.

1. **Higher Attenuation:**
    - Optical fibers exhibit slightly higher attenuation in the L-band than in the C-band. This means that signals in the L-band may require more amplification or shorter distances between amplifiers, potentially increasing the cost of deployment.
2. **More Expensive Amplification:**
    - While EDFA technology is available for the L-band, it tends to be more expensive and less efficient compared to C-band amplifiers. This adds to the operational cost of L-band deployment.
3. **Limited Availability of Components:**
    - The optical components ecosystem—such as **multiplexers**, **demultiplexers**, and **transceivers**—is more mature and widely available for C-band systems. While L-band components are available, they may not be as cost-effective or readily available in the market.
4. **Stimulated Raman Scattering (SRS):**
    - L-band systems are more susceptible to **Stimulated Raman Scattering (SRS)**, where power from shorter wavelengths (C-band) is transferred to longer wavelengths (L-band). This causes a power tilt across the spectrum, affecting the signal integrity in some cases.

Practical Example for L-Band implementation.

Imagine an optical network operator running a long-haul DWDM network in the C-band. As data traffic increases, the operator reaches the capacity limit of the C-band. Instead of deploying new fibers, which would be costly and time-consuming, the operator decides to expand into the L-band.

Capacity Expansion with C+L Band:

- C-Band Capacity (50GHz channel spacing):
    - Using **PM-QPSK modulation** and **33GB baud rate**, the operator can achieve **132 Gbps** per channel. With **80 channels** in the C-band, the total capacity becomes:

Total Capacity=132 Gbps×80=10.56 Tbps

- L-Band Capacity:
    - By adding another **80 channels** in the L-band with the same modulation and baud rate, the operator can double the capacity:

L-Band Capacity=132Gbps×80=10.56Tbps

- **Total Capacity with C+L Band:**
  Total Capacity=10.56 Tbps (C-Band)+10.56Tbps (L-Band)=21.12Tbps

By utilizing both the C and L bands, the network operator effectively doubles the transmission capacity without laying new fiber or changing the overall infrastructure.

When to Choose L-Band?

Choosing to implement L-band depends on several factors:

1. **When C-Band is Fully Utilized:**
    - If the current C-band system is at capacity, expanding into the L-band provides a cost-effective way to increase bandwidth without the need for additional fiber infrastructure.
2. **For High-Density, Long-Haul Networks:**
    - The L-band is particularly suited for high-density and long-haul optical networks where the need for additional channels outweighs the cost of more amplifiers and components.
3. **Mitigating Nonlinear Effects:**
    - In situations where nonlinear effects like four-wave mixing become a problem in the C-band, the L-band's lower signal power requirements can help reduce these impairments.

Advantages and Applications of DWDM

Advantages

- **Capacity Enhancement**
  - Theoretical capacity increase: **N × B**
  - N = number of wavelengths
  - B = bit rate per wavelength
  - Example: 40 channels × 100 Gbps = 4 Tbps total capacity
- **Protocol and Bit Rate Transparency**
  - Supports multiple protocols simultaneously
  - Can mix different bit rates on different wavelengths
- **Scalability**
  - Easy capacity upgrade by adding wavelengths
  - No need for new fiber installation
- **Cost Efficiency**
  - Cost per bit reduction
  - ROI calculation: Cost savings = (Cost of new fiber installation - Cost of DWDM equipment)

Applications

Long-haul Communications

- Submarine cables
- Terrestrial backbone networks
- Typical distances: 600-1500 km

Metro Networks

- Ring and mesh topologies
- Distance range: 40-80 km

Data Center Interconnection

- High-bandwidth requirements
- Low latency needs
- Typical capacity: 400G-1.6T per wavelength

DWDM Components

- Tx: Transmitter
- Rx: Receiver
- MUX: Multiplexer
- DEMUX: Demultiplexer
- EDFA: Erbium Doped Fiber Amplifier
- SMF: Single Mode Fiber
- NZDSF: Non-Zero Dispersion Shifted Fiber
- DCF: Dispersion Compensating Fiber

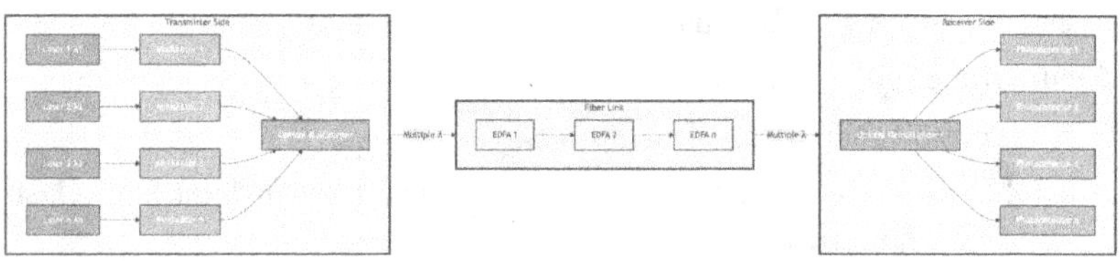

Transponders

Transponders are the interface between the client equipment and the DWDM system. They are classified into two main categories: coherent and non-coherent (direct-detection) transponders.

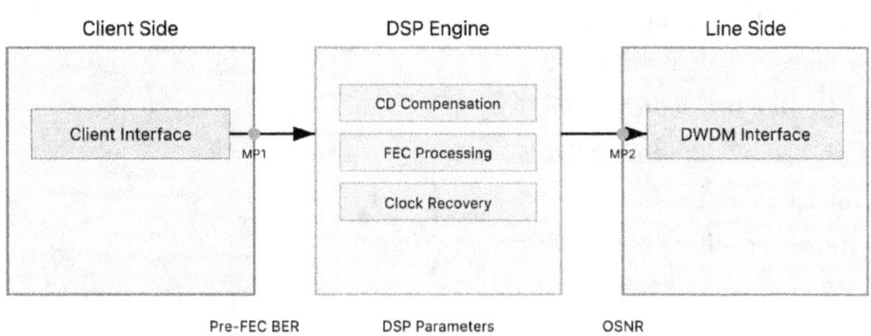

A. Non-Coherent (Direct-Detection) Transponders

Operating Principle

- Uses simple intensity modulation/direct detection (IM/DD)

- Binary representation through presence/absence of light
- Simpler and more cost-effective design

Modulation Formats

- On-Off Keying (OOK)
- Non-Return to Zero (NRZ)
- Return to Zero (RZ)
- Spectral efficiency: 0.5-1 bit/s/Hz

Performance Characteristics

- Reach: typically up to 80-120 km
- Data rates: up to 10G-40G per wavelength
- Receiver sensitivity: -22 to -18 dBm
- Cost-effective for metro applications

Applications

- Metro networks
- Enterprise connectivity
- Data center interconnection (short reach)
- Client-side interfaces

B. Coherent Transponders

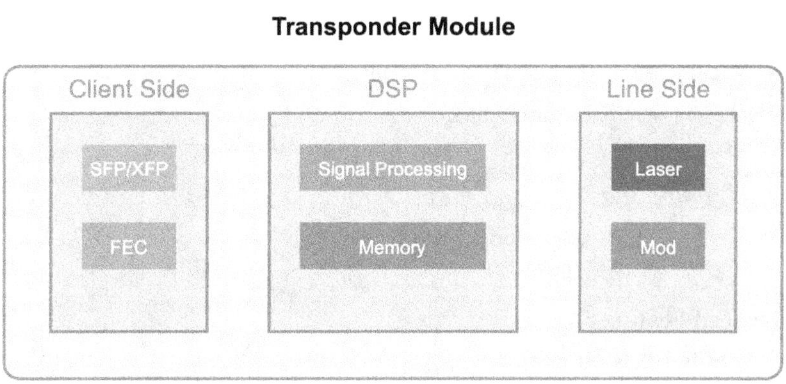

Operating Principle

- Uses coherent detection with local oscillator
- Preserves both amplitude and phase information
- Digital Signal Processing (DSP) enabled
- Complex modulation formats possible

Advanced Modulation Formats

- QPSK (2 bits/symbol)

$$\text{Spectral Efficiency} = 2 \text{ bits/symbol} \times \text{polarizations}$$

- 8QAM (3 bits/symbol)
- 16QAM (4 bits/symbol)
- 64QAM (6 bits/symbol)
- Polarization multiplexing doubles capacity

DSP Capabilities

- Chromatic Dispersion Compensation

$$CD(ps/nm) = D \times L$$

where:

  - D is dispersion parameter (ps/nm/km)
  - L is fiber length (km)
  - Polarization Mode Dispersion Compensation

$$PMD(ps) = PMD\_coefficient \times \sqrt{L}$$

- Frequency Offset Compensation
- Phase Noise Compensation
- Adaptive Equalization

Performance Characteristics

- Reach: 1000+ km (QPSK), 600+ km (16QAM)
- Data rates: 100G/200G/400G/800G per wavelength
- Receiver sensitivity: -45 to -35 dBm
- Higher OSNR requirements:

$$OSNR\_required = (Eb/N_0)\_required + 10\log_{10}(B/R)$$

where:

  - B is signal bandwidth
  - R is bit rate

Advanced Features

Soft-Decision FEC

- Net Coding Gain: 11-13 dB
- Pre-FEC BER threshold: $1\text{-}2 \times 10^{-2}$
- Post-FEC BER: 10^{-15}

Flexible Grid Support

- Channel spacing: 37.5/50/75/100 GHz
- Bandwidth allocation based on modulation:

$$Required\_BW = Symbol\_Rate \times (1 + Roll\_Off\_Factor)$$

Dynamic Modulation Adaptation

- Distance-based modulation selection
- SNR monitoring and adaptation
- Capacity versus reach trade-off:

$$\text{Capacity} = 2 \times R_s \times \log_2(M) \times \text{coding\_rate}$$

where:

  - R_s is symbol rate
  - M is modulation order

Application Scenarios

Long-haul/Submarine

- QPSK modulation
- Strong FEC
- Maximum reach priority

Metro/Regional

- 16QAM/64QAM
- Higher capacity
- Medium reach requirements

Data Center Interconnect

- Highest order modulation
- Maximum capacity
- Short reach optimization

C. Comparison Table: Coherent vs Non-Coherent Transponders

Parameter	Non-Coherent	Coherent
Cost	Lower	Higher
Reach	<120 km	>1000 km
Spectral Efficiency	0.5-1 bit/s/Hz	2-6 bit/s/Hz
Data Rate	Up to 40G	Up to 800G
CD Tolerance	Low	High
PMD Tolerance	Low	High
OSNR Requirement	Lower	Higher
Processing Complexity	Low	High
Power Consumption	Lower	Higher

D. Selection Criteria

Technical Considerations

- Required reach
- Target capacity

- Fiber type and quality
- OSNR budget
- Latency requirements

Economic Factors

- Cost per bit
- Power consumption
- Space requirements
- Network growth plans

Deployment Guidelines

Use non-coherent for:

- Short-reach applications (<80 km)
- Cost-sensitive deployments
- Simple point-to-point links

Use coherent for:

- Long-haul networks
- High-capacity requirements
- Complex optical paths
- Future-proof deployments

Multiplexers (Mux)

Multiplexers combine multiple wavelengths onto a single fiber. Key specifications include:

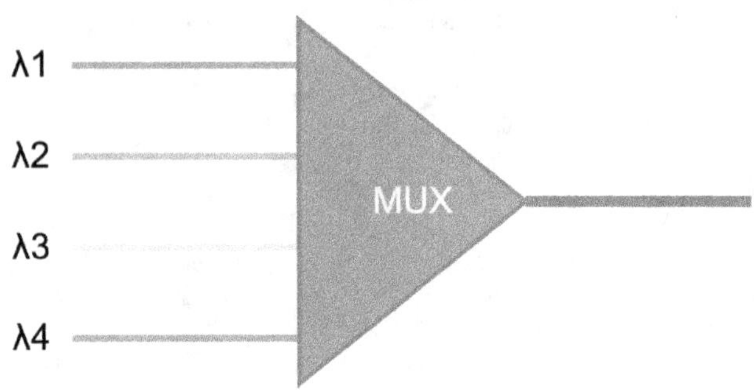

Insertion Loss

- Typical range: 3-7 dB
- Loss calculation:

$$IL(dB) = -10 \log_{10}(P\_out/P\_in)$$

Channel Isolation

- Minimum requirement: 25 dB
- Typical value: 30-40 dB

Passband Width

- Typically ±0.2nm around central wavelength
- Temperature dependence: ~0.01nm/°C

Multiplexers (Mux) and Their Types

Multiplexers in DWDM systems come in several technologies, each with specific characteristics and applications. Here's a detailed analysis of each type:

A. Arrayed Waveguide Grating (AWG)

Operating Principle

- Based on planar lightwave circuit technology
- Uses array of waveguides with incremental path lengths
- Constructive/destructive interference creates wavelength separation
- Phase difference calculation:

$$\Delta\Phi = 2\pi/\lambda \times (n_s \times \Delta L + n_c \times d \times \sin\theta)$$

where:

n_s: waveguide effective index

ΔL: path length difference

n_c: receiving waveguide index

d: waveguide spacing

θ: diffraction angle

Performance Characteristics

- Channel spacing: 50/100 GHz typical
- Insertion loss: 2-4 dB
- Channel isolation: >35 dB
- Polarization dependent loss: <0.5 dB
- Temperature sensitivity: ~0.01 nm/°C

Advantages

- High channel count (40+ channels)
- Compact size
- Good channel isolation
- Mass producible using semiconductor processes

Limitations

- Temperature sensitive
- Higher cost for low channel count
- Fixed channel spacing

B. Thin Film Filter (TFF)

Operating Principle

- Uses multiple dielectric layer interference
- Bragg reflection principle
- Filter response given by:

$$R(\lambda) = |r_1 + t_1t_2r_2e^{(-2i\beta L)}/(1 - r_1r_2e^{(-2i\beta L)})|^2$$

where:

r_1,r_2: reflection coefficients

t_1,t_2: transmission coefficients

β: propagation constant

L: cavity length

Performance Characteristics

- Channel spacing: 100/200 GHz typical
- Insertion loss: 0.5-1.5 dB per filter
- Channel isolation: >25 dB
- Thermal stability: <0.002 nm/°C
- Bandwidth: ±0.2 nm at -0.5 dB

Advantages

- Excellent thermal stability
- Low insertion loss
- Good for low channel count
- Cost-effective for simple systems

Limitations

- Cascading increases loss
- Limited channel count
- Physical size increases with channels

C. Fiber Bragg Grating (FBG)

Operating Principle

- Periodic variation in refractive index
- Bragg wavelength given by:

$$\lambda B = 2n_{eff}\Lambda$$

where:

n_{eff}: effective refractive index

Λ: grating period

Performance Characteristics

- Channel spacing: flexible
- Insertion loss: 0.1-0.3 dB per grating
- Reflection bandwidth: 0.1-1 nm
- Temperature sensitivity: ~0.01 nm/°C
- Reflection efficiency: >99%

Advantages

- Low insertion loss
- Flexible design
- All-fiber solution
- Good for add/drop applications

Limitations

- Temperature sensitive
- Requires circulators
- Complex for high channel count

D. Free Space Grating

Operating Principle

- Uses diffraction grating
- Grating equation:

$$d(\sin\theta_i + \sin\theta_r) = m\lambda$$

where:

d: grating spacing

θ_i: incident angle

θ_r: reflected angle

m: diffraction order

Performance Characteristics

- Channel count: >80 channels
- Insertion loss: 4-7 dB
- Channel isolation: >30 dB
- PDL: <0.3 dB
- Resolution: <0.2 nm

Advantages

- Very high channel count
- Flexible channel spacing
- Good for high-density systems

Limitations

- Higher insertion loss
- Mechanical stability issues
- Larger size

E. Interleaver-Based Systems

Operating Principle

- Separates odd/even channels
- Based on Mach-Zehnder interferometer
- Transfer function:

$$T(f) = \cos^2(\pi f/2f_0)$$

where f_0 is the free spectral range

Performance Characteristics

- Channel spacing: 50/100 GHz
- Insertion loss: 0.5-1.5 dB
- Channel isolation: >25 dB
- Bandwidth: 40% of channel spacing

Advantages

- Doubles spectral efficiency
- Good for upgrading systems
- Compatible with other technologies

Limitations

- Adds complexity
- Additional insertion loss
- Cost considerations

F. Technology Selection Guide

Application-based Selection

Application	Recommended Technology	Reason
Metro/Access	TFF	Cost-effective, moderate channel count
Long-haul	AWG	High channel count, good performance
Add/Drop	FBG	Low loss, flexible
Ultra-dense	Free Space Grating	Highest channel count

Decision Factors

- Channel count requirement
- Channel spacing needs
- Cost constraints
- Environmental conditions
- Maintenance requirements

Performance Trade-offs

Parameter	AWG	TFF	PLC	FBG	Interleaver
Insertion Loss	3-5 dB	1-2 dB/stage	4-6 dB	0.5-1 dB	2-3 dB
Channel Isolation	>30 dB	>45 dB	>25 dB	>30 dB	>25 dB
Channel Count	40-80	4-16	16-32	4-16	2x existing
Cost/Channel	Low	Medium	High	Medium	High

Parameter	AWG	TFF	FBG	Free Space
Loss	Medium	Low	Very Low	High
Channels	High	Low	Medium	Very High
Stability	Medium	High	Low	Medium
Cost/Ch	Low	High	Medium	Medium

Implementation Guidelines

Low Channel Count Systems (<8 channels)

- Prefer TFF
- Consider cost per channel
- Simpler maintenance

Medium Channel Count (8-32 channels)

- AWG becomes cost-effective
- Consider thermal management

- Balance performance/cost

High Channel Count (>32 channels)

- AWG or Free Space Grating
- Advanced monitoring required
- Professional maintenance needed

Additional Information about Mux selection

Type	Advantages	Disadvantages	Best Use Cases
AWG (Arrayed Waveguide Grating)	- High channel count - Low insertion loss - Compact size - Good thermal stability - Cost-effective for high channel count	- Temperature sensitive - Fixed channel spacing - Complex manufacturing - Limited flexibility	- DWDM systems - High-density applications - Metro networks
TFF (Thin Film Filter)	- Excellent channel isolation - Low crosstalk - Temperature independent - Simple structure	- Higher insertion loss - Cascaded design needed - Larger size - Cost increases with channels	- CWDM systems - Low channel count - Cost-sensitive applications
PLC (Planar Lightwave Circuit)	- High integration - Flexible design - Multiple functions - Mass production capable	- Higher cost - Temperature sensitive - Complex fabrication - Limited channel count	- Integrated solutions - Advanced functions - Metropolitan networks
FBG (Fiber Bragg Grating)	- Low insertion loss - High reflection - Fiber-based solution - Customizable spectrum	- Temperature sensitive - Limited channel count - Requires circulators - Higher component count	- Add/drop applications - Filtering - Sensor networks
Interleaver	- Doubles channel capacity - Low insertion loss - High isolation - Compact design	- Fixed spacing only - Higher cost - Complex alignment - Limited flexibility	- Channel spacing conversion - Capacity upgrade - Dense DWDM

Multiplexer Type Comparison

Type	Channel Spacing	Insertion Loss	Cost	Best Use Case
Fixed Grid	50/100 GHz	Low-Medium	Low	Metro, Cost-sensitive
Flexgrid	Variable (12.5 GHz steps)	Medium	High	Long-haul, High capacity
Flat-Top	50/100 GHz	Medium-High	Medium-High	Wavelength-drift sensitive
Gaussian	50/100 GHz	Low	Low	Short-reach, Basic DWDM
AWG	Fixed	Medium-High	Medium	High channel count DWDM

Typical Performance Metrics

Parameter	Fixed Grid	Flexgrid	Flat-Top
Bandwidth Utilization	80%	95%	85%

Typical Insertion Loss	3-4 dB	4-5 dB	5-6 dB
Channel Isolation	>25 dB	>30 dB	>35 dB

Frequency Domain Response

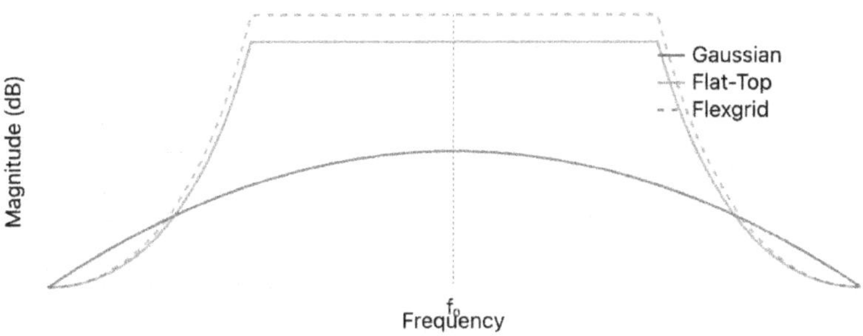

Key Considerations for SelectionIn the frequency response diagram above:

1. The blue line shows the Gaussian filter response:
    - Smooth bell-shaped curve
    - Gradual roll-off
    - More sensitive to frequency drift
2. The red line shows the Flat-top response:
    - Wide, flat passband
    - Steeper roll-off at edges
    - More tolerant to frequency drift

Key observations about the frequency responses:

- Flat-top provides better tolerance for wavelength drift but has higher insertion loss
- Gaussian is more efficient for insertion loss but requires better wavelength stability
- The steeper roll-off of flat-top helps in reducing cross-talk between adjacent channels

Filter Type	Time Domain Characteristics	Frequency Domain Characteristics	Key Parameters
Gaussian	- Smooth pulse response - Minimal ringing - Natural pulse shape - Low ISI	- Gradual roll-off - Symmetric response - No side lobes - -3dB at $\pm 0.707f_0$	- Bandwidth: standard - Group delay: constant - Phase response: linear - Insertion loss: 3-4dB
Flat-Top	- Sharp pulse edges - Some ringing - Rectangular-like - Higher ISI	- Steep roll-off - Flat passband - Small side lobes - -1dB bandwidth ≈ 80% of spacing	- Bandwidth: wider - Group delay: ripple - Phase response: non-linear - Insertion loss: 5-6dB
Flexgrid	- Adjustable response - Controlled ringing - Variable width - Optimized ISI	- Variable bandwidth - Programmable shape - Adaptive roll-off - 12.5 GHz granularity	- Bandwidth: variable - Group delay: managed - Phase response: optimized - Insertion loss: 6-7dB

Gaussian Filter Response

Advantages

- Better tolerance to frequency drift (±10 GHz)
- Reduced sensitivity to temperature variations
- Improved channel isolation
- Better for higher-order modulation formats
- Reduced maintenance requirements
- More forgiving in cascaded systems

Disadvantages

- Higher insertion loss (typically 5-6dB)
- More complex manufacturing
- Higher cost
- Increased group delay variation
- Limited scalability
- Fixed bandwidth constraints

Flat-Top Filter Response

Advantages

- Lower insertion loss (typically 3-4dB)
- Simple manufacturing process
- Cost-effective implementation
- Good for high-speed signals
- Minimal phase distortion
- Better chromatic dispersion tolerance

Disadvantages

- Poor tolerance to frequency drift
- Requires precise temperature control
- Lower spectral efficiency
- Less suitable for higher-order modulation
- More susceptible to cross-talk
- Needs higher power margin

Flexgrid Filter Response

Advantages

- Variable channel bandwidth support
- Optimized spectrum utilization
- Support for mixed bit rates
- Future-proof for higher speeds
- Dynamic bandwidth allocation
- Better for super-channels

Disadvantages

- Highest complexity
- Most expensive implementation
- Requires sophisticated control
- Higher power consumption
- More complex management
- Limited vendor support

Performance Comparison Table

Parameter	Gaussian	Flat-Top	Flexgrid
Insertion Loss	3-4 dB	5-6 dB	6-7 dB
Frequency Drift Tolerance	±2.5 GHz	±10 GHz	±12.5 GHz
Channel Isolation	>25 dB	>35 dB	>40 dB
Cost Factor	1x	1.5x	2-3x

Demultiplexers (Demux)

Demultiplexers separate combined wavelengths back into individual channels. Key parameters:

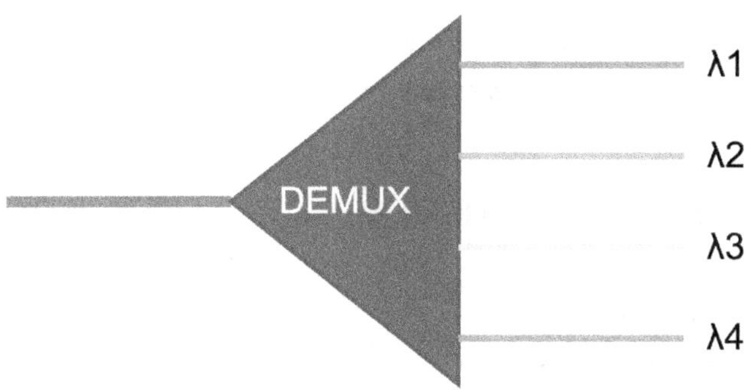

1. **Crosstalk**
   - Adjacent channel: < -30 dB
   - Non-adjacent: < -40 dB
   - Calculation:

$$\text{Crosstalk(dB)} = 10 \log_{10}(\text{P\_leaked/P\_signal})$$

2. **Wavelength Resolution**

- Typical value: 0.2nm
- Temperature stability: ±0.05nm over -5°C to +65°C

Amplifiers

DWDM systems employ various types of optical amplifiers:

1. **Erbium Doped Fiber Amplifiers (EDFA)**
    - Gain range: 20-35 dB
    - Noise figure: 4-6 dB
    - Gain calculation:

$$G(dB) = 10 \log_{10}(P\_out/P\_in)$$

2. **Raman Amplifiers**
    - Gain bandwidth: >100nm
    - Pump power requirements: 0.5-2W
    - Raman gain coefficient:

$$g\_R = (16\pi^2/n^2c\lambda\_s)\times(\partial\sigma/\partial\Omega)$$

    where:
    - n is the refractive index
    - λ_s is the signal wavelength
    - $\partial\sigma/\partial\Omega$ is the Raman cross-section

Erbium-Doped Fiber Amplifiers (EDFAs)

Introduction to EDFAs

Erbium-Doped Fiber Amplifiers (EDFAs) are one of the most widely used optical amplifiers in long-haul and dense wavelength division multiplexing (DWDM) systems. They work by amplifying light signals directly in the optical domain, avoiding the need for optical-electrical-optical conversion. EDFAs are crucial for extending transmission distances, boosting signal power, and maintaining the integrity of data in optical communication systems.

The basic principle of EDFA operation involves **stimulated emission** in a silica fiber doped with erbium ions, which amplifies the optical signals in the **C-band** (1530 nm–1565 nm) and **L-band** (1570 nm–1610 nm).

Gain Spectra Comparison

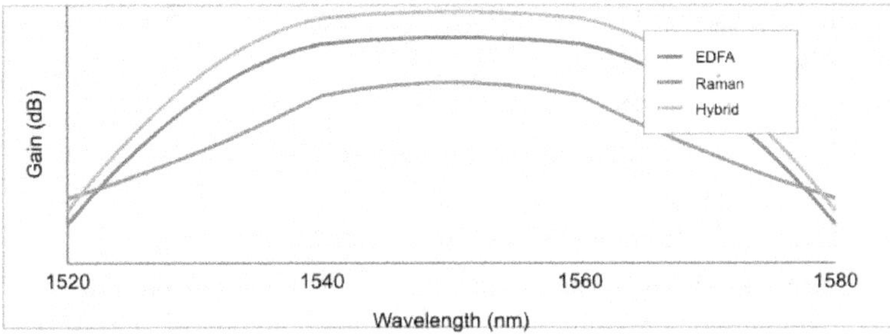

Noise Figure vs Gain

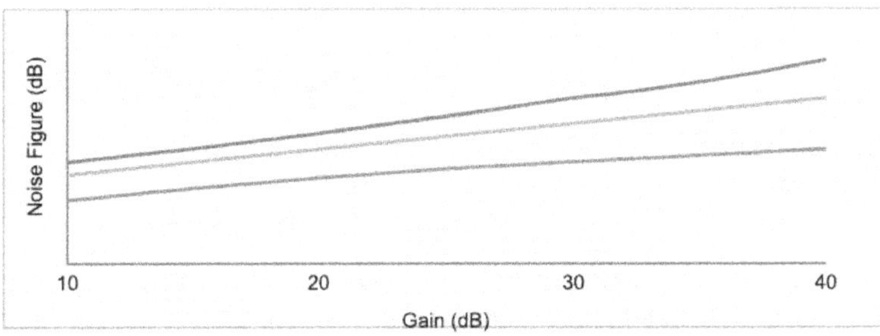

System Optimization Parameters

EDFA

- Pump Power: 20-30 dBm
- EDF Length: 10-30m
- Input Power: -30 to 0 dBm
- Gain Flatness: ±0.5 dB
- NF: 4-6 dB

Raman

- Pump Power: 27-33 dBm
- Fiber Length: 40-100km
- Stokes Shift: 13.2 THz
- Multiple Pumps: 3-4
- NF: 3-4 dB

Hybrid

- EDFA Gain: 15-20 dB
- Raman Gain: 10-15 dB
- Total Reach: >200km
- Combined NF: 3-5 dB
- OSNR: >30 dB

Working Principle of EDFAs

The operation of an EDFA revolves around the **three-level system** of erbium ions, as they transition between energy states. When erbium ions in the fiber are pumped using a laser at wavelengths such as **980 nm or 1480 nm**, they are excited to a higher energy level. These excited ions then undergo **stimulated emission** when they interact with incoming photons at signal wavelengths, amplifying the signal.

The following process occurs in an EDFA:

1. **Pump Source**: A high-power laser at 980 nm or 1480 nm pumps erbium ions.
2. **Excitation**: Erbium ions are excited to a higher energy level.
3. **Stimulated Emission**: As incoming signal photons pass through the erbium-doped region, they stimulate the emission of additional photons at the same wavelength, amplifying the signal.
4. **Amplification**: The signal is amplified as it travels through the erbium-doped fiber.

Key Parameters of EDFAs

Gain: The gain G of an EDFA is the ratio of output signal power P_{out} to input signal power P_{in}:

$$G=P_{out}/P_{in}$$

Gain depends on the pump power and the length of the erbium-doped fiber. Higher pump power and longer fiber lengths result in higher gain, but saturation effects limit the maximum achievable gain.

Noise Figure: The noise figure F quantifies the degradation of the signal-to-noise ratio (SNR) caused by the amplifier. It is primarily affected by **Amplified Spontaneous Emission (ASE)**, which introduces noise into the system. The noise figure for an EDFA is typically around 3–6 dB, depending on the operating conditions:

$$F\approx 2n_{sp}$$

Where n_{sp} is the population inversion factor. In practical systems, the noise figure is an important factor in determining overall system performance.

Saturation Power: The **saturation power** Psat of an EDFA refers to the input signal power at which the gain starts to decrease due to depletion of the pump energy. At high input powers, the amplifier becomes saturated, and the output power no longer increases linearly with input power.

Amplified Spontaneous Emission (ASE): ASE is generated by spontaneous emission from erbium ions and is a source of noise in the system. ASE propagates in both directions (forward and backward) and degrades the overall signal quality.

EDFA Gain and Noise Figure Calculations

The gain of an EDFA can be modeled as:

$$G=\exp(\sigma_e N_2 L)$$

Where:

- σ_e is the emission cross-section,
- N_2 is the population of excited erbium ions,
- L is the length of the erbium-doped fiber.

The noise figure F is given by:

$$F = 2n_{sp}\frac{G-1}{G}$$

Where:

- n_{sp} is the **spontaneous emission factor**, which describes how close the EDFA is to full inversion.

A noise figure of 3 dB (corresponding to $n_{sp}\approx 1$) is considered the best achievable in practical EDFAs.

EDFA Design Considerations

When designing an EDFA for optical networks, several key factors must be considered:

Pump Power: The pump power must be carefully selected to ensure efficient amplification. For example, using a 980 nm pump is more efficient for shorter fiber lengths, while a 1480 nm pump is often preferred for longer lengths due to reduced absorption losses.

Gain Flattening: In WDM systems, it is essential to maintain a flat gain spectrum across all channels. **Gain flattening filters** (GFFs) are used to equalize the gain across a broad wavelength range (1530–1565 nm). Without proper gain flattening, different channels in a DWDM system would experience varying levels of amplification, leading to performance degradation.

Cascaded EDFAs: In long-haul networks, multiple EDFAs are often cascaded to amplify signals over several hundred kilometers. Care must be taken to minimize the accumulation of noise from ASE, which can degrade the signal-to-noise ratio. A typical noise figure for cascaded EDFAs is around 5–6 dB.

EDFA in DWDM Systems

EDFA Key Advantages

EDFA has several key advantages that have made it a popular choice in modern optical communication systems, particularly in long-distance and high-capacity networks.

In-Line Amplification:

One of the primary benefits of EDFA is its ability to amplify an optical signal directly without requiring **optical-to-electrical** and **electrical-to-optical conversion**. This makes EDFA highly efficient for **DWDM** systems, where many channels are carried on the same fiber.

High Power Transfer Efficiency:

EDFA provides excellent power transfer efficiency from the pump laser to the signal. **1480 nm pumping** is particularly effective in providing high output power and superior conversion efficiency compared to other methods.

Wavelength Compatibility:

EDFA operates in the **C-band** (1530–1565 nm) and **L-band** (1565–1625 nm), which are the standard wavelength bands used in optical communication systems. This makes EDFA suitable for amplifying signals across a wide range of wavelengths without the need for complex adjustments.

Gain Flatness:

EDFA offers a relatively flat gain profile, meaning it can amplify multiple channels simultaneously with minimal variation in amplification levels. This is crucial for DWDM systems, where many different wavelength channels need to be amplified uniformly.

Data-Rate Independence:

EDFA amplifies signals independently of the data rate, meaning that it can be used in systems operating at different speeds. This versatility makes it future-proof for evolving communication technologies.

EDFA Pumping Methods: 980 nm vs. 1480 nm

EDFAs can be pumped using lasers at either **980 nm** or **1480 nm**, with each method offering unique advantages:

980 nm Pumping:

- Provides lower noise amplification, making it suitable for high-sensitivity applications.
- Reduces the likelihood of unwanted back-transitions of erbium ions to the ground state.
- Offers wider separation between the pump and signal wavelengths, further reducing noise.

1480 nm Pumping:

- Delivers better optical power conversion efficiency and higher output power.
- Ideal for high-power applications where maximum signal amplification is needed.

EDFA Gain: Typically ranges between **10 dB** to **30 dB**, depending on the system configuration and the pump power.

EDFA in Long-Haul and Metro Networks

Long-Haul Networks: EDFAs are used extensively in long-haul optical networks to extend transmission distances. A typical EDFA can provide gains of 20–40 dB and boost the signal enough to cover distances up to 80–100 km between amplifiers. In long-haul systems, the combination of EDFAs with dispersion compensation modules (DCMs) helps maintain signal integrity.

Metro Networks: In metro networks, EDFAs are used to boost signal power between shorter spans. The primary challenge in metro networks is to balance amplification while minimizing noise introduction, as the distances between nodes are shorter compared to long-haul networks.

Practical Example

Consider a 100 km DWDM system with a single EDFA providing a gain of 25 dB. The input signal power is -20 dBm per channel, and the ASE noise figure is 5 dB. To calculate the output signal power:

$$\mathbf{P_{out}=P_{in}+G}$$

$$\mathbf{P_{out}=-20\ dBm+25\ dB=5\ dBm}$$

The signal is amplified to 5 dBm, but ASE noise is introduced, which must be managed using appropriate filtering and gain control mechanisms.

Advanced EDFA Configurations

Hybrid Raman-EDFA Amplifiers: In some applications, hybrid Raman-EDFA amplifiers are used to extend the reach of optical signals by combining Raman amplification with EDFAs. This combination allows for better noise performance and higher signal power, particularly in long-haul submarine networks. Hybrid amplifiers provide a 3–5 dB improvement in noise figure compared to conventional EDFAs, making them ideal for high-capacity systems .

Gain-Clamped EDFAs: For systems with fluctuating input power levels, gain-clamped EDFAs are used to maintain a stable gain across all channels, regardless of variations in input power. This is particularly important in dynamic WDM networks, where channel conditions may vary over time.

Amplifier Chain Fault Characteristics

Position	Fault Type	Detection Method	System Impact
Pre-amp	Gain loss	Power monitoring	Signal loss
Line amp	ASE increase	OSNR degradation	BER increase
Booster	Power variation	Output monitoring	Range reduction
Post-amp	Gain tilt	Spectral analysis	Channel imbalance

Applications of EDFA in Optical Communication

EDFA's ability to amplify multiple wavelengths simultaneously has made it the amplifier of choice for various applications, particularly in long-distance and high-capacity networks.

DWDM Systems:

- EDFA is widely used in **Dense Wavelength Division Multiplexing** systems, where it can amplify numerous optical channels transmitted over a single fiber. By offering consistent amplification across all channels, EDFA supports efficient data transmission over long distances without the need for regenerators.

Long-Haul Fiber Networks:

- EDFA extends the transmission distance between costly regenerators, which are necessary for restoring signal quality over long distances. With EDFAs, signal amplification can extend transmission distances up to **120–140 km**, allowing for fewer repeater stations.

Submarine Cable Systems:

- In undersea communication cables, EDFAs are used to amplify signals over thousands of kilometers. Their ability to function in high-pressure environments without frequent maintenance makes them ideal for submarine networks.

Limitations and Challenges of EDFA

While EDFA has numerous advantages, it is not without limitations:

1. **Limited Gain Bandwidth:**
    - Although EDFA performs well in the C and L bands, its gain bandwidth is limited to these regions. This restricts its applicability in systems requiring wider bandwidth, such as **S-band** transmission.
2. **Saturation at High Power Levels:**
    - EDFA's amplification efficiency decreases at very high signal powers, leading to saturation effects that can degrade the signal-to-noise ratio (SNR).
3. **ASE Noise:**
    - **Amplified Spontaneous Emission (ASE)** noise is an inherent characteristic of EDFAs, where spontaneous emissions within the fiber are amplified alongside the signal. This can reduce the **Optical Signal-to-Noise Ratio (OSNR)**, particularly in systems with multiple EDFAs cascaded over long distances.

Raman Amplifiers

Introduction to Raman Amplifiers

Raman amplifiers are a critical component in modern optical networks, particularly for long-haul and ultra-long-haul systems. They utilize the process of **Stimulated Raman Scattering (SRS)** to amplify signals directly within the transmission fiber, offering unique advantages over traditional amplifiers like **Erbium-Doped Fiber Amplifiers (EDFAs)**. Unlike EDFAs, Raman amplifiers can operate across a broader range of wavelengths, making them highly versatile for Dense Wavelength Division Multiplexing (DWDM) systems.

Working Principle of Raman Amplifiers

The Raman amplification process is based on the interaction between light (photons) and the molecular vibrations of the optical fiber. When a high-power pump laser at frequency **ωp** propagates through the fiber, it transfers energy to a lower-frequency signal at **ωs** through stimulated Raman scattering, resulting in amplification.

$$P_s(L) = P_s(0)\exp\left(g_R P_p \frac{L_{\text{eff}}}{A_{\text{eff}}} - \alpha_s L\right)$$

Where:

- g_R is the Raman gain coefficient,
- P_p is the pump power,
- L_{eff} is the effective length of the fiber, and
- α_s is the signal loss due to fiber attenuation.

Types of Raman Amplifiers

There are two main types of Raman amplifiers:

1. **Distributed Raman Amplifiers (DRA)**: Amplification occurs along the transmission fiber itself, providing distributed gain over long distances. DRAs are often used in combination with EDFAs to extend the reach of long-haul links.
2. **Lumped (Discrete) Raman Amplifiers**: These amplifiers use a short length of specially prepared fiber (such as dispersion-compensating fiber) to provide localized amplification, similar to EDFAs.

Advantages of Distributed Raman Amplifiers

Advantages of Raman Amplifiers

Raman amplifiers offer several key benefits that make them an attractive choice for long-distance, high-capacity optical networks.

Extended Reach:

- Raman amplifiers are ideal for extending the reach of optical communication systems without the need for additional in-line amplifiers or repeaters. By amplifying the signal within the transmission fiber, Raman amplification can extend the transmission distance by several tens of kilometers.

Improved Optical Signal-to-Noise Ratio (OSNR):

- One of the primary advantages of Raman amplifiers is their ability to improve the **OSNR**. By providing amplification throughout the fiber rather than at discrete points, Raman amplifiers help maintain a higher signal quality, reducing the need for regeneration and ensuring clearer transmission over long distances.

Wavelength Flexibility:

- Raman amplification can occur at a wide range of wavelengths, making it highly adaptable to different optical bands, including **C-band** and **L-band**. This flexibility makes Raman amplifiers a versatile choice for DWDM systems, where multiple wavelengths are transmitted simultaneously.

Reduced Nonlinear Penalties:

- Raman amplifiers operate at lower power levels than EDFAs, which reduces nonlinear effects such as **self-phase modulation (SPM)** and **four-wave mixing (FWM)**. This makes Raman amplifiers particularly useful for high-capacity systems that require minimal signal distortion.

Improved Gain Flatness:

- Raman amplification provides a more uniform gain profile across multiple wavelengths, ensuring that all channels in a DWDM system are amplified evenly. This gain flatness reduces the likelihood of signal degradation and improves system performance.

Key Parameters of Raman Amplifiers

Raman Gain

The gain in a Raman amplifier is proportional to the pump power and the effective fiber length:

$$G_R = g_R P_p L_{\text{eff}} / A_{\text{eff}}$$

Where:

- g_R is the Raman gain coefficient (typically around **0.5 – 1 W^{-1}/km** for standard single-mode fibers),
- P_p is the pump power (typically **1 – 2 W** for high-power pumps),
- L_{eff} is the effective length of the fiber, and
- A_{eff} is the effective area of the fiber (smaller core fibers, like DCF, have higher Raman gain).

Noise Figure

The **Noise Figure (NF)** in Raman amplifiers is dominated by **Spontaneous Raman Scattering (SRS)**, which generates noise across all wavelengths. The **Spontaneous Emission Factor (n_{sp})** is a function of temperature and determines the level of noise introduced by the amplifier:

$$NF = 1 + \frac{h\nu B}{P_s G_R}$$

Where B is the bandwidth and P_s is the signal power. In general, distributed Raman amplifiers offer better noise performance than EDFAs.

Polarization-Dependent Gain (PDG)

PDG in Raman amplifiers arises because the Raman gain depends on the polarization of the signal relative to the pump. This can introduce signal distortion, particularly in high-data-rate systems. **Polarization diversity techniques** or depolarized pump sources are often used to mitigate PDG.

Design Considerations for Raman Amplifiers

Pump Configuration

Raman amplifiers can be **co-pumped**, **counter-pumped**, or use a combination of both. In **co-pumping**, the pump travels in the same direction as the signal, while in **counter-pumping**, the pump travels in the opposite direction. Counter-pumping is more commonly used in practice because it reduces **Rayleigh backscattering** and **pump-signal interactions**.

Types of Raman Amplifiers

There are two primary configurations of Raman amplifiers, each with its own set of benefits and applications:

Co-Propagating Raman Amplifier:

- In a co-propagating Raman amplifier, the pump laser and signal travel in the same direction. This configuration provides signal amplification at the beginning of the fiber span, helping to boost signal power before attenuation becomes significant.

Counter-Propagating Raman Amplifier:

- In a counter-propagating Raman amplifier, the pump laser is injected from the opposite end of the fiber, traveling in the reverse direction of the signal. This configuration amplifies the signal towards the end of the fiber span, helping to compensate for losses that occur as the signal propagates through the fiber.

Both co-propagating and counter-propagating Raman amplifiers can be used together in hybrid configurations to achieve optimal performance and extend transmission distances.

Applications of Raman Amplifiers

Long-Haul Optical Networks:

- Raman amplifiers are widely used in **long-haul networks**, where signal attenuation becomes a major concern over long distances. By amplifying the signal directly within the transmission fiber, Raman amplifiers extend the reach of optical networks, reducing the need for repeaters and improving overall network efficiency.

Submarine Cable Systems:

- **Submarine optical cables**, which carry a significant portion of the world's internet traffic, rely heavily on Raman amplifiers for long-distance signal transmission. The ability of Raman amplifiers to boost signal power without introducing significant noise is critical for ensuring the reliability of submarine cable systems.

Dense Wavelength Division Multiplexing (DWDM) Systems:

- In DWDM systems, multiple optical channels are transmitted simultaneously over a single fiber. Raman amplifiers are used to amplify all channels uniformly, ensuring that signal strength is maintained across the entire spectrum. This makes Raman amplifiers an essential component in high-capacity networks.

Multi-Pump Designs

To achieve broadband amplification, multiple pump lasers at different wavelengths are often used. This technique can flatten the gain spectrum across the **C-band (1530–1565 nm)** and **L-band (1565–1625 nm)**, enabling simultaneous amplification of multiple WDM channels. An example is shown in the following gain-flattened configuration:

$$G_{total}=G_1(\lambda_1)+G_2(\lambda_2)+\cdots+G_n(\lambda_n)$$

Where G_n represents the gain contribution from each individual pump.

Raman Amplification in DWDM Systems

In Dense Wavelength Division Multiplexing (DWDM) systems, Raman amplifiers are used to extend the reach of high-capacity optical links. By amplifying signals across a broad range of wavelengths, Raman amplifiers enable the transmission of **100G, 400G, and even 800G** signals over long distances without regeneration.

Case Study: Hybrid EDFA-Raman Systems

In hybrid systems, Raman amplifiers are used as pre-amplifiers, while EDFAs serve as booster amplifiers. This configuration provides both **low-noise pre-amplification** and **high-power post-amplification**, enabling ultra-long-haul transmission with minimal signal degradation.

Limitations and Challenges of Raman Amplifiers

While Raman amplifiers offer numerous advantages, they are not without limitations:

High Pump Power Requirement:

- Raman amplifiers require significant pump power to achieve the desired gain, particularly in long fiber spans. This increases the complexity and cost of the system.

Double Rayleigh Backscattering:

- **Double Rayleigh scattering** can introduce unwanted noise into the amplified signal, reducing the effectiveness of the Raman amplifier in certain configurations.

Pump Noise Transfer:

- Noise from the pump laser can be transferred to the amplified signal, potentially degrading the signal-to-noise ratio. Careful system design is required to minimize the impact of pump noise.

Higher Cost:

- Raman amplifiers tend to be more expensive than EDFAs due to the complexity of the pumping mechanism and the need for high-power pump lasers. This can make them less attractive for cost-sensitive applications.

Raman Amplifier Noise Figure vs EDFA and Their Use in Long-Haul Links

Introduction to Amplifier Noise Figures

In optical networks, noise figure (NF) is a critical parameter for evaluating the performance of amplifiers like Raman amplifiers and Erbium-Doped Fiber Amplifiers (EDFAs). The noise figure refers to the degradation in the signal-to-noise ratio (SNR) due to the amplifier's inherent noise processes, such as amplified spontaneous emission (ASE) in EDFAs or stimulated Raman scattering (SRS) noise in Raman amplifiers. An amplifier with a lower noise figure provides better signal quality and extended transmission distances.

In general, Raman amplifiers have a lower or even negative noise figure compared to EDFAs, especially when used in distributed configurations.

Why Raman Amplifier Noise Figure is Lower than EDFA?

Raman amplifiers achieve a lower noise figure for several reasons:

Distributed Amplification: Raman amplification occurs throughout the length of the transmission fiber, whereas EDFAs provide lumped amplification at discrete points along the link. This distributed nature means the signal is amplified before significant attenuation occurs, leading to an improved signal-to-noise ratio (SNR) across the entire fiber span. This improvement is quantified by an effective noise figure (Feff), which can be negative in some cases due to the way Raman gain compensates for fiber losses.

In contrast, EDFAs amplify the signal after it has already been attenuated by the fiber, which means the amplifier is amplifying both the signal and the noise that has accumulated along the fiber.

$$F_{eff}=F_n \cdot \exp(-\alpha_s \cdot L)$$

Where:

- F_{eff} is the effective noise figure,
- α_s is the signal attenuation coefficient, and
- L is the fiber length.

This formula demonstrates that the **effective noise figure can be less than 1** for distributed Raman amplifiers, leading to superior noise performance compared to EDFAs .

- **Improved OSNR**: By compensating for fiber losses throughout the transmission span, distributed Raman amplifiers improve the optical signal-to-noise ratio (OSNR) compared to lumped EDFA amplification, where ASE noise is added after significant signal attenuation . The distributed gain in Raman systems allows for more efficient use of the available signal power, leading to better system performance in terms of noise.
- **Negative Noise Figure**: In certain configurations, the effective noise figure of a distributed Raman amplifier can be negative on the decibel scale. This occurs because the distributed gain in Raman amplification effectively counteracts fiber attenuation. The Raman amplifier reduces the noise

figure so effectively that the SNR is improved relative to the unamplified fiber .

Hybrid Raman-EDFA Systems in Long-Haul Links

Hybrid systems that combine **Raman amplifiers** and **EDFAs** are commonly deployed in **long-haul** and **ultra-long-haul links**. These systems leverage the advantages of both amplifiers to achieve optimal performance.

Benefits of Hybrid Raman-EDFA Systems

- **Improved Noise Performance**: By placing a Raman amplifier at the start of the fiber span (acting as a pre-amplifier), followed by an EDFA, the overall **noise figure** of the system is greatly reduced. The Raman amplifier improves the SNR at the input of the EDFA, resulting in lower ASE noise generation and higher OSNR .
- **Extended Reach**: Hybrid systems extend the reach of optical links without regeneration. The Raman amplifier compensates for signal attenuation along the span, while the EDFA boosts the signal at the end of the span, enabling distances of **80–100 km** or more between amplifiers .
- **Enhanced Power Efficiency**: Raman amplifiers reduce the need for higher input powers into the EDFA, minimizing the effects of gain compression in the EDFA. This results in better power efficiency and improved system performance .

Example: Long-Haul DWDM Link

In a long-haul Dense Wavelength Division Multiplexing (DWDM) system, the use of backward-pumped Raman amplification in combination with EDFAs offers significant noise and reach improvements. For example:

1. **Raman Pre-Amplifier**: Provides **distributed gain** along the fiber span, improving the signal quality before it reaches the EDFA.
2. **EDFA Booster**: Amplifies the signal at the end of the span to compensate for any remaining losses and provide the necessary power for long-distance transmission.

The **noise figure** of the hybrid system is improved by **3.2 dB** on average compared to EDFA-only systems, providing **1.8 dB better nonlinear OSNR**. However, the increase in system capacity is only around **9.5%** due to nonlinear effects like **stimulated Brillouin scattering (SBS)** and **four-wave mixing (FWM)**, which limit the benefits of higher power .

Advantages and Disadvantages of Raman and EDFA Amplifiers

Advantages of Raman Amplifiers

- **Low Noise Figure**: As described, distributed Raman amplifiers can achieve very low or even negative noise figures, improving the OSNR and overall system performance.
- **Wider Gain Spectrum**: Raman amplifiers can provide gain over a broader range of wavelengths than EDFAs, including the **S-band**, **C-band**, and **L-band**, making them highly versatile in WDM systems .
- **Distributed Gain**: Amplification occurs throughout the fiber, leading to more uniform signal quality over long distances .

Disadvantages of Raman Amplifiers

- **Higher Pump Power Requirements**: Raman amplifiers require significant pump power (typically several watts) to achieve the necessary gain, increasing the complexity and cost of the system .
- **Nonlinear Effects**: The use of high pump powers can lead to nonlinear effects such as **SBS** and **FWM**, which degrade signal quality and limit the achievable system capacity .
- **Temperature Sensitivity**: Raman amplifiers are more sensitive to environmental conditions like temperature, which can affect their performance and stability .

Noise in EDFA and Raman Amplifiers

Both **Erbium-Doped Fiber Amplifiers (EDFAs)** and **Raman amplifiers** generate noise during signal amplification, but the mechanisms and characteristics of the noise generated by each type of amplifier are different. Understanding these noise mechanisms is crucial in designing optical networks, especially in long-haul and high-capacity Dense Wavelength Division Multiplexing (DWDM) systems. In optical systems, noise degrades the Optical Signal-to-Noise Ratio (OSNR) and can lead to increased Bit Error Rates (BER).

Noise in EDFAs

Amplified Spontaneous Emission (ASE)

The primary source of noise in EDFAs is Amplified Spontaneous Emission (ASE). This noise is generated as part of the process of signal amplification through stimulated emission, which amplifies not only the desired optical signal but also spontaneously emitted photons.

Mechanism of ASE Generation

EDFAs rely on the excitation of erbium ions using a pump laser, typically at 980 nm or 1480 nm. When the erbium ions return to their ground state from an excited state, they emit photons. These photons can either contribute to the amplification of the optical signal (desired process) or result in spontaneous emission. This spontaneous emission is inherently random and occurs in all directions. In an EDFA, these spontaneously emitted photons can themselves be amplified through the process of stimulated emission, producing ASE noise.

The ASE noise power PASE generated by the amplifier is proportional to the gain G, spontaneous emission factor nsp, and the bandwidth B of the optical system:

$$P_{ASE}=2n_{sp}(G-1)h\nu B$$

Where:

- n_{sp} is the spontaneous emission factor, which represents the population inversion efficiency.
- G is the gain of the EDFA.
- $h\nu$ is the photon energy (Planck's constant h times the frequency ν).
- B is the optical bandwidth.

Effect on OSNR

ASE degrades the **OSNR** by introducing noise across the entire bandwidth of the amplifier. Since ASE is amplified alongside the signal, the longer the optical path with multiple EDFAs, the more noise accumulates in the system, reducing the effective signal quality.

Noise Figure in EDFAs

The **noise figure (NF)** is a measure of the noise introduced by the amplifier, and it is directly related to the ASE noise. For EDFAs, the noise figure is given by:

$$NF\approx 2n_{sp}$$

For a typical EDFA, the noise figure ranges from **3 to 6 dB**, depending on the level of population inversion and operating conditions. A noise figure of **3 dB** represents the best performance possible in a fully inverted EDFA (i.e., when most erbium ions are in the excited state).

Factors Influencing ASE

- **Gain Level**: Higher gain levels lead to increased ASE noise, as more spontaneous emissions are amplified.
- **Pump Power**: A stronger pump power increases the number of excited erbium ions, which can increase the spontaneous emission rate and lead to higher ASE noise.
- **Spectral Bandwidth**: EDFAs have a gain bandwidth limited to the **C-band (1530–1565 nm)** and **L-band (1570–1610 nm)**, and ASE noise is distributed across this bandwidth.

Noise in Raman Amplifiers

Spontaneous Raman Scattering

The dominant noise mechanism in Raman amplifiers is Spontaneous Raman Scattering (SRS), which is different from the ASE found in EDFAs. In Raman amplification, signal amplification occurs through the interaction between a high-power pump and the optical signal via stimulated Raman scattering.

Mechanism of SRS Noise Generation

In a Raman amplifier, a high-power pump laser (usually around 1450 nm to 1500 nm) is injected into the transmission fiber. As the pump light interacts with the molecular vibrations of the fiber (phonons), it transfers energy to lower-frequency photons (the signal) via stimulated scattering. However, spontaneous Raman scattering occurs as well, where some of the pump light interacts randomly with phonons, producing scattered photons that are randomly distributed across the optical spectrum. These scattered photons are considered noise.

This spontaneous Raman scattering noise is then amplified by the pump, just as the desired signal is, contributing to the total noise in the system.

Polarization-Dependent Noise

One unique aspect of Raman amplifiers is **polarization-dependent gain (PDG)**, where the amplification efficiency depends on the relative polarization between the pump and signal. This can introduce additional noise and signal degradation, as the gain varies with changing polarization states along the fiber.

Noise Figure in Raman Amplifiers

In distributed Raman amplifiers, the noise figure is inherently lower than in EDFAs. This is because amplification occurs along the transmission fiber, before significant signal attenuation has taken place. The **effective noise figure** for a Raman amplifier is given by:

$$NF = \frac{P_{ASE}}{GP_{in}} + 1$$

Where:

- P_{ASE} is the noise power due to spontaneous Raman scattering.
- G is the Raman amplifier gain.
- P_{in} is the input signal power.

Since Raman amplification takes place **before** the signal experiences significant attenuation, the noise figure can be close to **0 dB** or even **negative** in some configurations, which is a significant improvement over EDFAs.

Comparison of Noise in EDFAs and Raman Amplifiers

Parameter	EDFA	Raman Amplifier
Main Noise Source	Amplified Spontaneous Emission (ASE)	Spontaneous Raman Scattering (SRS)
Noise Figure	3–6 dB	Typically lower, can be 0 dB or negative
Impact on OSNR	Adds significant ASE noise, especially in cascaded systems	Less noise due to distributed gain, improving OSNR
Gain Mechanism	Lumped amplification at discrete points	Distributed amplification along the transmission fiber
Polarization Sensitivity	Low (unless polarization-dependent configurations are used)	Higher due to polarization-dependent gain

Using Raman and EDFA Amplifiers Together in Long-Haul Links

In long-haul optical systems, hybrid Raman-EDFA amplifiers are often used to combine the benefits of both amplification technologies:

- Raman Amplifiers are typically used at the beginning of a fiber span to provide distributed gain, which amplifies the signal before significant attenuation occurs, improving the signal-to-noise ratio at the start of the span.
- EDFA Amplifiers are used as booster or in-line amplifiers after the Raman amplifier to provide a significant increase in signal power at the end of the span.

This hybrid configuration helps to mitigate the noise introduced by both amplifier types while extending the transmission distance without the need for regeneration. The combination of a low-noise Raman pre-amplifier and a high-gain EDFA booster allows for longer spans between amplifiers, making it ideal for ultra-long-haul networks.

Advantages of Using Hybrid Raman-EDFA Systems:

- **Lower Overall Noise**: The low noise figure of the Raman amplifier improves the OSNR, allowing for better signal quality over long distances.
- **Extended Reach**: By amplifying the signal throughout the fiber span, Raman amplifiers reduce the need for frequent amplification, while EDFAs provide the necessary high-power amplification at the end of the span.
- **Wider Bandwidth**: Raman amplifiers can amplify signals across a broader wavelength range (S-band, C-band, L-band), while EDFAs are limited to C-band and L-band amplification.

Disadvantages:

- **Higher Pump Power**: Raman amplifiers require high pump powers, which increases system complexity and cost.
- **Nonlinear Effects**: High pump powers in Raman amplifiers can induce nonlinear effects such as **Stimulated Brillouin Scattering (SBS)** and **Four-Wave Mixing (FWM)**, which degrade the signal quality.
- **Polarization Sensitivity**: Raman amplifiers are more sensitive to polarization effects, which can cause fluctuations in the gain.

Noise Optimization in Amplified Links

In optical communications, noise is a key factor that determines the quality of the signal and overall system performance. Different amplifiers, including Erbium-Doped Fiber Amplifiers (EDFAs) and Raman amplifiers, generate noise in different ways. While you can't completely eliminate noise, you can optimize system design and deployment to reduce noise and improve the signal-to-noise ratio (SNR), enhancing the overall performance of the system.

Can You Change Noise in an Optical Link?

Noise in optical amplifiers is primarily generated by amplified spontaneous emission (ASE) in EDFAs and spontaneous Raman scattering (SRS) in Raman amplifiers. While noise generation is an inherent part of amplification, certain strategies can minimize the noise and its impact on the system. Below are key approaches for controlling and optimizing noise in optical networks:

How to Optimize Noise in Optical Links

Amplifier Noise Optimization Techniques

Use of Hybrid Amplifiers (EDFA + Raman)

- By combining **Raman amplifiers** (with lower noise) and **EDFAs** (with high gain), you can balance **low noise figures** with sufficient amplification. Hybrid Raman-EDFA systems are commonly deployed in **long-haul links** because they offer the best of both worlds:
  - **Raman amplification** at the beginning of the span provides distributed gain, reducing noise figure.
  - **EDFA amplifiers** at the end boost signal power without adding significant noise .

Distributed Amplification

- Raman amplifiers provide **distributed amplification** along the transmission fiber, which prevents the signal from attenuating too much before being amplified. This is in contrast to lumped EDFAs, where the signal experiences more attenuation before amplification, increasing noise levels. Distributed amplification improves the **effective noise figure (Feff)** of the system, making it one of the most effective techniques to minimize noise .

Optimizing Gain Settings

- High gain settings amplify both the signal and noise, leading to higher noise accumulation over long distances. **Careful tuning of amplifier gain** can help reduce noise without compromising performance. Lowering gain but increasing the number of amplifiers along the route can reduce the **accumulation of ASE noise** .

Gain Flattening Filters (GFFs)

- Amplifiers like EDFAs experience **gain ripple** across different wavelengths, resulting in uneven noise distribution. Using **Gain Flattening Filters (GFFs)** smooths out the gain, providing more consistent amplification and reducing the noise impact on certain channels in **Wavelength Division Multiplexing (WDM)** systems .

Polarization Scrambling and Control

- Polarization-dependent noise, especially in Raman amplifiers, can be mitigated by **polarization scrambling**. Scrambling changes the relative polarization states between the signal and the pump light, averaging out polarization-related gain variations . This technique helps to reduce the **polarization-dependent gain (PDG)** noise, especially in systems using high symbol rates .

Noise Characteristics Based on Amplifier Position

Pre-Amplifiers (Typically Raman Amplifiers)

- **Pre-amplifiers** are placed at the beginning of a fiber span. Using a **Raman amplifier** in this position provides distributed gain, preventing the signal from experiencing significant attenuation before being amplified. This approach:
    - Reduces the noise figure by amplifying the signal close to the source.
    - Improves the **optical signal-to-noise ratio (OSNR)** by reducing the ASE noise generated by subsequent EDFAs .

In-Line Amplifiers (Typically EDFAs)

- **In-line amplifiers** are placed at regular intervals along the fiber. EDFAs are often used here due to their high gain capabilities. The noise figure of these amplifiers is directly affected by the **amount of gain** applied. Lowering the gain in each amplifier while increasing the number of amplifiers can help manage noise levels across long-haul links .

Booster Amplifiers

- **Booster amplifiers** are placed at the end of the fiber span and provide high output power to overcome signal attenuation. EDFAs are typically used in this position. While these amplifiers boost the signal, they also amplify any noise that has accumulated along the fiber, making it essential to have noise-minimizing strategies in earlier stages .

When to Use Different Amplifiers Based on Noise and Performance

When to Use Raman Amplifiers

- **Distributed Raman Amplifiers** should be used when you need to:
  - Improve **OSNR** in long-haul and ultra-long-haul systems.
  - Achieve **low noise amplification** with a noise figure that can be close to 0 dB or even negative in certain configurations.
  - Reduce **polarization-mode dispersion (PMD)** and other polarization-related noise .

When to Use EDFAs

- **EDFA Amplifiers** are preferred when:
  - You need high gain amplification in lumped form (ideal for **booster and in-line amplifier** positions).
  - Cost efficiency and simple deployment are important.
  - You are working with systems in the **C-band** and **L-band** .

How Noise Can Be Reduced in Long-Haul Links

1. **Power Optimization for Nonlinear Effects**
   - Noise optimization is not just about reducing ASE or Raman scattering noise but also involves minimizing nonlinear effects such as **stimulated Brillouin scattering (SBS), stimulated Raman scattering (SRS), four-wave mixing (FWM)**, and **cross-phase modulation (XPM)**. Operating amplifiers at optimized power levels reduces these nonlinear effects and helps minimize noise .
2. **Optimizing OSNR and Power**

- The **OSNR** can be optimized by choosing the right combination of Raman pre-amplifiers and EDFA boosters, along with the appropriate span length. Distributed Raman amplifiers help maintain a higher OSNR across longer spans .

3. **Using Hybrid Amplifiers**
    - Hybrid Raman-EDFA amplifiers are ideal for long-haul links where high OSNR is crucial. By providing distributed gain with Raman amplification and high-power boosting with EDFA, you can significantly reduce noise while maintaining high signal quality .

Optical Power Management in DWDM Networks

In dense wavelength division multiplexing (DWDM) systems, **power management** plays a critical role in determining the performance, reach, and longevity of the optical network. A key aspect of power management is ensuring that each channel's optical signal power is balanced and optimized to prevent degradation from both **high power nonlinearities** and **low power signal attenuation**. This chapter covers how to manage power effectively in DWDM networks, addresses the effects of high and low power on system performance, and provides guidelines for power management when dealing with hybrid channel configurations, different data rates, and modulation formats.

Optical Power Effects on DWDM Channels

Effects of High Power on DWDM Channels

Excessive optical power in DWDM channels can lead to several **nonlinear effects** within the fiber, which degrade signal quality and limit the system's overall performance. Some key nonlinear phenomena caused by high power include:

- **Stimulated Brillouin Scattering (SBS):** Occurs when the optical power exceeds a certain threshold, typically around 5 mW. SBS can limit the amount of power that can be launched into the fiber, particularly in systems with **narrow channel spacings**. For WDM systems with channel spacings greater than **50 GHz**, SBS becomes a key limiting factor .
- **Stimulated Raman Scattering (SRS):** In WDM systems, high-power signals can transfer energy from shorter wavelengths to longer wave-

lengths, amplifying the longer-wavelength channels and attenuating the shorter-wavelength ones. This **Raman crosstalk** can significantly degrade the system's **optical signal-to-noise ratio (OSNR)**, especially in systems with large channel counts .

- **Four-Wave Mixing (FWM):** This nonlinear effect arises when multiple optical channels interact within the fiber, creating additional spurious signals that interfere with the original data. FWM is particularly significant when the fiber operates near the **zero-dispersion wavelength**, as the efficiency of FWM increases in low-dispersion regions. High channel power increases the likelihood of FWM .
- **Cross-Phase Modulation (XPM):** In WDM systems, high-power signals from one channel can induce phase changes in adjacent channels, leading to signal distortion. The phase shift depends on both the power of the affected channel and the power of the adjacent channels .

Effects of Low Power on DWDM Channels

Insufficient power can result in **signal attenuation** that degrades signal quality over long distances. Low-power signals are more susceptible to attenuation due to:

- **Fiber Losses:** Typical attenuation rates in optical fibers are around **0.2 dB/km** for standard single-mode fibers. Without sufficient power, signals can be weakened significantly over long distances, leading to degraded OSNR .
- **Noise Accumulation:** Lower power levels make signals more vulnerable to noise introduced by amplifiers, including **amplified spontaneous emission (ASE)** noise from EDFAs. This can reduce the **signal-to-noise ratio (SNR)** and increase **bit error rates (BER)** .

Optical Power Management Techniques for DWDM Networks

Ideal Power Management for Uniform Channels

For a DWDM system where all channels are operating at the same **data rate** and **modulation format**, maintaining equal power levels across all channels is essential. In such systems:

- **Launch Power Control:** The **launch power** of each channel should be carefully calibrated to ensure that all channels have similar power levels to minimize **crosstalk** and nonlinear effects like FWM and XPM .
- **Gain Equalization:** Amplifiers, particularly EDFAs, can introduce **gain variations** across different wavelengths, leading to uneven power levels. Using **gain flattening filters (GFFs)** ensures consistent amplifi-

cation across all channels, preventing some channels from experiencing higher power and others from falling below the noise floor .

- **OSNR Optimization:** In uniformly loaded systems, the OSNR should be optimized to achieve the required performance. A higher launch power increases OSNR but at the risk of triggering nonlinear effects, so balancing power is key .

Power Management for Mixed/Hybrid Channels

In systems where channels have **different data rates** and **modulation formats** (e.g., a mix of 100G DP-QPSK and 200G DP-16QAM), power management becomes more complex. Higher data rates and more advanced modulation formats (like 16QAM) require better OSNR, but these signals are more sensitive to nonlinear effects, so careful power control is required:

- **Lower Power for Higher Modulation Channels:** Higher-order modulation formats like **DP-16QAM** are more prone to nonlinearities. Therefore, channels using these formats should be operated at lower power compared to channels with simpler modulations like **DP-QPSK**. This reduces the risk of FWM, XPM, and SPM .
- **Dynamic Power Adjustment:** Systems with mixed channels benefit from **dynamic power management**, where power levels are adjusted in real-time based on network conditions. **Software-defined networking (SDN)** platforms can be used to optimize power levels dynamically based on traffic patterns and channel configurations .

Steps for Upgrading Channels from 100G to 200G or 400G or more.

When upgrading a DWDM network to higher data rates (e.g., from 100G to 200G or 400G), several power management considerations must be taken into account:

- **Signal Power Adjustments:** Channels carrying higher data rates and more complex modulations need **more precise power control**. **400G DP-16QAM** channels, for instance, should be operated at lower power than **100G DP-QPSK** channels to avoid nonlinear impairments.
- **Amplifier Gain Optimization:** Upgrading to higher data rates often requires **re-tuning amplifier gain** settings to accommodate the new channel configuration. Amplifiers should be optimized to provide suffi-

cient gain for all channels without amplifying noise or introducing non-linear effects .

- **OSNR Calculations:** Higher data rates generally require better OSNR for reliable operation. When upgrading channels, **OSNR budgets** need to be recalculated based on the new modulation formats and channel spacing .
- **Nonlinear Effect Mitigation:** As the network moves to higher data rates, the risk of nonlinear effects increases. Techniques like **nonlinear compensation** and **digital signal processing (DSP)** can be used to mitigate these effects in real-time .

Power Optimization Based on Channel Loading and Network Conditions

Impact of Channel Loading

The **loading condition** of the DWDM system (i.e., the number of channels in use) can significantly affect the ideal power levels for each channel. Fully loaded systems are more susceptible to **nonlinear effects**, while under-loaded systems can tolerate higher per-channel power:

- **Fully Loaded Systems:** In systems with high channel counts, power must be kept low to minimize **cross-channel interference** caused by nonlinearities like **SPM** and **XPM** .
- **Partially Loaded Systems:** When fewer channels are in use, individual channel power can be increased without triggering nonlinear effects, as the total power density in the fiber is lower. However, care must still be taken to avoid **SRS-induced crosstalk**, where higher power channels deplete the power of neighboring lower-power channels .

Power Management During Network Upgrades

When adding new channels or upgrading to higher data rates, several steps should be followed:

- **Re-evaluate Power Budgets:** Ensure that the total power across all channels is within the system's limits, taking into account nonlinear effects like FWM and XPM.
- **Amplifier Tuning:** Adjust the gain of inline and booster amplifiers to maintain consistent OSNR across the new channels.
- **Channel Spacing Optimization:** Consider using **flex-grid technology** to adjust channel spacing dynamically. Higher modulation formats may benefit from **wider channel spacing** to reduce crosstalk and interference .

ROADMs (Reconfigurable Optical Add/Drop Multiplexers)

ROADMs (Reconfigurable Optical Add/Drop Multiplexers) Theory and Architectures

Reconfigurable Optical Add-Drop Multiplexers (ROADMs) have evolved significantly from simple, fixed-grid devices to highly flexible, colorless, directionless, contentionless (CDC) architectures. Modern ROADM systems allow network operators to dynamically manage optical paths, making optical networks more resilient, scalable, and efficient. This chapter delves into the various stages of ROADM evolution, explores the latest advancements such as flex-grid

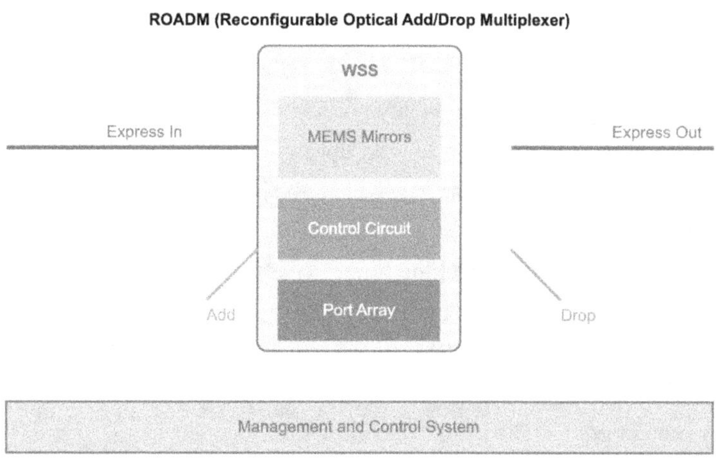

ROADMs, and includes practical examples demonstrating how they improve network flexibility and reduce operational complexity.

ROADM Capabilities

Feature	Description	Benefit
Colorless	Any wavelength on any port	Flexible wavelength assignment
Directionless	Any direction on any port	Routing flexibility
Contentionless	Multiple same wavelengths	Enhanced capacity

Architectural Types
- Broadcast-and-Select
- Route-and-Select
- Wavelength-Selective

Performance Metrics
- Insertion Loss: 10-15 dB
- Isolation: >40 dB
- Switching Time: <50 ms

ROADMs provide dynamic wavelength management capabilities such as

Degrees of Freedom

- Colorless: Any wavelength on any port
- Directionless: Any direction for add/drop
- Contentionless: Multiple same-wavelength signals

Switching Technologies

- MEMS-based: <50ms switching time
- WSS-based: <20ms switching time
- Typical insertion loss: 5-7 dB

Protection Schemes

- 1+1 protection
- Ring protection
- Mesh restoration
- Protection switching time: <50ms

Practical Implementation Considerations

1. **Power Budget Calculation**

$$P\_receiver = P\_transmitter - \Sigma(losses) + \Sigma(gains)$$

where losses include:

- Fiber attenuation (0.2 dB/km at 1550nm)
- Connector losses (0.5 dB per connector)
- Splice losses (0.1 dB per splice)
- Mux/Demux losses

2. **System Design Guidelines**

- Maximum span length without amplification: 80-120 km
- Minimum OSNR requirement: 18-20 dB
- Maximum number of cascaded ROADMs: 15-20
- Channel power flatness: ±1 dB

3. **Maintenance and Troubleshooting**
    - Regular OSNR measurements
    - Chromatic dispersion monitoring
    - Polarization mode dispersion checks
    - Bit error rate testing
4. **Network Management**
    - Performance monitoring thresholds
    - Protection switching criteria
    - Wavelength routing algorithms
    - Power leveling procedures

Evolution of ROADM Technologies

Fixed-Grid ROADMs

- **Initial Technology**: The first generation of ROADMs operated on a fixed-grid architecture, where wavelengths were constrained to predefined channel spacings, typically 50 GHz or 100 GHz. These ROADMs were limited in flexibility, allowing only specific wavelengths to be added or dropped at certain nodes.
- **Limitations**: Fixed-grid ROADMs could not accommodate the demand for higher-capacity channels such as 400G or 1T, which require broader bandwidth.
- **Example**: In early DWDM systems, a fixed-grid ROADM was used in metro networks, enabling static wavelength routing for 10G or 40G signals. As demand grew, the network struggled to support higher-speed signals efficiently due to the rigid channel grid.

Wavelength Selective Switch (WSS)

- **Advancement**: The introduction of WSS-based ROADMs marked a significant advancement by allowing the dynamic switching of wavelengths. WSS enables flexible routing of any wavelength to any direction in the network, supporting mesh networking and reducing the need for manual intervention.
- **Example**: A regional operator deployed WSS-based ROADMs in a long-haul network, allowing real-time routing changes as traffic patterns shifted, reducing downtime during maintenance.

Colorless, Directionless, and Contentionless (CDC) ROADMs

- **Colorless**: Allows any wavelength to be added/dropped at any port without being tied to a specific port.
- **Directionless**: Permits traffic to flow in any direction (e.g., east, west, north, south) without physical reconnections.
- **Contentionless**: Prevents wavelength contention, ensuring that the same wavelength can be routed through multiple paths in the same node without interference.
- **Example**: In a nationwide optical backbone, the deployment of CDC-ROADM nodes enabled the carrier to add or drop any wavelength on any fiber without wavelength blocking, enhancing the flexibility to route 100G and 400G channels dynamically.

Flex-Grid ROADMs and the Move Beyond 100G

Flex-Grid Technology

- **What is Flex-Grid**: Traditional ROADMs work on a fixed wavelength grid, usually spaced at 50 GHz or 100 GHz. Flex-grid ROADMs, on the other hand, enable variable bandwidth allocation per channel. Instead of confining channels to a fixed width, flex-grid allows channels to occupy only the spectrum they require, enabling the support of 400G, 800G, or even 1T channels.
- **Practical Impact**: Flex-grid allows more efficient use of the fiber spectrum, increasing total capacity by packing channels closer together while avoiding underutilization.
- **Example**: A flex-grid ROADM was deployed in a high-capacity metro network where both 100G and 400G signals needed to coexist. Flex-grid allowed the operator to dynamically adjust channel spacing, optimizing spectrum use and enabling the seamless upgrade from 100G to 400G without adding new hardware.

Use Cases and Practical Applications of ROADMs

Dynamic Service Provisioning

- ROADMs enable on-demand provisioning of wavelengths, allowing network operators to react quickly to new service requests. For example, in a data center interconnect network, dynamic wavelength provisioning enables faster deployment of additional capacity to meet unexpected traffic surges.
- **Use Case**: A large financial institution needed to increase its inter-data-center bandwidth during market hours. Using CDC-ROADM technolo-

gy, the operator was able to provision additional 100G channels dynamically, ensuring uninterrupted connectivity during peak trading periods.

Disaster Recovery and Protection

- **ROADM-Based Protection**: ROADMs allow optical networks to automatically reroute traffic in the event of a fiber cut or node failure. This is particularly important in disaster recovery scenarios, where service continuity is critical.
- **Use Case**: In a long-haul fiber network, a major fiber cut disrupted the primary path. The ROADM nodes automatically switched traffic to an alternate path within seconds, maintaining service availability for critical customers like emergency services and financial institutions.

Multi-Rate Support in Flex-Grid Networks

- **Challenge**: In modern networks, there is a need to support a mix of 100G, 200G, 400G, and 800G traffic on the same infrastructure.
- **Solution**: Flex-grid ROADMs dynamically allocate bandwidth based on the specific needs of each service, enabling the coexistence of multiple data rates on the same fiber.
- **Example**: A cloud service provider uses flex-grid ROADMs to allocate variable bandwidth per channel in its data center interconnects. As some data centers require 400G channels and others 100G channels, flex-grid allows the provider to optimize spectrum usage, avoiding the need to deploy additional fiber.

Link Control and G-OSNR Calculations for ROADMs

Generalized Optical Signal-to-Noise Ratio (G-OSNR)

- **Definition**: G-OSNR is a metric that extends traditional OSNR by considering all noise sources, including those introduced by ROADMs, amplifiers, and other network elements. G-OSNR helps operators understand the overall signal quality across multiple spans and through several ROADMs.
- **Example**: In a 400G metro network, G-OSNR was calculated at various points along the network path, accounting for losses introduced by WSS modules and amplifiers. The network was optimized to ensure that G-OSNR stayed above the required threshold for error-free operation.

Practical G-OSNR Calculation for a ROADM Network

- Given a network with multiple ROADMs, amplifiers, and fiber spans:
  - **G-OSNR** is calculated by summing the contributions of noise from each element along the path.

- Formula: G-OSNR=PsignalNtotal where Psignal is the total signal power and Ntotal is the accumulated noise power along the path.
- **Use Case**: An operator planning a long-haul link with several ROADM nodes calculated G-OSNR to ensure that a new 400G service could be deployed without exceeding the network's noise tolerance. Based on G-OSNR calculations, adjustments to amplifier settings and signal launch power were made to maintain error-free transmission.

The Role of ROADM in 5G and Beyond

1. **5G Backhaul and ROADM Integration**
   - ROADMs play a critical role in 5G backhaul, where dynamic wavelength provisioning and high-capacity links are essential to meet the low-latency requirements of 5G applications.
   - **Example**: A 5G network operator used ROADM-based backhaul links to dynamically allocate bandwidth for different regions based on real-time traffic needs, reducing congestion and improving network performance during peak hours.
2. **Future of ROADM in 6G and Beyond**
   - As networks evolve toward 6G, the need for more dynamic, flexible optical infrastructures will continue to grow. ROADMs, particularly those with CDC and flex-grid capabilities, will be integral to managing the increased data rates and ultra-low latency requirements of future networks.

Non-Linearity in Optical Fiber

Nonlinearities in optical fibers occur when the intensity of the optical signal becomes sufficiently high that the response of the fiber medium deviates from being linear. In a linear regime, the relationship between input power and the transmitted signal is proportional. However, in the nonlinear regime, high-intensity optical fields cause changes in the refractive index of the fiber, leading to phenomena that affect the integrity of the transmitted signal. .Nonlinearities in optical fibers represent one of the most significant challenges in high-capacity optical networks, particularly as we push toward higher data rates and denser channel spacing in DWDM systems. Understanding the causes, types, and effects of nonlinearities is essential for designing robust optical networks.

Why Nonlinearities Happen

- **High Power Levels**: As the intensity of the optical signal increases (due to higher baud rates, more densely packed wavelengths in DWDM systems, or long fiber spans), the fiber's refractive index starts to change in response to the electric field of the light.
- **Long Transmission Distances**: Nonlinear effects accumulate over distance, so in long-haul and ultra-long-haul optical networks, even moderate power levels can lead to significant nonlinear impairments.
- **Dense Wavelength Division Multiplexing (DWDM)**: In DWDM systems, multiple optical channels are tightly spaced in the same fiber. The interactions between closely spaced wavelengths lead to additional nonlinear effects.

Formula for Nonlinear Refractive Index:

$$n_{\text{eff}} = n_0 + n_2 \cdot I$$

Where:

- n_0 is the linear refractive index,
- n_2 is the nonlinear index coefficient,
- I is the intensity of the optical field.

As I increases, the nonlinear term ($n_2 \cdot I$) becomes significant, leading to various nonlinear effects.

Types of Nonlinearities in Optical Fibers

Nonlinearities are broadly categorized into two types: **Kerr effects** and **Scattering effects**.

Kerr Effects

The Kerr effect refers to the intensity-dependent change in the refractive index of the fiber. The most common types of Kerr nonlinearities include:

- **Self-Phase Modulation (SPM)**: Occurs when the phase of the optical signal is modulated by its own intensity. This leads to spectral broadening of the signal, which can degrade signal quality, especially over long distances.

  - **Example**: In a 100G coherent system, the phase of the transmitted signal gets modulated due to high input power, causing temporal pulse spreading and resulting in inter-symbol interference (ISI).
- **Cross-Phase Modulation (XPM)**: In DWDM systems, the intensity of one channel affects the phase of another co-propagating channel. XPM is particularly troublesome in multi-channel systems and leads to crosstalk between adjacent wavelengths.
  - **Example**: In a 400G DWDM link with 40 channels, the phase of one channel is altered by fluctuations in the power of neighboring channels, leading to signal distortion and increased BER.

- **Four-Wave Mixing (FWM)**: This occurs when three optical waves interact within the fiber to generate a fourth wave. FWM is highly dependent on the channel spacing and the chromatic dispersion of the fiber. It is more pronounced in systems with tightly spaced DWDM channels.
  - **Example**: In a metro network operating with 50 GHz channel spacing, FWM generates additional spurious signals at new frequencies, causing interference with the main channels.

Scattering Effects

Scattering refers to the interaction between the light signal and the material of the fiber, leading to energy being transferred from one part of the signal to another. The primary scattering effects include:

- **Stimulated Brillouin Scattering (SBS)**: Occurs when light is scattered by acoustic phonons within the fiber. SBS becomes significant at high optical power levels, causing backscattering and limiting the amount of power that can be transmitted through the fiber.
  - **Example**: In a long-haul 100G link operating at high power, SBS backscattering results in signal loss, limiting the effective reach of the transmission.

- **Stimulated Raman Scattering (SRS)**: Involves the scattering of light by optical phonons. SRS transfers power from shorter wavelengths to longer wavelengths in a DWDM system. This leads to signal degradation, especially for shorter-wavelength channels.
  - **Example**: In a DWDM system with 40 channels, SRS reduces the power of channels at the shorter wavelengths, while increasing the power of channels at longer wavelengths, leading to imbalance and degradation.

Detecting Nonlinearities in Optical Networks

Symptoms of Nonlinearity in a Link

- **Increased Bit Error Rate (BER)**: Nonlinear effects can introduce noise and distortions, leading to an increased BER, especially on high-speed links (e.g., 400G or 800G).

- **Optical Signal-to-Noise Ratio (OSNR) Degradation**: As nonlinearities accumulate, the OSNR degrades, leading to poor signal quality at the receiver.

- **Power Imbalance Between Channels**: In DWDM systems, SBS and SRS can cause power fluctuations between channels, leading to some channels becoming underpowered while others are overpowered.

Practical Example: In a 400G DWDM system operating over 1,500 km, engineers notice that the BER on specific channels has increased. Using an optical spectrum analyzer, they detect that the power levels of neighboring channels are fluctuating, indicating the presence of XPM or SRS.

Tools for Detecting Nonlinearity

- **Optical Spectrum Analyzer (OSA)**: An OSA can detect the presence of spurious signals generated by nonlinear effects such as FWM or the power shifts caused by SRS.
- **Bit Error Rate Tester (BERT)**: BERT is used to measure the BER of a link. A sudden increase in BER, especially as power levels increase, is a strong indicator of nonlinear impairments.
- **Optical Performance Monitoring (OPM)**: OPM tools provide real-time monitoring of key parameters such as OSNR, power levels, and chromatic dispersion, helping to detect when nonlinear effects are becoming problematic.

Fiber Nonlinearity Thresholds

Effect	Power Threshold	Impact Level	Mitigation
SBS	+5 dBm	Severe	Frequency dithering
SRS	+10 dBm	Moderate	Channel spacing
FWM	+3 dBm	High	Dispersion management
XPM	+7 dBm	Moderate	Power reduction
SPM	+8 dBm	Low	Dispersion compensation

Countering Nonlinearities in Optical Fibers

- **Reducing Input Power**
  - **Power Optimization**: The simplest and most effective way to mitigate nonlinearities is by reducing the input power to the optical fiber. Lower power levels reduce the intensity of the optical field, thus limiting the occurrence of nonlinear effects such as SPM and XPM.
  - **Example**: In a metro network operating at 200G per channel, engineers reduce the launch power of each channel by 3 dB to mitigate FWM and XPM. This allows for better signal integrity over shorter distances.

- **Channel Spacing Optimization in DWDM Systems**
  - **Wider Channel Spacing**: Increasing the spacing between DWDM channels reduces the interaction between channels, mitigating FWM and XPM. While this reduces spectral efficiency, it is effective in long-haul systems where maintaining signal integrity is more critical than maximizing capacity.
  - **Example**: A service provider widens the channel spacing from 50 GHz to 100 GHz in its 800G DWDM system to reduce the effects of FWM, improving the OSNR and extending the transmission distance by 200 km.

- **Dispersion Management**
  - **Chromatic Dispersion Compensation**: Chromatic dispersion spreads the optical pulse over time, which can mitigate nonlinearities like FWM by preventing multiple channels from interacting at the same point in the fiber. Dispersion-compensating modules (DCMs) or digital signal processing (DSP) techniques can be used to manage dispersion in real time.
  - **Practical Example**: A long-haul 100G system uses dispersion-compensating fiber (DCF) to manage the accumulated chromatic dispersion, reducing the impact of XPM and FWM on the link's performance.

- **Use of Advanced Modulation Formats**

- **QPSK and BPSK for Long-Haul Networks**: Lower-order modulation formats like QPSK and BPSK are more resistant to nonlinear effects compared to higher-order formats like 16QAM or 64QAM. While these formats provide lower spectral efficiency, they offer better reach and reliability in the presence of nonlinearities.
- **Example**: A 100G transoceanic link uses QPSK modulation to extend the transmission distance to 3,000 km without requiring regeneration, minimizing the impact of SPM and XPM.

- **Raman Amplification**
  - **Distributed Raman Amplification**: Raman amplifiers provide distributed gain along the length of the fiber, rather than at discrete points. This reduces the required input power and helps to mitigate nonlinearities by lowering the optical power over long spans.
  - **Use Case**: In a 400G long-haul link, the use of Raman amplifiers helps reduce the launch power by 5 dB, mitigating the effects of SPM and allowing for a longer transmission distance with lower nonlinear penalties.

Practical Example: Nonlinearity in a 400G DWDM Network

Let's walk through an example of how an engineer might detect and resolve nonlinearities in a 400G DWDM network:

- **Scenario**: A network operator is deploying a 400G DWDM link over 1,500 km. After deployment, engineers notice that the BER on several channels has increased, particularly during periods of high traffic. The OSNR on these channels is also lower than expected.
- **Diagnosis**: Using an OSA, the engineers detect the presence of spurious signals generated by FWM. The power levels of neighboring channels are fluctuating, indicating the presence of SRS. The engineers also notice that some channels are experiencing phase distortions due to XPM.
- **Solution**: The engineers lower the launch power on each channel by 3 dB, mitigating the effects of SPM and XPM. They also widen the channel spacing from 50 GHz to 75 GHz to reduce FWM. Finally, they install DCMs to manage chromatic dispersion, further mitigating nonlinear impairments. After these adjustments, the BER and OSNR improve, and the network stabilizes.

Stimulated Brillouin Scattering (SBS)

Stimulated Brillouin Scattering (SBS) is one of the most significant nonlinear effects in optical fiber communication, particularly for systems that transmit high-power signals. SBS is a backward-scattering phenomenon, where a portion of the optical signal is reflected back toward the source, limiting the amount of optical power that can be effectively transmitted through the fiber.

SBS can significantly degrade the performance of long-haul fiber optic communication systems, causing power loss, signal distortion, and degradation in **Optical Signal-to-Noise Ratio (OSNR)**. Therefore, understanding and mitigating SBS is critical in designing high-performance optical networks.

How SBS Occurs?

SBS arises due to the interaction between the optical field (the transmitted light) and acoustic waves in the fiber. When the optical power exceeds a certain threshold, the light waves interact with density fluctuations in the fiber, which generates an acoustic wave (phonons). This acoustic wave scatters the light back toward the source, causing **Brillouin backscattering**.

The scattered light has a slightly lower frequency than the incident light due to the Doppler effect caused by the motion of the acoustic wave. The frequency shift (or **Brillouin frequency shift**) is typically in the range of **10-11 GHz** in standard single-mode fibers (SMF) and depends on the optical wavelength and the properties of the fiber material.

The basic mechanism of SBS can be summarized as follows:

- Incident light interacts with the material's density fluctuations (phonons) within the fiber.
- This interaction generates an acoustic wave.
- The acoustic wave scatters light back in the direction of the source (backscattering).
- The backscattered light is downshifted in frequency, and this scattering grows exponentially with increasing signal power.

Theoretical Background and Equations

The **Brillouin frequency shift** vB is given by:

$$\nu_B = \frac{2nV_A}{\lambda}$$

Where:

- n is the refractive index of the fiber.
- V_A is the acoustic velocity in the fiber (around 5,960 m/s for silica fibers).
- λ is the wavelength of the optical signal.

For a typical fiber and signal in the **1550 nm** range, this results in a Brillouin frequency shift of approximately **11 GHz.**

The **Brillouin gain spectrum** is very narrow, typically only a few tens of MHz wide, making SBS sensitive to continuous-wave (CW) signals. The narrow linewidth is a significant challenge because even relatively small power increases can push the signal into the SBS regime.

The critical parameter for SBS is the **Brillouin threshold** Pth, which represents the maximum optical power that can be transmitted through the fiber without significant SBS backscattering. The Brillouin threshold can be approximated as:

$$P_{\text{th}} = \frac{21A_{\text{eff}}}{g_B L_{\text{eff}}}$$

Where:

- Aeff is the effective area of the fiber core.
- g_B is the Brillouin gain coefficient, typically on the order of **10^{-11} , \text{m/W}**.
- L_{eff} is the effective fiber length, accounting for fiber attenuation over distance.

The key observation here is that **SBS is a power-limited effect**: the higher the input power, the more pronounced the backscattering. This puts a practical upper limit on the optical power that can be transmitted through the fiber without SBS mitigation techniques.

Effects of SBS on System Performance

- **Power Limitation** The primary impact of SBS is the limitation it places on the optical power that can be launched into the fiber. When the transmitted power exceeds the SBS threshold, a significant portion of the light is backscattered, reducing the power delivered to the receiver. This power loss leads to a reduction in the **OSNR** and increases the bit error rate (BER) in high-capacity systems.

- **Spectral Broadening and Backscattering** SBS causes spectral broadening of the backscattered signal. Since SBS reflects the light in the reverse direction, it interferes with the forward-propagating signal, causing signal degradation. For single-channel systems, this is less problematic; however, in **Wavelength-Division Multiplexing (WDM)** systems with multiple channels, SBS can result in channel interference and cross-talk between channels.
- **Impact on High-Power Systems** In long-haul DWDM systems that employ high-power optical amplifiers such as EDFAs or Raman amplifiers, SBS becomes a significant limiting factor. Without proper mitigation, SBS can reduce the maximum launch power to levels that are insufficient for long-distance transmission.

SBS Mitigation Techniques

Given that SBS limits the launch power, a variety of mitigation techniques have been developed to allow for higher power transmission while minimizing the effects of SBS.

- **Broadening the Laser Linewidth**
  - Since SBS has a very narrow gain bandwidth (typically less than 50 MHz), one of the most effective ways to mitigate SBS is to broaden the linewidth of the transmitted optical signal. By spreading the signal over a wider frequency range, the interaction with the acoustic wave is reduced, lowering the SBS gain and increasing the SBS threshold.Techniques for broadening the linewidth include:
    - **Laser Chirping**: Modifying the laser's frequency over time, which effectively spreads the power across a broader spectrum.
    - **Phase Modulation**: Adding a small amount of phase modulation to the optical signal can also broaden the effective linewidth.
- **Reducing Fiber Length**
  - Since SBS grows exponentially with fiber length, reducing the effective length of the fiber can increase the SBS threshold. This can be done by using:
    - **Distributed Raman Amplification**: By amplifying the signal along the entire length of the fiber rather than at discrete points, the launch power at the input of the fiber can be reduced, thus reducing the chance of SBS.
- **Temperature and Strain Management**
  - SBS is sensitive to environmental factors such as **temperature** and **strain** in the fiber, which affect the fiber's acoustic properties. By ap-

plying controlled strain or temperature gradients along the fiber, the Brillouin frequency can be shifted, reducing the SBS gain.

- **Use of Polarization Control**
  - The interaction between the optical signal and acoustic waves is polarization-dependent. By controlling the state of polarization of the signal, SBS can be reduced.
- **Reducing Input Power**
  - If the power is reduced below the SBS threshold, the scattering effect can be minimized. However, this can limit the transmission distance, so it is often used in conjunction with amplification strategies like distributed Raman amplification or lower-gain EDFAs.
- **Modulation Formats**
  - Using higher-order modulation formats like **Quadrature Phase Shift Keying (QPSK)** or **16-QAM** can also mitigate SBS, as these modulation schemes typically require lower peak power compared to simpler modulation formats like **On-Off Keying (OOK)**.

Practical Example of SBS Management

Consider a long-haul **DWDM** system operating over **200 km** of single-mode fiber with an EDFA providing an optical output power of **10 dBm** per channel. The SBS threshold for the fiber is calculated to be around **7 dBm** without mitigation. To avoid SBS while maintaining the required power levels for long-distance transmission, engineers could employ **phase modulation** to broaden the signal's linewidth and use **distributed Raman amplification** to keep the launch power below the SBS threshold.

After applying these techniques, the effective SBS threshold could be raised to **12 dBm**, allowing the system to transmit at the desired power level without significant backscattering.

SBS is a critical limitation in high-power optical fiber systems, particularly for long-haul transmission and DWDM systems. By understanding the underlying mechanisms and applying appropriate mitigation techniques—such as linewidth broadening, reducing effective fiber length, and using advanced modulation formats—engineers can significantly reduce the impact of SBS, allowing for higher transmission power and more reliable system performance.

Four-Wave Mixing (FWM)

Four-Wave Mixing (FWM) is a significant nonlinear effect that occurs in optical fiber communication systems, particularly in Dense Wavelength Division Multiplexing (DWDM) systems. FWM arises from the interaction of multiple optical wavelengths within the fiber, resulting in the generation of new frequencies that can interfere with the original signals.

FWM is more pronounced in **low-dispersion fibers** and systems with tightly spaced channels, where the interaction between different wavelength channels becomes stronger. FWM leads to **crosstalk**, **signal distortion**, and **channel interference**, all of which degrade the system's **Optical Signal-to-Noise Ratio (OSNR)** and overall performance.

How FWM Occurs?

FWM is a third-order nonlinear effect where three optical signals at different frequencies mix within the fiber to generate a new signal at a fourth frequency. This effect occurs when the electric fields of the three interacting waves overlap within the fiber's core, giving rise to nonlinear polarization, which produces additional frequencies.

For three input frequencies f_1, f_2, and f_3, the new frequency components generated by FWM are:

$$f_{\text{new}} = f_i + f_j - f_k$$

Where i, j, and k represent different input wavelengths. The number of new frequencies generated depends on the number of channels involved, leading to substantial crosstalk in densely packed DWDM systems.

Conditions for Strong FWM

FWM becomes significant under the following conditions:

- **Low Chromatic Dispersion**: In fibers with low dispersion (near zero dispersion), the interacting waves travel at nearly the same speed, increasing the efficiency of FWM.
- **High Channel Power**: FWM efficiency increases with higher optical power in each channel, leading to stronger signal mixing.
- **Close Channel Spacing**: FWM is more pronounced in systems where the channel spacing is narrow (e.g., **50 GHz** or **100 GHz** in DWDM systems).

Theoretical Background and Equations

The **FWM power** generated in a fiber is governed by several factors, including channel power, fiber length, and chromatic dispersion. The efficiency of FWM can be quantified using the following relation:

$$P_{\text{FWM}} = \eta \cdot P_1 \cdot P_2 \cdot P_3 \cdot L_{\text{eff}}^2$$

Where:

- P_1, P_2, and P_3 are the optical powers of the interacting channels.
- L_{eff} is the effective fiber length, accounting for fiber attenuation.
- η is the **FWM efficiency**, which depends on chromatic dispersion and channel spacing.

FWM Efficiency and Chromatic Dispersion

The efficiency of FWM is inversely proportional to the fiber's chromatic dispersion. In fibers with zero or near-zero dispersion, the interacting waves remain phase-matched over long distances, increasing the FWM efficiency. Dispersion disrupts this phase matching, reducing the FWM effect.

The **FWM efficiency factor** η can be written as:

$$\eta \propto \frac{1}{(D \cdot \Delta f)^2}$$

Where:

- D is the chromatic dispersion in the fiber (ps/nm/km).
- Δf is the frequency spacing between the channels.

This equation shows that increasing dispersion and/or channel spacing reduces the FWM power.

Channel Spacing and FWM Power

For closely spaced channels, such as **50 GHz** or **100 GHz** in DWDM systems, the proximity of the wavelengths increases the likelihood of FWM interactions. The number of new frequency components generated by FWM increases exponentially as the number of channels grows, leading to significant crosstalk and signal degradation.

Impact of FWM on System Performance

FWM can have a number of detrimental effects on optical communication systems, particularly in high-capacity DWDM systems:

1. **Crosstalk Between Channels**:
    - The new frequency components generated by FWM can overlap with existing data channels, leading

to **interference** and **crosstalk**. This degrades the signal-to-noise ratio (SNR) and increases the **bit-error rate (BER)**.

2. **Signal Distortion**:
   - FWM can cause **signal distortion**, especially in systems with small channel spacing and high optical power levels. This reduces the system's overall performance and limits the effective transmission distance.
3. **Performance Degradation**:
   - FWM becomes more pronounced in **low-dispersion fibers** and **systems with small channel spacing**. In DWDM systems, where many channels are spaced closely together, FWM can significantly reduce system performance by introducing interference between the channels.

FWM in Single-Channel vs. Multi-Channel Systems

In single-channel systems, FWM does not occur because there are no other channels with which the signal can mix. In multi-channel systems, however, the presence of several wavelengths increases the likelihood of FWM, especially in tightly spaced channels.

Techniques to Mitigate FWM

Since FWM is a power-dependent effect, several mitigation techniques can be used to reduce its impact on DWDM systems.

- **Increasing Chromatic Dispersion**
  - One of the most effective ways to reduce FWM is to increase the chromatic dispersion in the fiber. Dispersion disrupts the phase matching between the interacting wavelengths, significantly reducing the FWM efficiency.
    - **Dispersion-Managed Fiber**: Using fibers with controlled levels of dispersion helps balance the trade-off between managing nonlinear effects (like FWM) and chromatic dispersion effects (like pulse broadening).
    - **Dispersion Compensation Modules (DCMs)**: DCMs can be strategically placed along the fiber to maintain a higher level of dispersion and mitigate FWM.

- **Increasing Channel Spacing**
  - Increasing the channel spacing in DWDM systems reduces the likelihood of FWM interactions. By spacing the channels further apart, the phase-matching condition required for FWM becomes less likely, reducing the strength of the generated new frequencies.
    - **100 GHz Spacing**: Systems with 100 GHz channel spacing experience significantly less FWM than systems with 50 GHz spacing.
    - **Coarse WDM (CWDM)**: CWDM systems with much wider channel spacing (20 nm or more) are typically immune to FWM effects.

- **Reducing Launch Power**
  - Since FWM power increases with higher channel power, reducing the launch power per channel can significantly mitigate FWM. However, reducing power can limit the transmission distance, so this technique is often used alongside amplification strategies.
    - **Optimum Power Levels**: Systems can be designed to operate at power levels just below the FWM threshold, balancing between power efficiency and FWM suppression.

- **Using Nonlinear Optical Fibers**
  - Nonlinear fibers with optimized core sizes and refractive index profiles can be designed to reduce FWM. By altering the fiber's dispersion characteristics, the efficiency of FWM can be minimized.
    - **Non-Zero Dispersion-Shifted Fibers (NZDSF)**: These fibers have a small amount of chromatic dispersion, designed to reduce both FWM and chromatic dispersion effects in high-capacity systems.

- **Polarization Control**
  - FWM is polarization-dependent, meaning that the interaction between different wavelength channels is influenced by their polarization states. By ensuring that the interacting channels have different polarization states, FWM can be reduced.
    - **Polarization-Multiplexed Signals**: By transmitting channels with orthogonal polarization states, the likelihood of FWM can be reduced.

- **Modulation Formats**
  - Advanced modulation formats, such as **Quadrature Phase Shift Keying (QPSK)** or **16-QAM**, require lower peak power levels compared to traditional On-Off Keying (OOK), which can help mitigate FWM.

Practical Example of FWM Management

Consider a 100 km DWDM link with 50 GHz channel spacing and an EDFA providing an optical output power of 5 dBm per channel. The system operates in a fiber with near-zero dispersion, making it highly susceptible to FWM.To mitigate FWM, engineers can:

- Increase the chromatic dispersion by using a **dispersion-compensating fiber (DCF)** at regular intervals along the link.
- Reduce the launch power to **0 dBm per channel** to minimize FWM generation.
- Increase the channel spacing to **100 GHz** in future upgrades to further reduce FWM effects.

FWM management is essential in modern high-capacity optical systems, especially as demand for higher bandwidth and tighter channel spacing grows. Proper planning and mitigation techniques ensure the longevity and efficiency of DWDM systems.

Stimulated Raman Scattering (SRS)

Stimulated Raman Scattering (SRS) is one of the key nonlinear effects that can occur in optical fiber communication systems, especially in Wavelength Division Multiplexing (WDM) systems. SRS causes power to be transferred from shorter-wavelength signals (higher frequencies) to longer-wavelength signals (lower frequencies), leading to degradation in the system performance.

Unlike Stimulated Brillouin Scattering (SBS), which primarily affects single-channel systems, SRS has a significant impact on multi-channel systems such as DWDM networks. It is particularly problematic when optical power is high, as the power transfer between channels leads to crosstalk and signal degradation.

Mechanism of SRS

SRS is a phenomenon where photons from a high-frequency signal (shorter wavelength) lose energy by scattering and generating **optical phonons** (vibrations in the fiber medium), which in turn transfer power to lower-frequency signals (longer wavelength). This effect occurs in both the forward and backward directions within the fiber.

- **Forward SRS**: The scattered light propagates in the same direction as the original signal.
- **Backward SRS**: The scattered light propagates opposite to the original signal, similar to SBS.

The **Raman gain** is relatively broad compared to SBS, with a bandwidth extending over several **terahertz (THz)**, which allows it to affect multiple wavelength channels in WDM systems. SRS gain depends on the power of the incident light and the fiber material properties, with silica fibers commonly used in telecommunications having an SRS gain peak around **13 THz** away from the pump signal.

Key Equations and Parameters

The power transferred between two signals due to SRS can be modeled using coupled equations. For forward-propagating SRS, the equations are:

$$\frac{dI_p}{dz} = -g_R I_p I_s - \alpha_p I_p$$

$$\frac{dI_s}{dz} = g_R I_p I_s - \alpha_s I_s$$

Where:

- Ip and Is are the powers of the pump and Stokes (lower frequency) signals.
- g_R is the **Raman gain coefficient**, typically in the range of **1 × 10^{-13} m/W** for silica fibers.
- α_p and α_s are the attenuation coefficients for the pump and Stokes signals.
- z is the distance along the fiber.

The **threshold power** Pth for SRS is the power level at which a significant amount of energy is transferred from the higher-frequency signals to the lower-frequency signals. It can be estimated using the following equation:

$$P_{\text{th}} \approx \frac{16\alpha(\pi w^2)}{g_R}$$

Where:

- w is the mode field radius of the fiber (typically around 10 microns).
- α is the attenuation coefficient (around 0.2 dB/km).
- g_R is the Raman gain coefficient.

For typical telecommunication fibers, the threshold for SRS is around **500 mW to 1 W**.

Impact of SRS on System Performance

In **DWDM systems**, where multiple channels are transmitted simultaneously over a single fiber, SRS can cause power to be transferred between adjacent channels. This power transfer degrades the **signal-to-noise ratio (SNR)** of shorter-wavelength channels, while longer-wavelength channels experience a gain, leading to **inter-channel crosstalk** and performance degradation.

- Power Penalty
  - The redistribution of power between channels can cause **uneven power levels** across the spectrum, which increases the system's **bit error rate (BER)** and reduces the overall system capacity.
- OSNR Degradation
  - SRS affects the **optical signal-to-noise ratio (OSNR)** of the system. The channels at the lower end of the spectrum lose power, reducing their OSNR, while channels at the higher end gain power, but with accompanying **interference** from the added energy of the scattered photons.
- Crosstalk
  - SRS can induce **nonlinear crosstalk**, which leads to increased noise and potential data errors in adjacent channels, particularly in systems with tightly spaced wavelengths (e.g., 50 GHz or 100 GHz channel spacing).

SRS in Short vs. Long-Haul Systems

Short-Haul Systems:

- In systems with shorter fiber lengths, SRS may not play a significant role due to the relatively short interaction distance between channels. The **threshold power** for SRS in short-haul systems is generally higher, and thus, the effect is less pronounced.

Long-Haul Systems:

- In long-haul transmission systems, where optical amplifiers (e.g., **EDFA**, **Raman amplifiers**) are used to boost the signal, the higher power levels combined with long interaction lengths make SRS a critical issue. Power redistribution between channels can become a serious problem if not properly mitigated.

Techniques to Mitigate SRS

Several techniques can be employed to mitigate the effects of SRS in optical communication systems, particularly in high-power, long-haul WDM systems.

- Power Equalization
  - By equalizing the power levels across all channels before transmission, the power transfer due to SRS can be minimized. This ensures that no channel is disproportionately affected.
- Reducing Channel Power
  - Lowering the launch power per channel reduces the severity of SRS. However, this can limit the transmission distance, so a balance must be struck between mitigating SRS and maintaining system performance.
- Wavelength Spacing
  - Wider **channel spacing** can help reduce the impact of SRS because the power transfer between widely spaced channels is less efficient. For example, **100 GHz channel spacing** results in lower SRS crosstalk compared to **50 GHz** spacing.
- Raman Amplification
  - **Distributed Raman amplification** can be used to counteract SRS by boosting the signal strength in all channels simultaneously, helping maintain a balanced power profile along the fiber.
- Advanced Modulation Formats
  - Using higher-order modulation formats such as **QPSK** or **16-QAM** can reduce the per-channel power, thereby lowering the likelihood of SRS-induced power transfer.

Practical Example of SRS in a DWDM System

Consider a 200 km DWDM link with 100 GHz channel spacing and a total launched power of 1 W. Without SRS mitigation, power will transfer from the shorter-wavelength channels (e.g., 1530 nm) to longer-wavelength channels (e.g., 1560 nm), leading to a power penalty in the shorter-wavelength channels. By employing distributed Raman amplification and adjusting the launch power to 500 mW, the effects of SRS can be significantly reduced, ensuring consistent performance across all channels.

Stimulated Raman Scattering (SRS) in C+L Band Optical Networks

In modern Dense Wavelength Division Multiplexing (DWDM) systems, capacity expansion is crucial for accommodating the increasing data traffic demands. This need has led to the widespread use of **C+L band optical networks**. By leveraging both the **C-band** (1530 nm - 1565 nm) and the **L-band** (1565 nm - 1625 nm), operators can significantly enhance the available spectrum for data transmission. However, this approach introduces challenges, one of the most significant being **Stimulated Raman Scattering (SRS)**.In this article, we'll explore how **SRS** affects C+L band networks, the mechanisms behind it, its impact on optical transmission, and potential mitigation techniques.

What is Stimulated Raman Scattering (SRS)?

Stimulated Raman Scattering (SRS) is a nonlinear optical effect that occurs when intense light interacts with the molecular vibrations in an optical fiber. It results in the transfer of energy from higher-frequency (shorter wavelength) channels, primarily in the **C-band**, to lower-frequency (longer wavelength) channels in the **L-band**. This energy transfer creates an **SRS tilt**, causing a **linear power tilt** across the transmission spectrum.

SRS in C+L Band Systems:

In C+L band systems, both **C-band** and **L-band** signals are transmitted simultaneously through the same optical fiber. As they propagate, SRS leads to the transfer of power from the C-band to the L-band channels. This phenomenon results in a tilt, or **power imbalance**, across the two bands, leading to **up to 8 dB** of power tilt per span .

How Does SRS Work in C+L Band Links?

1. **Energy Transfer:**

    - **SRS** causes energy transfer from shorter wavelengths (C-band) to longer wavelengths (L-band) as the light signals propagate through the fiber.
    - This transfer leads to **SRS tilt**, where the L-band channels receive increased power while the C-band channels experience a reduction in power.
2. **Loading Dependency:**
    - The degree of SRS tilt depends on the network load. A heavily loaded system with higher channel powers will experience a more pronounced tilt than a lightly loaded one.
3. **Add/Drop Transients:**
    - When traffic is added or removed from the network, **transient effects** can cause sudden changes in the SRS tilt, affecting the signal power of both C-band and L-band channels. This can lead to **instability** in the network, which requires rapid **amplifier gain adjustments** to maintain signal integrity .

Impact of SRS in Optical Networks

The impact of SRS in a C+L link is multifaceted, leading to both performance degradation and operational challenges. Some of the key effects include:

1. **Power Imbalance (Tilt):**
    - The most direct impact of SRS is the **linear power tilt** that develops between the C-band and L-band channels. As the C-band loses power, the L-band channels receive excess power. This imbalance can degrade the signal quality, particularly in networks that rely on precise power levels for optimal performance.
2. **Amplification Challenges:**
    - Amplifiers such as **erbium-doped fiber amplifiers (EDFAs)** and **Raman amplifiers** are commonly used to boost signals in optical networks. In C+L band systems, these amplifiers must be carefully configured to compensate for the SRS-induced power tilt. Amplifiers need to provide **tilt correction** to ensure consistent gain across the entire spectrum .
3. **Nonlinear Effects:**
    - SRS can exacerbate other **nonlinear effects**, such as **self-phase modulation (SPM)** and **four-wave mixing (FWM)**, further impacting the network's performance.

Mitigation Techniques for SRS

To manage and mitigate the effects of **SRS** in C+L band optical systems, several strategies can be employed:

1. **Tilt Compensation:**
    - **Tilt correction** techniques are implemented during both **Raman** and **EDFA** amplification stages. This involves dynamically adjusting the gain of the amplifiers to compensate for the SRS-induced tilt.
2. **Traffic Orchestration:**
    - Automated systems can be used to manage the addition or removal of traffic channels. By coordinating the **turn-up** or **turn-down** of channels, network operators can minimize **SRS transients**, reducing the risk of power imbalances during traffic changes .
3. **Raman Amplification:**
    - **Raman amplifiers** are particularly useful in mitigating the effects of SRS. These amplifiers help **boost the power** of the L-band channels early in the transmission span, counteracting the power loss experienced by the C-band channels .
4. **Lowering Channel Power:**
    - Reducing the power of individual channels can limit the severity of SRS. While this approach may reduce the network's overall capacity, it helps maintain a more balanced power distribution across the C+L bands.

Example of SRS in a C+L Band Link

In a typical C+L band DWDM system:

- **C-band:** 1530 nm - 1565 nm
- **L-band:** 1565 nm - 1625 nm

Assume a 100 km fiber span where both C-band and L-band channels are actively transmitting data. As the signal propagates through the fiber, **SRS** causes a gradual transfer of energy from the C-band to the L-band channels. At the end of the span, the **L-band** channels have **8 dB more power** than they had at the beginning, while the **C-band** channels have lost an equivalent amount of power.

This imbalance can severely degrade the performance of C-band channels if not properly mitigated using **tilt correction** or **Raman amplification** .

Stimulated Raman Scattering (SRS) is a significant challenge in C+L band optical networks. As data channels in the C-band and L-band are coupled during transmission, SRS transfers power from C-band channels to L-band channels, causing a **power tilt**. This tilt, if left unchecked, can degrade network performance and reduce the effective reach of the optical system.

To manage the effects of SRS, network operators must employ **tilt correction**, **Raman amplification**, and careful orchestration of traffic. These techniques help maintain signal integrity and ensure that the network can deliver high-capacity, long-distance transmission across both the C-band and L-band.

As optical networks continue to evolve, understanding and mitigating SRS will be critical for operators seeking to maximize the performance and capacity of their C+L band systems.

Cross-Phase Modulation (XPM)

Cross-Phase Modulation (XPM) is a nonlinear effect in optical fiber communication that results from the intensity dependence of the refractive index of the fiber. In **Wavelength Division Multiplexing (WDM)** systems, when two or more optical signals travel simultaneously through the fiber, the power of one signal can influence the phase of the other signals, leading to XPM.

XPM is particularly problematic in **Dense Wavelength Division Multiplexing (DWDM)** systems where multiple closely spaced channels are transmitted. As the optical signals from different channels interact, the phase modulation caused by one channel affects the neighboring channels, degrading their signal integrity and increasing **bit error rates (BER)**.

Mechanism of XPM

In WDM systems, when several channels are transmitted through the same fiber, the refractive index of the fiber is affected by the combined optical power of all channels. The refractive index varies proportionally to the intensity of the propagating signals, and this variation leads to a **phase shift** in all channels.

The nonlinear phase shift experienced by a specific channel i can be described by the following equation:

$$\phi_{i,NL} = \gamma L_{\text{eff}}\left(P_i + 2\sum_{j \neq i} P_j\right)$$

Where:

- $\phi_{i,NL}$ is the total nonlinear phase shift for channel i,
- γ is the nonlinear coefficient of the fiber (related to the fiber's effective area and nonlinear refractive index),

- Leff is the effective length of the fiber,
- Pi is the power of the i-th channel, and
- Pj is the power of the j-th interfering channel.

XPM is **twice as effective** as **Self-Phase Modulation (SPM)** because the intensity of neighboring channels contributes to the total phase shift experienced by the signal. This inter-channel interaction distorts the signal, causing **timing jitter**, **phase noise**, and **spectral broadening**.

Theoretical Description and Equations

XPM-induced phase shifts are dependent on the **power of all copropagating channels**. For **two copropagating channels** with powers P1 and P2, the XPM phase shift for each channel is given by:

$$\Delta\phi = 2\gamma L_{\text{eff}} P_{\text{other}}$$

Where:

- γ is the nonlinear coefficient of the fiber,
- L_{eff} is the effective length over which the interaction takes place,
- P_{other} is the power of the other channel.

The total **XPM-induced chirp** (frequency shift due to XPM) can be expressed as:

$$\delta\omega_{\text{XPM}} = -2\gamma P_{\text{other}} \frac{dI(t)}{dt}$$

Where δωXPM represents the **XPM-induced frequency chirp**, and dI(t)dt is the time derivative of the signal's intensity, which shows that the chirp is proportional to the time variation in the intensity of the copropagating signal.

Impact of XPM on System Performance

XPM introduces significant **cross-talk** in WDM systems, especially when:

- The **channel spacing** is narrow (e.g., 50 GHz or 100 GHz in DWDM systems).
- The **channel power** is high, which increases the strength of the nonlinear interaction.
- The **dispersion** of the fiber is low, allowing for longer interactions between channels.

Timing Jitter

XPM-induced phase modulation causes fluctuations in the timing of the signal pulses, leading to **timing jitter**. The timing jitter increases with the number of channels and the overall channel power.

Power Penalty

The power penalty due to XPM arises from the distortion of the signal, which reduces the **signal-to-noise ratio (SNR)** and leads to **bit errors**. As the number of WDM channels increases, the power penalty due to XPM becomes more significant, requiring careful power management to avoid excessive degradation.

OSNR Degradation

XPM affects the **optical signal-to-noise ratio (OSNR)** of the system, especially in long-haul systems where signals traverse multiple fiber spans. The phase modulation from XPM leads to inter-channel interference, degrading the OSNR and increasing the **bit error rate (BER)**.

XPM in Short-Haul vs. Long-Haul Systems

In **short-haul systems**, the impact of XPM may be limited due to the relatively short fiber lengths and lower power levels. However, in **long-haul systems** with **high-power channels** and **dense channel spacing**, XPM becomes a significant issue.

For example, in **multi-span systems** with **erbium-doped fiber amplifiers (EDFA)**, the cumulative effect of XPM across multiple spans can severely degrade system performance. As the number of spans increases, the XPM-induced noise and phase distortions also accumulate, requiring **dispersion management** and **power equalization** to mitigate these effects.

Techniques to Mitigate XPM

Several strategies can be used to mitigate the effects of XPM in WDM systems:

- **Increasing Channel Spacing**
  - By increasing the **spacing between channels**, the phase modulation caused by XPM is reduced. Systems with **50 GHz** or **100 GHz spacing** experience less XPM than systems with tighter channel spacing.

- **Reducing Channel Power**
  - Lowering the power of individual channels reduces the strength of the XPM effect. However, this approach may require the use of additional **optical amplifiers** to maintain sufficient signal strength.

- **Dispersion Management**
    - By carefully managing the dispersion of the fiber, it is possible to reduce the interaction time between channels and minimize the impact of XPM. **Dispersion-compensating fibers (DCFs)** or **digital signal processing (DSP)** techniques can be used to control the phase distortions caused by XPM.

- **Polarization Multiplexing**
    - Since XPM is polarization-dependent, using **polarization multiplexing** can help reduce the interaction between channels. By ensuring that neighboring channels have orthogonal polarization states, XPM-induced phase shifts can be minimized.

Practical Example of XPM in a DWDM System

Consider a **200 km** DWDM link with **50 GHz channel spacing** and a total launched power of **500 mW** per channel. In this system, XPM can cause significant phase modulation between adjacent channels, leading to timing jitter and phase noise.

To mitigate the effects of XPM, engineers could:

- Increase the channel spacing to **100 GHz** to reduce inter-channel interaction.
- Use **dispersion-compensating modules (DCMs)** to manage the fiber's chromatic dispersion.
- Reduce the launched power to **250 mW** per channel to lower the XPM-induced phase shifts.

Self-Phase Modulation (SPM)

Self-Phase Modulation (SPM) is a significant nonlinear effect in optical fibers where the intensity of an optical signal influences its own phase. SPM occurs because the refractive index of the fiber depends on the intensity of the propagating signal. This intensity-dependent refractive index causes a **nonlinear phase shift** within the signal, leading to signal distortion, frequency chirping, and spectral broadening.

SPM predominantly affects **single-channel systems** and becomes more prominent at high power levels and in long-haul systems. In **Wavelength Division Multiplexing (WDM)** systems, while **Cross-Phase Modulation (XPM)** affects neighboring channels, SPM only influences the channel it originates from.

Mechanism of SPM

The refractive index of an optical fiber changes in response to the optical power traveling through it. This nonlinear effect can be described by the Kerr nonlinearity, where the refractive index n is related to the signal power P as:

$$n = n_0 + n_2 I$$

Where:

- n_0 is the linear refractive index,
- n_2 is the nonlinear index coefficient,
- I is the intensity of the optical signal.

This intensity-dependent refractive index induces a phase shift in the optical signal, which can be expressed as:

$$\Delta\phi = \gamma P_{\text{in}} L_{\text{eff}}$$

Where:

- $\Delta\phi$ is the nonlinear phase shift,
- γ is the **nonlinear coefficient** of the fiber, defined as $\gamma = 2\pi n_2 / \lambda A_{eff}$,
- P_{in} is the input power,
- L_{eff} is the effective fiber length, defined as $L_{eff} = (1 - e^{-\alpha L}) / \alpha$, where α is the fiber loss coefficient and L is the fiber length.

SPM causes **frequency chirping** (variation of frequency within the pulse), and this frequency shift is proportional to the derivative of the signal's intensity with respect to time:

$$\delta\omega_{\text{SPM}} = -\gamma P_{\text{in}} \frac{dI(t)}{dt}$$

The **temporal variation** of the intensity creates **spectral broadening** of the signal, leading to a broader pulse width over time. This spectral broadening limits the capacity of the system by increasing **inter-symbol interference** (ISI) and distorting the signal's shape.

Key Equations and Parameters

The **nonlinear Schrödinger equation (NLS)** is often used to model the propagation of optical pulses in a fiber. In the context of SPM, the NLS equation is:

$$\frac{\partial A}{\partial z} + \frac{i\beta_2}{2}\frac{\partial^2 A}{\partial t^2} = i\gamma |A|^2 A - \frac{\alpha}{2} A$$

Where:

- A(z,t) is the slowly varying envelope of the pulse,

- β_2 is the group velocity dispersion (GVD) coefficient,
- $\gamma|A|2A$ represents the nonlinear phase modulation due to SPM,
- α accounts for fiber attenuation.

The solution of this equation shows that SPM leads to a **chirped pulse** as the signal propagates along the fiber, meaning the frequency shifts continuously within the pulse.

Impact of SPM on System Performance

- **Spectral Broadening**
  - One of the most notable effects of SPM is **spectral broadening**. As the signal propagates, its bandwidth increases due to the self-induced phase modulation. This can reduce the overall performance of optical systems, particularly in systems with narrow spectral spacing or long transmission distances.
  - For **Gaussian pulses**, the nonlinear phase shift and chirping can cause the pulse to broaden, which ultimately increases the **bit error rate (BER)** due to inter-symbol interference (ISI).
- **Timing Jitter and Phase Noise**
  - SPM introduces timing jitter and phase noise as the pulse's intensity variations cause nonlinear changes in the signal's phase. This effect is exacerbated in long-haul systems where multiple amplification stages are employed, and the phase modulation accumulates over distance.
- **Interaction with Dispersion**
  - SPM interacts with **chromatic dispersion (CD)** and **polarization mode dispersion (PMD)**, further complicating signal transmission. The combination of SPM and **anomalous GVD** can lead to **modulation instability**, where signal energy is transferred from one frequency component to another, further distorting the signal.
  - The balance between SPM and GVD can also be beneficial in certain cases. For example, in **anomalous dispersion regimes**, SPM can balance the pulse broadening due to GVD, stabilizing the pulse width.

SPM in Short-Haul vs. Long-Haul Systems

In **short-haul systems**, the impact of SPM may be minimal because the nonlinear phase shift does not accumulate significantly over short distances. However, in **long-haul systems**, where signals travel over hundreds or thousands of kilometers and pass through multiple **optical amplifiers (e.g., EDFA)**, the nonlinear phase shift accumulates with each span, leading to significant signal degradation.

For instance, in systems with **multiple spans** of 80 km, the nonlinear phase shift can accumulate to a point where the SPM-induced phase noise severely degrades system performance. **Amplification schemes** such as **Raman amplification** can reduce the severity of SPM by maintaining a low input power, but this only partially mitigates the problem.

Techniques to Mitigate SPM

Several techniques can be used to mitigate the effects of SPM in optical communication systems:

- **Power Optimization**
  - One of the simplest ways to mitigate SPM is to lower the input power. By reducing the optical power launched into the fiber, the nonlinear phase shift is minimized. However, this approach may limit the transmission distance and require additional optical amplifiers.

- **Dispersion Compensation**
  - Managing **dispersion** can help mitigate SPM effects. By using **dispersion-compensating fibers (DCFs)** or **digital signal processing (DSP)** techniques, the combined effects of SPM and dispersion can be controlled to minimize signal distortion.

- **Large Effective Area Fibers**
  - Fibers with a **large effective area (A_eff)** can reduce the nonlinear coefficient γ, thereby reducing the nonlinear phase shift induced by SPM. **Large-effective-area fibers (LEAF)** are often used in long-haul systems to combat nonlinear effects such as SPM.

Practical Example of SPM in a DWDM System

Consider a **400 km DWDM link** operating with **100 GHz channel spacing**. At an input power of **10 mW** per channel, the nonlinear phase shift due to SPM causes significant spectral broadening and phase noise. By employing **dispersion management** with alternating spans of normal and anomalous dispersion fiber, the system can balance the effects of SPM and GVD, reducing signal distortion and maintaining a lower BER.

If the input power is reduced to **5 mW** per channel, the nonlinear phase shift is halved, reducing the spectral broadening. However, this may require additional amplification to maintain sufficient signal strength at the receiver.

Leveraging the Full Potential of Fiber Optic Networks

Dense Wavelength Division Multiplexing (DWDM) has become the backbone of modern fiber-optic communication systems, allowing for the transmission of vast amounts of data over long distances. A key component in the evolution of DWDM systems is the ability to scale optical capacity. This article will explore **DWDM optical capacity scaling**, covering key concepts such as **symbols per second (baud rate)**, **bits per symbol (modulation order)**, and **multi-carrier integration**.

Key Concepts of Optical Capacity Scaling

Symbols per Second (Baud Rate)

The number of symbols transmitted per second is referred to as the **baud rate**. This rate directly impacts the spectral bandwidth of the transmitted signal. A higher baud rate increases the capacity by transmitting more symbols per second, but it also requires more bandwidth.

Formula:

$$\text{Baud Rate} = \frac{\text{Total Capacity}}{\text{Bits per Symbol} \times \text{Channel Width}}$$

Where:

- **Total Capacity** is the overall data rate (in bits/second),
- **Bits per Symbol** is determined by the modulation format (e.g., QPSK, 16-QAM),
- **Channel Width** refers to the bandwidth allocated for a single channel.

Example: If the baud rate is 33GB (33 Giga Bauds), using PM-QPSK (2 bits per symbol per polarization) over a 50 GHz channel width, the total capacity becomes:

$$\text{Data Rate}=\text{Baud Rate}\times\text{Bits per Symbol}=33\text{GB}\times 4=132\text{Gbps}$$

Bits per Symbol (Modulation Order)

The modulation format determines how many bits are transmitted per symbol. In DWDM systems, higher-order modulation formats such as **Quadrature Phase Shift Keying (QPSK)** or **m-QAM (Quadrature Amplitude Modulation)** are employed to increase spectral efficiency. By transmitting more bits per symbol, higher capacity can be achieved without increasing the baud rate.

Common Modulation Schemes:

- **QPSK** (Quadrature Phase Shift Keying): 2 bits per symbol,
- **16-QAM**: 4 bits per symbol,
- **64-QAM**: 6 bits per symbol.

Formula:

$$\text{Total Capacity} = \text{Baud Rate} \times \text{Bits per Symbol}$$

Example: Using **16-QAM** with 33GB (baud rate), we get:

$$\text{Data Rate} = 33\ \text{GB} \times 8 = 264\text{Gbps}$$

Multi-Carrier Integration

Multi-carrier integration refers to **superchannels** or the use of **multiple carriers** within the same transmission system. Instead of a single wavelength channel, several wavelength channels are combined into a "superchannel," which can greatly increase total capacity.

Superchannel Example: If a DWDM system uses 12 carriers, each with a channel width of 200 GHz and a data rate of 264 Gbps, the total capacity for the system can be calculated as:

$$\text{Total Capacity} = 12 \times 264\ \text{Gbps} = 3.168\ \text{Tbps}$$

This allows the optical system to handle large-scale data transmission without significantly increasing the complexity of the system design.

DWDM Scaling Benefits

Scaling the optical capacity of DWDM networks is crucial in modern communication systems, where data demands continue to grow exponentially. Key drivers include:

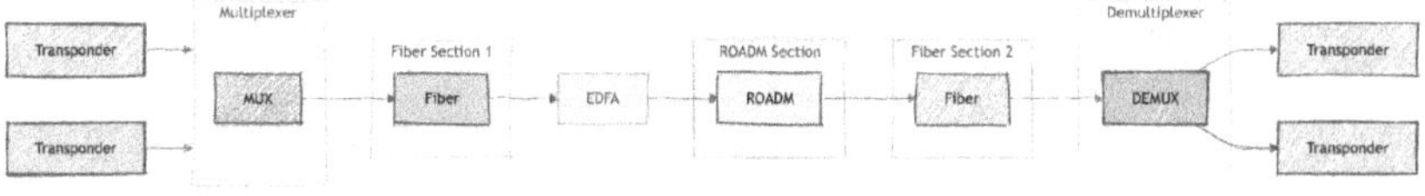

- **Increased Data Traffic:** The need to accommodate high-capacity services like video streaming, cloud computing, and IoT applications.
- **Cost-Effectiveness:** Higher-order modulation and multi-carrier systems allow operators to maximize the use of existing fiber infrastructure without laying new fibers.

- **Future-Proofing Networks:** Higher baud rates and advanced modulation schemes enable optical systems to handle future data demands, ensuring long-term viability.

Chapter 6

Optical Transport Network (OTN)

Chapter 6
Optical Transport Network (OTN)

"OTN is the container that carries our digital world." - Peter Winzer

---

Optical Transport Network (OTN) is a telecommunication standard developed by the ITU-T (International Telecommunication Union Telecommunication Standardization Sector) under the G.709 recommendation. It was designed to address the limitations of legacy technologies like SONET/SDH (Synchronous Optical Network/Synchronous Digital Hierarchy) while leveraging the advancements in Wavelength Division Multiplexing (WDM). OTN offers more flexibility, scalability, and efficiency in transporting a wide variety of client signals, such as IP, Ethernet, Fibre Channel, and TDM (Time Division Multiplexing).

The architecture of OTN is layered, enabling it to provide transparent transport for multiple types of data services, including Ethernet and IP traffic, across long distances. This chapter explores the principles, architecture, components, and use cases of OTN, which has become a foundational technology in modern optical communication systems.

Definition of OTN

- **Optical Transport Network (OTN)** is a network layer designed to enable the transparent transport of data across optical networks. It includes both **optical (physical) and electrical (digital) layers**, enabling efficient management of different traffic types, including Ethernet, SDH, and other high-speed data streams.
- OTN enables **multiplexing, switching, routing, and transport** of data across large geographical areas, with support for **Forward Error Correction (FEC)**, framing, and management functions.

Key Functions of OTN:

- Multiplexing of multiple client signals into a single higher-capacity optical transport unit (OTU).

- End-to-end management and monitoring of optical signals, including support for alarms and fault detection.
- Provision of FEC for improved signal quality and transmission distance.

Why OTN?

Benefits of OTN Over Traditional Networks OTN provides several key advantages compared to older technologies like SONET/SDH:

- **Higher Capacity**: OTN supports data rates up to 400 Gbps and beyond, making it suitable for high-bandwidth applications.
- **Transparency**: OTN can carry multiple types of traffic (e.g., Ethernet, SONET, SDH, IP) in their native formats without altering the client data.
- **Efficient Multiplexing**: It provides efficient multiplexing of lower data rate signals into higher-capacity data streams (OTU frames).
- **Improved Error Correction**: The use of FEC improves the reliability of long-distance transmissions by correcting errors caused by noise and signal degradation.
- **Flexible Bandwidth Allocation**: OTN allows for flexible, scalable bandwidth allocation, optimizing the use of available resources.
- **Service Separation and Isolation**: Different traffic types are encapsulated and transported separately, ensuring that the failure of one service does not affect others.

Features of OTN

OTN is defined by several features that make it a robust and versatile transport system:

Multi-Layered Structure

- **Optical Layer (Physical)**: This layer is responsible for the physical transmission of light signals across the fiber. It deals with signal modulation, amplification, and wavelength multiplexing.
- **Electrical Layer (Digital)**: The electrical layer adds framing, FEC, and management capabilities to the signal, ensuring that data can be monitored, switched, and managed efficiently.

Forward Error Correction (FEC)

- FEC is a key feature of OTN, helping to extend the reach of optical networks by correcting errors introduced during transmission. FEC adds extra data to the transmitted signal, allowing the receiver to detect and correct errors without the need for retransmission.

Management and Control

- OTN supports comprehensive management features, including alarms, monitoring, and fault isolation. These capabilities make OTN highly reliable, as issues can be detected and resolved before they impact service.

OTN Frame Structure

OTU (Optical Transport Unit)

- **OTU** represents the basic building block in OTN, carrying user data encapsulated in a digital wrapper. OTUs come in different rates depending on the capacity and requirements of the network (e.g., OTU1, OTU2, OTU3, OTU4 for 10G, 40G, 100G, 400G systems).
- **OTU Frame Structure**: Each OTU frame is composed of an overhead section, payload section, and Forward Error Correction (FEC) section.
- The **OTU layer** is responsible for the transmission and reception of optical signals. It provides functions like **Forward Error Correction (FEC)**, enabling longer transmission distances by correcting errors. OTU is classified into different levels, such as OTU1 (2.5 Gbps), OTU2 (10 Gbps), OTU3 (40 Gbps), and OTU4 (100 Gbps), to support various data rates.

ODU (Optical Data Unit)

- The **ODU** layer provides a structure for switching and routing data within the OTN. It is the client-independent layer of OTN, allowing it to transport different client signals (Ethernet, SDH, etc.).
- The **ODU layer** handles the mapping of client data. The ODU encapsulates client signals and provides the necessary overheads for monitoring and managing the data as it moves through the network. There are several ODU types, including **ODU0 (1.25 Gbps)** for 1 Gbps Ethernet, **ODU1 (2.5 Gbps)** for OC-48/STM-16, **ODU2 (10 Gbps)** for OC-192/STM-64, and **ODU4 (100 Gbps)** for 100 Gbps Ethernet. The **ODUflex** is a variable-rate container used for services that do not fit into the fixed rates of other ODUs.

OPU (Optical Payload Unit)

- **OPU** is responsible for carrying the actual client data within the OTN frame. The OPU contains the payload area where the client signal is mapped.
- The **OPU layer** is responsible for carrying the actual client data. The OPU layer encapsulates the client signal and includes information about the signal type and rate. The payload can include services like Ethernet, SDH/SONET, and Fibre Channel. The **OPUk** frame includes overheads for error monitoring, payload type indication, and rate adaptation.

OTN Frame Layers:

- **OTU (Optical Transport Unit)**: Adds FEC to the data for error correction.
- **ODU (Optical Data Unit)**: Adds management and routing information.
- **OPU (Optical Payload Unit)**: Encapsulates the actual client data.

Components of OTN Systems

OTN systems include several key components that work together to ensure efficient transport and management of optical signals across the network. These components are critical to the overall performance and reliability of OTN networks.

Transponders

Transponders convert client signals (electrical or optical) into a specific OTN frame, wrapping the signal with FEC and other necessary overheads. This conversion allows the client signal to be transported over an OTN network at a specific wavelength.

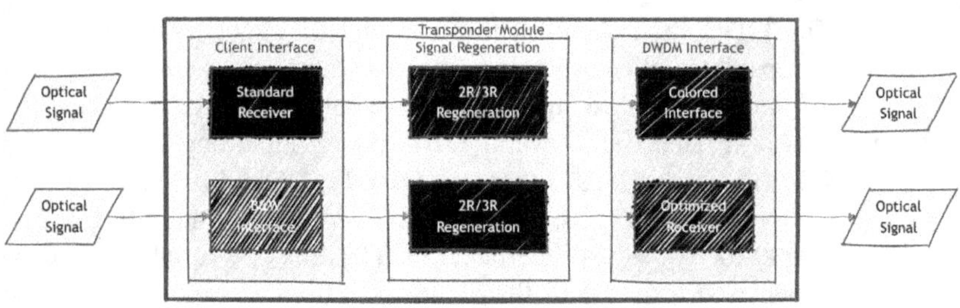

- **Functions**:

- Termination of client signal.
- Conversion of signal to OTN frame.
- Addition of Forward Error Correction (FEC).
- Transmission over DWDM wavelengths.

Muxponders

A **muxponder** is a multiplexing transponder that aggregates multiple lower-speed client signals into a single higher-speed OTN frame. For instance, several ODU0 containers (1.25 Gbps) can be multiplexed into an ODU2 container (10 Gbps).

- **Functions**:
  - Termination of multiple client signals.
  - Multiplexing of signals into a single high-speed OTN container.
  - Addition of FEC for long-distance transmission.

OTN Switches

OTN switches perform the cross-connection of ODU containers, allowing signals to be switched dynamically across the network. This process is essential for grooming traffic and efficiently utilizing network resources.

- **Functions:**
  - Cross-connection of ODU containers.
  - Grooming of lower-speed signals into higher-speed circuits.
  - Dynamic wavelength routing.

Forward Error Correction (FEC)

FEC is used in OTN systems to improve the robustness of data transmission by detecting and correcting errors in the signal. This allows the signal to travel longer distances without degradation.

- **Benefits**:
  - Extends transmission distance.
  - Improves signal quality.
  - Reduces the need for regeneration points.

OTN and DWDM Integration

OTN and Dense Wavelength Division Multiplexing (DWDM) are often used together in modern optical networks. DWDM enables multiple optical signals to be transmitted over a single fiber, while OTN provides the management, switching, and error correction functions.

OTN can encapsulate client signals into wavelengths that are transmitted over a DWDM system. By combining these technologies, network operators can maximize fiber capacity and improve network efficiency.

- **Advantages**:
  - Increased fiber capacity through wavelength multiplexing.
  - Efficient use of bandwidth.
  - Long-distance transmission with FEC.

OTN Switching in DWDM Networks

OTN switching is used in DWDM networks to dynamically switch signals between different wavelengths. This allows for more flexible network configurations and better resource utilization.

OTN Frame information

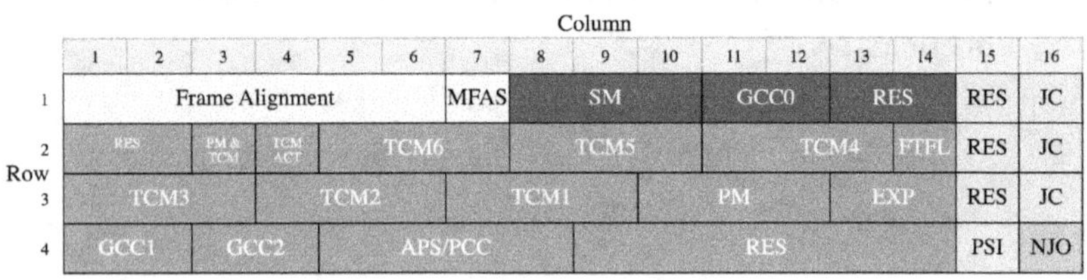

OTN frame for reference

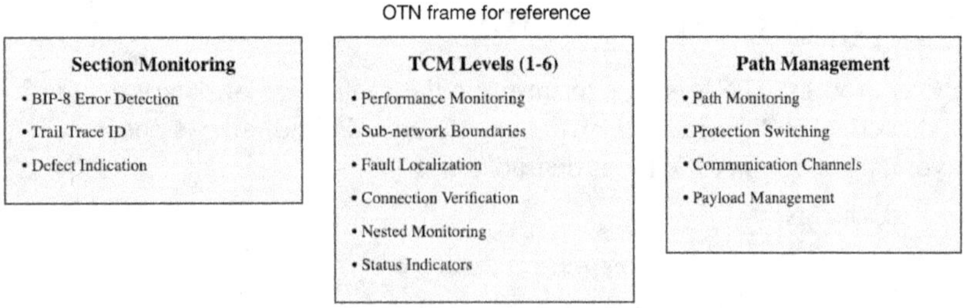

Communication Channels

GCC0: Section Level Management
GCC1: Path Level Management
GCC2: Protection Coordination

OTN Frame Explanation

Row	Component	Columns	Description
1	Frame Alignment	1-6	Contains Fixed Frame Alignment Signal (FAS) for frame synchronization. Pattern: F6F6F6282828 (hexadecimal). Alarms: Loss of Frame (LOF), Out of Frame (OOF).
1	MFAS	7	Multi-frame Alignment Signal with 256 multi-frame counter for multi-frame alignment. Alarms: Loss of Multi-frame (LOM).
1	SM	8-10	Section Monitoring includes BIP-8 error detection, Trail Trace Identifier (TTI), Backward Error Indication (BEI), Backward Defect Indication (BDI), and Status Indications. Alarms: Trail Trace Identifier Mismatch (TIM), Backward Defect Indication (BDI).
1	GCC0	11-12	General Communication Channel 0 used for management communication, supports section level messaging.
1	RES	13-14	Reserved for future standardization, must be set to '0' when not used.
2	RES	1	Reserved byte.
2	PM & TCM	2	Path Monitoring and TCM activation control, controls TCM level functionality.
2	TCM ACT	3	TCM Activation/Deactivation, controls which TCM levels are active.

2	TCM6-TCM4	4-12	Tandem Connection Monitoring levels 6-4, each includes BIP-8 error monitoring, Trail Trace Identifier, Backward Error Indication, Backward Defect Indication, and Status indicators. Alarms: TCM-Level Loss of Tandem Connection (LTC), TCM-BDI.
2	FTFL	13	Fault Type and Fault Location, carries fault information used for maintenance purposes.
2	RES	14-16	Reserved for future use.
3	TCM3-TCM1	1-9	Lower level Tandem Connection Monitoring, similar functionality to TCM6-4, used for nested monitoring levels.
3	PM	10-12	Path Monitoring, includes Path-level BIP-8, Path Trace Identifier, and Path Status indicators. Alarms: Path Trace Identifier Mismatch, Path BDI.
3	EXP	13-14	Experimental use, vendor-specific functions.
3	RES	9-14	Reserved for future use.
4	GCC1/GCC2	1-2	General Communication Channels, management communication at path level.
4	APS/PCC	3-4	Automatic Protection Switching and Protection Communication Channel, coordinates protection switching. Alarms: Protection Switching Byte Mismatch.
4	RES	9-14	Reserved for future use.
4	PSI	15	Payload Structure Identifier, indicates payload type, supports different client signals.
4	NJO	16	Negative Justification Opportunity, supports bit-rate adaptation, part of justification control mechanism.

In OTN, the frame structure is critical for efficient transport, error correction, and management of client data. Let's look at the components in more depth:

OTU Frame Structure (Optical Transport Unit)

The **OTU frame** is the foundation of OTN, providing the structure that carries the client data, management information, and Forward Error Correction (FEC). Here's a detailed breakdown of the OTU frame:

- **Frame Length**: Each OTU frame has a constant length of 4 rows of overhead and 4080 rows of payload data.
- **Overhead Section**: The overhead is used for network management, error monitoring, and control purposes. It includes fields such as:
    - **Section Monitoring (SM)**: Used to monitor the quality of the OTU frame across the entire link.
    - **General Communication Channel (GCC)**: Provides in-band communication for network management and control signals.
    - **Path Monitoring (PM)**: Monitors the performance of the optical path and detects issues such as loss of signal (LOS) or bit errors.

ODU Frame Structure (Optical Data Unit)

The **ODU frame** is an abstraction layer in the OTN hierarchy, encapsulating the client signal and adding additional overhead for path monitoring and management.

- **ODU Overhead**: This includes the **Path Monitoring (PM)** field, which provides end-to-end path monitoring information, including signal degradation and error detection.
- **Client Mapping**: The client data is mapped into the **Optical Payload Unit (OPU)**, which resides inside the ODU frame. The client data could be Ethernet, SONET, or other traffic types.

OPU Frame Structure (Optical Payload Unit)

The **OPU frame** carries the actual client data. It contains fields for client mapping and flexible payload area. It supports different traffic types and ensures that data integrity is maintained.

- **Payload Structure**: The OPU maps client signals, ensuring that different services (e.g., 10GbE, SDH) can be transported over the same optical link while maintaining their native properties.

Key Advantage: The OPU supports **asynchronous mapping**, which allows different client signals with different bit rates to be efficiently carried without synchronization issues.

OTN Speed and Frame Rates

ODUk Rates

Rate Level	Bit Rate (bps)	Frame Size (bits)	Frame Rate (µs)	Frame Frequency (KHz)
		ODUk		
ODU0	1,244,160,000	122,368	98.35390947	10,167.36402
ODU1	2,498,775,126	122,368	48.97119342	20,420.16807
ODU2	10,037,273,924	122,368	12.19135802	82,025.31646
ODU2e	10,399,525,316	122,368	11.76751592	84,978.91991
ODU3	40,319,218,983	122,368	3.03497942	329,491.5254
ODU4	104,794,445,815	122,368	1.16769547	856,387.6652
ODU5	408,346,841,112	122,368	0.29966822	3,337,039.431

Here is a table summarizing the different speeds, data rates, and frame rates for OTU, ODU, and OPU in OTN:

- **OTU (Optical Transport Unit)**: Responsible for end-to-end transport of client data, including FEC for error correction.

OTUk Rates

Rate Level	Bit Rate (bps)	Frame Size (bits)	Frame Rate (µs)	Frame Frequency (KHz)
		OTUk		
OTU1	2,666,057,143	130,560	48.97119342	20,420.16807
OTU2	10,709,225,316	130,560	12.19135802	82,025.31646
OTU2e	11,095,727,848	130,560	11.76751592	84,978.91991
OTU3	43,018,413,559	130,560	3.03497942	329,491.5254
OTU4	111,809,973,568	130,560	1.16769547	856,387.6652
OTU5	433,860,923,077	130,560	0.30092593	3,323,076.923

- **ODU (Optical Data Unit)**: Acts as the switching layer in OTN, encapsulating client data and providing routing information.
- **OPU (Optical Payload Unit)**: Carries the actual client data payload, such as Ethernet, SDH, or other protocols.

OPUk Rates

Rate Level	Bit Rate (bps)	Frame Size (bits)	Frame Rate (µs)	Frame Frequency (KHz)
		OPUk		
OPU0	1,238,954,310	121,856	98.35390947	10,167.36402
OPU1	2,488,320,000	121,856	48.97119342	20,420.16807
OPU2	9,995,276,962	121,856	12.19135802	82,025.31646
OPU3	40,150,519,322	121,856	3.03497942	329,491.5254
OPU4	104,355,975,330	121,856	1.16769547	856,387.6652
OPU5	406,033,906,250	121,856	0.30092593	3,323,076.923

OTN Alarms and Monitoring

Alarms in OTN are essential for detecting and resolving issues in optical networks. Key OTN alarms include:

- **Loss of Signal (LOS)**: Indicates that the optical signal has been lost.
- **Loss of Frame (LOF)**: Occurs when the frame structure is not detected, suggesting an issue with signal integrity.

- **Backward Defect Indicator (BDI)**: Signals that a downstream network element has detected an issue and is reporting it back to the upstream network element.
- **Bit Error Rate (BER) Thresholds**: High BER may indicate issues with transmission, and thresholds can be set to trigger alarms when errors exceed acceptable limits.

Common Alarms and Notifications

Signal Failure	Signal Degraded	Maintenance
• Loss of Frame (LOF)	• BIP-8 Errors	• AIS
• Loss of Signal (LOS)	• BER Threshold	• RDI
• Loss of Multi-frame	• Error Indicators	• FDI

Example of Alarm Workflow:

1. **LOS Detected**: An LOS alarm triggers when the optical signal drops, signaling a potential fiber cut or transmitter failure.
2. **Automatic Protection Switching (APS)**: The OTN system automatically reroutes traffic via a protection path to maintain service continuity.

OTN Alarms and Actions Flowchart

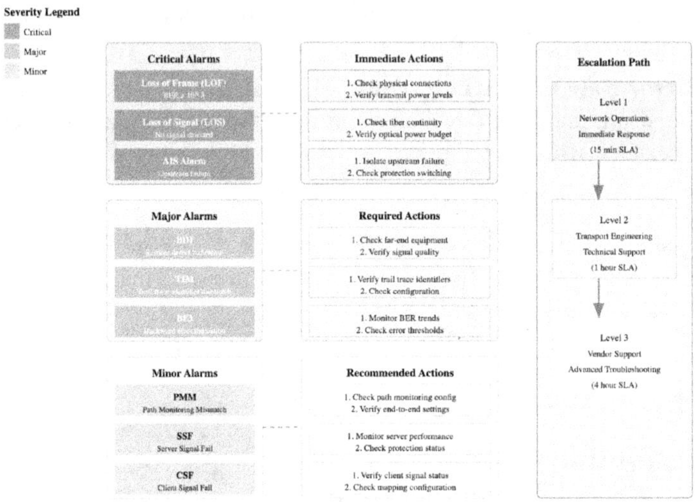

OTN Alarm Correlation: A-Z End

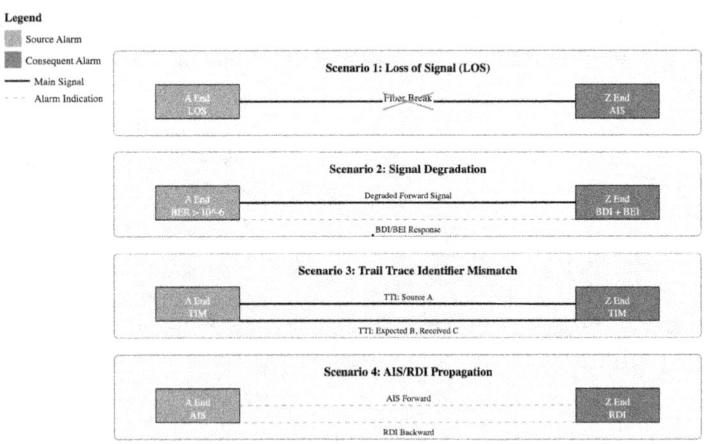

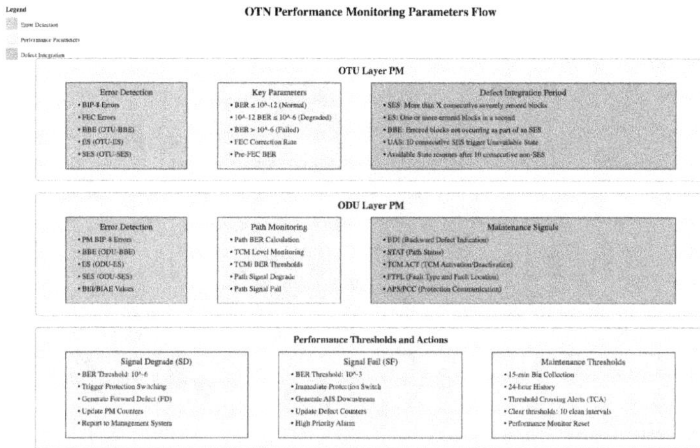

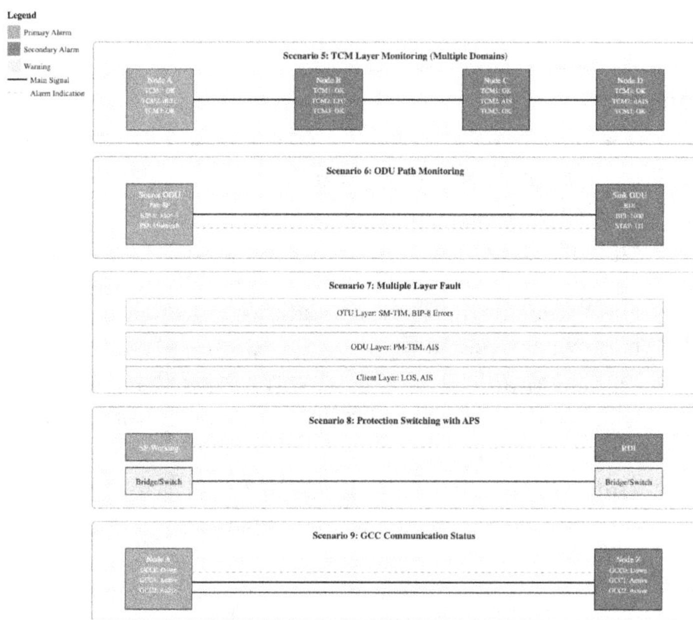

Optical and Electrical Layers in OTN

OTN is defined by its **multi-layered architecture**, which includes both optical (physical) and electrical (digital) layers:

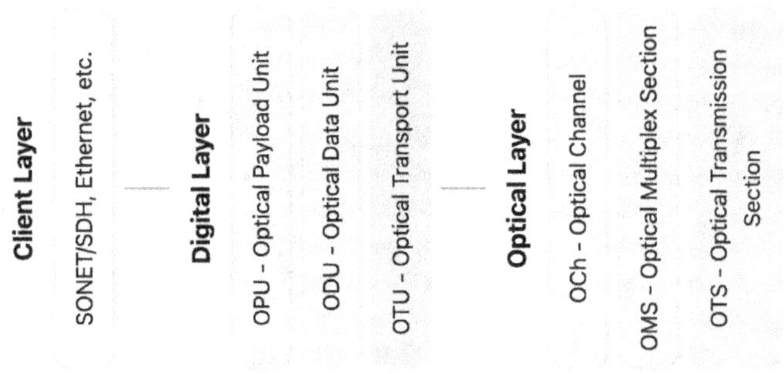

Optical Layer

- Responsible for the physical transmission of the optical signal, including wavelength multiplexing, signal amplification, and transmission across fibers.
- **Optical Channel Layer (OCh)**: Responsible for transporting client signals over a wavelength in DWDM systems. The OCh layer maps client data to optical channels, allowing the transport of multiple signals over a single fiber.
- **Optical Multiplex Section (OMS) Layer**: Manages the multiplexing and routing of wavelengths in the network, ensuring efficient use of fiber resources.
- **Optical Transport Section (OTS) Layer**: This layer is responsible for the optical transmission and regeneration of signals in long-haul networks.

Electrical Layer

- The electrical layer manages the digital data that is carried within the optical signals. This layer handles switching, multiplexing, and framing, as well as adding management and error correction overheads to ensure the integrity of the transmitted data.

Layer Interactions:

- The **optical layer** ensures that the light signals are transmitted efficiently across fibers, while the **electrical layer** manages the client data, routing it appropriately and ensuring it is protected from errors during transmission.

Advanced Features of OTN

OTN is not only known for its core capabilities but also for a range of advanced features that enhance its functionality for modern networks.

OTN Multiplexing and Grooming

Hierarchical Multiplexing: OTN supports the hierarchical multiplexing of lower-rate signals into higher-rate Optical Data Units (ODUs). Multiplexing at various levels allows for the aggregation of multiple client signals (such as Ethernet, SONET/SDH) into a single optical channel, optimizing fiber utilization.

Multiplexing Example:

- **ODU0 (1.25 Gbps)** signals can be multiplexed into an **ODU1 (2.5 Gbps)** container.
- **ODU1** containers can then be multiplexed into an **ODU2 (10 Gbps)** signal.
- This hierarchical structure continues up to **ODU4 (100 Gbps)** and beyond.

Practical Use: In a metro network, ODU0 signals (from individual client connections) are multiplexed into an ODU2 frame for transport over a 10G DWDM link. This ensures efficient use of the available bandwidth while maintaining separation between the different client services.

OTN Cross-Connect (OTN Switch)

Cross-Connect Functionality: OTN cross-connects, or switches, are used to manage and route data streams within the OTN network. These switches allow different client services to be switched and routed dynamically at the ODU layer, ensuring flexibility and efficiency in traffic management.

Layer 1 Switching: OTN provides Layer 1 (optical layer) switching capabilities, which means the network can manage traffic at the wavelength level without needing to convert the signal back to an electrical format. This allows for more efficient management of large volumes of data in a transparent manner.

Use Case: A national service provider uses OTN cross-connects to dynamically switch and manage 100G and 400G channels across its backbone network. This enables the provider to adjust bandwidth allocation based on demand, improving resource utilization and reducing operational costs.

Sub-Lambda Multiplexing

Efficient Bandwidth Utilization: OTN also supports sub-lambda multiplexing, where client signals that do not fully utilize a single wavelength (lambda) can be aggregated. This is critical in scenarios where services like 10G, 40G, and 100G must coexist on a single fiber but don't need the entire bandwidth of the wavelength.

Example: A 100G OTN system can multiplex multiple 10G client signals onto the same wavelength using sub-lambda multiplexing, ensuring efficient utilization of the available spectrum.

OTN Protection and Restoration

Protection Mechanisms in OTN

Linear Protection

Linear protection in OTN provides dedicated backup paths for traffic between two network elements. The primary mechanisms include:

1. **1+1 Protection**
    - Simultaneous transmission on working and protection paths
    - Receiving end selects better signal
    - Fastest switching time but highest resource usage
    - Commonly used for critical services requiring sub-50ms recovery
2. **1:1 Protection**
    - Protection path available but not actively carrying traffic
    - More efficient resource utilization than 1+1
    - Protection path can carry low-priority traffic during normal operation
    - Slightly longer switching time compared to 1+1

Ring Protection

Ring protection architectures provide multiple paths between network nodes arranged in a circular topology:

1. **Dedicated Ring Protection**
    - Similar to 1+1 linear protection but in a ring topology
    - Traffic sent in both directions around the ring
    - Automatic protection switching upon failure
    - High availability but resource-intensive

2. **Shared Ring Protection**
   - Protection capacity shared among multiple working paths
   - More efficient resource utilization
   - Multiple protection domains possible within single ring
   - Complex protection switching protocols required

Restoration Techniques

Unlike protection, restoration involves dynamic recovery from failures:

Mesh Restoration

- Dynamic calculation of alternate paths
- More efficient resource utilization than protection
- Longer recovery times (typically seconds to minutes)
- Greater flexibility in handling multiple failures

Path Restoration

- End-to-end restoration of affected paths
- Can utilize multiple alternate routes
- More complex than link restoration
- Better optimization of network resources

OTN Protection Switching

Triggers for Protection Switching

- Signal failure (SF)
- Signal degradation (SD)
- Administrative commands
- External commands (forced switch, manual switch)

Protection Switching Time

1. Detection Time
   - Time to detect failure condition
   - Typically few milliseconds for hardware-based detection
2. Switching Time
   - Time to activate protection path
   - Usually under 50ms for protection schemes
   - Several seconds for restoration

Implementation Considerations

Network Planning

- Protection path diversity
- Resource allocation for protection
- Failure scenario analysis
- Quality of service requirements

Management Aspects

1. Configuration Management
    - Protection group setup
    - Protection policy definition
    - Priority settings
2. Performance Monitoring
    - Protection switching events
    - Restoration success rate
    - Recovery time measurements

Interworking

- Protection interworking with client layers
- Coordination with higher layer protection
- Multi-vendor compatibility considerations

Advanced Protection Features

Sub-Network Connection Protection (SNCP)

- Path-level protection within sub-networks
- Independent of network topology
- Flexible protection domains
- Enhanced scalability

Dual-Node Interconnection (DNI)

- Protection against node failures
- Dual homing of critical nodes
- Load sharing capabilities
- Geographic redundancy

Best Practices

1. Design Recommendations
    - Implement diverse routing for working and protection paths
    - Consider hybrid protection/restoration schemes
    - Plan for future capacity needs
    - Document protection domains and policies
2. Operational Guidelines
    - Regular testing of protection mechanisms
    - Maintenance procedures for protected services
    - Clear escalation procedures
    - Change management processes

Comparative Analysis of OTN Protection Mechanisms

Protection Type	Recovery Time	Resource Utilization	Complexity	Traffic Impact	Common Applications
1+1 Linear	< 50ms	High (100% redundancy)	Low	No traffic loss	Critical services, financial networks
1:1 Linear	50-100ms	Medium	Medium	Minimal loss	Enterprise services
1:N Linear	100-200ms	Low	High	Possible loss	Best-effort services
Dedicated Ring	< 50ms	High	Medium	No traffic loss	Metro networks
Shared Ring	50-150ms	Medium	High	Minimal loss	Regional networks
Mesh Protection	< 50ms	Medium-High	High	No traffic loss	Core networks
Path Restoration	200ms-2s	Low	Very High	Service interruption	Backup recovery
SNCP	< 50ms	High	Medium	No traffic loss	Sub-network protection

Protection Mechanism Selection Criteria

Criterion	Description	Importance
Service Level Agreement (SLA)	Required recovery time and availability	Critical
Cost	CAPEX and OPEX considerations	High
Network Topology	Physical network layout and constraints	High
Scalability	Ability to grow with network expansion	Medium
Management Complexity	Operational overhead and expertise required	Medium
Traffic Type	Critical vs non-critical traffic	High

Performance Metrics Comparison

Metric	1+1 Protection	1:1 Protection	Mesh Restoration
Switching Time	<50ms	50-100ms	>200ms
Resource Efficiency	Low	Medium	High
Failure Coverage	Single	Single	Multiple
Implementation Cost	High	Medium	Low
Operation Complexity	Low	Medium	High

OTN Performance Metrics and Monitoring

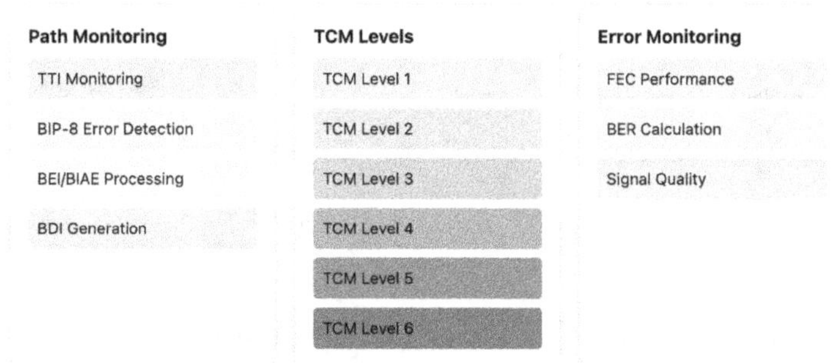

Analysis of OTN Performance Metrics

Forward Error Correction (FEC) in Detail

FEC is one of the most critical features of OTN because it enables long-distance transmission by correcting errors introduced during optical transmission.

How FEC Works: FEC adds redundancy to the transmitted data, allowing the receiver to detect and correct errors without needing retransmission. In OTN, **Reed-Solomon FEC** is commonly used, which can correct a certain number of errors in each block of data.

Reed-Solomon FEC Formula:

$$RS(n,k)=n-k$$

Where:

- n is the total number of symbols (data and FEC),
- k is the number of data symbols,
- n−k represents the number of symbols added for error correction.

Example: A 100G OTU4 link with FEC can transmit data over 1,500 km without signal regeneration by correcting errors caused by fiber attenuation and noise.

Bit Error Rate (BER) Thresholds in OTN

BER Monitoring: OTN continuously monitors the **Bit Error Rate (BER)**, which is a measure of how many bits in the data stream have been altered during transmission. The **pre-FEC BER** gives an indication of the raw error rate before FEC correction, while the **post-FEC BER** reflects the errors that remain after FEC has been applied.

Typical BER Levels:

- Pre-FEC BER: 10−3
- Post-FEC BER: 10−15 (Ideal scenario with errors corrected by FEC)

Example: In a 400G link, a pre-FEC BER of 10−3 might indicate significant noise or nonlinear effects. After FEC is applied, the BER might drop to 10−15, ensuring error-free transmission.

Optical Signal-to-Noise Ratio (OSNR) in OTN

OSNR Importance: OSNR is a key performance metric in optical networks, especially in long-haul systems. It measures the ratio of the signal power to the noise power and indicates the quality of the received optical signal.

OSNR Thresholds:

- For QPSK (Quadrature Phase-Shift Keying) modulation, a minimum OSNR of 15 dB is typically required for error-free transmission.
- For higher-order modulation formats like 16-QAM (Quadrature Amplitude Modulation), the required OSNR may increase to 25 dB or more.

Example: In a 200G metro network using 16-QAM, the OSNR must be carefully monitored. A drop below 25 dB might trigger alarms, indicating that the link is close to failure or is experiencing heavy degradation due to noise or nonlinearities.

Real-World OTN Deployment and Use Cases

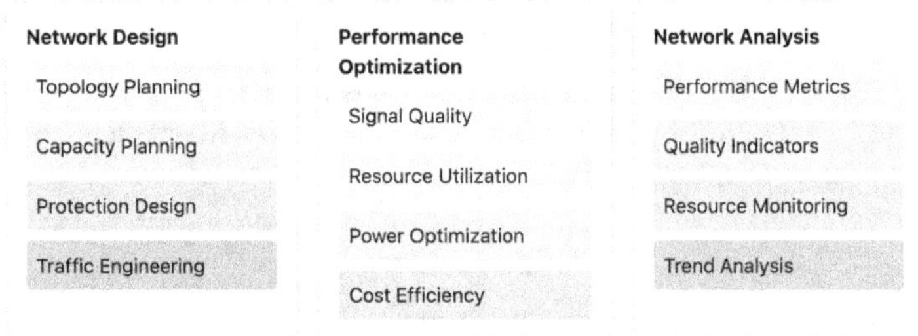

OTN in Data Center Interconnects (DCI)

Data centers are rapidly adopting OTN to interconnect multiple facilities across cities or regions. OTN's ability to transport multiple types of data (e.g., Ethernet, Fibre Channel, SONET/SDH) over a single network makes it ideal for DCI applications.

Use Case: A cloud provider uses OTN to interconnect its data centers in three major cities, multiplexing 100G Ethernet traffic and 40G Fibre Channel storage traffic into a single OTN frame. The provider leverages OTN's efficient multiplexing and error correction to ensure seamless data transfer with low latency.

OTN in Long-Haul Networks

OTN is extensively used in long-haul networks because it offers high capacity, error correction, and management features over long distances. FEC and amplification ensure that optical signals can travel thousands of kilometers without the need for electrical regeneration.

Use Case: A telecommunications company deploys OTN for a 2,500 km long-haul link. By using OTN's FEC and optical amplification, the company eliminates the need for frequent signal regeneration, reducing both operational costs and latency.

Metro and Regional Networks

In metro networks, OTN is used to aggregate traffic from different access points and deliver it to core networks. The scalability and flexibility of OTN allow metro networks to handle the increasing demand for high-bandwidth services like video streaming and cloud computing.

Additional OTN Use Cases in Various Network Architectures

OTN in 5G Transport Networks

With the rollout of 5G, OTN plays a crucial role in backhauling traffic from 5G cell sites to the core network.

Low Latency and High Bandwidth: 5G networks require extremely low-latency and high-bandwidth transport, which OTN provides. Its ability to aggregate different types of traffic (e.g., CPRI, Ethernet, IP) into a single optical channel makes it ideal for 5G backhaul.

Use Case: A mobile operator uses OTN to aggregate 10G and 25G Ethernet traffic from 5G base stations into a single 100G OTN stream, transporting it to the core network with minimal latency.

OTN for Cloud and Enterprise Connectivity

As cloud computing and enterprise services grow, data centers require robust and scalable transport networks. OTN offers the reliability and capacity needed for data center interconnects (DCI).

Multi-Service Support: OTN can carry multiple services, such as Ethernet for data services and Fibre Channel for storage traffic, in a single optical channel. This reduces the complexity and cost of managing multiple transport layers.

Use Case: A cloud provider uses OTN to transport 100G Ethernet and 40G Fibre Channel from its data centers in one city to another, using a single OTN frame for efficiency. OTN's management capabilities ensure that data integrity is maintained throughout the journey.

Advanced OTN Protection and Restoration Mechanisms

1+1 and 1:1 Protection in OTN

1+1 Protection: In 1+1 protection, two identical signals are sent over separate paths, and the receiving equipment selects the best signal. This is useful for highly critical services where any downtime is unacceptable.

Example: In a financial trading network, 1+1 protection ensures zero downtime by transmitting data simultaneously over two independent paths. If one path fails, the other path takes over instantly.

1:1 Protection: In this scheme, the backup path remains idle until the primary path fails. This is more efficient in terms of resource utilization compared to 1+1 protection, but it introduces a small delay during switching.

Use Case: A telecom operator uses 1:1 protection in its OTN network to ensure backup paths are available in case of failure. While this method saves bandwidth, it still provides a safety net for critical services.

Shared Mesh Protection (SMP) in OTN

Shared Mesh Protection (SMP): SMP allows multiple links to share backup resources, reducing the amount of spare capacity needed for protection. When a failure occurs, traffic is dynamically rerouted through the shared backup resources.

Example: In a long-haul OTN network spanning continents, SMP allows multiple 100G and 400G links to share backup capacity. If a fiber cut occurs, the affected traffic is rerouted through the backup channels, minimizing service disruption.

Automatic Protection Switching (APS)

APS Mechanism: OTN networks use APS to automatically switch to a backup path when a failure or degradation is detected on the primary path. This process occurs in milliseconds, ensuring that services continue without interruption.

APS Use Case: A metro network uses APS to protect its 100G OTN links. If a fiber cut occurs or the OSNR drops below a predefined threshold, the system automatically switches traffic to a preconfigured backup path, ensuring minimal downtime.

Cost and Power Optimization with OTN

Cost-Benefit Analysis of OTN Deployment

- **Cost Efficiency**: OTN reduces overall costs by multiplexing multiple services into a single optical channel, reducing the need for additional fiber and equipment. The use of FEC also reduces the number of optical amplifiers and regenerators required.
- **Operational Efficiency**: OTN's built-in management and monitoring systems lower operational costs by simplifying troubleshooting and reducing downtime.

Power Efficiency in OTN Networks

Per-Bit Power Consumption: OTN is optimized for low power consumption, particularly in comparison to earlier technologies like SONET/SDH. Higher-capacity OTU frames (e.g., OTU4, OTUCn) provide higher data throughput without significantly increasing the power required per bit of data.

Example: A metro network using 400G OTN systems achieves a lower power consumption per bit compared to a network using multiple 100G SONET/SDH channels.

Why Clock Synchronization is Not Needed in OTN

In traditional systems like SONET/SDH, clock synchronization is critical because these systems rely on synchronous transmission, where all network elements must be precisely synchronized to the same clock source to maintain proper timing for data transfer. OTN, however, is designed to be asynchronous, which eliminates the need for strict clock synchronization.

Asynchronous Nature of OTN

Client Signals Are Decoupled from Network Clock: In OTN, the client signal (e.g., Ethernet, SDH, etc.) is decoupled from the transport network's clock. This means that the OTN network can carry data without requiring the client signal and the network to be synchronized to the same clock.

Example: An Ethernet signal transported over OTN does not need to adhere to the same clock as the OTN network, unlike in SONET/SDH, where precise timing alignment is essential.

Digital Wrapper and Justification Mechanism: OTN uses a concept known as the **"digital wrapper"** to transport client data. The client signal is encapsulated within the Optical Payload Unit (OPU) and then mapped into the Optical Data Unit (ODU), which is transmitted over the network. To handle differences in the client signal's clock and the OTN network clock, **stuffing bytes** (or justification bytes) are used.

- **Positive Stuffing**: If the client signal's rate is lower than the OTN signal, extra "stuffing" bits are added to adjust for the timing mismatch.
- **Negative Stuffing**: If the client signal's rate is higher, the OTN frame accommodates this by reducing the number of stuffing bits.

This dynamic adjustment between the client and network timing allows OTN to transport signals asynchronously without needing all elements to operate on the same clock.

Forward Error Correction (FEC) and Robust Framing

- **Error Correction and Recovery**: OTN's Forward Error Correction (FEC) feature improves data transmission quality by correcting errors during transmission. Thiş is another reason OTN can operate asynchronously, as FEC helps ensure that minor clock mismatches or timing errors are corrected without requiring strict synchronization across the network.
- **Framing Structure**: The OTN frame includes overhead fields that provide framing and management information, including bytes for **frame alignment** and error detection/correction. This allows the receiving end to detect the boundaries of each OTN frame even if the data is transmitted asynchronously.

How Frame Synchronization Works in OTN

Despite OTN being asynchronous in nature, it still needs to ensure that the frames are correctly synchronized at the receiving end. OTN achieves this through a robust **frame alignment** process.

Frame Alignment in OTN

Frame synchronization is the process by which the receiving equipment identifies the start and end of each OTN frame. This is done through specific bytes in the overhead section of the frame.

Frame Alignment Signals (FAS): The first few bytes of every OTN frame contain the **Frame Alignment Signal (FAS)**, which is a unique pattern that helps the receiver identify the beginning of each frame. The FAS is part of the OTU overhead, and it repeats at regular intervals to maintain synchronization between the transmitter and the receiver.

FAS Structure:

- The FAS occupies the first three bytes of the OTU frame and contains a fixed 6-bit pattern (e.g., 0xF6). This pattern helps the receiver detect frame boundaries and re-synchronize if the frame alignment is lost.

Practical Example: In a 100G OTN link, the receiver monitors the incoming data stream for the FAS. When it detects the unique pattern, it locks onto the frame structure, allowing the receiver to interpret the payload correctly.

Out-of-Band Signaling for Synchronization

OTN Overhead: In addition to the FAS, OTN frames include various overhead bytes that provide critical signaling and management functions, such as section monitoring (SM), path monitoring (PM), and general communication channels (GCC). These overhead fields ensure that the frames remain aligned and synchronized even if there are minor transmission errors or jitter.

Overhead in Synchronization:

- The **Section Monitoring (SM)** bytes continuously monitor the quality of the transmission section and can trigger alarms if issues like loss of frame (LOF) or loss of signal (LOS) occur.
- The **Path Monitoring (PM)** bytes help monitor the end-to-end integrity of the data path, ensuring that frames remain properly aligned throughout the transmission.

Justification in OTN

As mentioned earlier, OTN uses a **justification mechanism** to account for differences in timing between the client signal and the OTN network. This process adjusts the timing dynamically, ensuring that data can be transmitted asynchronously.

Positive and Negative Justification: OTN employs positive and negative stuffing bytes to handle the slight variations in clock rates between the client signal and the OTN frame. These bytes allow the client data to fit into the OTN frame without requiring both the client and network clocks to be synchronized.

Example: If the client signal is slightly faster than the OTN frame rate, the justification bytes are reduced (negative justification). Conversely, if the client signal is slower, extra justification bytes are added (positive justification) to align the data.

Comparing Framing Technologies

As data transmission needs continue to grow exponentially, various framing technologies have emerged, each offering distinct advantages and capabilities. In this chapter, we delve into the key differences between **Optical Transport Network (OTN)**, **Synchronous Digital Hierarchy (SDH)**, **Synchronous Optical Networking (SONET)**, and **Dense Wavelength Division Multiplexing (DWDM)**. These technologies play crucial roles in the management and transmission of high-speed data across vast distances, and understanding their characteristics is essential for making informed network design decisions.

Overview of Framing Technologies

Optical Transport Network (OTN)

OTN is defined by the **ITU-T G.709** standard and is the latest in a long evolution of optical transport technologies. It was designed to address the limitations of SONET/SDH, providing a more flexible, efficient, and scalable method to transport various client signals, such as Ethernet, SDH, SONET, and Fibre Channel. OTN also introduces robust **Forward Error Correction (FEC)**, which enhances transmission distance and minimizes error rates.

- **Main Features:**
  - **Support for Multiple Client Signals**: OTN can transport a range of signal types, making it highly flexible.
  - **Forward Error Correction (FEC)**: Extends transmission distances by correcting errors at the receiver end.
  - **Sub-Wavelength Networking**: With its flexible frame structure (ODUk, OTUk, OPUk), OTN enables multiplexing and efficient network usage.

Synchronous Digital Hierarchy (SDH) and Synchronous Optical Networking (SONET)

SDH and SONET are both time-division multiplexing (TDM) technologies. While **SONET** is primarily used in North America and **SDH** is used internationally, the two are largely compatible and operate under similar principles. SDH/SONET were designed to transport voice data and were dominant technologies in the late 20th century. However, their rigid hierarchies make them less adaptable to modern, data-centric traffic.

- **Main Features:**
  - **Circuit-Switched**: Designed to handle TDM voice traffic.
  - **Hierarchical Structure**: Uses rigid multiplexing hierarchies, including STM (Synchronous Transport Module) in SDH and OC (Optical Carrier) levels in SONET.
  - **Fast Restoration**: Offers rapid restoration times (50 ms) in case of network failure.

Dense Wavelength Division Multiplexing (DWDM)

DWDM operates on a different principle from OTN, SDH, and SONET, utilizing multiple wavelengths (channels) of light to transmit data simultaneously over a single fiber. It does not perform any framing but works with technologies like OTN to encapsulate and transport data over long distances.

- **Main Features:**
  - **Wavelength-Based Multiplexing**: DWDM allows for the transmission of multiple optical signals (wavelengths) over the same fiber.
  - **High Capacity**: DWDM can support up to 160 wavelengths per fiber, each carrying up to 100 Gbps, providing significant bandwidth.
  - **Scalable**: Easily scaled by adding more wavelengths to the network.

Comparison of OTN, SDH, SONET, and DWDM

Each of these technologies serves different purposes in optical transport networks, and the choice of which to use depends on the specific application and traffic requirements.

Framing and Signal Multiplexing

- **OTN**:
  - Uses a **frame-based structure** (OTUk, ODUk, OPUk) to multiplex and encapsulate client signals. It can carry both packet-switched and circuit-switched traffic.
  - OTN provides more efficient bandwidth management, with the ability to transport signals of varying rates using ODU0, ODU1, ODU2, ODU3, and ODUflex.
  - **Standards**: ITU-T G.709 defines OTN's frame format and multiplexing hierarchy.
- **SDH/SONET:**
  - Both SDH and SONET use a strict **time-division multiplexing (TDM)** method. SDH uses STM frames, while SONET uses OC levels.
  - **Standards**: ITU-T G.707 (SDH) and ANSI T1.105 (SONET) define the respective frame formats.
- **DWDM:**
  - DWDM does not perform framing but rather multiplexes data on different wavelengths of light. DWDM systems often rely on OTN or Ethernet framing for encapsulating client signals.

- **Standards**: ITU-T G.694 defines the channel spacing for DWDM.

Error Handling and Performance

- **OTN**:
    - OTN introduces **FEC (Forward Error Correction)**, which allows it to extend transmission distances while minimizing errors.
    - By correcting bit errors at the receiver end, OTN ensures high-performance transmission, even over long distances.
- **SDH/SONET:**
    - SDH/SONET have limited error correction capabilities and rely more on network redundancy for error handling.
    - Restoration times are fast (50 ms), making them suitable for networks where high availability is crucial, such as in voice communications.
- **DWDM:**
    - DWDM depends on other technologies (such as OTN or Ethernet) for error handling. DWDM amplifies signals using **Erbium-Doped Fiber Amplifiers (EDFAs)**, which are crucial for long-distance transmission.

Scalability

- **OTN**:
    - OTN is highly scalable, supporting data rates up to 100 Gbps and beyond with OTU4. It also supports **sub-wavelength multiplexing** with ODUflex, allowing network operators to use bandwidth more efficiently.
- **SDH/SONET:**
    - SDH/SONET were designed with fixed data rates, which makes them less scalable for modern networks. The highest rate supported by SONET is OC-768 (40 Gbps), while SDH can support STM-256 (also 40 Gbps).
- **DWDM**:
    - DWDM is inherently scalable. By adding more wavelengths (channels), network operators can significantly increase the capacity of the fiber without laying additional cables.

Flexibility and Client Support

- **OTN**:
    - OTN is **client-agnostic**, supporting a wide range of client types, including Ethernet, SONET/SDH, and Fibre Channel. Its flexibility makes it ideal for networks carrying mixed traffic.
- **SDH/SONET:**
    - SDH/SONET were primarily designed for **voice traffic** and TDM-based services, making them less adaptable to packet-switched networks like Ethernet or IP.
- **DWDM**:
    - DWDM can transport any data type over its optical channels, making it flexible for both circuit-switched and packet-switched services. However, it depends on technologies like OTN or Ethernet to manage client signals.

When to Use Each Technology ?

OTN:

- **Best for**: Transporting diverse types of client signals (e.g., Ethernet, SDH, SONET) across long distances. OTN is ideal for backbone and core networks where flexibility and error correction are critical.
- **Advantages**: Supports a wide range of client types, highly scalable, efficient bandwidth usage, error correction with FEC.

SDH/SONET:

- **Best for**: Legacy networks, especially those focused on voice and TDM traffic. SONET/SDH are still used in some metropolitan and long-haul networks but are being phased out in favor of newer technologies like OTN.
- **Advantages**: High availability with fast restoration times, ideal for TDM voice traffic.

DWDM:

- **Best for**: Maximizing the capacity of existing fiber infrastructure. DWDM is commonly used in high-capacity backbone networks where multiple channels of data need to be transmitted simultaneously over a single fiber.
- **Advantages**: Scalable, high-capacity transport, compatible with a wide range of client signals through OTN or Ethernet framing.

Comparative Analysis of Framing Technologies

Core Technology Characteristics

Feature	OTN	SDH	SONET	DWDM
Primary Standard	ITU-T G.709	ITU-T G.707	ANSI T1.105	ITU-T G.694
Main Purpose	Multi-service transport	TDM voice/data	TDM voice/data	Wavelength multiplexing
Frame Structure	OTUk/ODUk/OPUk	STM	OC levels	N/A (wavelength-based)
Maximum Data Rate	100+ Gbps (OTU4)	40 Gbps (STM-256)	40 Gbps (OC-768)	100+ Gbps per wavelength
Error Correction	Advanced FEC	Limited	Limited	Depends on framing tech
Geographic Usage	Worldwide	International	North America	Worldwide

Technical Capabilities

Capability	OTN	SDH/SONET	DWDM
Multiplexing Method	Digital wrapper	Time-division	Wavelength-based
Signal Types Supported	Multiple (Ethernet, SDH, FC)	Primarily TDM	Any (with proper framing)
Restoration Time	Variable	< 50ms	Depends on control plane
Scalability	High	Limited	Very High
Network Layer	Layer 1	Layer 1	Physical Layer

Bandwidth Management	Flexible	Fixed hierarchy	Wavelength-based

Use Cases and Applications

Aspect	OTN	SDH/SONET	DWDM
Best Application	Core networks, mixed traffic	Legacy voice networks	Long-haul, high capacity
Network Type	Metro, Regional, Long-haul	Metro, Regional	Long-haul, Submarine
Client Services	Mixed packet/TDM	Primarily TDM	Any (technology agnostic)
Typical Deployment	Modern networks	Legacy networks	All optical networks
Cost Efficiency	High	Medium	Very High
Management Complexity	Medium	Low	High

Performance and Features

Feature	OTN	SDH/SONET	DWDM
Error Handling	Strong (FEC)	Basic	Technology dependent
Distance Support	Long	Medium	Very Long
Channel Capacity	High	Medium	Very High
Service Flexibility	High	Low	Very High

Protection Options	Multiple	Ring/Linear	Wavelength-based
QoS Support	Yes	Limited	Technology dependent

Implementation Considerations

Consideration	OTN	SDH/SONET	DWDM
Initial Cost	High	Medium	Very High
Operational Cost	Medium	Low	High
Expertise Required	High	Medium	Very High
Migration Path	Flexible	Limited	Technology agnostic
Future-proofing	High	Low	Very High
Interoperability	Excellent	Good	Excellent

Standards and Protocols

Aspect	OTN	SDH	SONET	DWDM
Main Standards Body	ITU-T	ITU-T	ANSI	ITU-T
Frame Format	G.709	G.707	T1.105	G.694
Management Protocol	G.874	G.783	T1.111	G.695

Protection Standard	G.873	G.841	GR-1230	G.692
Synchronization	G.8251	G.803	T1.101	N/A

Chapter 7

Understanding Bit Rate, Baud Rate, and Spectral Width

Chapter 7
Understanding Bit Rate, Baud Rate, and Spectral Width

"Every bit matters, but how you transmit them matters more." - Andrew Chraplyvy

---

As optical networks continue to evolve, understanding key concepts like bit rate, baud rate, spectral width, single-carrier and multi-carrier systems, super channels, and modulation schemes is essential for designing efficient, high-capacity, and cost-effective networks. This chapter explores each of these concepts in depth, providing clear explanations, real-world examples, and the latest data on their impact on network performance, capacity, reach, and power consumption.

Bit Rate vs. Baud Rate

What is Bit Rate?

Definition: Bit rate refers to the number of bits transmitted per second in a communication system. It's often expressed in gigabits per second (Gbps) or terabits per second (Tbps). In optical networks, the bit rate is a key indicator of the network's capacity.

$$\text{Bit Rate (R)} = \text{Baud Rate (B)} \times \text{Number of Bits per Symbol (M)}$$

Example: A 100G optical link using polarization-division multiplexing quadrature phase-shift keying (PDM-QPSK) modulation has a bit rate of 100 Gbps, where each symbol represents 2 bits, and polarization-division multiplexing doubles the data throughput.

What is Baud Rate?

Definition: Baud rate refers to the number of symbols transmitted per second. While the bit rate indicates how many bits are transmitted, the baud rate represents how many times the signal changes per second. Increasing the baud rate improves the data transmission rate but also increases the spectral width (discussed later).

$$B_{\min} = \frac{\text{Baud Rate}}{2}$$

Example: In a 100G coherent system using PDM-QPSK, a baud rate of 32 Gbaud corresponds to 32 billion symbols transmitted per second. Since each symbol carries 2 bits (in QPSK), the system achieves a bit rate of 100 Gbps.

Bit Rate (R):
- Number of bits transmitted per second
- Measured in bits per second (bps)
- Formula: R = Baud Rate × bits per symbol

Baud Rate (S):
- Number of symbols per second
- One symbol can represent multiple bits
- Symbol Rate = 1/T (T = symbol period)

Modulation:
- Process of encoding information
- Changes carrier signal properties
- Amplitude, Phase, Frequency

Bit Rate and Baud Rate Relationship

Higher Baud Rate vs. Higher Modulation: Increasing the baud rate improves the bit rate but requires more bandwidth. Alternatively, using higher-order modulation formats increases the number of bits transmitted per symbol without increasing the baud rate, but it also requires a higher optical signal-to-noise ratio (OSNR).

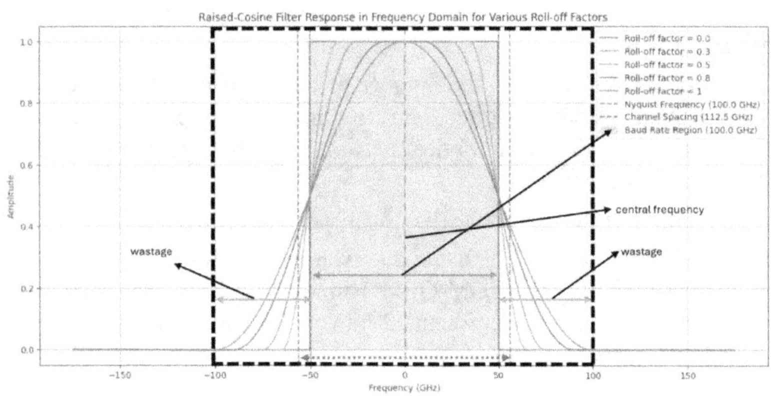

Fig. Raised-cosine filter response showing the effect of various roll-off factors on bandwidth efficiency. Highlighted are the central frequency, Nyquist bandwidth, and wasted spectral bandwidth due to roll-off.

Practical Use Case: A 400G coherent optical transceiver operates at 64 Gbaud using 16QAM modulation. Each symbol represents 4 bits, and the polarization-division multiplexing technique doubles the effective bit rate, allowing 400 Gbps transmission over a single wavelength.

The Nyquist Theorem and Roll-Off Factor

The Nyquist theorem sets a theoretical limit on the minimum bandwidth required to transmit data without ISI. According to this theorem, the minimum bandwidth Bmin for a signal is half the baud rate:

In practical systems, the actual bandwidth exceeds this minimum due to imperfections in filters and other system limitations. The roll-off factor r typically ranging from 0 to 1, defines the excess bandwidth required beyond the Nyquist limit. The actual bandwidth with a roll-off factor is:

$$B_{actual} = \text{Baud Rate} \times (1+r)$$

Choosing an appropriate roll-off factor involves balancing bandwidth efficiency with system robustness. A higher roll-off factor results in smoother transitions between symbols and reduced ISI but at the cost of increased bandwidth consumption.

Spectral Width and Its Impact on Optical Transmission

Definition of Spectral Width

What is Spectral Width?: Spectral width refers to the range of frequencies over which the optical signal is transmitted. It is closely related to the baud rate—the higher the baud rate, the broader the spectral width. Spectral width is typically measured in GHz, and for dense wavelength-division multiplexing (DWDM) systems, it determines how closely spaced the optical channels can be.

Formula:

$$\text{Spectral Width} = \text{Baud Rate} \times \text{Spectral Efficiency}$$

Example: A 32 Gbaud signal with a spectral efficiency of 1 bit/Hz has a spectral width of 32 GHz. For higher spectral efficiency modulation formats, such as 16QAM, the spectral width increases due to the need for higher OSNR and more robust transmission.

Significance of Spectral Width in Capacity and Reach

Capacity: Narrower spectral width allows more optical channels to be packed into the available fiber bandwidth, increasing the total network capacity. However, increasing the baud rate (and thus the spectral width) allows for higher bit rates but reduces the number of channels that can fit within the same fiber.

Reach: A broader spectral width requires higher OSNR, which affects the reach of the signal. Narrow spectral width channels are more resistant to chromatic dispersion and nonlinear effects, enabling longer reach.

Use Case: A 400G superchannel operating at 64 Gbaud with 64QAM modulation has a spectral width of approximately 96 GHz. This wider spectral width reduces the number of channels that can be packed into a DWDM system, but it maximizes the data rate on each channel. By contrast, a 100G system using 32 Gbaud PDM-QPSK has a narrower spectral width, allowing more channels to be placed on the fiber.

Trade-offs Between Baud Rate, Bit Rate and Modulation Formats

In optical communication systems, higher baud rates allow for the transmission of more symbols per second, but they require broader spectral widths (i.e., more bandwidth). Conversely, higher-order modulation formats allow more bits per symbol, reducing the required baud rate for the same bit rate, but they increase system complexity and susceptibility to impairments.

For instance, if we aim to transmit a 400 Gbps signal, we have two general options:

1. Increasing the Baud Rate: Keeping a lower modulation format (e.g., QPSK), we can increase the baud rate. For instance, a 400 Gbps signal using QPSK requires a 200 GBaud rate.
2. Using Higher-Order Modulation: With 64-QAM, which transmits 6 bits per symbol, we could transmit the same 400 Gbps with a baud rate of approximately 66.67 GBaud.

While higher baud rates increase the spectral width requirement, they are generally less sensitive to noise. Higher-order modulation schemes, on the other hand, require less spectral width but need a higher optical signal-to-noise ratio (OSNR) to maintain performance. Engineers need to carefully balance baud rate and modulation formats based on system requirements and constraints.

Single Carrier vs. Multi-Carrier Systems

Single Carrier Systems

Overview: In single-carrier systems, the entire data stream is transmitted over a single optical carrier frequency. These systems are simpler to implement but have limitations in terms of capacity, reach, and resilience to impairments like chromatic dispersion and fiber nonlinearities.

Example: A traditional 100G DWDM system using PDM-QPSK is a single-carrier system. It transmits all 100 Gbps over a single optical carrier with a typical spectral width of 50 GHz.

Multi-Carrier Systems

- **Overview**: Multi-carrier systems (such as orthogonal frequency-division multiplexing or OFDM) transmit data over multiple subcarriers, each occupying a smaller portion of the total available spectrum. Multi-carrier systems improve resilience to impairments and allow more flexible use of the available spectral bandwidth.
- **Benefits**:
    - **Higher Capacity**: Multi-carrier systems enable the transmission of more data by using multiple carriers within the same optical channel.
    - **Resilience to Impairments**: Subcarriers can be individually modulated, making the system more robust to fiber impairments like chromatic dispersion and nonlinearities.

Example: A multi-carrier system using OFDM splits a 400G signal into multiple subcarriers, each modulated independently. This improves spectral efficiency and resilience to fiber impairments compared to a single-carrier system.

Super Channels and Their Role in High-Capacity Networks

What are Super Channels?

- **Definition**: Super channels are high-capacity optical channels that aggregate multiple subcarriers into a single logical channel. They are used to increase the overall data rate on a single wavelength, typically beyond 400G, while optimizing the use of available spectrum.
- **Benefits**:
    - **Spectral Efficiency**: Super channels make better use of the available spectrum by packing subcarriers closely together.

- **Higher Data Rates**: Super channels enable the transmission of data at rates beyond 400G and 1T, using a combination of multiple subcarriers and advanced modulation formats.

Example: A 1T optical super channel is created by combining ten 100G subcarriers into a single logical channel. Each subcarrier is modulated using QPSK and transmitted over a tightly packed spectrum of approximately 500 GHz.

Super Channels in Practical Use

Flex-Grid ROADMs: Super channels are often deployed in flex-grid reconfigurable optical add-drop multiplexer (ROADM) networks, which allow dynamic allocation of spectral bandwidth based on the number of subcarriers and modulation format. This improves network flexibility and scalability.

Reach and Power Consumption: Super channels improve the power efficiency of optical networks by reducing the need for multiple transponders. However, their reach is typically shorter than single-carrier systems due to higher OSNR requirements.

Use Case: A data center interconnect (DCI) network deploys 800G super channels using a flex-grid ROADM. The system uses eight 100G subcarriers modulated with QPSK, occupying 400 GHz of spectrum and transmitting over a 1,000 km reach with reduced power consumption compared to deploying individual 100G transponders.

Modulation Formats and Their Impact on Optical Networks

Common Modulation Formats

Binary Phase-Shift Keying (BPSK): A simple modulation format where each symbol represents 1 bit, typically used in long-haul networks due to its resilience to noise.

Quadrature Phase-Shift Keying (QPSK): Each symbol represents 2 bits, providing a balance between spectral efficiency and reach. QPSK is commonly used in 100G systems.

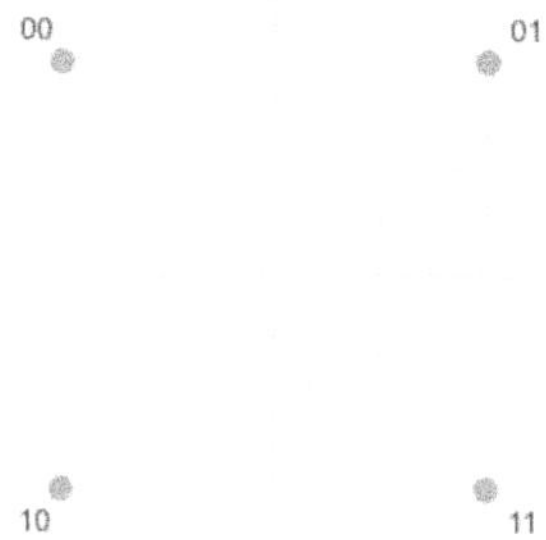

16-Quadrature Amplitude Modulation (16QAM): Each symbol represents 4 bits, doubling the data rate compared to QPSK but requiring a higher OSNR.

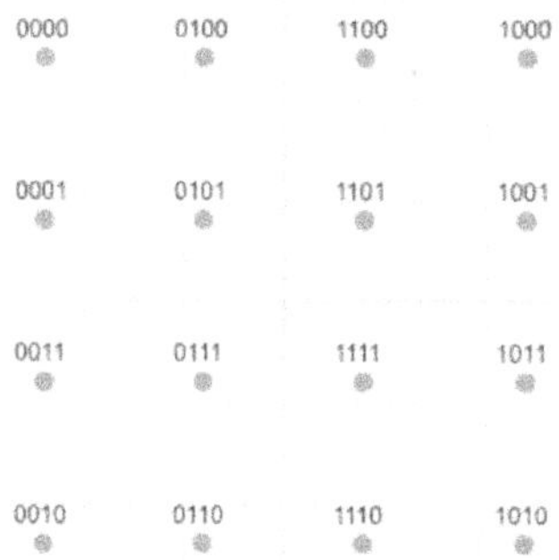

64QAM: Each symbol represents 6 bits, offering very high spectral efficiency but with limited reach due to high OSNR requirements.

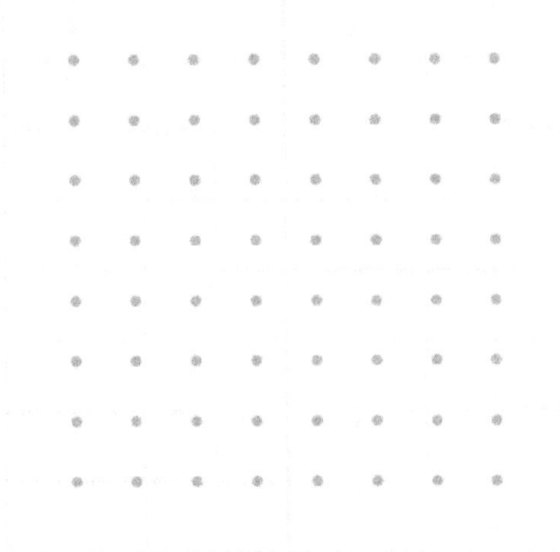

Use Case: A national carrier uses QPSK modulation for its 100G long-haul optical backbone, ensuring reliable transmission over distances exceeding 2,000 km. In contrast, the carrier uses 16QAM modulation for its metro network, where the shorter distances allow for higher spectral efficiency and 200G data rates.

Modulation and Power Consumption

Higher-Order Modulation and Power Efficiency: Higher-order modulation formats (such as 16QAM and 64QAM) require more precise signal processing and higher OSNR, leading to increased power consumption. However, they provide higher data rates and spectral efficiency.

Trade-Offs Between Reach and Power Consumption: Using higher-order modulation formats improves spectral efficiency but shortens reach due to increased sensitivity to noise and fiber impairments. Operators must balance power consumption, capacity, and reach to optimize network performance.

Example: A 400G system using 16QAM requires more amplification and power compared to a 100G QPSK system. However, the overall power consumption per gigabit is lower in the 400G system due to its higher data throughput.

Capacity, Reach, and Cost Optimization

Capacity and Reach Trade-Off

Spectral Efficiency vs. Reach: Higher spectral efficiency modulation formats (e.g., 64QAM) increase the capacity of each optical channel but reduce the maximum transmission distance due to higher OSNR requirements. Lower-order formats (e.g., BPSK) provide longer reach but with lower capacity.

Use Case: A service provider designs its network to use QPSK modulation for long-haul links where reach is critical and 16QAM for metro networks where capacity is more important than distance.

Power Consumption per Gigabit

Impact of Baud Rate: Increasing the baud rate reduces the number of transceivers and amplifiers required for a given capacity, improving power efficiency. However, higher baud rates also require more advanced digital signal processing (DSP), which increases the overall power consumption of the network.

Energy-Efficient Modulation: Lower-order modulation formats (e.g., BPSK and QPSK) are more energy-efficient in long-haul applications, while higher-order formats like 16QAM and 64QAM offer better energy efficiency per gigabit in short-reach, high-capacity scenarios.

Practical Example: A metro network using 16QAM modulation achieves a power consumption of 0.5 watts per gigabit, while a long-haul network using QPSK consumes 1 watt per gigabit due to the additional amplification required for extended reach.

Insights on High Bit Rate, Modulation Formats, and Probabilistic Constellation Shaping (PCS)

Advanced Modulation Formats for High Bit Rate Optical Transmission

Quadrature Amplitude Modulation (QAM)

- **QAM Overview**: Quadrature Amplitude Modulation (QAM) is one of the most commonly used modulation formats in high-speed optical communication. QAM encodes data by varying both the phase and the amplitude of the optical signal, which increases spectral efficiency and maximizes the bit rate over a given optical channel.
- **Higher-Order QAM**: As we move towards 400G, 800G, and even 1T optical transmission systems, higher-order QAM formats like 16QAM, 64QAM, and 256QAM are being employed. Each increase in modulation order allows more bits to be transmitted per symbol but requires better signal-to-noise ratios (SNR) and higher OSNR to maintain error-free transmission.
- **Example**: In 16QAM, each symbol encodes 4 bits, providing twice the capacity of QPSK for the same baud rate. However, it requires higher OSNR (approximately 3 dB higher) to achieve the same level of performance, limiting the transmission distance in long-haul networks.

Challenges with Higher-Order Modulation Formats

- **Signal-to-Noise Ratio (SNR)**: As the order of modulation increases (e.g., from QPSK to 64QAM), the signal becomes more sensitive to noise. The higher the modulation format, the smaller the distance between the constellation points in the signal space, making the system more prone to errors caused by noise and impairments.
- **Chromatic and Polarization Mode Dispersion**: Higher-order modulation formats are also more affected by chromatic dispersion and polarization mode dispersion (PMD). These impairments spread the optical pulses and introduce inter-symbol interference (ISI), which can significantly degrade the signal.
- **Use Case**: A 400G system using 64QAM modulation for short-haul data center interconnects (DCI) is capable of achieving high spectral efficiency. However, the same system would face reach limitations in long-haul deployments due to OSNR constraints and dispersion issues.

Dual Polarization (DP) and Polarization-Division Multiplexing (PDM)

DP-QPSK and DP-16QAM: Polarization-division multiplexing (PDM) is used in combination with advanced modulation formats like

QPSK and QAM to double the data rate without increasing the baud rate. In DP-QPSK, data is transmitted on two orthogonal polarizations, effectively doubling the capacity over the same wavelength.

Example: A 100G coherent system using DP-QPSK transmits 50 Gbps on each polarization, achieving a total bit rate of 100 Gbps. Similarly, a 400G system using DP-16QAM transmits 200 Gbps on each polarization, achieving a total bit rate of 400 Gbps.

Probabilistic Constellation Shaping (PCS) for High Spectral Efficiency

What is Probabilistic Constellation Shaping (PCS)?

Overview: PCS is a novel modulation technique that optimizes the use of the signal constellation by adjusting the probability with which different symbols are transmitted. In traditional QAM systems, all symbols in the constellation are equally likely to occur, but in PCS, symbols near the center of the constellation (which are less susceptible to noise) are transmitted more frequently than those at the outer edges.

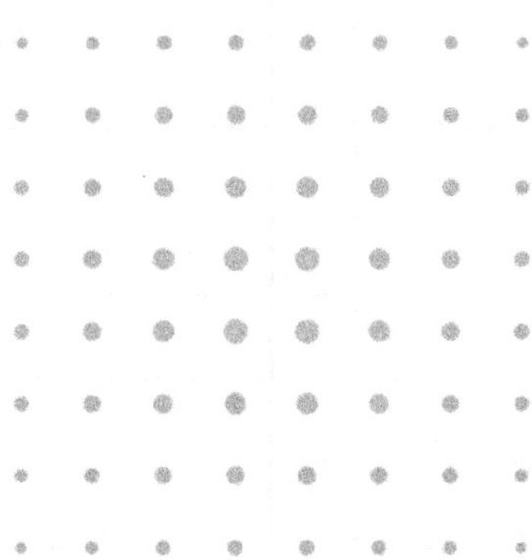

Benefits of PCS:

- **Improved OSNR**: By reducing the probability of transmitting symbols with high amplitude (which are more susceptible to noise), PCS can operate at lower OSNR, enabling higher data rates over longer distances without sacrificing performance.

- **Higher Spectral Efficiency**: PCS allows optical systems to approach the Shannon limit (the theoretical maximum capacity of a communication channel) more closely than traditional QAM systems. This results in greater spectral efficiency and higher capacity over the same bandwidth.

Example: A 400G optical transceiver using DP-16QAM with PCS can achieve better performance at lower OSNR levels than a traditional DP-16QAM transceiver, extending the transmission distance and reducing the need for amplification.

How PCS Works in Practice

- **Variable Probability Constellation**: In PCS, the probability distribution of the constellation points is shaped such that points closer to the origin (which have lower amplitude and are more resistant to noise) are used more often than those farther from the origin. This effectively reduces the likelihood of transmitting high-power symbols that are more prone to errors in noisy environments.
- **Example Use Case**: A service provider uses 800G transceivers with DP-64QAM and PCS for short-haul metro networks. By shaping the constellation, the provider can extend the reach of 800G signals without compromising spectral efficiency, allowing them to transmit at high data rates over longer distances.

Impact of Modulation, Bit Rate, and Baud Rate on Power Consumption

Power Consumption and Modulation Formats

- **Power vs. Capacity Trade-Off**: As modulation formats become more complex (e.g., moving from QPSK to 64QAM), the power required for signal processing increases. Coherent transceivers using advanced modulation formats require more sophisticated DSP algorithms and higher-speed analog-to-digital converters (ADCs), both of which contribute to higher power consumption.
- **Use Case**: In a data center interconnect (DCI) network, 400G coherent transceivers using 64QAM consume more power per transceiver compared to 100G systems using QPSK. However, the overall power consumption per gigabit is lower because fewer transceivers are needed to achieve the same capacity.

Per-Gigabit Power Consumption

- **Lower Baud Rate and Power Efficiency**: While increasing the baud rate reduces the number of transceivers required for a given capacity, it can also increase power consumption due to the need for more advanced DSP algorithms and higher-speed ADCs. The key to optimizing power consumption is balancing baud rate, modulation format, and OSNR requirements.
- **Example**: A 400G transceiver operating at 64 Gbaud with DP-16QAM consumes approximately 2.5 watts per gigabit, while a 100G transceiver operating at 32 Gbaud with QPSK consumes about 4 watts per gigabit. The higher baud rate and modulation efficiency of the 400G transceiver allow it to deliver higher capacity with lower per-gigabit power consumption.

Energy-Efficient Modulation for Long-Haul Networks

- **BPSK for Long-Haul**: Lower-order modulation formats like BPSK and QPSK are typically used in long-haul networks because they offer greater reach and resilience to noise at the expense of spectral efficiency. These formats are more power-efficient for long-distance transmission because they require less complex signal processing.
- **Example**: In a transoceanic optical cable system, BPSK is used for 100G long-haul transmission due to its robustness in noisy environments. Although BPSK is less spectrally efficient, its lower OSNR requirements allow for longer reach without requiring expensive optical amplification.

Practical Considerations for Capacity, Reach, and Cost Optimization

Balancing Capacity and Reach

- **Reach vs. Modulation Complexity**: Higher-order modulation formats like 64QAM provide higher spectral efficiency but reduce the transmission reach due to their higher OSNR requirements. In contrast, lower-order formats like BPSK and QPSK provide longer reach but with reduced capacity. Network operators must balance these trade-offs when designing optical links.
- **Use Case**: A cloud provider uses DP-16QAM for 200G metro links with a reach of 500 km, while DP-QPSK is used for long-haul links of 1,500 km at 100G. This balance allows the provider to optimize capacity where possible and ensure reliable performance over longer distances.

Cost Considerations for High Bit Rate Systems

- **Cost per Transceiver**: Higher bit rate transceivers (e.g., 400G or 800G) are typically more expensive due to the complexity of the DSP and modulation techniques required. However, these costs are offset by the reduced need for parallel fiber deployment and the lower overall power consumption per gigabit.
- **Total Cost of Ownership (TCO)**: The cost savings from using higher-capacity transceivers come from reduced fiber infrastructure, fewer amplifiers, and lower operational costs. The move to flex-grid ROADMs and programmable transceivers further reduces the TCO by enabling dynamic bandwidth allocation and more efficient use of available spectral resources.
- **Example**: A telecom operator upgrades its metro network from 100G QPSK transceivers to 400G DP-16QAM transceivers. While the upfront cost of the 400G transceivers is higher, the operator saves on fiber deployment and reduces power consumption by consolidating multiple 100G links into a single 400G link.

Modulation Formats, Bandwidth, and Data Rates Table

Format	Bits/Symbol	Baud Rate	E-Bandwidth	O-Bandwidth	Data Rate	Reach	Application
BPSK	1	100 GBaud	50 GHz	100 GHz	100 Gbps	Longest	Submarine
QPSK	2	100 GBaud	50 GHz	100 GHz	200 Gbps	Very Long	Long-haul
8QAM	3	100 GBaud	50 GHz	100 GHz	300 Gbps	Long	Regional
16QAM	4	100 GBaud	50 GHz	100 GHz	400 Gbps	Medium	Metro
32QAM	5	100 GBaud	50 GHz	100 GHz	500 Gbps	Short	DCI
64QAM	6	100 GBaud	50 GHz	100 GHz	600 Gbps	Very Short	Campus
PCS-64QAM	~5.5	140 GBaud	70 GHz	140 GHz	800 Gbps	Short+	DCI/Metro

Key Formulas:

1. Data Rate = Baud Rate × Bits per Symbol
2. Electrical Bandwidth = Baud Rate/2 (Nyquist)
3. Optical Bandwidth ≈ Baud Rate

Notes:

- Higher order modulations (>64QAM) require better SNR and limit reach-
- PCS helps optimize spectral efficiency vs reach trade-off
- 140 GBaud systems require 3nm technology for RF performance

Modulation Format	Bits per Symbol	Baud Rate Range	Typical Data Rates	Maximum Reach	Applications
Basic Digital Modulation					
NRZ (Non-Return to Zero)	1	1-28 GBaud	1-28 Gbps	80-100 km	Short-reach optical, Direct Detect
PAM-4	2	26.5625 GBaud	53.125 Gbps 100 Gbps with FEC	500m-2km	400G Ethernet Data Center
PAM-8	3	20-30 GBaud	60-90 Gbps	100m	Next-gen Data Center
Basic Coherent Formats					
BPSK	1	28-35 GBaud	28-35 Gbps	4000+ km	Ultra-long-haul legacy
QPSK	2	28-35 GBaud	56-70 Gbps	2000+ km	Long-haul transmission
8-QAM	3	32-35 GBaud	96-105 Gbps	1000-1500 km	Metro/Regional
16-QAM	4	32-35 GBaud	128-140 Gbps	500-800 km	Metro/Regional
Advanced Coherent Formats (with Dual Polarization)					
DP-QPSK	4	32-35 GBaud	128-140 Gbps	2000+ km	100G Long-haul
DP-8QAM	6	32-35 GBaud	192-210 Gbps	1000-1500 km	200G Metro/Regional
DP-16QAM	8	32-35 GBaud	256-280 Gbps	500-800 km	200G/400G Metro
DP-64QAM	12	32-35 GBaud	384-420 Gbps	80-120 km	400G/600G Short-reach
400G ZR/OpenZR+ Formats					
400G ZR (DP-16QAM)	8	59.84 GBaud	400 Gbps	80-120 km	Data Center Interconnect
OpenZR+ (DP-16QAM)	8	60.14 GBaud	400 Gbps	120-480 km	Metro/Regional
OpenZR+ (DP-8QAM)	6	60.14 GBaud	300 Gbps	400-800 km	Long-haul
OpenZR+ (DP-QPSK)	4	60.14 GBaud	200 Gbps	1000-2000 km	Ultra-long-haul
Emerging/Future Formats					
DP-256QAM	16	60-100 GBaud	800-1200 Gbps	40-80 km	Next-gen Metro
Probabilistic Shaping	Variable	60-100 GBaud	400-800 Gbps	Varies	Flexible Rate/Distance

Detailed Modulation Analysis: 100G to 1.6T

Speed	Modulation	Bits/Symbol	Baud Rate	E-Bandwidth	O-Bandwidth	Cycles/sec	Channel	Node Tech	Reach
100G	BPSK	1	100G	50GHz	100GHz	50B	75GHz	5nm	10000km
200G	QPSK	2	100G	50GHz	100GHz	50B	75GHz	5nm	5000km
400G	16QAM	4	100G	50GHz	100GHz	50B	75GHz	5nm	2000km
600G	64QAM	6	100G	50GHz	100GHz	50B	75GHz	5nm	1000km
800G	PCS-64QAM	5.5	140G	70GHz	140GHz	70B	150GHz	3nm	800km
1.2T	PCS-64QAM	5.5	200G	100GHz	200GHz	100B	150GHz	3nm	500km
1.6T	PCS-64QAM	5.5	280G	140GHz	280GHz	140B	150GHz	3nm	400km

Important Notes:

1. Higher modulation = more bits/symbol but shorter reach
2. 3nm enables higher baud rates through better RF performance
3. PCS optimizes constellation for better performance4. Channel width increases with baud rate

Chapter 8

Coherent Optics and Modulation Formats

Chapter 8
Coherent Optics and Modulation Formats

"The future belongs to those who can master the phase of light." - Peter Winzer

---

Coherent detection is an advanced optical signal processing technique that allows both the **amplitude** and **phase** of an optical signal to be accurately detected. Unlike traditional **Intensity Modulation with Direct Detection (IMDD)**, which only captures signal intensity, coherent detection uses a **local oscillator** (LO) to mix the incoming optical signal with a reference signal, making it possible to recover both the phase and polarization state of the signal.This ability to detect the phase of the signal allows coherent detection systems to utilize **phase-modulated formats**, such as **Quadrature Phase-Shift Keying (QPSK)** and **Quadrature Amplitude Modulation (QAM)**, which encode more bits per symbol and greatly enhance spectral efficiency.

Key Components of a Coherent Receiver:

1. **Local Oscillator (LO):** Generates a stable reference signal that helps extract amplitude and phase information from the received signal.
2. **Digital Signal Processor (DSP):** Crucial for recovering the transmitted data, compensating for impairments like chromatic dispersion (CD) and polarization mode dispersion (PMD).
3. **Phase Modulation Formats:** Coherent systems support advanced modulation formats like **BPSK**, **QPSK**, **16-QAM**, and **64-QAM**, which improve data rates and spectral efficiency.

The Evolution of Coherent Technology

Coherent optical detection technology was introduced to address the limitations of traditional IMDD systems, particularly as network operators sought to scale data rates beyond **10 Gbps**. While IMDD works well at lower data rates, it faces challenges at higher rates, particularly with chromatic dispersion and polarization mode dispersion.

The industry's first **coherent 40G** optical transport solution was unveiled in **2008**, marking a significant leap forward in optical communication. This solution combined advanced digital signal processing (DSP) with **dual-polarization quadrature phase-shift keying (DP-QPSK)** modulation, allowing for a substantial increase in transmission speed and reach.

Advantages of Coherent Detection

Coherent detection offers numerous advantages over traditional optical transmission methods, making it the technology of choice for high-capacity, long-haul DWDM systems.

1. Improved Noise Tolerance:

- Coherent detection improves the **optical signal-to-noise ratio (OSNR)**. For example, a **coherent BPSK** system can operate with an OSNR up to **6 dB lower** than a corresponding IMDD system, allowing for longer transmission distances and higher system margins.

2. Spectrally Efficient Modulation Formats:

- By enabling the use of **phase-modulated formats** like **QPSK** and higher-order QAM (e.g., 16-QAM, 64-QAM), coherent systems can encode multiple bits per symbol. This allows operators to significantly increase the data rate without requiring more bandwidth.

3. Compensation for Fiber Impairments:

- One of the key benefits of coherent detection is its ability to **digitally compensate** for impairments such as **chromatic dispersion (CD)**, **polarization mode dispersion (PMD)**, and **polarization-dependent loss (PDL)**. This reduces the need for **dispersion compensation modules (DCMs)**, thereby lowering costs and simplifying network architecture.
- **Digital signal processing (DSP)** in coherent systems can correct for thousands of kilometers of accumulated chromatic dispersion, allowing for longer, uncompensated spans.

4. Increased Fiber Capacity:

- Coherent detection allows operators to scale up fiber capacity significantly without increasing the bandwidth of the optical amplifiers. For example, moving from **BPSK** to **16-QAM** can increase fiber capacity by a factor of four, without modifying the underlying fiber infrastructure.

5. Higher Data Rates:

- Coherent systems enable **data rates of 400G and beyond**, and are paving the way for **800G** and **1.6 Tbps** networks. This is particularly important for addressing the exponential growth in data traffic driven by video streaming, cloud services, and the Internet of Things (IoT).

Capacity Expansion and Reach with Coherent Technology

The use of coherent detection technology allows for significant capacity expansion in both **C-band** and **C+L band** systems, which are commonly used in DWDM networks. As shown in the table below, coherent systems support a range of modulation formats that offer a trade-off between capacity and reach:

Modulation Format	C-Band Capacity (Tb/s)	C-Band Reach (km)	C+L Band Capacity (Tb/s)	C+L Band Reach (km)
BPSK	6	10,000	12	9,000
QPSK	12	6,000	24	4,800
8-QAM	18	2,200	36	1,800
16-QAM	24	800	48	700
64-QAM	36	80	72	60

Key Observations:

- As the **modulation order** increases (e.g., from QPSK to 16-QAM), the system's **spectral efficiency** improves, allowing more data to be transmitted over the same bandwidth.
- However, higher-order modulation schemes typically have a shorter **reach**, requiring more frequent amplification and regeneration.

Why Coherent Detection is Essential for Next-Generation Networks?

With the exponential growth in global data traffic, driven by applications such as 4K video streaming, cloud computing, and IoT, the need for scalable and efficient optical networks has never been more critical. **Coherent detection** is a key enabler for scaling capacity in long-haul and metro optical networks.

Future-Proofing Networks:

- **800G and 1.6 Tbps transmission:** Coherent technology supports higher data rates, making it suitable for future network upgrades.
- **Increased Spectral Efficiency:** By enabling more bits per symbol, coherent systems maximize the use of available bandwidth, which is essential for meeting the growing demand for capacity.
- **Digital Compensation:** The ability to correct for impairments digitally reduces the complexity and cost of optical networks, making them more flexible and easier to scale.

Modulation Formats in Coherent Optics

Quadrature Phase-Shift Keying (QPSK)

- **Description**: QPSK is a four-state modulation format where data is encoded onto two orthogonal components of the signal (in-phase and quadrature). This doubles the spectral efficiency compared to binary phase-shift keying (BPSK).
- **PDM-QPSK**: In coherent optics, polarization-division multiplexing (PDM) is combined with QPSK, effectively doubling the capacity by transmitting separate data streams on two orthogonal polarizations of light.
- **Example**: A 100G coherent system uses PDM-QPSK modulation, allowing it to transmit 50G per polarization, for a total of 100G per wavelength.

16-Quadrature Amplitude Modulation (16QAM)

- **Description**: 16QAM is a higher-order modulation format that encodes data onto both the amplitude and phase of the light signal. Each symbol represents one of 16 possible states, allowing 4 bits of data to be encoded per symbol.
- **Spectral Efficiency**: 16QAM offers higher spectral efficiency than QPSK, but at the cost of increased sensitivity to noise and nonlinearity.
- **Use Case**: In metro networks, 16QAM is used for 200G systems due to its high spectral efficiency. However, it requires a higher optical signal-to-noise ratio (OSNR) than QPSK.

64-Quadrature Amplitude Modulation (64QAM)

Modulation Format	Spectral Efficiency	Complexity	Reach	Cost
OOK	1 bit/s/Hz	Low	Short-Medium	Low
QPSK	2 bits/s/Hz	Medium	Long	Medium
16-QAM	4 bits/s/Hz	High	Medium	High
64-QAM	6 bits/s/Hz	Very High	Short	Very High

- **Description**: 64QAM pushes the limits of spectral efficiency by encoding 6 bits of data per symbol. This format is ideal for short-reach, high-capacity applications but is more susceptible to signal degradation from noise, dispersion, and nonlinear effects.
- **Use Case**: 64QAM is often used in data center interconnect (DCI) networks for 400G and 800G links, where distances are short, and the OSNR is high enough to support the format.

Major Modulation Techniques

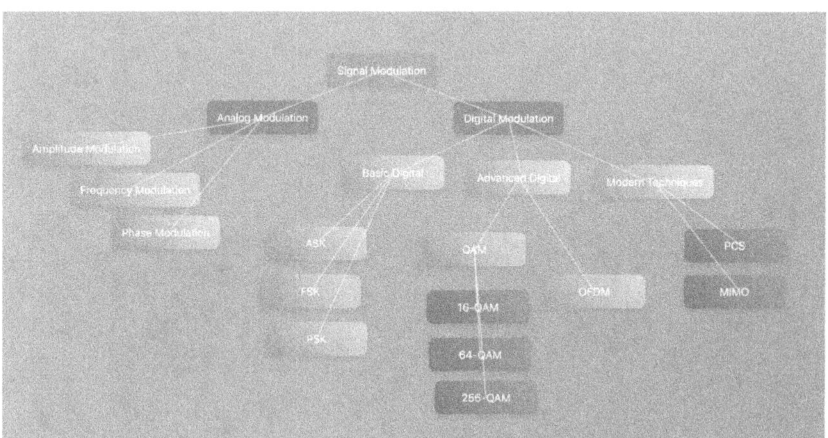

Intensity Modulation (IM)

The simplest form of optical modulation where the intensity of light is varied to represent data.

- On-Off Keying (OOK)
- Pulse Amplitude Modulation (PAM)
- Pulse Position Modulation (PPM)

Phase Modulation (PM)

Involves changing the phase of the optical carrier to encode information.

- Binary Phase Shift Keying (BPSK)
- Quadrature Phase Shift Keying (QPSK)
- Differential Phase Shift Keying (DPSK)

Advanced Modulation Formats

- Quadrature Amplitude Modulation (QAM)
- Polarization Multiplexed QAM (PM-QAM)
- Coherent Optical OFDM (CO-OFDM)

Comparative Analysis

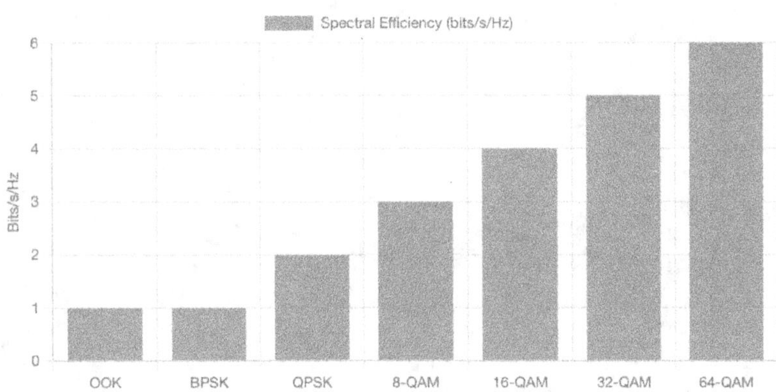

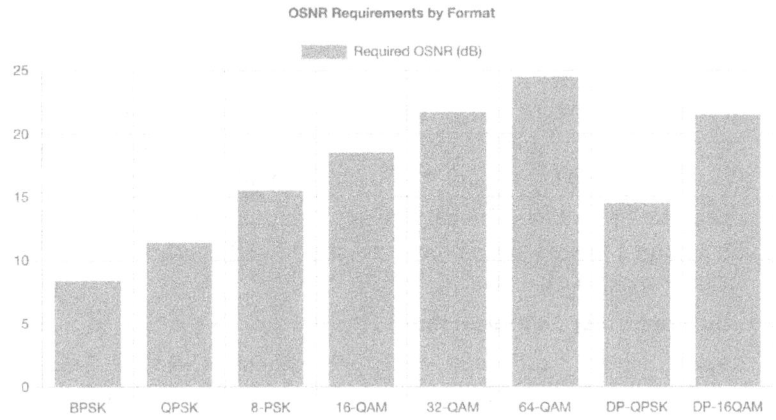

Flowchart to decide modulation scheme

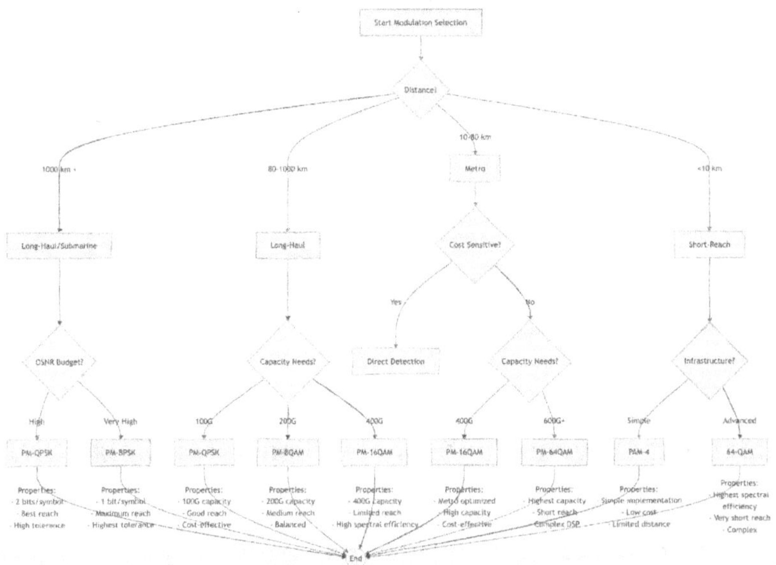

Advancements in Baud Rate and Symbol Rate

What is Baud Rate?

- **Definition**: Baud rate refers to the number of symbols transmitted per second in an optical communication system. A higher baud rate increases the data throughput by transmitting more symbols in the same time period.
- **Relation to Bit Rate**: The bit rate is related to the baud rate and modulation format. For example, a 32 Gbaud system using 16QAM transmits 128 Gbps of data (32 Gbaud × 4 bits per symbol).
- **Example**: In a 400G coherent system, increasing the baud rate from 32 Gbaud to 64 Gbaud allows the same spectral efficiency while doubling the transmission capacity.

Baud Rate and Fiber Nonlinearities

- **Impact**: Higher baud rates reduce the number of symbols needed to encode the same amount of data, which improves transmission efficiency. However, higher baud rates are more susceptible to fiber nonlinearities, such as self-phase modulation (SPM) and cross-phase modulation (XPM).
- **Mitigation**: Advanced digital signal processing (DSP) techniques are used to compensate for the distortions caused by nonlinearities and chromatic dispersion at higher baud rates.

Practical Example: A telecom operator increases the baud rate to 64 Gbaud in its long-haul 400G system but uses advanced DSP techniques to mitigate nonlinear effects, ensuring signal integrity over long distances.

Key Concepts:

- Bit Rate: Number of bits transmitted per second
- Baud Rate: Number of symbol changes per second
- Spectral Efficiency: Bits per second per Hz of bandwidth

Coherent Detection and Digital Signal Processing (DSP)

Coherent Detection Process

- **Phase and Amplitude Detection**: In coherent systems, both the amplitude and phase of the incoming signal are detected using a local oscillator. This allows the receiver to recover more information from the signal compared to direct detection systems.
- **Polarization Multiplexing**: Coherent systems also use polarization-division multiplexing (PDM) to transmit two independent data streams on orthogonal polarizations. The coherent receiver demultiplexes these streams and recovers the original data.

- **Example**: In a 400G coherent system using PDM-16QAM, the receiver uses coherent detection to recover both polarizations and extract the phase and amplitude information for each symbol.

Role of Digital Signal Processing (DSP)

- **Signal Recovery**: DSP algorithms are critical in recovering the transmitted signal in the presence of fiber impairments. These algorithms compensate for chromatic dispersion, polarization-mode dispersion, and nonlinearities.
- **Carrier Recovery and Timing Synchronization**: DSP also handles carrier recovery, timing synchronization, and forward error correction (FEC), ensuring that the transmitted data is accurately recovered despite channel impairments.
- **Practical Example**: A 400G long-haul network uses DSP to compensate for chromatic dispersion accumulated over 2,000 km of fiber, allowing error-free transmission without the need for optical dispersion compensating modules.

Real-World Use Cases of Coherent Optics

100G Coherent Systems

- **Use Case**: A national carrier deploys 100G coherent PDM-QPSK in its long-haul network, replacing multiple 10G channels with a single 100G channel. The carrier significantly reduces the number of transponders required, improving power efficiency and reducing operational complexity.

400G and 800G Coherent Systems

- **Use Case**: A cloud service provider uses 400G coherent optics with PDM-16QAM to connect data centers over a 500 km distance. By using flex-grid ROADMs and coherent detection, the network can support high-capacity traffic with minimal latency.
- **Baud Rate Consideration**: The provider initially deploys 32 Gbaud transceivers but later upgrades to 64 Gbaud to double capacity without requiring new fiber infrastructure.

1T Coherent Optical Systems

- **Use Case**: In preparation for the next generation of optical networks, an operator trials 1T coherent systems using 64QAM and 128 Gbaud transceivers. Although still in early stages, these systems promise to deliver the capacity needed for future 6G backhaul and ultra-high-capacity DCI networks.

Coherent Optics in Metro vs. Long-Haul Networks

1. **Metro Networks**
   - Coherent optics in metro networks prioritize spectral efficiency and high data rates. In these networks, higher-order modulation formats such as 64QAM and 16QAM are feasible due to the shorter distances and higher available OSNR.
   - **Example**: A city's data center interconnect (DCI) network uses 64QAM modulation to maximize capacity across its metro ring, supporting 400G and 800G connections over 100 km distances.
2. **Long-Haul Networks**
   - In long-haul networks, coherent optics must balance data rate, baud rate, and resilience to impairments. Lower-order modulation formats, such as QPSK, are often preferred for distances exceeding 1,000 km.
   - **Example**: A long-haul link spanning 2,000 km uses PDM-QPSK to achieve 100G per wavelength while maintaining a high OSNR over multiple spans.

Future of Coherent Optics

Terabit Coherent Systems

- As 1T systems begin to emerge, coherent optics will continue to play a pivotal role in increasing data rates while maintaining efficiency. These systems will likely use advanced DSP and machine learning techniques to optimize signal recovery and mitigate fiber impairments.

Coherent Pluggables

- Coherent optics are now moving into smaller form factors such as CFP2-DCO and QSFP-DD, making it easier to deploy coherent optics in data center environments. These pluggable modules support flexible rates from 100G to 800G, providing scalability for future network growth.

Integration with Machine Learning

- Machine learning algorithms are being integrated into DSP to improve adaptive modulation, power optimization, and real-time network monitoring. This will further enhance the performance and efficiency of coherent optical systems.

Part III

Network Design and Implementation

Chapter 9

Planning and Design of Networks

Chapter 9
Planning and Design of Networks

"The best network design is one that anticipates tomorrow's needs."
- Rod C. Alferness

Effective planning and design are fundamental to the success of optical networks. This chapter delves into the principles, methodologies, and practical considerations for planning and designing robust, scalable, and efficient optical networks, with a focus on link planning examples involving various amplifier setups and OSNR calculations.

Principles of Network Planning and Design

Network planning and design involve several core principles to ensure the network meets technical and business requirements:

- **Scalability**: Designing networks that can easily scale to accommodate future growth.
- **Reliability**: Ensuring the network is resilient to failures and provides high availability.
- **Performance**: Optimizing the network for high performance, including low latency and high throughput.
- **Cost-effectiveness**: Balancing performance and reliability with cost considerations.
- **Flexibility**: Designing networks that can adapt to changing requirements and technologies.

Steps in Network Planning and Design

1. **Assessing Network Requirements**
    - **Capacity and Bandwidth Needs**: Determine the current and future bandwidth requirements based on user demands and application needs.
    - **Geographical Coverage**: Define the areas that need to be covered, including urban, suburban, and rural regions.

- **Scalability and Future-Proofing**: Plan for future expansion and technological advancements to avoid obsolescence.
- **Reliability and Redundancy**: Ensure high availability and fault tolerance by incorporating redundancy and backup paths.
- **Example**: A telecom operator plans to upgrade its metropolitan network to support 100G and 400G connections. The assessment includes analyzing traffic growth, user distribution, and critical service areas.

2. **Choosing the Appropriate Network Topology**
   - **Point-to-Point**: Simple and direct connections suitable for short distances and low-complexity networks.
   - **Ring**: Provides redundancy and reliability, suitable for metropolitan and regional networks.
   - **Mesh**: Offers high resilience and flexibility, ideal for large-scale and high-availability networks.
   - **Example**: A metropolitan network adopts a ring topology to ensure continuous service even if a segment fails, while a core backbone network uses a mesh topology for maximum resilience.
3. **Selecting Optical Components and Technologies**
   - **Fiber Types**: Choose between single-mode, multimode, or specialized fibers like low water peak or bend-insensitive fibers based on application and distance.
   - **Transceivers and Amplifiers**: Select appropriate transceivers (e.g., SFP+, QSFP28, ZR, ZR+) and amplifiers (e.g., EDFAs, Raman amplifiers) to meet performance and distance requirements.
   - **Wavelength Division Multiplexing (WDM)**: Implement CWDM or DWDM to increase bandwidth over existing fiber infrastructure.
   - **Example**: For a long-haul network, the design includes single-mode fibers with DWDM technology, using EDFAs to extend the reach and maintain signal quality.
4. **Calculating Link Budget**
   - **Transmitter Power**: Determine the output power of the transmitter.
   - **Fiber Losses**: Account for fiber attenuation, splice losses, and connector losses.

- **Amplification and Gain**: Include the gain provided by optical amplifiers.
- **Safety Margin**: Add a safety margin to account for unforeseen losses and ensure reliable operation.
- **Example**: A link budget calculation for a 200 km link with DWDM technology includes the transmitter power, fiber attenuation of 0.25 dB/km, splice losses, and the gain from EDFAs. The calculation ensures the received power is within acceptable limits.

5. **Managing Dispersion**
    - **Chromatic Dispersion (CD)**: Use dispersion-compensating fibers (DCFs) or modules to mitigate the effects of CD.
    - **Polarization Mode Dispersion (PMD)**: Ensure fiber quality and installation practices minimize PMD.
    - **Example**: In a high-speed long-haul network, dispersion compensation modules are placed at regular intervals to counteract the effects of CD, maintaining signal integrity.
6. **Ensuring Network Security and Monitoring**
    - **Security Measures**: Implement encryption and access controls to protect data integrity and confidentiality.
    - **Monitoring Tools**: Use network monitoring systems (NMS) to continuously track network performance, detect faults, and optimize operations.
    - **Example**: A service provider deploys an NMS to monitor a nationwide optical network, using real-time data to proactively address issues and optimize network performance.

Practical Examples and Case Studies

1. Urban Fiber Network Planning

Scenario: A city plans to deploy a new fiber optic network to support smart city applications, including IoT sensors, public Wi-Fi, and high-speed internet.

Implementation:

- **Assessment**: Determine bandwidth requirements and identify key areas for connectivity.
- **Design**: Use a ring topology to ensure reliability and integrate single-mode fibers with DWDM technology for scalability.
- **Outcome**: The network supports current applications and is scalable for future growth, providing robust connectivity across the city.

2. Enterprise Data Center Interconnect (DCI)

Scenario: A large enterprise needs to interconnect multiple data centers to support high-speed data transfer and redundancy.

Implementation:

- **Assessment**: Analyze data traffic patterns and redundancy requirements.
- **Design**: Deploy a mesh topology with QSFP28 transceivers and DWDM technology, incorporating EDFAs for long-distance links.
- **Outcome**: The network provides high-capacity, low-latency connections with built-in redundancy, ensuring continuous operation.

Link Planning Examples

Calculating OSNR for a DWDM Link

The **Optical Signal-to-Noise Ratio (OSNR)** is a critical performance metric in DWDM systems. It quantifies the ratio of the signal power to the noise power, and is essential for evaluating signal quality in optical communication systems. OSNR determines the quality of data transmission over long distances and is affected by a variety of factors such as **amplifier noise**, **fiber non-linearities**, **link attenuation**, and the number of components in the system.

Definition and Importance of OSNR

The OSNR is generally defined as the ratio of the optical signal power to the noise power in a given reference bandwidth (typically 12.5 GHz for standard calculations):

$$OSNR = \frac{P_{\text{signal}}}{P_{\text{noise}}}$$

Where:

- P_{signal} is the optical power of the signal.
- P_{noise} is the noise power introduced primarily by amplifiers (such as ASE noise).

In DWDM systems, the OSNR is a key parameter because it directly impacts the **Bit Error Rate (BER)** and the system's ability to recover data reliably.

An insufficient OSNR can result in increased errors and degraded system performance.

OSNR Calculation Methods

Link Budget-Based OSNR Calculation

The simplest method to calculate OSNR is through the **link budget**. This involves computing the signal power at the receiver, considering all the losses (attenuation, component insertion losses, etc.), and then determining the noise accumulated across amplifiers.

OSNR Formula:

$$OSNR_{\text{dB}} = P_{\text{TX}} - \sum \text{Losses} + G_{\text{amp}} - NF_{\text{amp}} - M$$

Where:

- P_{TX} is the transmitter output power (in dBm).
- ∑Losses is the sum of all losses along the link (in dB), including fiber attenuation and component insertion losses.
- G_{amp} is the gain of the amplifiers (in dB).
- NF_{amp} is the noise figure of the amplifiers.
- M is the safety margin (usually 3-6 dB).

Spectral Approach to OSNR

A more precise method involves measuring the OSNR directly from an **optical spectrum analyzer (OSA)**, where the signal power and noise power are measured within a 0.1 nm bandwidth (approximately 12.5 GHz).

The OSNR is then calculated as:

$$OSNR_{\text{dB}} = 10 \log_{10} \left(\frac{P_{\text{signal}}}{P_{\text{noise}}} \right)$$

OSNR Example Calculations for Different DWDM Scenarios

Short-Distance Point-to-Point Link (No Amplifier)

Consider a 10 km point-to-point link without amplification. The main factors affecting OSNR are **fiber attenuation** and **component insertion losses**. Assume the following:

- **Transmit Power**: 0 dBm
- **Fiber Attenuation**: 0.25 dB/km
- **Mux/Demux Insertion Loss**: 4 dB
- **Receiver Sensitivity**: -10 dBm

The total fiber loss is:

$$\text{Loss}_{\text{fiber}} = 0.25\,\text{dB/km} \times 10\,\text{km} = 2.5\,\text{dB}$$

The total link loss is:

$$\text{Loss}_{\text{total}} = 2.5\,\text{dB (fiber)} + 4\,\text{dB (insertion loss)} = 6.5\,\text{dB}$$

Thus, the received signal power is:

$$P_{\text{RX}} = P_{\text{TX}} - \text{Loss}_{\text{total}} = 0\,\text{dBm} - 6.5\,\text{dB} = -6.5\,\text{dBm}$$

In this case, OSNR is mostly dependent on the noise from the receiver, and no amplifier noise is introduced.

Long-Haul Link with Multiple Amplifiers

Consider a long-haul link of 400 km with **Erbium-Doped Fiber Amplifiers (EDFAs)** placed every 80 km. Assume:

- **Transmit Power**: 0 dBm
- **Fiber Attenuation**: 0.25 dB/km
- **Amplifier Gain**: 20 dB
- **Amplifier Noise Figure**: 5 dB
- **Mux/Demux Insertion Loss**: 5 dB

Step-by-Step OSNR Calculation:

1. **Fiber Loss per Span**:

$$Loss_{fiber}=0.25\ dB/km \times 80\ km=20\ dB$$

2. **OSNR After Each Amplifier**: The OSNR after one amplifier can be calculated as:

$$OSNR_{span}=P_{TX}+G_{amp}-Loss_{fiber}-NF_{amp}$$

$$OSNR_{span}=0+20-20-5=-5\ dB$$

If Tx OSNR is provided, below formula can be used.

$$OSNR_{out} = -10\log\left(10^{-\left(\frac{OSNR_{in}}{10}\right)}+10^{-\left(\frac{P_{in}-NF-10\log(h\nu\nu_r)}{10}\right)}\right)$$

Where:

$OSNR_{out}$: log OSNR (dB) at the output port of the ONE

$OSNR_{in}$: log OSNR (dB) at the input port of the ONE

P_{in} : channel power (dBm) at the input port of the ONE

NF : noise figure (dB) of the relevant path through the ONE

h : Planck's constant (in mJ•s to be consistent with in Pin (dBm))

v : optical frequency in Hz

v_r : reference bandwidth in Hz (usually the frequency equivalent of 0.1 nm)

Below formula can be used to calculate OSNR for a point to point link with chain of amplifiers.

$$OSNR_{out} = -10\log\left(10^{-\left(\frac{P_{in1}-NF_1-10\log(h\nu\nu_r)}{10}\right)}+10^{-\left(\frac{P_{in2}-NF_2-10\log(h\nu\nu_r)}{10}\right)}+\ldots+10^{-\left(\frac{P_{inN}-NF_N-10\log(h\nu\nu_r)}{10}\right)}\right)$$

Where:

P_{in1}, P_{in2} to P_{inN} : channel powers (dBm) at the inputs of the amplifiers or ONEs on the relevant path through the network

NF_1, NF_2 to NF_N : noise figures (dB) of the amplifiers or ONEs on the relevant path through the network

The OSNR degrades with each amplifier because of the noise figure of the amplifier. After multiple spans, the cumulative OSNR degrades according to the number of amplifiers and total losses.

OSNR Impact of Modulation Formats and System Loading

Modulation Format Impact

Higher-order modulation formats (e.g., **16-QAM** or **64-QAM**) require higher OSNR compared to simpler formats (e.g., **QPSK**). This is because higher-order formats are more susceptible to noise and require higher signal quality to maintain a low bit error rate (BER).

For instance:

- **QPSK**: Can operate with an OSNR as low as 13-15 dB for 100G transmission.
- **16-QAM**: Requires a higher OSNR, typically around 21-23 dB for 200G or 400G systems.

Multi-Channel vs. Single-Channel Systems

In fully loaded DWDM systems, **cross-talk** and **nonlinear effects** (such as **Four-Wave Mixing (FWM)** and **Stimulated Raman Scattering (SRS)**) degrade OSNR. These effects are less pronounced in single-channel systems but become significant in dense multi-channel deployments.

Example Calculation for Nonlinearities: Nonlinear impairments such as **self-phase modulation (SPM)** and **cross-phase modulation (XPM)** introduce penalties to the OSNR. The penalty can be estimated based on the power levels of the channels and the **fiber nonlinear coefficient**.

OSNR Degradation from Nonlinear Effects

Stimulated Raman Scattering (SRS)

SRS causes power transfer between channels in a WDM system, reducing the signal power in lower-wavelength channels and introducing noise in higher-wavelength channels. SRS becomes significant at higher power levels and when channel spacing is reduced.

Four-Wave Mixing (FWM)

FWM generates new frequency components in a DWDM system when three or more wavelengths interact. FWM is particularly problematic in systems with low dispersion and high power.

Stimulated Brillouin Scattering (SBS)

SBS causes a reflection of the transmitted signal, limiting the launch power of the system. SBS can be mitigated by reducing the power of individual channels or by using broader linewidth sources.

OSNR Calculation for Multi-Span Systems

In multi-span long-haul DWDM networks, where amplifiers are placed at regular intervals, it's crucial to consider the cumulative impact of each span on the overall OSNR. Each amplifier introduces noise (amplifier spontaneous emission or ASE noise), which degrades the OSNR progressively as the signal traverses multiple spans.

OSNR Accumulation Over Multiple Spans

In multi-span systems, OSNR degrades after each amplifier, and the final OSNR at the receiver is the cumulative result of all amplifiers and spans.

For an N-span system, the total OSNR at the receiver is given by:

$$\frac{1}{OSNR_{\text{total}}} = \frac{1}{OSNR_{\text{span 1}}} + \frac{1}{OSNR_{\text{span 2}}} + \cdots + \frac{1}{OSNR_{\text{span N}}}$$

$$osnr_{out} = \frac{1}{\frac{1}{osnr_{in}} + \frac{1}{osnr_{one}}}$$

$osnr_{out}$: linear OSNR at the output port of the ONE

$osnr_{in}$: linear OSNR at the input port of the ONE

$osnr_{one}$: linear OSNR that would appear at the output port of the ONE for a noise free input signal

Where:

- $OSNR_{span}$ is the OSNR contribution of each span.

Example: Consider a 400 km long-haul DWDM system with **5 spans** of **80 km** each. Assuming that each span has an OSNR of 15 dB due to fiber attenuation and EDFA noise:

$$\frac{1}{OSNR_{\text{total}}} = \frac{1}{15} + \frac{1}{15} + \frac{1}{15} + \frac{1}{15} + \frac{1}{15}$$

$$OSNR_{\text{total}} = \frac{15}{5} = 3\,\text{dB}$$

Thus, the cumulative OSNR at the receiver would be 3 dB after traversing five amplifiers, indicating significant degradation in signal quality due to noise accumulation.

Amplifier Noise Figure Impact

The **noise figure (NF)** of amplifiers has a direct impact on OSNR. A lower noise figure results in less ASE noise, improving OSNR. Typical EDFA noise figures range from 4-6 dB.

When designing a multi-span system, it's important to select amplifiers with a low noise figure to maintain a high OSNR, especially in systems with many spans. **Hybrid amplifiers** (e.g., EDFA combined with Raman amplifiers) can be used to reduce the noise figure and extend reach.

Example: Multi-Span 100G QPSK System

Let's consider a long-haul **100G QPSK** system spanning 800 km, with amplifiers placed every 100 km. We assume the following:

- **Transmit Power**: 0 dBm
- **Amplifier Gain**: 20 dB
- **Fiber Attenuation**: 0.25 dB/km
- **Amplifier Noise Figure**: 5 dB

Step-by-Step OSNR Calculation:

1. **Loss per Span**:

$$\text{Loss}_{\text{fiber}} = 0.25\ \text{dB/km} \times 100\ \text{km} = 25\ \text{dB}$$

2. **OSNR for One Span**:

$$OSNR_{\text{span}} = P_{\text{TX}} + G_{\text{amp}} - \text{Loss}_{\text{fiber}} - NF_{\text{amp}}$$

$$OSNR_{\text{span}} = 0 + 20 - 25 - 5 = -10\,\text{dB}$$

Since OSNR is calculated logarithmically, a value of -10 dB for one span is acceptable, and the OSNR at the receiver will degrade with each additional span.

3. **Cumulative OSNR**: After 8 spans:

$$\frac{1}{OSNR_{\text{total}}} = \frac{1}{OSNR_{\text{span}}} + \cdots \text{(for 8 spans)}$$

The cumulative OSNR would show substantial degradation, so **regenerators** or **improved amplifiers (e.g., Raman amplifiers)** may be required to maintain acceptable signal quality.

Nonlinearity and OSNR

Nonlinear effects in the fiber can significantly degrade OSNR in high-capacity, long-haul DWDM systems. Nonlinearities are more pronounced in fully loaded systems with high optical power and dense channel spacing.

Types of Nonlinear Effects

- **Self-Phase Modulation (SPM)**: SPM is a phenomenon where the phase of the optical signal is modulated by its own intensity. This effect increases with higher optical power and shortens the system reach.
- **Cross-Phase Modulation (XPM)**: XPM occurs when the phase of one wavelength is modulated by the intensity of another wavelength in a multi-channel system. It introduces cross-talk between channels and affects the system's OSNR.
- **Four-Wave Mixing (FWM)**: FWM generates new optical frequencies when multiple wavelengths interact in the fiber. It is more pronounced in systems with low chromatic dispersion and closely spaced wavelengths. FWM leads to channel interference and a reduction in OSNR.

Nonlinearity and OSNR Penalties

Nonlinearities introduce additional noise into the system, effectively degrading the OSNR. The penalty due to nonlinearities can be modeled and estimated for DWDM systems using the following formula:

$$\mathrm{OSNR}_{\mathrm{NL}} = \frac{P_{\mathrm{signal}}}{P_{\mathrm{noise}} + P_{\mathrm{NL}}}$$

Where:

- P_{signal} is the signal power.
- P_{noise} is the noise power.
- P_{NL} is the power due to nonlinear effects.

Example: In a **200G DWDM** link with 16-QAM modulation, nonlinear effects such as SPM and XPM can degrade the OSNR by 3-5 dB, especially in fully loaded systems. To counteract this, techniques such as **dispersion compensation** or **reduced launch power** may be used to mitigate nonlinearity.

Mitigating Nonlinear Effects

- **Lowering Launch Power**: Reducing the power per channel can help mitigate nonlinear effects, but it must be balanced against the need to maintain sufficient OSNR.
- **Dispersion Management**: Proper dispersion management helps minimize FWM and XPM by introducing controlled dispersion in the fiber.
- **Raman Amplifiers**: These amplifiers can provide distributed gain along the fiber, reducing the need for high launch power at the transmitter, thus mitigating nonlinear effects.

Advanced OSNR Calculation Considerations

OSNR in Single-Channel vs. Fully Loaded Systems

In a single-channel system, the primary contributors to OSNR degradation are fiber attenuation and amplifier noise. However, in a fully loaded multi-channel DWDM system, **cross-talk** and **nonlinearities** between channels become dominant, especially as the number of channels increases.

Single-Channel OSNR: In a single-channel system, OSNR is primarily determined by **amplifier noise** and **fiber attenuation**. The formula remains simple:

$$OSNR_{\text{single}} = \frac{P_{\text{signal}}}{P_{\text{ASE}}}$$

Where P_{ASE} represents the ASE noise from amplifiers.

Multi-Channel OSNR: In a fully loaded system, OSNR is affected by **cross-channel interference**, requiring a more complex model:

$$OSNR_{\text{multi}} = \frac{P_{\text{signal}}}{P_{\text{ASE}} + P_{\text{XPM}} + P_{\text{FWM}}}$$

Where PXPM and PFWM represent the noise contributions from cross-phase modulation and four-wave mixing, respectively.

OSNR Penalties Due to Modulation Formats

Higher-order modulation formats (e.g., 16-QAM, 64-QAM) are more susceptible to noise and nonlinear effects, and thus require a higher OSNR to maintain acceptable performance.

Modulation Format OSNR Requirements:

- **QPSK**: Requires an OSNR of ~13-15 dB.
- **16-QAM**: Requires an OSNR of ~21-23 dB.
- **64-QAM**: Requires an OSNR of ~27-30 dB, making it much more sensitive to both noise and nonlinear effects.

Channel Power Thresholds for Nonlinearities

For multi-channel DWDM systems, it is important to ensure that the **launch power per channel** does not exceed the threshold where nonlinearities become dominant. Typical power thresholds:

- **SPM/XPM threshold**: ~0 dBm per channel.
- **FWM threshold**: Closely spaced channels (100 GHz or less) require lower power to avoid FWM, with ~-2 dBm per channel.

In a fully loaded system, the optimal power per channel must be carefully balanced to minimize nonlinear penalties while maintaining a good OSNR.

Summary and Best Practices for OSNR Calculation

Key Takeaways

- **OSNR Calculation Methods**: For single-span, unamplified links, a simple link budget approach suffices. For multi-span systems with amplifiers, cumulative OSNR must be calculated considering amplifier noise, attenuation, and nonlinear effects.
- **Nonlinear Effects**: FWM, XPM, and SRS must be accounted for in fully loaded systems. These effects degrade OSNR, especially as channel count and power increase.
- **Modulation Format Impact**: Higher-order modulation formats (e.g., 16-QAM, 64-QAM) require higher OSNR, making them more sensitive to noise and fiber impairments.
- **Amplifier Selection**: Using low-noise amplifiers (e.g., EDFA with a noise figure of 5 dB or less) is crucial for maintaining high OSNR, especially in long-haul systems.

Best Practices for Optimizing OSNR

- **Lower Launch Power**: Reducing the launch power per channel minimizes nonlinear effects such as SPM and FWM.
- **Amplifier Placement**: Optimal placement of amplifiers and minimizing their noise figure (NF) is key for maintaining high OSNR in long-haul systems.
- **Use of Hybrid Amplifiers**: Raman amplifiers in combination with EDFAs can extend the reach while keeping noise levels low.
- **Regular Monitoring**: Continuous monitoring using **optical spectrum analyzers (OSA)** helps ensure that OSNR remains within acceptable limits throughout the system's lifespan.

Key Design Considerations for C+L Band Systems in Optical Communication

In modern optical communication systems, especially those that employ Dense Wavelength Division Multiplexing (DWDM), the C-band and L-band are essential for expanding the capacity of fiber-optic networks. By utilizing both bands, operators can effectively double the transmission capacity without the need for new infrastructure. However, designing systems that operate across both the C and L bands presents unique challenges, including managing **Stimulated Raman Scattering (SRS)**, fiber attenuation, and amplifier noise. This article discusses the key design considerations for **C+L band systems** and how to address these challenges.

Key Challenges in C+L Band Systems

Large Spectral Tilt Due to SRS

Stimulated Raman Scattering (SRS) is a non-linear optical effect that occurs when multiple wavelengths are transmitted simultaneously through a fiber. In C+L band systems, this effect is particularly pronounced. SRS causes energy to transfer from **C-band channels** (shorter wavelengths) to **L-band channels** (longer wavelengths), resulting in a power imbalance or **tilt** between the bands.

Solution: Tilt Compensation in Amplifiers

To mitigate the effects of SRS, it is crucial to use amplifiers capable of correcting for this power tilt. Both **Raman amplifiers** and **Erbium-Doped Fiber Amplifiers (EDFA)** are used to provide **tilt correction**. These amplifiers dynamically adjust the gain to balance the power levels between the C-band and L-band channels, ensuring uniform signal strength throughout the fiber span.

For example, modern EDFA systems offer a **large range of tilt correction** to compensate for the SRS tilt, which can reach up to 8 dB per span.

SRS Power Transfer Along Fiber Length

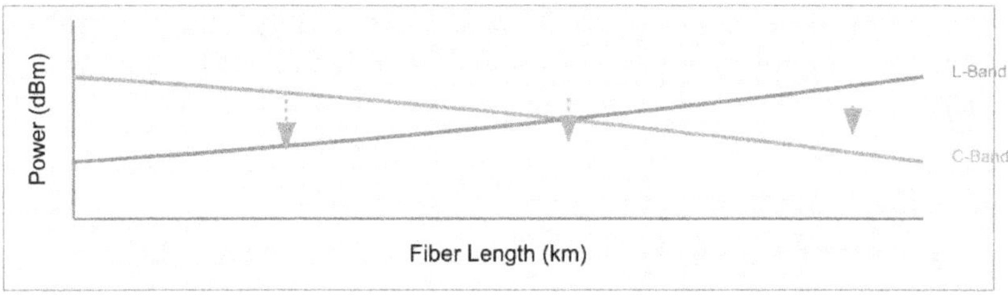

SRS Tilt Changes Due to Traffic Addition or Removal

In systems where traffic channels are dynamically added or removed, the SRS tilt can change rapidly. When channels are introduced or dropped, the balance of power between the C-band and L-band shifts, causing transient power imbalances. These sudden changes can degrade the **optical signal-to-noise ratio (OSNR)** and increase **bit-error rates (BER)** if not properly managed.

Solution: Orchestrated Traffic Management

To address this issue, C+L band systems implement **orchestrated turn-up and turn-down** of traffic channels. This approach ensures that changes in channel power are controlled and gradual, reducing the risk of transients affecting the system. **Automation software**, such as Ribbon's control systems, can be used to manage traffic changes and ensure that amplifier gain and tilt setpoints are optimized in real time. This allows for **fast detection** of changes and rapid recovery of amplifier performance, maintaining a stable transmission environment.

SRS Tilt Effect Across C+L Band

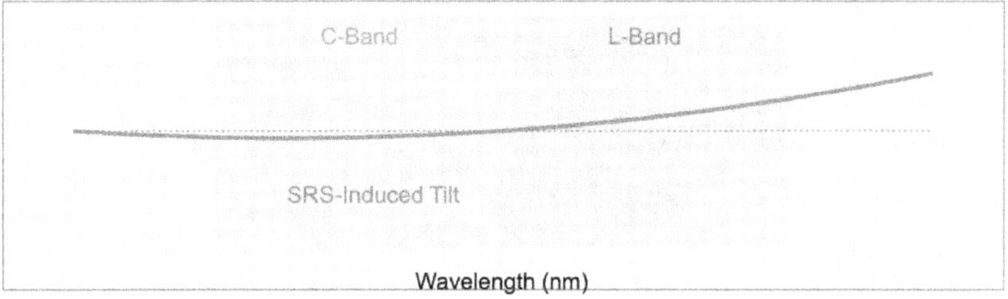

Higher L-Band Fiber Loss and Amplifier Noise

The L-band operates at longer wavelengths, where fiber attenuation is higher compared to the C-band. Additionally, **EDFA noise figures** are typically higher in the L-band, which can degrade signal quality. However, L-band systems also benefit from **lower non-linear penalties**, which can help offset the higher loss.

Solution: L-Band Raman Amplification

To compensate for the higher loss and noise in the L-band, **Raman amplifiers** are often used. Raman amplification provides a **lower noise figure (NF)** in the L-band, improving the overall performance of the system. By boosting L-band power through Raman amplification, operators can mitigate the higher attenuation and ensure that the signal maintains adequate strength for long-distance transmission.

Additionally, the higher power available in the L-band due to **high SRS effects** can be leveraged to balance the system, resulting in more consistent performance across both bands.

Design Considerations for Optical Amplifiers in C+L Band Systems

Optical amplifiers are a key component in managing the challenges of C+L band systems. Both **EDFA** and **Raman amplifiers** play essential roles in compensating for signal loss, managing SRS tilt, and ensuring that the optical signal remains strong across long distances.

Optical Band Spectrum Analysis

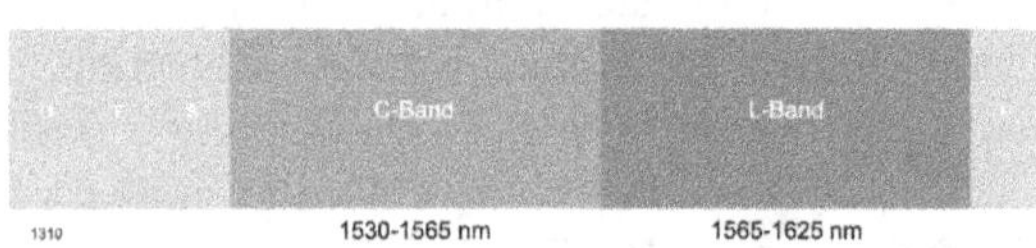

Band Characteristics

C-Band

- Wavelength: 1530-1565 nm
- Channel Count: 80 (50GHz)
- Gain: 20-25 dB
- NF: 4-6 dB
- Applications: Core Networks

L-Band

- Wavelength: 1565-1625 nm
- Channel Count: 80 (50GHz)
- Gain: 18-23 dB
- NF: 5-7 dB
- Applications: Capacity Expansion

C+L Band Amplification System

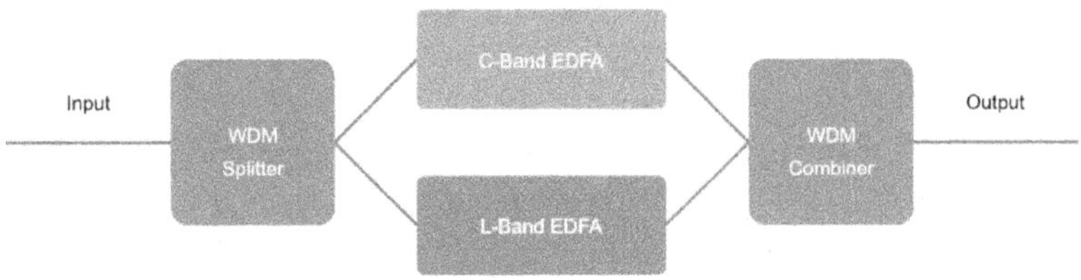

EDFA Design for C+L Bands

EDFAs are widely used for amplifying optical signals in both C-band and L-band systems. However, the design of EDFA amplifiers for C+L band operation must account for the different noise figures and gain characteristics of each band.

Combined C+L Band Gain Profile

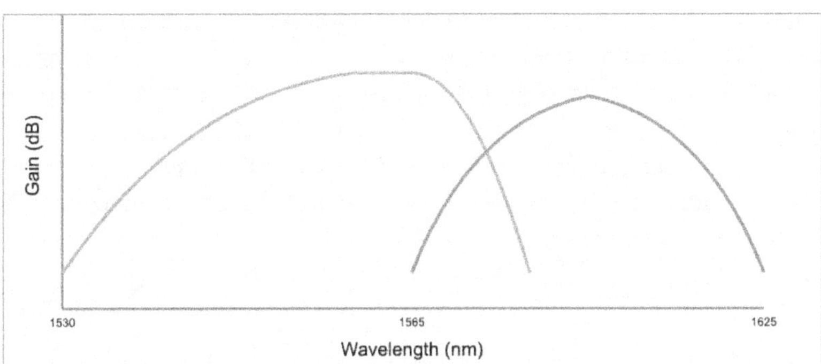

- **C-Band**: EDFAs typically provide a flatter gain profile and lower noise figures in the C-band, making them ideal for amplifying shorter wavelengths.
- **L-Band**: EDFAs for L-band systems are designed to deliver higher gain to compensate for increased fiber loss. However, they may also introduce higher noise, which needs to be managed through careful system design.

Raman Amplifiers for C+L Systems

Raman amplifiers provide **distributed amplification**, meaning they amplify the signal directly within the transmission fiber. This is particularly useful in C+L band systems, as Raman amplification can be used to provide **tilt compensation** and improve the OSNR in both bands.

For example, Raman amplifiers are often used in conjunction with EDFAs to extend the transmission distance and compensate for the higher loss in the L-band. By providing distributed gain throughout the fiber span, Raman amplification helps to maintain consistent signal quality across long distances.

Practical Example: A 100 km C+L Band Link

*Consider a DWDM system using both C-band and L-band channels to transmit data over a **100 km** fiber span. Without proper tilt compensation, the system would experience significant power imbalances due to SRS, with C-band channels losing power to L-band channels. This power imbalance could reach up to **8 dB** per span, severely affecting system performance.*

To address this, the system uses **Raman amplification** to provide distributed gain throughout the fiber. At the same time, **EDFAs** at key points along the span are used to apply tilt correction, ensuring that both C-band and L-band channels maintain consistent power levels. Additionally, **automatic traffic management software** monitors channel power in real-time, ensuring that any changes in traffic are controlled to prevent transients from affecting the system.

By using a combination of Raman and EDFA amplification, the system is able to maintain high OSNR across both bands, enabling **error-free transmission** over long distances.

Designing C+L band systems for optical communication requires careful consideration of non-linear effects like SRS, higher attenuation in the L-band, and the challenges of amplifier noise. By employing **tilt correction** techniques, **orchestrated traffic management**, and a combination of **EDFA** and **Raman amplification**, network operators can overcome these challenges and maximize the capacity of their optical networks.

As demand for bandwidth continues to grow, **C+L band systems** will remain a critical solution for expanding the capacity of fiber-optic networks without the need for additional infrastructure. With proper design and optimization, these systems can deliver reliable, high-performance transmission for the next generation of communication networks.

Link with No Amplifier

Scenario: A short-distance link of 50 km that does not require amplification.
Calculation Steps:

1. **Fiber Attenuation**: Assume fiber attenuation is 0.25 dB/km.
2. **Total Attenuation**: Total Attenuation=Fiber Attenuation×Distance

$$\text{Total Attenuation}=0.25\ \text{dB/km}\times 50\ \text{km}=12.5\ \text{dB}$$

3. **OSNR Calculation**:
   - Assume transmitted power P_{TX}=0 dBm.
   - Receiver sensitivity P_{RX} threshold = -28 dBm.

$$P_{RX}=P_{TX}-\text{Total Attenuation}$$

$$P_{RX}=0\ \text{dBm}-12.5\ \text{dB}=-12.5\ \text{dBm}$$

   - Check if P_{RX} is above the sensitivity threshold.

Link with Multiple Amplifiers

Scenario: A long-distance link of 400 km with multiple EDFAs.
Calculation Steps:

1. **Fiber Attenuation**: Assume fiber attenuation is 0.25 dB/km.
2. **Amplifier Spacing**: EDFAs are spaced 80 km apart.
3. **Number of Amplifiers**:

$$\text{Number of Amplifiers}=\text{Total Distance}/\text{Amplifier Spacing}$$

$$=400\ \text{km}/80\ \text{km}=5$$

4. **Total Attenuation per Span**:

$$\text{Attenuation per Span}=0.25\ \text{dB/km}\times 80\ \text{km}=20\ \text{dB}$$

5. **Gain per Amplifier**: Assume each EDFA provides 20 dB gain.
6. **OSNR Calculation**:
   - Calculate OSNR degradation per amplifier: $\text{OSNR}_{\text{span}}=\frac{P_{TX}-\text{Attenuation per Span}+\text{Gain per Amplifier}}{\text{Noise Figure}}$
     - Example noise figure = 5 dB.
   - Aggregate OSNR for the link using the formula: $\text{OSNR}_{\text{total}}=\frac{1}{\left(\frac{1}{\text{OSNR}_{\text{span}1}}\right)+\left(\frac{1}{\text{OSNR}_{\text{span}2}}\right)+\cdots+\left(\frac{1}{\text{OSNR}_{\text{span}n}}\right)}$

Example: If each span has an OSNR of 30 dB, and there are 5 spans: $\text{OSNR}_{\text{total}}=\frac{1}{\left(\frac{1}{30}+\frac{1}{30}+\frac{1}{30}+\frac{1}{30}+\frac{1}{30}\right)}=\frac{1}{\frac{5}{30}}=\frac{30}{5}=6\ \text{dB}$

Link with EDFA and Raman Amplification

Scenario: A link of 600 km using both EDFAs and Raman amplifiers.

Calculation Steps:

1. **Fiber Attenuation**: Assume fiber attenuation is 0.25 dB/km.
2. **Amplifier Types**: Use EDFAs every 80 km and Raman amplifiers every 200 km.
3. **Total Attenuation**:
    - **EDFAs:**
    - Total EDFA Gain=Number of EDFAs×Gain per EDFA
        - Number of EDFAs = 600/80=7.5
        - Gain per EDFA = 20 dB.
    - **Raman Amplifiers:**
    - Total Raman Gain=Number of Raman Amplifiers×Gain per Raman
        - Number of Raman Amplifiers = 600/200=3
        - Gain per Raman = 15 dB.
4. **OSNR Calculation**:
    - Combine gains and attenuations to find total OSNR.
    - Assume Raman amplifiers have lower noise figures (e.g., 3 dB).
    - Calculate composite OSNR for the link:

$$\mathrm{OSNR}_{\mathrm{total}} = \frac{1}{\left(\frac{1}{\mathrm{OSNR}_{\mathrm{EDFA}}}\right) + \left(\frac{1}{\mathrm{OSNR}_{\mathrm{Raman}}}\right)}$$

Link with ROADMs

Scenario: A dynamic optical network with reconfigurable optical add-drop multiplexers (ROADMs) over 500 km.

Calculation Steps:

1. **Fiber Attenuation**: Assume fiber attenuation is 0.25 dB/km.
2. **ROADM Insertion Loss**: Assume each ROADM introduces a 5 dB insertion loss.
3. **Number of ROADMs**: Assume 5 ROADMs in the link.
4. **Total Attenuation**:

Total Attenuation=Fiber Attenuation×Distance+Number of ROADMs×Insertion Loss

Total Attenuation=0.25 dB/km×500 km+5×5 dB=125 dB+25 dB=150 dB

5. **Amplifier Planning**: Place EDFAs between ROADMs.
   - Assume EDFA gain = 20 dB per amplifier.
   - Calculate total required amplification: Total Gain Required=Total Attenuation
6. **OSNR Calculation**:

- Calculate OSNR for each span and aggregate: $\mathrm{OSNR}_{\mathrm{span}} = \frac{P_{TX} - \text{Attenuation per Span} + \text{Gain per Amplifier}}{\text{Noise Figure}}$
  - Aggregate OSNR over all spans using the formula: $\mathrm{OSNR}_{\mathrm{total}} = \frac{1}{\left(\frac{1}{\mathrm{OSNR}_{\mathrm{span}1}}\right) + \left(\frac{1}{\mathrm{OSNR}_{\mathrm{span}2}}\right) + \cdots + \left(\frac{1}{\mathrm{OSNR}_{\mathrm{span}n}}\right)}$

Mathematical Formulas and Examples

Link Budget Calculation

The link budget ensures that the signal strength is sufficient to reach the receiver. It is calculated as: $P_{RX}=P_{TX}-\alpha\times L-M+G$

Where:

- P_{RX} = Received power
- P_{TX} = Transmitted power
- α = Fiber attenuation (dB/km)
- L = Fiber length (km)
- M = Margin for safety and additional losses (dB)
- G = Gain from optical amplifiers (dB)

Example: If P_{TX}=0 dBm, α=0.25 dB/km, L=100 km, M=3 dB, and G=20 dB:

$$P_{RX}=0\text{ dBm}-(0.25\text{ dB/km}\times 100\text{ km})-3\text{ dB}+20\text{ dB}$$

$$P_{RX}=0\text{ dBm}-25\text{ dB}-3\text{ dB}+20\text{ dB}=-8\text{ dBm}$$

Shannon Capacity Limit

The Shannon Capacity Limit defines the maximum data rate that can be transmitted over a communication channel without error, given the channel's bandwidth and signal-to-noise ratio (SNR). It is calculated using the formula:

$$C=B * \log_2(1+SNR)$$

Where:

- C = Channel capacity (bps)
- B = Bandwidth (Hz)

- SNR = Signal-to-noise ratio (linear scale)

Example: For a DWDM channel with a bandwidth of 50 GHz and an SNR of 20 dB (which corresponds to an SNR linear value of 100):

$$C=50\times10^9\log_2(1+100)$$

$$C=50\times10^9\log_2(101)$$

$$C\approx50\times10^9\times6.6582$$

$$C\approx332.91 \text{ Gbps}$$

OSNR Calculation Using the 58+ Formula

The 58+ formula is a practical method to estimate the required OSNR for a given modulation format and data rate.

$$OSNR = P_{out} - L - NF - 10\log\left(N + \frac{10^{G_{BA}/10}}{10^{L/10}}\right) - 10\log(\eta v_r)$$

Where:

P_{out}: Output power (per channel) of the booster and line amplifiers (dBm)
L: Span loss (dB) (assumed equal to line amplifiers gain)
G_{BA}: Gain of the optical booster amplifier (dB)
NF: Signal-spontaneous noise figure of the optical amplifier (dB)
h: Planck's constant (mJ·s)
v: Optical frequency (Hz)
v_r: Reference bandwidth (Hz), typically 0.1 nm
N - 1: Total number of line amplifiers

Note: For v = 193.4 THz and vr = 12.48 GHz (0.1nm), 10log(hvvr) = -58.0dBm

Simplified Cases

Case 1: When GBA ≈ L

$$OSNR = P_{out} - L - NF - 10\log(N+1) - 10\log(h\nu v_r)$$

Case 2: When L >> GBA (Negligible Booster ASE)

$$OSNR = P_{out} - L - NF - 10\log(N) - 10\log(h\nu v_r)$$

Case 3: Single Span with Booster Amplifier Only

$$OSNR = P_{out} - G_{BA} - NF - 10\log(h\nu v_r)$$

Case 4: Single Span with Pre-amplifier Only

$$OSNR = P_{out} - L - NF - 10\log(h\nu v_r)$$

Practical Systems with Unequal Span Losses

For systems where span losses vary, the general equation becomes:

$$OSNR = -10\log\left[\sum_{i=1}^{N} 10^{(NF_i - P_{in_i})/10}\right]$$

$$OSNR_{out} = -10\log\left[10^{-\frac{P_{in1}-NF_1-10\log(h\nu v_r)}{10}} + 10^{-\frac{P_{in2}-NF_2-10\log(h\nu v_r)}{10}} + \ldots + 10^{-\frac{P_{inN}-NF_N-10\log(h\nu v_r)}{10}}\right]$$

Where:

- **P_{in1}, P_{in2}, ..., P_{inN}**: Channel powers (dBm) at amplifier inputs
- **NF_1, NF_2, ..., NF_N**: Noise figures (dB) at channel wavelength of amplifiers

Key Implications

- OSNR decreases with increasing span loss (L) and number of amplifiers (N)
- For terrestrial links (≤2000km): repeater spacing can be 80-100km
- For submarine links (6000-8000km): maximum repeater spacing ≈50km
- Amplifier output power must balance between maintaining good OSNR and avoiding fiber nonlinearities

Data and Statistics

Recent data and statistics highlight the importance of effective network planning and design:

- **Global Data Traffic**: Global IP traffic is expected to reach 396 exabytes per month by 2025, necessitating robust network planning.
- **Cost of Downtime**: Network downtime can cost enterprises up to $5,600 per minute, emphasizing the need for reliable and resilient network designs.
- **Market Growth**: The optical networking market is projected to grow from $14.9 billion in 2020 to $24.4 billion by 2026, driven by the need for advanced network designs to support increasing data demands.

Network Design Flowchart

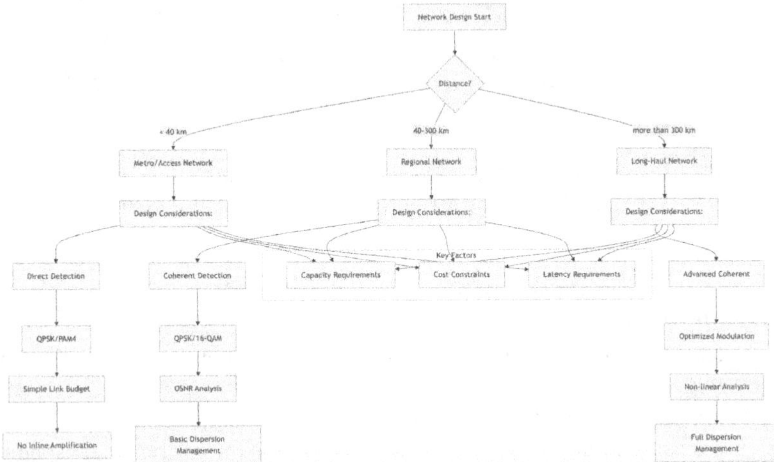

Optical Link Design: Thumb Rules & Methods

1. Quick Reference Rules

Power Budget Rules

- Maximum launch power: +1 dBm per channel
- Minimum receiver sensitivity: -20 dBm
- System margin: 3 dB minimum
- Repair margin: 2 dB

Span Design Rules

- EDFA spacing: 80-100 km
- Raman spacing: 60-80 km
- Maximum span loss: 25 dB
- Typical fiber loss: 0.2 dB/km

2. OSNR Calculation Methods

$$10\ \text{Log}\left[h\,\nu \triangle \nu 0\right] = -58\ \text{dBm}\quad (1.55\mu\text{m},\ 0.1\text{nm spectrum width})$$

Simple OSNR (58 Rule)

```
OSNR = 58 - Span Loss
When to use: Quick field estimates, single span
```

Detailed OSNR

```
OSNR = Pin - NF - 10log₁₀(N) - 10log₁₀(hνΔf)
When to use: System design, multi-span
```

GSNR Method

```
1/GSNR = 1/OSNR_ASE + 1/OSNR_NL
When to use: Modern coherent systems
```

3. Modulation Format Requirements

Format	Min OSNR	Max Distance	Spectral Efficiency
QPSK	8.5 dB	4000 km	2 bits/symbol
8QAM	12.5 dB	2000 km	3 bits/symbol
16QAM	15.5 dB	1000 km	4 bits/symbol
64QAM	22 dB	300 km	6 bits/symbol

4. Design Methods by Network Type

Metro Networks (<100 km)

- Use simple link budget
- Direct detection possible
- Minimal dispersion compensation
- Power optimization not critical

Regional Networks (100-800 km)

- Use detailed OSNR calculations
- Consider amplifier placement
- Basic non-linear compensation
- Moderate power optimization

Long-Haul Networks (>800 km)

- Use GSNR calculations
- Full non-linear compensation
- Critical power optimization
- Advanced dispersion management

5. Component Rules

Connectors & Splices

- Connector loss: 0.5 dB max
- Splice loss: 0.1 dB typical
- Reflection: -45 dB max
- Minimum bend radius: 30mm

Amplifiers

- Noise Figure: 5-6 dB
- Gain flatness: ±0.5 dB
- Input power: -30 to -20 dBm
- Output power: +17 to +20 dBm

6. System Margins

Required Design Margins

- Aging margin: 3 dB
- Repair margin: 2 dB
- Implementation penalty: 2 dB
- Polarization penalty: 1 dB
- Temperature effect: 1 dB

7. Best Practices

Design Phase

- Always include system margins
- Consider future upgrades
- Use appropriate calculation method
- Document all assumptions

Implementation Phase

- Verify all component specifications
- Measure actual losses
- Document as-built values
- Perform end-to-end testing

Chapter 10

Network Architectures and Topologies

Chapter 10
Network Architectures and Topologies

"Network architecture is like city planning - it must serve both present and future generations." - Ivan Kaminow

---

Optical network architectures form the backbone of modern data communication, enabling high-speed, high-capacity transmission with resilience and scalability. Different architectures support various applications, from metro networks to long-haul and access networks, each with unique design needs. This chapter explores the primary optical network architectures—Point-to-Point, Ring, Mesh, and Star—along with their specific applications and use cases.

Network Architectures and Use Cases

The architecture chosen for an optical network dictates its resilience, efficiency, and scalability. Each architecture provides different benefits and drawbacks, making it essential to understand its use cases and limitations before deployment.

Types of Optical Network Architectures

The four major architectures in optical networks are

- Point-to-Point
- Ring
- Mesh
- Star

Each architecture has specific advantages and applications, impacting how data is transmitted, managed, and protected across the network.

Point-to-Point Architecture

Following are some of the types of Point to point networks.

Point-to-Point Network

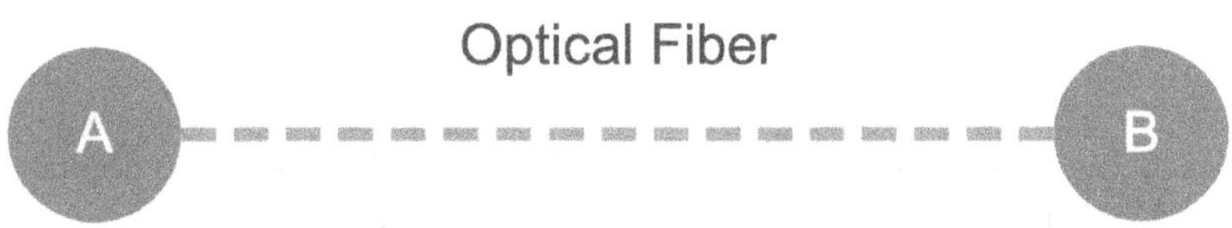

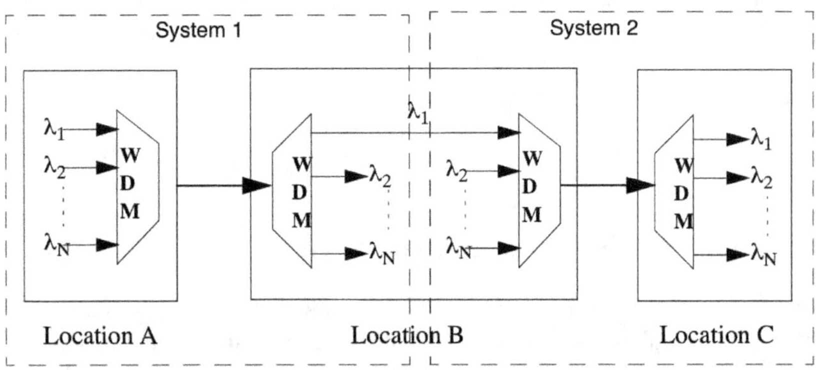

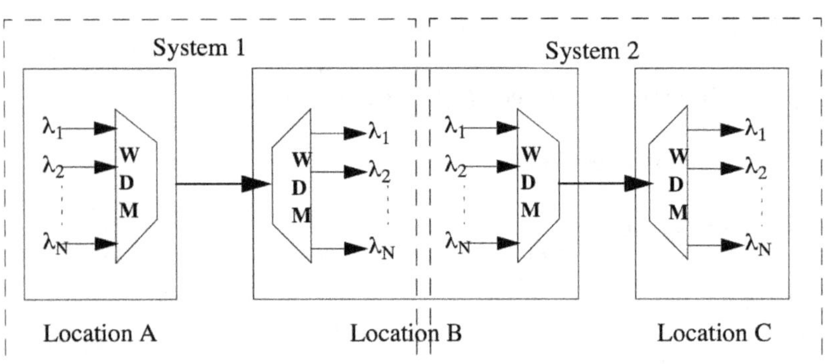

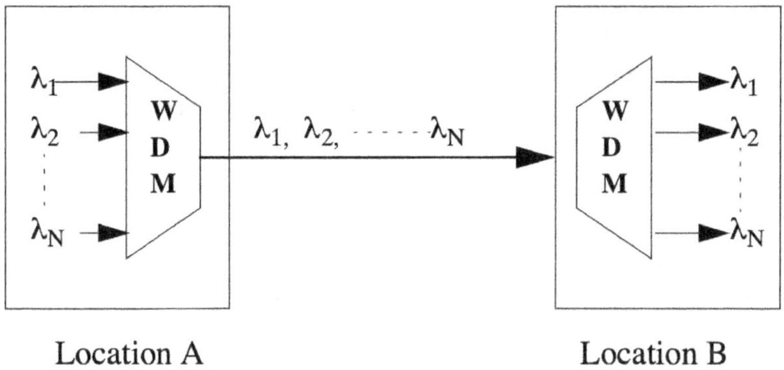

Point-to-Point WDM Systems with Wavelength Pass-Through

Point-to-Point (PtP) is the simplest form of network architecture, providing a direct link between two nodes. It's widely used in long-haul communication because of its high capacity and straightforward configuration.

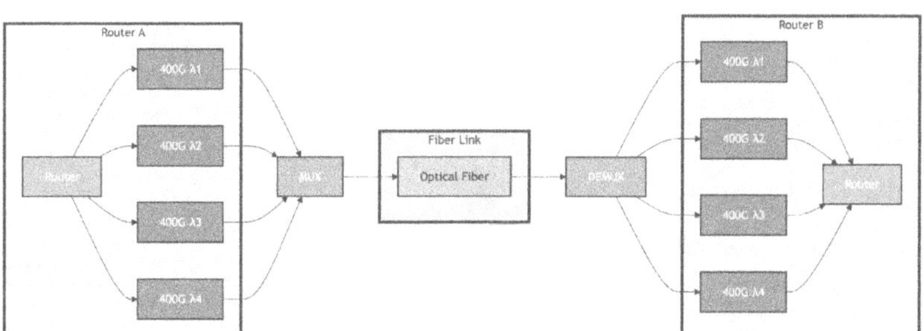

Structure: In PtP networks, data flows directly from a transmitter (Tx) to a receiver (Rx) over a dedicated fiber, providing high-speed, low-latency links.

Common Applications:

Long-Haul Transmission: PtP links are ideal for intercity and intercontinental connections requiring dedicated bandwidth and minimal latency.

Data Center Interconnect (DCI): PtP links connect data centers within metropolitan areas, supporting fast, secure communication.

Advantages:

- **Low Complexity**: The simple design reduces operational complexity and maintenance requirements.
- **High Bandwidth**: PtP links provide high data rates with minimal interference, making them ideal for bandwidth-intensive applications.

Disadvantages:

- **Lack of Redundancy**: A single failure can disrupt communication unless a secondary PtP link is provided.
- **High Cost for Redundancy**: Dedicated links require significant infrastructure investment to maintain high reliability over long distances.

Ring Architecture

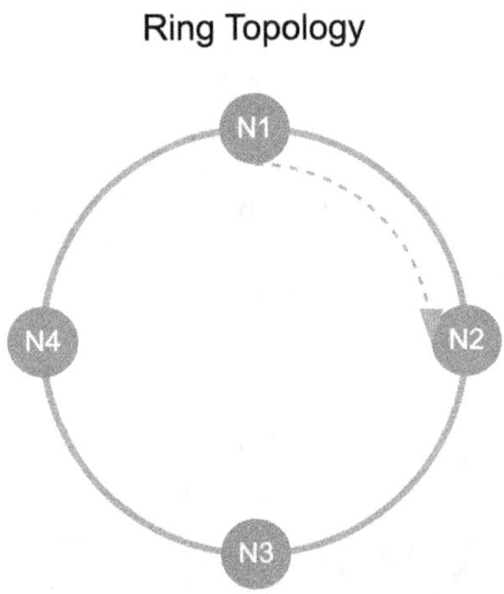

A **Ring Architecture** connects nodes in a closed-loop, providing resilience by allowing data to flow in both directions. This setup is common in metro networks, where redundancy is essential for ensuring uninterrupted service.

- **Structure**: Each node is connected to two other nodes in a circular pattern. If a link between two nodes fails, data can reroute in the opposite direction.
- **Applications**:
  - **Metro Networks**: Ring topologies are ideal for urban and regional networks, offering high redundancy for densely connected areas.

- **Access Networks**: Ring architecture provides robust connectivity for access networks, supporting broadband, voice, and data services.

- **Advantages**:
    - **High Reliability**: The looped structure allows for immediate rerouting in the case of a failure, reducing downtime.
    - **Efficient Resource Utilization**: Ring networks typically require less cabling compared to mesh networks, making them more cost-effective for medium-scale deployments.
- **Disadvantages**:
    - **Limited Scalability**: Adding more nodes can increase complexity and latency, making it less suitable for expansive networks.
    - **Latency**: The more nodes in the ring, the higher the latency as signals travel around the loop.
- **Example**:
    - In a metropolitan area, a **dual-ring topology** with Automatic Protection Switching (APS) ensures that if one ring fails, traffic automatically switches to the secondary ring, maintaining service continuity.

Mesh Architecture

Mesh Architecture offers multiple interconnections between nodes, allowing data to be transmitted over various paths. This setup enhances fault tolerance and scalability, making it ideal for large-scale networks.

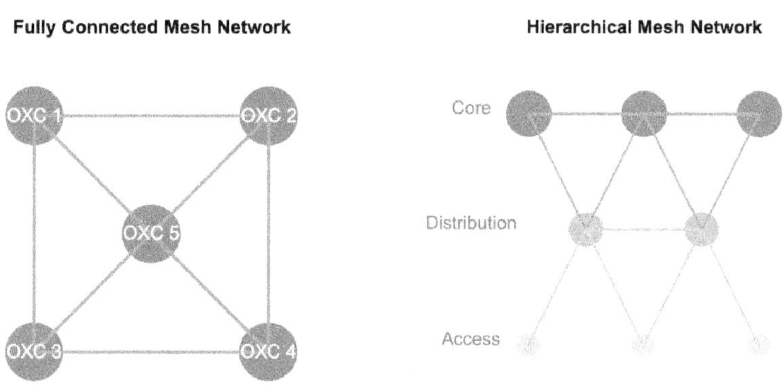

- **Structure**: Nodes in a mesh network are connected to several other nodes, providing numerous paths for data to reach its destination.

- **Applications**:
  - **Core and Backbone Networks**: Mesh architectures are commonly used in backbone networks, where high reliability and low latency are crucial.
  - **Data Centers and Cloud Networks**: In data centers, mesh topologies support large-scale, dynamic environments requiring multiple data paths.
- **Advantages**:
  - **High Fault Tolerance**: Multiple paths provide redundancy, allowing data to reroute around failed nodes or links.
  - **Scalability**: Mesh networks are easy to expand by adding new nodes and connections.
- **Disadvantages**:
  - **Complexity and Cost**: The extensive cabling and infrastructure required increase both capital and operational expenditures.
  - **Management Overhead**: Routing and traffic management are more complex due to multiple available paths.
- **Example Calculation for Path Diversity**:
  - For a mesh network with four nodes (A, B, C, D), each connected to multiple nodes:

▪ **Possible Paths**: Each pair of nodes has multiple available paths, such as A -> B -> D and A -> C -> D.

▪ **Redundancy**: In the event of a link failure between A and B, traffic can reroute via A -> C -> B.

Star Architecture

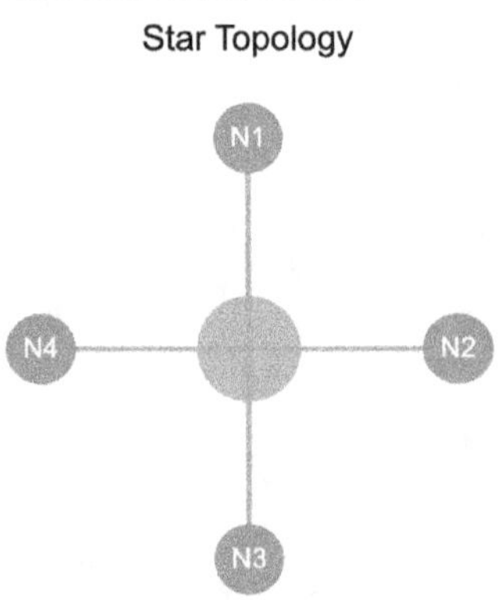

In a **Star Topology**, all nodes connect to a central hub, making it suitable for access networks or smaller networks with limited redundancy requirements.

- **Structure**: A single central node connects to multiple endpoints, which are not interconnected. All traffic flows through the central hub.
- **Applications**:
  - **Access Networks**: Star topology is used in passive optical networks (PONs) and fiber-to-the-home (FTTH) setups to connect end-users to a central office.
  - **Local Area Networks (LANs)**: Frequently used in small office or residential settings for simplicity and cost-effectiveness.
- **Advantages**:
  - **Ease of Management**: The central hub simplifies monitoring, control, and management of the network.
  - **Cost-Effective**: Less cabling is required compared to mesh or ring networks, making star topology affordable for access networks.
- **Disadvantages**:
  - **Single Point of Failure**: If the central hub fails, all connected nodes lose connectivity.
  - **Limited Scalability**: Expanding the network puts a strain on the central hub, which can limit scalability.
- **Example**:

  In a **PON network** serving a residential area, a single hub at the central office connects to multiple endpoints at user premises, providing broadband access over fiber.

Specific Applications of Optical Network Architectures

Each architecture has unique strengths and is suited to different types of optical networks, depending on the operational requirements, geographical layout, and redundancy needs.

Metro Networks

Metro networks connect various locations within a city or metropolitan area, such as data centers, offices, and internet exchange points (IXPs).

Common Architecture: Ring and mesh topologies are commonly used in metro networks, providing resilience and flexibility to accommodate high-density traffic.

Metro Network Architecture

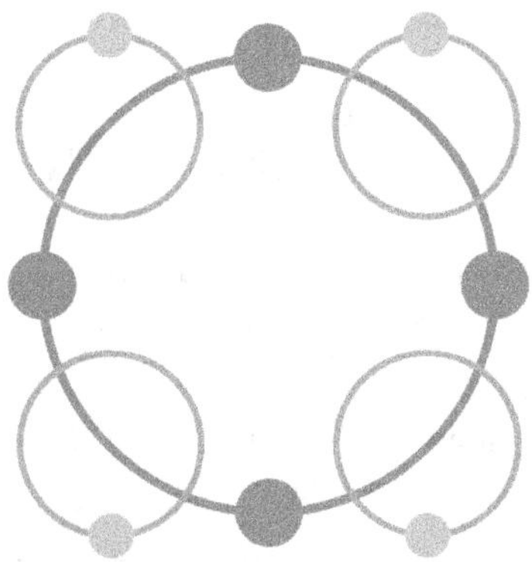

Core Ring with Edge Access Rings

Key Requirements:

- **High Redundancy**: Ensures minimal downtime in case of failures, especially for business-critical applications.
- **Low Latency**: Required for real-time services and applications like video conferencing, financial trading, and data exchange.

Example:

- A metro network in a city may use a **dual-ring topology** with each ring serving different parts of the city, providing redundancy by connecting both rings at key locations.

Long-Haul Networks

Long-haul networks connect distant locations, often spanning hundreds or thousands of kilometers. They are crucial for national and international connectivity, linking data centers and exchange points over large distances.

Common Architecture: Point-to-point and mesh topologies are prevalent in long-haul networks to support high-capacity transmission with extensive redundancy.

Key Requirements:

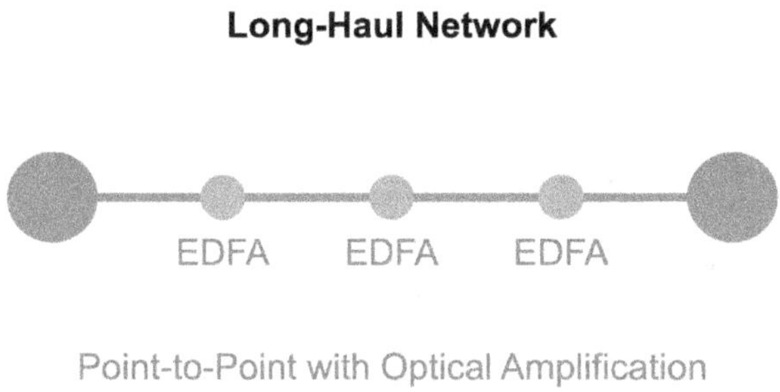

- **Amplification**: Long-haul links require EDFAs or Raman amplifiers to boost signal strength over extended distances.
- **Protection Mechanisms**: Ensuring high reliability through 1+1 or 1:1 protection is essential to prevent service interruptions.

Example:

- An undersea fiber link connecting two continents may utilize **point-to-point architecture** with repeaters and amplifiers spaced at intervals to maintain signal integrity across thousands of kilometers.

Access Networks

Access networks deliver connectivity from the central network to end-users, commonly employing cost-effective topologies suited for high-volume connections.

Common Architecture: Star and tree topologies are widely used, particularly in FTTH and FTTx networks.

Key Requirements:

- **Cost-Effective Deployment**: Minimizes installation and maintenance costs while ensuring reliable last-mile connectivity.
- **Scalability**: Access networks need to support a growing number of users as broadband demand rises.

Example:

A fiber-to-the-home (FTTH) network in a residential area uses a **star topology** to connect multiple homes to a central hub, ensuring affordable and efficient connectivity.

Network Architectures and Use Cases

Point-to-Point Architecture

Theory and Principles

Point-to-point architecture represents the simplest form of optical networking, establishing a direct connection between two nodes. The fundamental capacity equation for a point-to-point link is:

$$C = B \times \log_2(1 + SNR) \times N$$

where:

- C = Total capacity (bits/s)
- B = Bandwidth per wavelength (Hz)
- SNR = Signal-to-noise ratio
- N = Number of wavelengths

Design Considerations

Power Budget Analysis:

$$P_{Rx} = P_{Tx} - \alpha * L - \Sigma(\text{connector losses}) - \Sigma(\text{splice losses}) + G - \text{Margin}$$

where:

- P_{Rx} = Received power (dBm)
- P_{Tx} = Transmitted power (dBm)
- α = Fiber attenuation (dB/km)
- L = Link length (km)
- G = Amplifier gain (dB)

Span Loss Calculation:

```
Total_span_loss = (α × L) + MUX_loss + DEMUX_loss + Connector_loss

Where:
- α: Fiber attenuation (0.25 dB/km)
- L: Span length (km)
- MUX_loss: Typically 4-5 dB
- DEMUX_loss: Typically 4-5 dB
- Connector_loss: ~0.5 dB per connector
```

Protection Schemes:

Protection Type	Switching Time	Resource Usage
1+1	< 50ms	200%
1:1	< 100ms	100%
Unprotected	N/A	100%

Implementation Example

```
[Tx Site]──────────[EDFA]──────────[EDFA]──────────[Rx Site]
   │                                                   │
   └──────────────────────Protection Path──────────────┘
```

Typical specifications:

- Distance: 10-1000 km
- Capacity: Up to 800G per wavelength
- OSNR requirement: >18 dB
- Maximum span length: 80-100 km

Ring Architecture

Theory and Principles

Ring architectures provide enhanced reliability through built-in protection mechanisms. The ring's capacity is determined by:

$$\text{Ring Capacity} = \Sigma(C_i \times HP_i)$$

where: - C_i = Capacity of channel i - HP_i = Working path ratio for channel i

Types of Ring Protection

UPSR (Unidirectional Path Switched Ring):

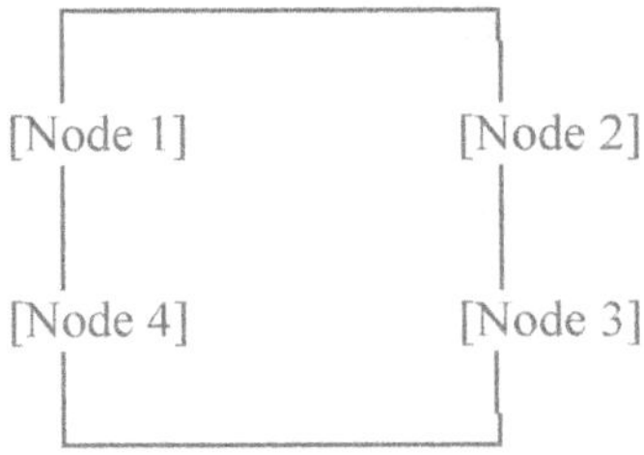

Working Path: Clockwise
Protection Path: Counter-clockwise

BLSR (Bidirectional Line Switched Ring):

Protection switching time calculation:

$$T_{switch} = T_{detect} + T_{notify} + T_{config}$$

where:

- Tdetect: Fault detection time (typically 10ms)
- Tnotify: Notification propagation time
- Tconfig: Protection path configuration time

Design Parameters

Parameter	2-Fiber Ring	4-Fiber Ring
Working capacity	50%	75%
Protection capacity	50%	25%
Switching time	< 50ms	< 50ms
Node count	2-16	2-32
Maximum circumference	1200km	2400km

Mesh Architecture

Theory and Principles

Mesh networks provide multiple paths between nodes, offering superior reliability and flexibility. The mesh degree is calculated as:

$$MD = 2E/[N(N-1)]$$

where:

- MD = Mesh degree

- E = Number of edges (links)
- N = Number of nodes

Protection Schemes

Path Protection:

$$\text{Availability} = 1 - \Pi(1-a_i)$$

where a_i is the availability of path i

Link Protection:

$$\text{Resource efficiency} = \text{Protected capacity}/\text{Total capacity}$$

Routing and Wavelength Assignment (RWA)

RWA constraint equations:

$$\text{Wavelength continuity: } \lambda_{i,p} = \lambda_{j,p} \text{ (for all i,j in path p)}$$
$$\text{Link capacity: } \Sigma(\lambda_{i,p}) \leq W \text{ (for all links i)}$$

where:

- $\lambda_{i,p}$ = Wavelength assignment on link i for path p
- W = Number of wavelengths per fiber

Star Architecture

Theory and Principles

Star topology connects all nodes to a central hub. The required hub capacity is:

$$C_{Hub} = N \times C_{avg} \times (1 + OF)$$

where:

- N = Number of nodes
- C_{avg} = Average node capacity
- OF = Oversubscription factor

Implementation Considerations

Parameter	Passive Star	Active Star
Max distance	20km	80km

Split ratio	1:32 typical	N/A
Insertion loss	17-20 dB	Variable
Cost per user	Lower	Higher

Specific Applications

Metro Networks

Design Parameters

Parameter	Value Range	Optimization Goal
Network diameter	10-300km	Minimize latency
Node count	5-50	Balance cost/flexibility
Protection scheme	Ring/Mesh	99.999% availability
Channel spacing	50/100 GHz	Maximize capacity

Traffic Engineering

$$\text{Required capacity} = \Sigma(Di \times Gi \times Si)$$

where:

- Di = Demand for service i
- Gi = Growth factor
- Si = Service multiplication factor

Long-Haul Networks

Technical Requirements

Parameter	Specification	Critical Threshold
OSNR margin	> 3 dB	< 2 dB
Dispersion tolerance	±800 ps/nm	> ±1000 ps/nm
PMD tolerance	< 10 ps	> 12 ps
Span length	80-100 km	> 120 km

Implementation Considerations

Component	Specification	Alternative
Fiber type	G.655/G.654	G.652
Amplification	EDFA+Raman	EDFA only
Modulation	DP-QPSK	16-QAM
FEC	SD-FEC	HD-FEC

Access Networks

PON Architecture

```
            [OLT]
              |
            [1:3]
           /  |  \
      [ONU][ONU][ONU]
```

Split ratio optimization:

$$SNR\_min = SNR\_input - 10\log_{10}(N)$$

where N is the split ratio

Technology Comparison

Parameter	GPON	XGS-PON	TWDM-PON
Down/Up (Gbps)	2.5/1.25	10/10	40/10
Split ratio	1:32	1:64	1:64
Reach (km)	20	20	40
λ count	1	1	4
Cost per user	Low	Medium	High

Network Architecture Availability Comparison

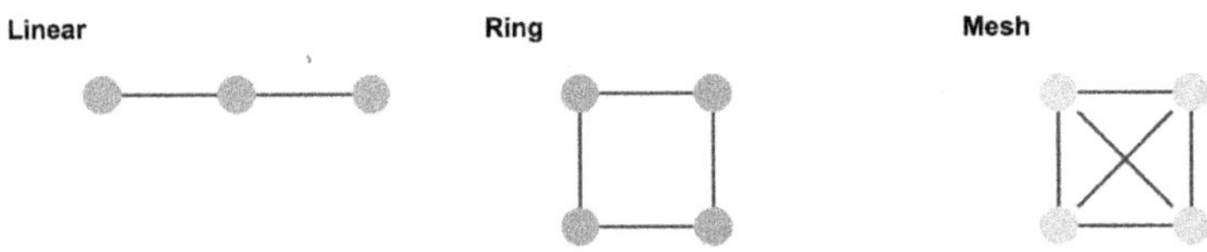

Architecture Comparison

Type	Availability	Recovery Time	Cost Factor	Complexity
Linear	99.9%	Hours	1x	Low
Ring	99.999%	50ms	2.5x	Medium
Mesh	99.9999%	10ms	3-4x	High

Chapter 11

How to Choose DWDM Link Components

Chapter 11
How to Choose DWDM Link Components

"Choosing components is like choosing ingredients - they must work together perfectly." - David Chaffee

---

A DWDM system is a complex network designed to transmit multiple data signals across a single optical fiber by using different wavelengths (lambdas). Choosing the right components is crucial for achieving optimal performance in terms of bandwidth, power consumption, and overall network reach. This chapter will break down the essential DWDM components, providing a detailed understanding of their roles, features, and how to choose the right variant for your network.

Transponders: What, Why, and How to Choose?

What is a Transponder?

A **transponder** is a key component in a DWDM system responsible for converting client data signals into optical wavelengths that can be transmitted over a DWDM network. It performs both the **electrical-to-optical (E/O) conversion** and the reverse **optical-to-electrical (O/E) conversion**.

When and Why to Choose a Transponder?

- **Functionality**: Transponders are required when client signals (e.g., Ethernet, Fibre Channel, SONET/SDH) need to be transported over the DWDM network. These signals may not be natively compatible with the optical wavelengths used in DWDM.
- **Multiplexing Compatibility**: In cases where the client devices do not natively support WDM wavelengths, transponders enable the conversion of the electrical signals into WDM optical signals.

Types of Transponders

There are various types of transponders depending on the data rate and the distance requirements:

- **100G and 400G Transponders**: For high-capacity metro, long-haul, or data center interconnect (DCI) applications.
- **Coherent Transponders**: These transponders support coherent modulation formats (such as QPSK, 16-QAM), allowing for better performance over long distances and in networks with lower OSNR.

Advantages and Disadvantages of Transponders

Advantages:

- **Protocol Agnostic**: Can convert various types of client signals into WDM wavelengths.
- **Modulation Flexibility**: Coherent transponders support advanced modulation formats, improving capacity and reach.
- **Reach Extension**: They provide the capability to extend network reach by using Forward Error Correction (FEC) and other performance-enhancing techniques.

Disadvantages:

- **Power Consumption**: Transponders can be power-hungry, especially when supporting high data rates and coherent technologies.
- **Cost**: High-end transponders with advanced features (e.g., coherent detection) can be expensive.

Example Use Case

In a 400G metro DWDM network, **coherent transponders** are deployed to convert 100G Ethernet signals from client routers into optical wavelengths. By using coherent detection, these transponders enable long-reach transmission (up to 1000 km) without signal regeneration.

Muxponders: Multiplexing and More

What is a Muxponder?

A **muxponder** combines (multiplexes) multiple lower-speed client signals into a single higher-speed wavelength for transmission over the DWDM system. It performs both the E/O and O/E conversions for each individual client signal.

When and Why to Choose a Muxponder?

- **Capacity Optimization**: Muxponders are ideal when you need to maximize the capacity of your DWDM network by combining multiple low-speed services (e.g., 10G, 25G) into a single higher-speed optical channel (e.g., 100G, 200G).
- **Cost Efficiency**: They provide a cost-effective way to utilize available spectrum efficiently by aggregating multiple client signals onto a single wavelength.

Types of Muxponders

- **10G to 100G Muxponders**: These muxponders aggregate multiple 10G client signals onto a single 100G wavelength.
- **100G to 400G Muxponders**: These aggregate multiple 100G client signals onto a single 400G wavelength, optimizing high-bandwidth applications.

Advantages and Disadvantages of Muxponders

- **Advantages**:
  - **Increased Capacity**: Maximizes the utilization of available fiber by aggregating multiple client signals into fewer wavelengths.
  - **Simplified Management**: Reduces the number of optical wavelengths needed, simplifying the management of the DWDM system.
- **Disadvantages**:
  - **Latency**: The process of aggregating and de-multiplexing multiple signals can introduce slight latency.
  - **Limited Flexibility**: Muxponders are generally optimized for specific data rates and may lack flexibility in terms of adding more channels in the future.

Example Use Case

In a regional DWDM network, a 100G muxponder aggregates multiple 10G Ethernet services from various enterprises into a single 100G wavelength for efficient transport across the network, reducing the number of active wavelengths and simplifying fiber management.

Optical Transceivers: The Eyes of the Network

What is an Optical Transceiver?

An **optical transceiver** is a device that transmits and receives data in the form of light over fiber optic cables. It consists of both a transmitter and a receiver module, allowing bi-directional communication. In DWDM systems, optical transceivers are critical for enabling data transport over individual wavelengths.

When and Why to Choose an Optical Transceiver?

- **Client-Side and Line-Side Interface**: Optical transceivers are typically chosen when you need to interface between the DWDM system and the client equipment. They are also used on the **line side** for the transmission of DWDM wavelengths.
- **Modular Design**: Optical transceivers come in a variety of form factors (e.g., SFP, QSFP, CFP) and can be easily swapped, offering modularity and flexibility in network design.

Types of Optical Transceivers

- **SFP+ (10G)**: Commonly used for short- and long-distance 10G connections.
- **QSFP+ (40G)**: Aggregates four 10G lanes into a single 40G transceiver.
- **QSFP28 (100G)**: A widely used form factor for high-speed 100G connections.
- **400G ZR/ZR+**: Designed for 400G transmission over longer distances, leveraging coherent technology.

Advantages and Disadvantages of Optical Transceivers

Advantages:

- o **Modularity**: Transceivers can be easily swapped or upgraded to accommodate new data rates and technologies.
- o **Range of Options**: Available in multiple variants to support different distances (e.g., 10 km, 80 km) and types of fiber (e.g., single-mode, multi-mode).

Disadvantages:

- o **Distance Limitations**: Standard transceivers (e.g., SFP, QSFP) may have limitations in terms of reach, requiring amplification or regeneration for long-haul networks.

- **Power Consumption**: Higher-capacity transceivers (e.g., 400G ZR) can consume significant amounts of power, impacting the overall energy efficiency of the network.

Example Use Case

In a data center interconnect (DCI) network, **QSFP28 transceivers** are used to link 100G client devices to the DWDM system. These transceivers provide a cost-effective and modular solution for high-bandwidth data transmission over distances up to 80 km.

Multiplexers: The Backbone of DWDM

What is a Multiplexer (MUX)?

A **multiplexer** is a device that combines multiple optical signals (wavelengths) onto a single fiber for transmission. In DWDM systems, multiplexers are used to aggregate wavelengths into a single optical fiber, increasing the overall capacity of the network.

When and Why to Choose a Multiplexer?

- **Capacity Expansion**: Multiplexers allow network operators to expand the capacity of their fiber infrastructure by transmitting multiple data streams (each on a different wavelength) over the same fiber.
- **Flexibility**: Multiplexers can be used to build flexible DWDM networks, enabling the transport of multiple services (e.g., Ethernet, SDH) over a single fiber.

Types of Multiplexers

- **Passive Multiplexers**: These are unpowered devices that use fixed wavelength filters to combine or separate signals. They are simple and cost-effective but offer limited flexibility.
- **Active Multiplexers**: These devices can dynamically manage and adjust wavelengths, allowing for more flexible and programmable network architectures.

Advantages and Disadvantages of Multiplexers

- **Advantages**:
    - **Cost Efficiency**: Multiplexers enable multiple services to be carried over a single fiber, reducing the need for additional fiber infrastructure.

- **Scalability**: They support scaling up the network capacity by simply adding more wavelengths.

- **Disadvantages**:
  - **Insertion Loss**: Each multiplexer introduces insertion loss, which can degrade the signal quality over long distances. Careful planning is required to ensure that the loss does not exceed acceptable limits.
  - **Limited Flexibility (Passive Mux)**: Passive multiplexers do not allow for dynamic reconfiguration, which can be a limitation in highly dynamic networks.

Example Use Case

In a long-haul DWDM system, a **passive DWDM multiplexer** is used to aggregate up to 40 different wavelengths (40 channels) onto a single fiber. This setup allows the network to transmit multiple 10G, 40G, and 100G services simultaneously, without needing additional fiber infrastructure.

Insertion Loss in DWDM Systems

What is Insertion Loss?

Insertion loss refers to the loss of signal power that occurs when an optical component (e.g., multiplexer, coupler, connector) is inserted into the optical link. In DWDM systems, minimizing insertion loss is critical for maintaining signal quality over long distances.

Insertion Loss Calculation

Insertion loss is typically measured in decibels (dB) and is calculated as:

$$\text{Insertion Loss (dB)} = 10 \cdot \log_{10}\left(\frac{P_{\text{out}}}{P_{\text{in}}}\right)$$

Where:

- P_{out} is the output power,
- P_{in} is the input power.

Factors Affecting Insertion Loss

- **Fiber Length**: The longer the fiber, the greater the insertion loss due to attenuation.
- **Connectors and Splices**: Each connector and splice introduces additional loss, which can accumulate over long distances.

- **Multiplexers and Demultiplexers**: These components can introduce loss depending on their design and the number of channels being multiplexed.

Managing Insertion Loss

To mitigate insertion loss, network planners must carefully design the optical path and select components that introduce minimal loss. In some cases, optical amplifiers (such as EDFAs) are used to boost signal strength and compensate for the loss introduced by these components.

ROADMs (Reconfigurable Optical Add-Drop Multiplexers)

What is a ROADM?

A **Reconfigurable Optical Add-Drop Multiplexer (ROADM)** is a critical component in modern DWDM networks that provides the flexibility to dynamically add, drop, or pass through individual wavelengths without requiring optical-electrical-optical (OEO) conversion. Unlike fixed add-drop multiplexers (ADMs), ROADMs allow for remote configuration, making them ideal for **flex-grid** networks where bandwidth can be adjusted as needed.

When and Why to Choose a ROADM?

- **Flexibility**: ROADMs provide the ability to add or drop specific wavelengths at any node in the network without disrupting other wavelengths. This flexibility is vital for building **dynamic, multi-service, and scalable networks**.
- **Cost Efficiency**: ROADMs eliminate the need for electrical conversion at every switching point, reducing power consumption and equipment costs in long-haul or metro networks.
- **Wavelength Management**: They allow the network operator to manage wavelengths in real-time, adjusting bandwidth and rerouting traffic based on demand.

Types of ROADMs

- **Fixed ROADMs**: These support adding/dropping of a fixed number of channels at specific wavelengths. They are suitable for static networks but lack flexibility for future changes.

- **Dynamic ROADMs**: These enable full flexibility in adding or dropping any wavelength at any node, making them ideal for scalable and dynamic networks.
- **Colorless, Directionless, and Contentionless (CDC) ROADMs**: The latest ROADM technology that provides full flexibility in selecting the wavelength (color), direction, and number of channels that can be added or dropped without contention between channels.

Advantages and Disadvantages of ROADMs

- **Advantages**:
  - **Scalability**: ROADMs provide the ability to scale DWDM networks dynamically without disrupting existing services.
  - **Cost Savings**: Reduced need for electrical processing at intermediate nodes, leading to lower power consumption and fewer active components.
  - **Real-Time Reconfigurability**: ROADMs can be managed and reconfigured remotely, offering more efficient use of fiber resources and better network resilience.
- **Disadvantages**:
  - **Initial Cost**: ROADMs, especially CDC ROADMs, can be expensive to deploy initially compared to fixed multiplexers or passive components.
  - **Insertion Loss**: Due to the complexity of the optical switches, ROADMs can introduce higher insertion loss than simpler passive components.

Example Use Case

In a large metro DWDM network, **CDC ROADMs** are deployed at key aggregation points. These ROADMs enable the operator to add or drop any wavelength without manual intervention, allowing for the rapid provisioning of new services or bandwidth adjustments in response to demand.

Fibers: Choosing the Right Optical Fiber for DWDM Networks

Types of Fiber Used in DWDM

Different types of fiber are used depending on the distance, capacity, and specific requirements of the DWDM system.

Standard Single-Mode Fiber (SMF): This is the most common fiber used in DWDM networks. SMF has a core diameter of about 9 microns and supports long-distance, high-capacity data transmission by minimizing attenuation and chromatic dispersion.

Advantages:

- Supports long-distance communication.
- Low attenuation and dispersion at the 1550 nm wavelength band (C-band), ideal for DWDM systems.

Disadvantages:

- More prone to **nonlinearities** (e.g., self-phase modulation, four-wave mixing) at high power levels.

Dispersion-Shifted Fiber (DSF): DSF is designed to minimize chromatic dispersion around the 1550 nm region, but it can be more susceptible to nonlinear effects like four-wave mixing (FWM) in DWDM systems.

Non-Zero Dispersion-Shifted Fiber (NZDSF): This fiber type provides low dispersion but avoids the nonlinear effects of DSF, making it better suited for high-capacity DWDM networks.

When and Why to Choose Specific Fiber Types?

- **SMF for Long-Haul Networks**: Standard SMF is typically used for long-haul transmission due to its low attenuation and wide availability.
- **NZDSF for Dense DWDM Systems**: Non-zero dispersion-shifted fiber is ideal for systems with dense wavelength spacing because it balances the dispersion and nonlinearities in high-capacity DWDM systems.

Fiber Characteristics to Consider

Attenuation: The loss of signal power over distance, typically measured in dB/km. For SMF, attenuation rates are typically around **0.2 dB/km** in the C-band.

Dispersion: The spreading of light pulses over time. While some dispersion is desirable to counteract nonlinear effects, excessive dispersion can cause signal degradation. In long-haul networks, **dispersion compensation** or dispersion-managed fibers are often used.

Example Use Case

In a 1000 km long-haul DWDM link, **NZDSF fiber** is chosen to minimize chromatic dispersion while avoiding the nonlinear effects that would occur with DSF. The low attenuation of the fiber ensures that signal quality remains high, even across long distances.

Optical Amplifiers: Boosting Signal Strength

What is an Optical Amplifier?

An **optical amplifier** is a device used to boost the strength of an optical signal without converting it into an electrical signal. Amplifiers are essential in DWDM systems to extend the transmission distance between nodes without signal degradation.

Types of Optical Amplifiers

Erbium-Doped Fiber Amplifier (EDFA)

The most commonly used amplifier in DWDM systems. EDFAs are optimized for the C-band (1530-1565 nm) and L-band (1565-1625 nm) and provide high-gain, low-noise amplification for multiple wavelengths simultaneously.

Advantages:

- Efficient amplification of multiple DWDM channels in the C-band or L-band.
- Low noise figure (~5 dB), making them ideal for long-haul systems.

Disadvantages:

- Limited gain bandwidth in the S-band (lower wavelengths).

Raman Amplifier

A distributed amplification technique where the signal is amplified along the entire fiber length using the Raman effect.

Advantages:

- Can extend the amplification range beyond the C-band, including the S-band.
- Distributed amplification reduces the nonlinear effects seen in discrete amplifiers.

Disadvantages:

- More complex to implement than EDFAs, and can introduce noise if not properly managed.

Hybrid Amplifier (EDFA + Raman)

These amplifiers combine the strengths of both EDFAs and Raman amplifiers to extend the gain bandwidth while reducing the overall noise.

When and Why to Choose a Specific Amplifier?

- **EDFA for Long-Haul DWDM**: EDFAs are typically used in long-haul DWDM systems where multiple channels in the C-band need to be amplified efficiently.
- **Raman for Ultra-Long Haul and High-Capacity Systems**: Raman amplifiers or hybrid amplifiers are used in ultra-long-haul systems or when higher capacity (beyond the C-band) is required.

Example Use Case

In a 100G long-haul DWDM system spanning 1500 km, **EDFA amplifiers** are deployed at regular intervals to boost the signal strength without the need for electrical regeneration. In a submarine optical cable system requiring ultra-long distances, **Raman amplifiers** are combined with EDFAs to ensure low-noise amplification across the entire fiber span.

Power and Reach Considerations in DWDM Networks

Power Budget and Signal Reach

The power budget of a DWDM system determines how far a signal can travel before it needs amplification or regeneration. It depends on the **transmit power**, **insertion loss**, and **receiver sensitivity**.

Transmit Power:

The optical power output of the transceivers or transponders, typically measured in dBm. Higher power transceivers can extend the reach of the signal.

Example: A transceiver with a power output of 0 dBm can transmit over 80 km without amplification, but over longer distances, the signal will degrade without amplification.

Insertion Loss:

Each component (e.g., multiplexers, connectors, fibers) introduces insertion loss, which reduces the signal power. In long-haul systems, insertion loss must be carefully managed to prevent signal degradation.

Receiver Sensitivity:

The minimum optical power level at which the receiver can detect the signal without errors. Advanced modulation formats (e.g., QPSK, 16-QAM) may require higher signal quality, reducing the allowable transmission distance before signal regeneration is needed.

Power Budget Calculation:

```
Power Budget (dB) = Tx_power - Rx_sensitivity
Max_allowable_loss = Power Budget - System_margin

Where:
- Tx_power: Transmitter output power (dBm)
- Rx_sensitivity: Receiver sensitivity (dBm)
- System_margin: Typically 3-4 dB
```

Link Budget Calculation

The link budget is the calculation used to determine whether the optical signal will reach the receiver with enough power for error-free communication.

$$\text{Link Budget} = P_{TX} - \sum \text{Losses} + G_{amp} - M$$

Where:

- P_{TX} is the transmit power (dBm),
- $\sum$Losses is the total insertion loss along the link (dB),
- G_{amp} is the gain from amplifiers (dB),
- M is the margin for safety (dB).

Example Use Case

In a 200G DWDM system, a link budget calculation shows that a transponder with an output power of 5 dBm, coupled with EDFA amplification, can achieve a reach of 600 km. The total insertion loss of the fiber, multiplexers, and ROADMs is calculated to be 15 dB. With a safety margin of 3 dB, the network is designed to meet the required reach without signal regeneration.

Modulation Formats in DWDM Systems

Modulation formats in DWDM systems determine how data is encoded onto the optical carrier, impacting both the **capacity** and **reach** of the system. As network speeds increase, advanced modulation formats enable more data to be transmitted over each wavelength, but they also introduce trade-offs in terms of complexity, power consumption, and sensitivity to impairments.

What is Optical Modulation?

Optical modulation refers to the process of encoding data onto an optical carrier wave (light) by varying one or more of its properties, such as amplitude, phase, or frequency. The choice of modulation format directly influences the **spectral efficiency**, **reach**, and **OSNR (Optical Signal-to-Noise Ratio)** requirements of the DWDM system.

Key Modulation Formats in DWDM

On-Off Keying (OOK):

The simplest form of modulation where the light is either turned on (representing a "1") or off (representing a "0"). This format is used in lower-speed systems but lacks spectral efficiency.

Advantages:

- Simple and inexpensive to implement.
- Low complexity, making it suitable for short-reach applications.

Disadvantages:

- Poor spectral efficiency.
- Limited reach and high power consumption at higher data rates.

Use Case: OOK is often used in **10G DWDM** links for short-distance transmission (up to 80 km) where power consumption and complexity are less of a concern.

Quadrature Phase-Shift Keying (QPSK):

QPSK modulates the phase of the carrier wave to encode two bits of information per symbol, offering better spectral efficiency than OOK. It is widely used in **100G** coherent DWDM systems.

Advantages:

- Better spectral efficiency compared to OOK.
- Improved reach and OSNR tolerance, especially in coherent systems.

Disadvantages:

- Higher complexity in signal generation and detection.
- Increased power consumption due to the need for digital signal processing (DSP).

Use Case: QPSK is used in **100G and 200G DWDM** links for metro and long-haul transmission, balancing capacity and reach.

16-QAM (Quadrature Amplitude Modulation):

This format combines both amplitude and phase modulation to encode four bits per symbol, providing higher spectral efficiency than QPSK. However, it requires higher OSNR and is more susceptible to fiber impairments.

Advantages:

- High spectral efficiency, enabling higher capacity on each wavelength.
- Suitable for high-bandwidth applications, such as **400G** networks.

Disadvantages:

- Requires higher OSNR, making it less suitable for long-haul transmission without amplification.
- More sensitive to nonlinear effects and chromatic dispersion.

Use Case: **16-QAM** is commonly used in **400G DWDM** systems for **metro** networks, where higher capacity is needed, and transmission distances are moderate.

64-QAM:

A higher-order modulation format that encodes six bits per symbol. It offers even greater spectral efficiency than 16-QAM but requires very high OSNR and is limited to short-reach applications.

Use Case: **64-QAM** is typically used in **data center interconnect (DCI)** applications where the transmission distance is short, but the demand for bandwidth is very high.

Coherent Modulation

Coherent detection and modulation are key advancements in DWDM technology, enabling higher data rates (100G, 200G, 400G, and beyond) while extending reach. Coherent systems use advanced DSP techniques to mitigate impairments such as chromatic dispersion and polarization mode dispersion (PMD).

Advantages of Coherent Modulation:

- **Longer Reach**: Coherent systems can achieve transmission distances of over 1000 km without regeneration.
- **Better OSNR Performance**: Coherent detection improves the system's tolerance to noise and other impairments.
- **Spectral Efficiency**: Higher-order modulation formats (e.g., 16-QAM) are supported, increasing capacity per wavelength.

Example: In a long-haul **400G DWDM** network, coherent QPSK modulation allows for long-distance transmission with minimal signal degradation. The use of DSP compensates for dispersion and nonlinearities, extending the reach of the system.

Modulation Format Selection Criteria

- **Capacity Requirements**: Higher-order modulation formats (e.g., 16-QAM, 64-QAM) provide greater capacity but require better OSNR and shorter transmission distances.
- **Reach Requirements**: For long-haul networks, lower-order modulation formats (e.g., QPSK) offer better reach and resilience to impairments.
- **Power and Complexity**: Advanced modulation formats require more power and DSP resources, increasing the complexity and cost of the transceiver.

Practical Example: A service provider deploying a **200G metro DWDM** network selects **16-QAM modulation** for its high capacity and moderate reach, ensuring that bandwidth demands are met without the need for excessive amplification.

Network Design Considerations: Power, Reach, and Amplification

Power Budget and Signal Reach in DWDM Networks

Designing a DWDM network requires careful calculation of the power budget, ensuring that the transmitted signal reaches the receiver with sufficient power for error-free detection. The power budget must account for **attenuation, insertion loss**, and **amplifier gain**.

Power Budget Formula:

$$P_{RX}=P_{TX}-\sum(\text{Losses})+G_{amp}-M$$

Where:

- P_{RX} is the received power,
- P_{TX} is the transmit power,

- $\sum$(Losses) is the total loss from fibers, connectors, and multiplexers,
- G_{amp} is the gain from amplifiers,
- M is the safety margin (typically 3-5 dB).

Example Calculation: For a 200 km long-haul link using **100G QPSK**, the transmit power is 5 dBm, and the total loss (fiber + components) is calculated to be 30 dB. Using EDFAs with a gain of 20 dB, the system achieves a power budget that supports the required reach.

Amplification and Signal Regeneration

Amplifiers are essential for extending the reach of DWDM systems, compensating for signal loss over long distances. However, the placement and type of amplifier depend on the system's design and requirements.

Erbium-Doped Fiber Amplifier (EDFA): Used for amplifying multiple DWDM channels simultaneously in the C-band or L-band. EDFAs are widely used in both metro and long-haul networks.

Example: In a **100G long-haul DWDM** system, EDFAs are placed at intervals of 80-100 km to compensate for fiber attenuation, allowing the signal to travel up to 1000 km without regeneration.

Raman Amplifier: Distributed amplification that boosts the signal along the entire fiber length, rather than at discrete points, improving performance over ultra-long distances.

Dispersion Compensation

Chromatic dispersion causes light pulses to spread as they travel through fiber, leading to inter-symbol interference and signal degradation, especially in long-haul systems. To manage this, **dispersion compensation** techniques are used:

Dispersion-Compensating Fiber (DCF): Specialized fiber that compensates for chromatic dispersion by introducing negative dispersion.

Digital Signal Processing (DSP): In coherent systems, DSP is used to digitally compensate for dispersion, eliminating the need for DCF.

Example: In a **400G coherent DWDM** system, DSP compensates for chromatic dispersion, ensuring clear signal reception over distances of up to 2000 km.

Chromatic Dispersion (CD) and Polarization Mode Dispersion (PMD) in DWDM Systems

Chromatic dispersion (CD) and polarization mode dispersion (PMD) are two critical impairments that can significantly degrade OSNR and performance in DWDM systems. Both CD and PMD cause pulse broadening, leading to increased intersymbol interference (ISI) and thus degrading system performance.

Chromatic Dispersion (CD)

Chromatic Dispersion (CD) is a critical factor that affects the transmission performance of optical fiber communication systems. As we move towards higher data rates and longer transmission distances, understanding and mitigating the effects of chromatic dispersion becomes essential for maintaining signal integrity and optimizing network performance. This article delves into what chromatic dispersion is, its causes, and how it affects optical communication systems, along with methods of compensation.

What is Chromatic Dispersion?

Chromatic dispersion is the phenomenon where different wavelengths of light travel at different speeds through an optical fiber. In essence, dispersion causes the broadening of optical pulses as they propagate through the fiber. This pulse broadening leads to inter-symbol interference (ISI), limiting the maximum transmission distance and data rate.

How Chromatic Dispersion Occurs

Optical signals transmitted through fiber consist of multiple wavelengths. These different wavelength components travel at different velocities, resulting in **group velocity dispersion (GVD)**. This effect is especially pronounced when the **laser source** is imperfect, meaning that it emits multiple frequencies/wavelengths instead of a single wavelength. The velocity of light at a specific wavelength (λ) can be expressed as:

$$V = \frac{C}{n(\lambda)}$$

Where:

- V is the velocity of light in the fiber,
- C is the speed of light in a vacuum,
- n(λ) is the refractive index of the fiber for a given wavelength.

Types of Dispersion

1. **Material Dispersion:** Material dispersion arises due to the wavelength dependence of the refractive index of the core material in the fiber. As the refractive index changes with wavelength, different wavelength components of the light pulse travel at different speeds, leading to pulse broadening.
2. **Waveguide Dispersion:** Waveguide dispersion occurs because light travels differently in the core and cladding of the optical fiber. This dispersion is related to the fiber's structure, particularly the size of the core and the refractive index difference between the core and cladding.

Zero-Dispersion Wavelength (λD)

In single-mode fibers (SMFs), **zero-dispersion wavelength** is the point at which material dispersion and waveguide dispersion cancel each other out, resulting in minimal dispersion. For most **pure silica fibers**, the zero-dispersion wavelength occurs around **1273 nm**. However, in silica fibers doped with **germanium dioxide (GeO2)**, the zero-dispersion wavelength shifts towards **1310 nm**, which is an important wavelength for optical communications.

Zero-Dispersion Wavelength in G.652 Fiber:

- **Pure Silica:** Zero-dispersion at 1273 nm,
- **Silica + GeO2:** Zero-dispersion at 1310 nm.

For long-distance transmission, modern optical fibers are designed to shift the zero-dispersion wavelength closer to the minimum-loss window at around **1550 nm**, where attenuation is minimal, making it ideal for high-capacity and long-haul communications.

The Impact of Chromatic Dispersion on Optical Networks

Chromatic dispersion can cause significant degradation in the performance of optical networks, especially at higher data rates and over longer distances.

Effects of Dispersion:

1. **Pulse Broadening:** As the optical signal travels through the fiber, different wavelength components arrive at the receiver at different times due to chromatic dispersion, leading to pulse broadening. This broadening reduces the distinction between consecutive pulses, leading to **inter-symbol interference (ISI)**, which limits data rates and transmission distances.
2. **Signal Distortion:** Dispersion-induced pulse broadening leads to **signal distortion**, particularly in systems operating at high data rates. This distortion causes overlap between adjacent pulses, further exacerbating ISI.

3. **Transmission Limitations:** Chromatic dispersion restricts the maximum transmission distance of optical signals. If left uncompensated, it can lead to increased bit-error rates (BER) and necessitate more frequent signal regeneration or amplification.

Methods for Compensating Chromatic Dispersion

To ensure efficient transmission over long distances, optical networks employ various techniques to mitigate the effects of chromatic dispersion. The most common methods include:

1. **Dispersion Compensating Fiber (DCF):** DCF is a type of fiber that has a high negative dispersion coefficient, typically used to compensate for the positive dispersion of standard single-mode fibers. A spool of DCF can be inserted into the optical link to counteract the dispersion accumulated over a longer transmission distance.
   - Typical dispersion of DCF: -80 ps/(nm·km),
   - **Example:** A 20 km length of DCF can compensate for the dispersion in a 100 km span of standard single-mode fiber (SMF).
2. **Fiber Bragg Grating (FBG):** FBGs are another form of dispersion compensation, where a series of FBGs or a long FBG is written into a fiber segment to perform dispersion compensation. This method is efficient but has relatively high insertion loss.
   - FBG-based compensators are typically co-located with **erbium-doped fiber amplifiers (EDFAs)** to counteract the insertion loss.
3. **Coherent Detection and Digital Signal Processing (DSP):** Modern high-speed coherent optical systems use **digital signal processing (DSP)** to compensate for chromatic dispersion and other impairments. This approach eliminates the need for physical compensating devices, making it highly effective for high-capacity long-haul networks.
   - DSP-based compensation allows for real-time correction of dispersion and polarization mode dispersion (PMD) in the digital domain.

Chromatic dispersion is one of the most significant impairments in optical communication systems, especially as we move towards higher data rates and longer transmission distances. By understanding the mechanisms behind chromatic dispersion and employing compensation techniques such as **dispersion compensating fibers (DCF)**, **Fiber Bragg Gratings (FBG)**, and **digital signal processing (DSP)**, network operators can ensure efficient and reliable transmission in modern DWDM systems.

As optical networks continue to evolve, mitigating chromatic dispersion will remain a critical factor in optimizing performance, reducing costs, and enabling the high-capacity, long-distance communication required by today's data-driven world.

Polarization Mode Dispersion (PMD)

Polarization Mode Dispersion (PMD) results from imperfections in the optical fiber that cause the different polarization modes of light to travel at different speeds, leading to differential group delay (DGD). Unlike CD, PMD is a random, time-varying effect and is more challenging to compensate for.

PMD Formula

The time delay Δt_{PMD} caused by PMD over a fiber length L is given by:

$$\Delta t_{PMD} = D_{PMD} \cdot \sqrt{L}$$

Where:

- D_{PMD} is the PMD coefficient in ps/sqrt(km).
- L is the fiber length in km.

Typical values of DPMD for standard single-mode fibers range from **0.1 to 1 ps/km**. For modern fibers, the PMD coefficient is usually kept below **0.2 ps/km**.

PMD Tolerance

The tolerance to PMD decreases as the bit rate increases. PMD causes signal distortion that can reduce the effective signal-to-noise ratio (SNR), requiring advanced compensation techniques, such as **adaptive PMD compensators** that use feedback loops to reduce the impact of DGD.

Compensation Techniques

- **Optical PMD Compensators**: These are typically deployed in long-haul systems and can adapt to the changing PMD characteristics of the fiber.
- **Digital Signal Processing (DSP)**: In coherent systems, DSP techniques are used to mitigate PMD effects by dynamically adjusting the signal to compensate for time-varying delays.

Impact on OSNR

Both CD and PMD directly impact the **Optical Signal-to-Noise Ratio (OSNR)** by causing pulse broadening and intersymbol interference (ISI). For long-haul DWDM systems, CD and PMD must be carefully managed to prevent OSNR degradation.

OSNR Penalty Due to CD and PMD

The **OSNR penalty** caused by chromatic dispersion and PMD can be calculated using empirical models that take into account the pulse broadening and DGD introduced by the fiber. The penalty increases exponentially with the accumulated dispersion or DGD:

$$\text{OSNR Penalty (dB)} = 10\log_{10}\left(\frac{1}{1 - f(\Delta t, \Delta t_{PMD})}\right)$$

Where $f(\Delta t, \Delta t_{PMD})$ is a function of the accumulated dispersion and DGD.

Example: 100G Coherent DWDM System

In a **100G coherent DWDM system** spanning 500 km, with a PMD coefficient of **0.2 ps/km** and a chromatic dispersion of **16 ps/nm/km**, the accumulated PMD and CD would result in significant OSNR penalties without compensation.

For a **500 km link**:

- **Accumulated CD** = 16 ps/nm/km×500 km=8000 ps/nm.
- **Accumulated PMD** = 0.2 ps/sqrt(km)×500 km=4.47 ps.

With compensation applied (DCF and DSP), the OSNR can be restored to acceptable levels, ensuring error-free transmission.

Nonlinear Effects and OSNR

In addition to CD and PMD, **nonlinear effects** such as **Four-Wave Mixing (FWM)**, **Self-Phase Modulation (SPM)**, and **Stimulated Raman Scattering (SRS)** can further degrade OSNR, particularly in fully loaded DWDM systems with high power levels.

Nonlinear Penalties

Nonlinear effects introduce additional noise, reducing the effective OSNR. The nonlinear OSNR penalty can be calculated as:

$$\text{OSNR}_{\text{NL}} = \frac{P_{\text{signal}}}{P_{\text{ASE}} + P_{\text{NL}}}$$

Where P_{NL} is the noise power due to nonlinear effects.

For example, **Four-Wave Mixing (FWM)** is more prominent in systems with dense channel spacing and low chromatic dispersion. It generates new frequencies that interfere with adjacent channels, leading to cross-talk and OSNR degradation.

Compensation for Nonlinear Effects

- **Power Reduction**: Reducing the launch power per channel can minimize nonlinear effects.
- **Dispersion Compensation**: Proper dispersion management can mitigate FWM and other nonlinear impairments.
- **Advanced Modulation Formats**: Coherent detection and advanced modulation formats (e.g., QPSK, 16-QAM) with DSP can help mitigate the impact of nonlinearities on OSNR.

Network Design: Choosing Components for Power, Reach, and Cost Optimization

Trade-offs Between Capacity, Power, and Reach

When designing a DWDM network, trade-offs between **capacity**, **power consumption**, and **reach** are critical. Higher-capacity systems (e.g., 400G, 800G) often require more advanced modulation formats, which increase power consumption and reduce reach due to higher OSNR requirements.

Power Consumption per Gigabit: Lower-order modulation formats (e.g., QPSK) may consume more power per gigabit due to longer transmission distances and the need for amplification. However, higher-order formats (e.g., 16-QAM) offer better spectral efficiency but require higher power to maintain signal quality.

Example: In a **400G metro DWDM network**, operators choose **16-QAM modulation** for its spectral efficiency, even though it increases power consumption. To mitigate this, they optimize the network by using shorter amplifier spans and fewer regeneration points.

Cost Optimization Through Component Selection

Transponders and Amplifiers: Selecting the appropriate transponder and amplifier combination is key to balancing cost and performance. Lower-cost **direct-detection transponders** may be suitable for short-haul links, while **coherent transponders** with advanced DSP are required for long-haul networks.

ROADM Complexity: While ROADMs provide flexibility and scalability, they also increase initial deployment costs. In static networks, **fixed multiplexers** might offer a more cost-effective solution.

Example: In a **regional DWDM network**, fixed multiplexers are used at edge nodes to reduce costs, while **dynamic ROADMs** are deployed at core nodes for flexibility and bandwidth management.

Chapter 12

Network Protection and Reliability

Chapter 12
Network Protection and Reliability

"In optical networks, failure is not an option, it's a scenario to be managed." - Alan Huang

---

The evolution of optical networks has brought unprecedented capacity and speed to modern communications. However, with increased dependency on these networks comes the need to ensure their reliability and minimize downtime during failures. Failures in optical networks can be caused by fiber cuts, equipment malfunctions, environmental disruptions, or human errors.This chapter delves into the various protection mechanisms employed in optical networks to ensure reliability, ranging from link and line protection to ring and client-layer protections. Each protection mechanism has its distinct role, implementation techniques, and trade-offs. A detailed understanding of these systems enables network architects to design robust and efficient networks that minimize downtime and ensure business continuity.

Fundamentals of Network Protection

Network protection is categorized into **proactive** and **reactive** approaches:

- **Proactive Protection**: Preconfigured backup paths or resources that are activated automatically upon failure (e.g., 1+1 protection).
- **Reactive Restoration**: Dynamic rerouting of traffic using available network resources after failure detection (e.g., mesh restoration).

Key metrics for assessing protection mechanisms:

- **Switching Time**: Time required to switch from a working to a protection path.
- **Resource Utilization**: Amount of additional resources required for protection.
- **Cost Efficiency**: Balance between reliability and the cost of implementation.
- **Scalability**: Ability to adapt to growing network requirements.

Categories of Network Protection

Network protection mechanisms are broadly classified as:

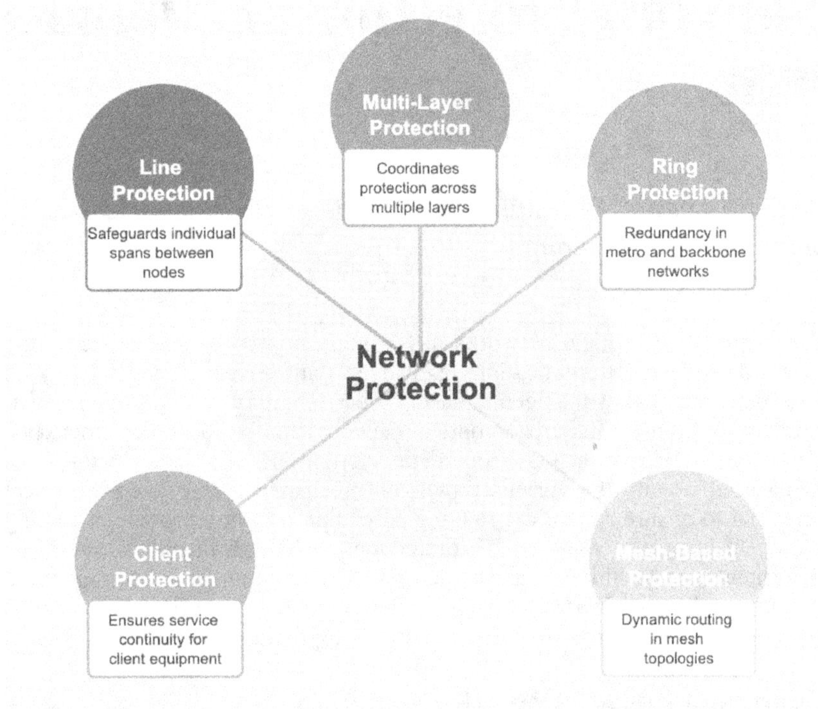

Category	Description
Line Protection	Safeguards individual spans or links between two nodes.
Ring Protection	Provides redundancy in ring topologies, commonly used in metro and backbone networks.
Client Protection	Operates at higher layers, ensuring service continuity for client equipment.
Mesh-Based Protection	Dynamically reroutes traffic in mesh topologies, optimizing resource utilization.
Multi-Layer Protection	Coordinates protection across multiple network layers for comprehensive reliability.

Line Protection Mechanisms

Optical Line Protection (OLP)

OLP provides fiber-level redundancy and is essential for safeguarding critical spans.

Type	Working Principle	Advantages	Disadvantages	Applications
1+1 OLP	Transmits traffic over both working and protection fibers simultaneously; receiver selects best signal.	Fast switching; high reliability.	High resource usage.	Long-haul critical links.
1:1 OLP	Uses protection fiber only during failure; traffic is switched to protection path upon failure.	Efficient resource utilization.	Slight switchover delay.	Regional and metro networks.

Y-Cable Protection

Uses a Y-splitter to duplicate signals for two transponders (working and protection).

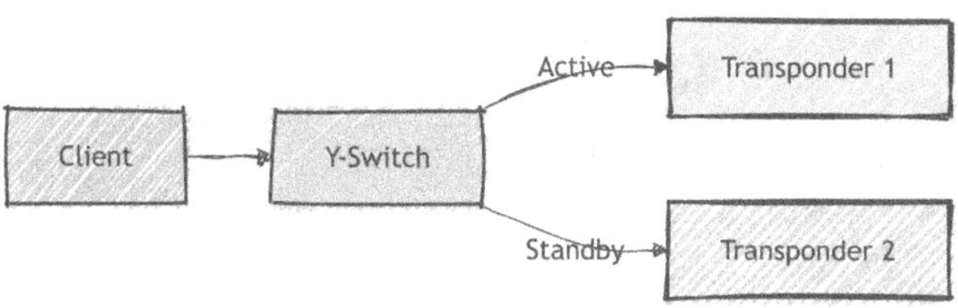

Advantages	Disadvantages
Simple and cost-effective for short spans.	Signal splitting reduces optical power.
Protects against transponder failures.	Not suitable for long-haul spans.

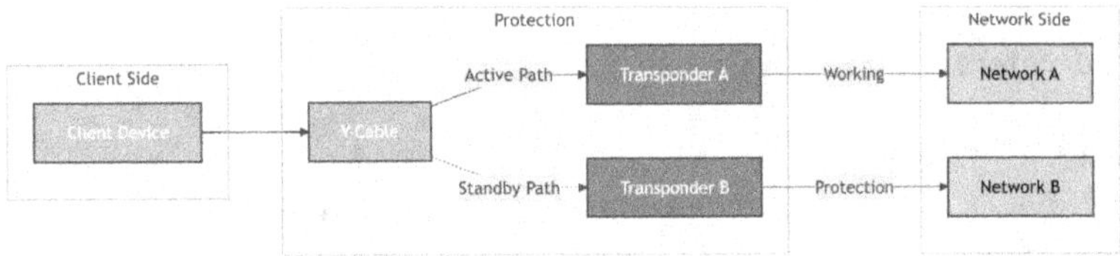

Multiplex Section Protection (MSP)

- Protects multiplexed sections in SDH/SONET systems.
- Configurations:
    - **1+1 MSP**: Always active backup.
    - **1:N MSP**: One protection path shared among multiple working paths.

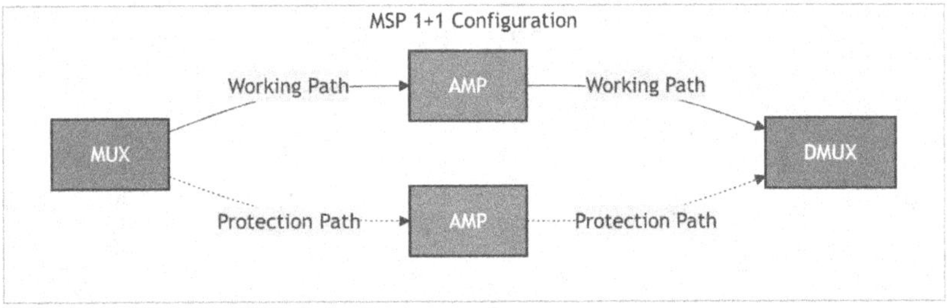

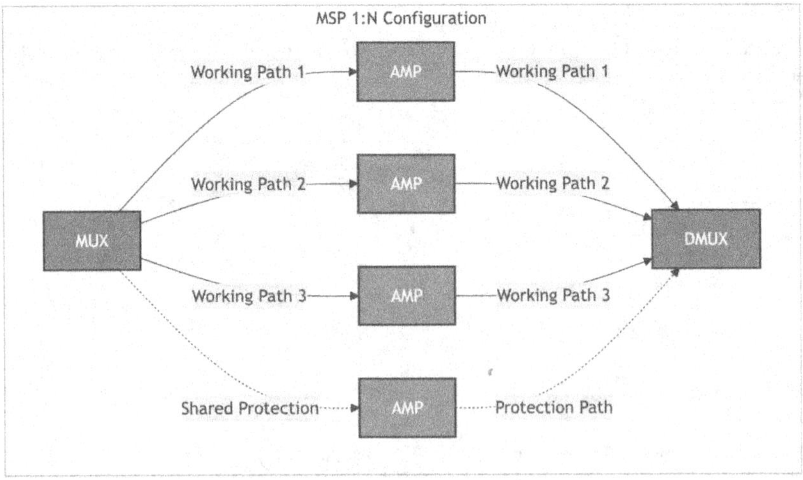

Ring Protection Mechanisms

Ring protection is commonly used in metro and backbone networks where nodes are interconnected in circular layouts.

Type	Description	Advantages	Disadvantages	Applications
Unidirectional Path-Switched Ring (UPSR)	Traffic flows in one direction; backup paths are pre-configured.	Low latency; fast restoration.	Idle bandwidth on protection paths.	Metro and access networks.
Bidirectional Line-Switched Ring (BLSR)	Traffic flows in both directions; uses opposite direction for protection.	Efficient resource utilization.	More complex management.	Backbone networks.
2-Fiber BLSR	Both working and protection paths share the same fibers.	Suitable for medium-capacity networks.	Limited capacity compared to 4-fiber.	Metro networks.
4-Fiber BLSR	Separate fibers for working and protection paths.	High capacity; resilient to failures.	Higher cost and complexity.	High-capacity backbones.

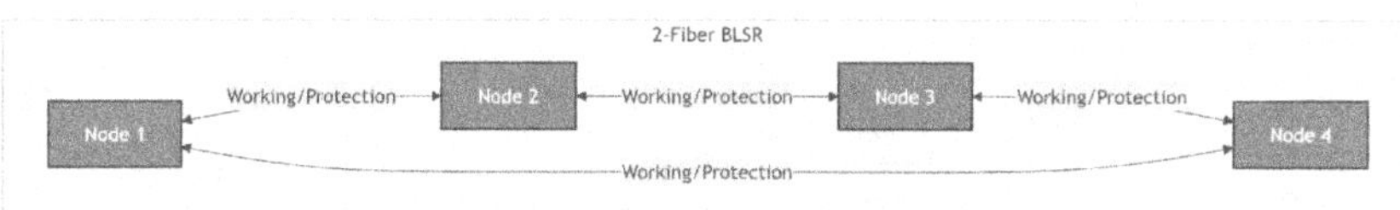

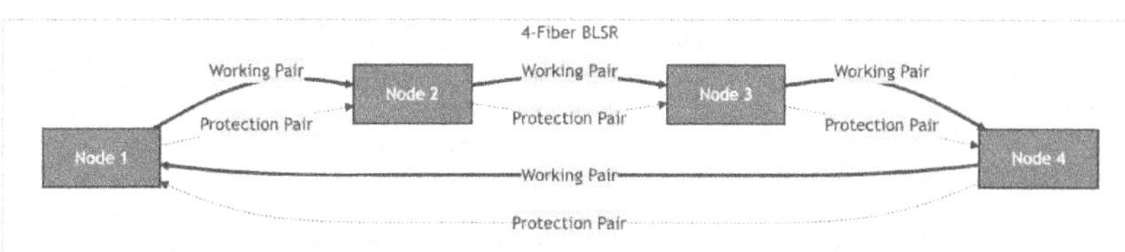

Client Protection Mechanisms

Ethernet Protection

Redundancy at the Ethernet layer ensures continuity for client services.

- **Mechanisms**: Link Aggregation (LAG), Rapid Spanning Tree Protocol (RSTP), and Ethernet Ring Protection Switching (ERPS).

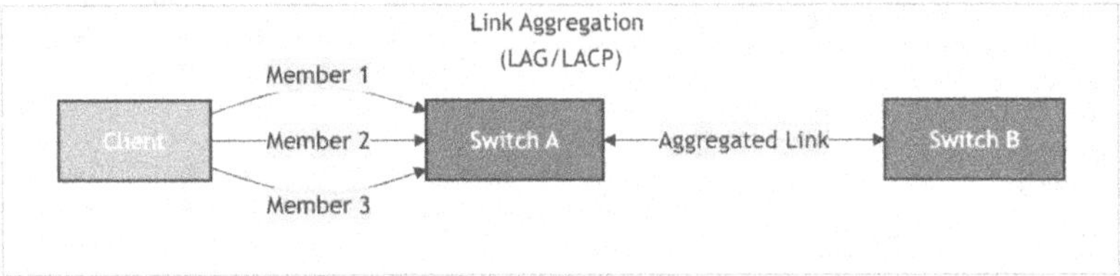

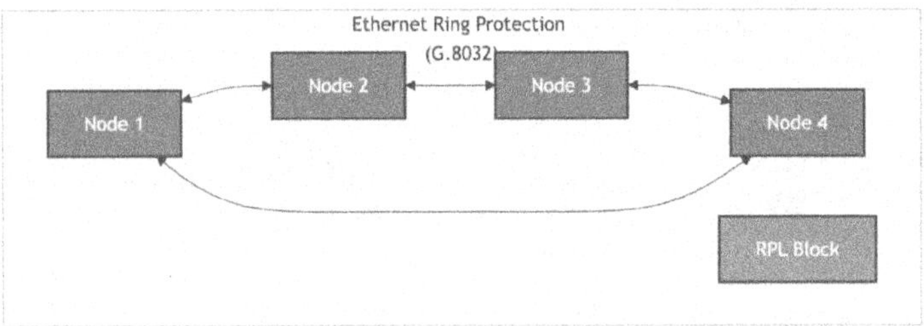

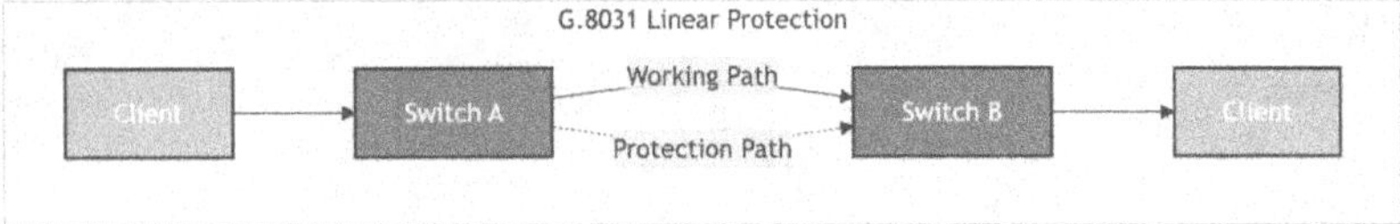

Advantages	**Disadvantages**
Universal compatibility across systems.	Latency during failover.
Operates above the optical layer.	Less granular than OTN-level protection.

OTN Sub-Network Connection (SNC) Protection

Provides circuit-level protection at the ODUk layer.

Type	Description	Advantages	Disadvantages
1+1 SNC	Dual signals for highest reliability.	High reliability; fast recovery.	Resource-intensive.
1:1 SNC	Reserved backup path used only during failure.	Efficient resource utilization.	Slight switching delay.

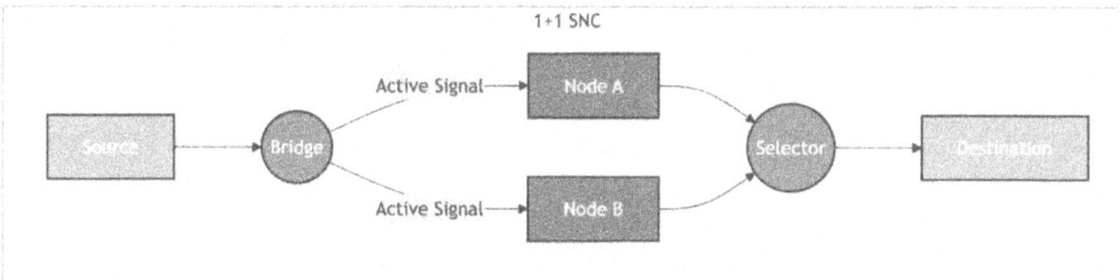

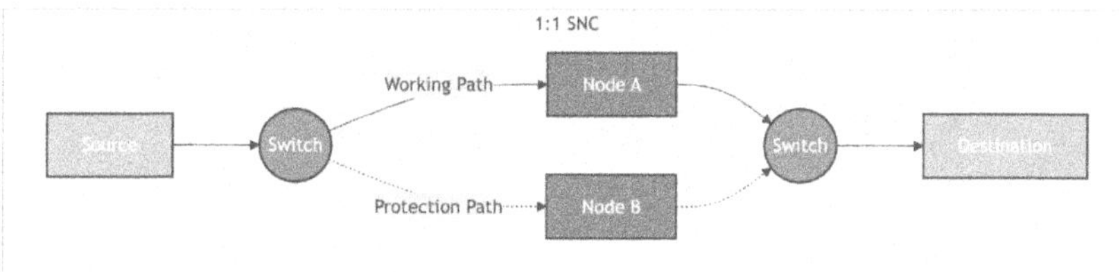

Mesh-Based Protection

Type	Description	Advantages	Disadvantages
Shared Mesh Protection (SMP)	Dynamically shares backup resources among multiple connections.	Optimizes resource usage.	Higher switching times compared to pre-configured paths.
Dedicated Mesh Restoration	Precomputed backup paths activated only during failures.	Fast restoration.	Consumes more resources than SMP.

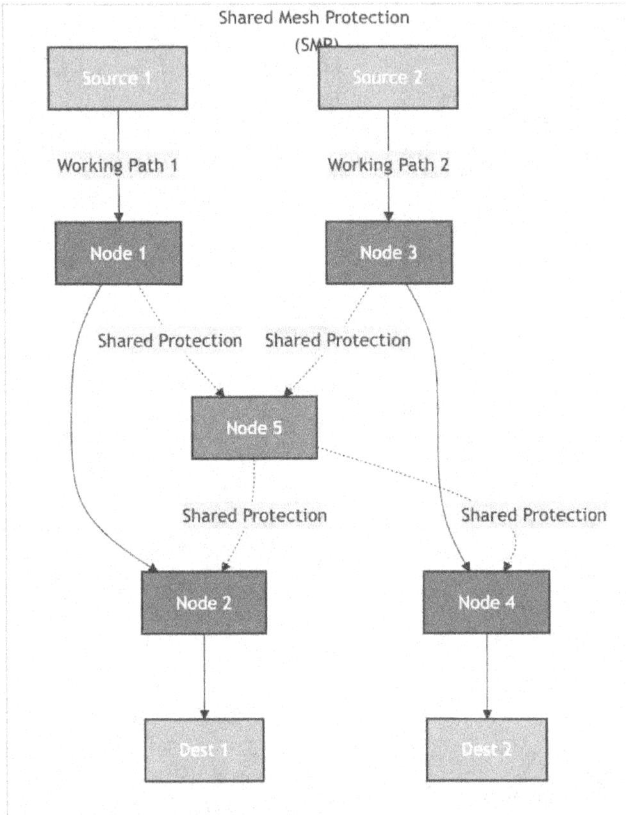

Restoration vs. Protection

Restoration and protection are two complementary approaches to ensure network reliability. While protection involves pre-configured paths for instant failover, restoration dynamically reroutes traffic after a failure has occurred.

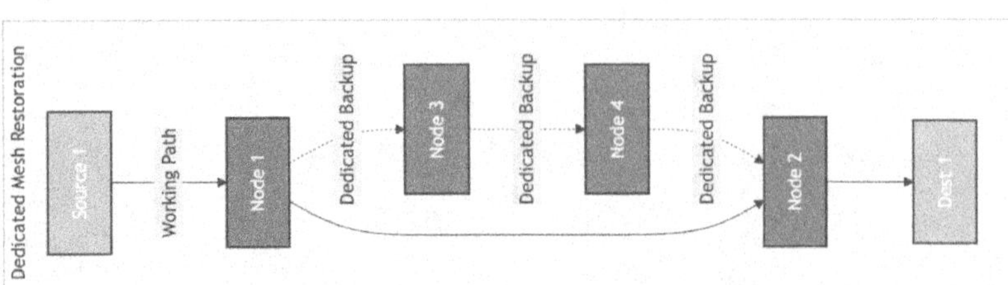

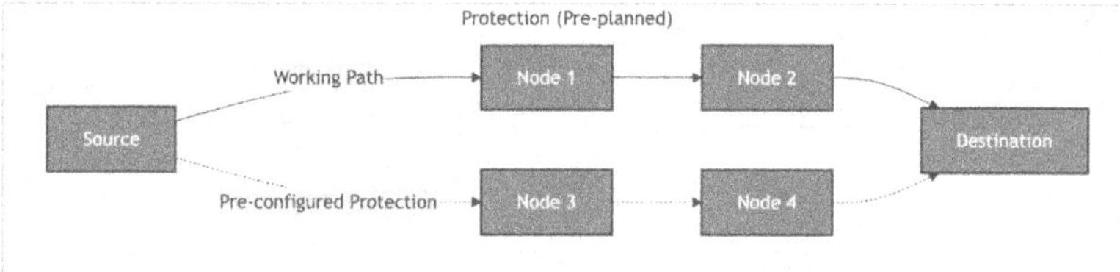

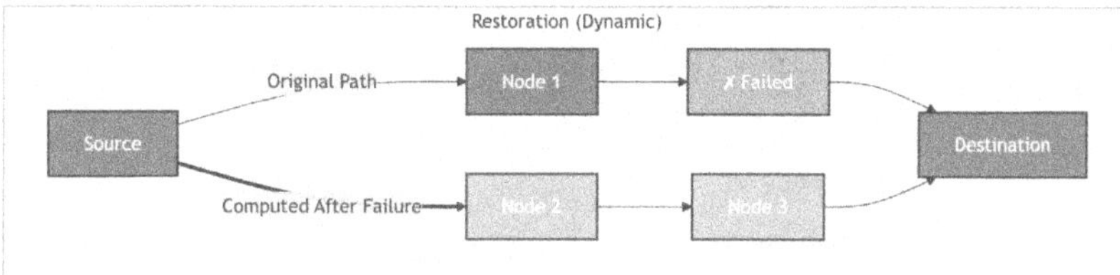

Aspect	Protection	Restoration
Switching Time	Sub-50ms (very fast).	Seconds to minutes (slower).
Resource Usage	Pre-allocated resources (higher usage).	Utilizes spare capacity dynamically.
Cost	Higher due to dedicated paths.	Lower due to shared resources.
Scalability	Limited by pre-configured paths.	Highly scalable for large networks.
Complexity	Relatively simple.	Higher due to real-time computation.

Advanced Protection Mechanisms

Dual-Homing Protection

Dual-homing involves connecting a network device (e.g., client equipment) to two different nodes or networks, ensuring redundancy in case one fails.

Advantages	Disadvantages
Protects against node and network failures.	Requires additional hardware and configuration.
Provides path diversity for higher reliability.	Complex routing policies may be needed.

Applications:

- Data center interconnects.
- Mission-critical services requiring ultra-high availability.

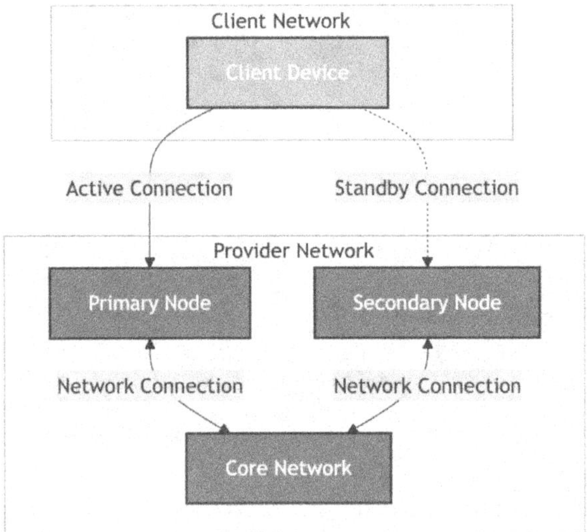

SDN-Controlled Protection

Software-Defined Networking (SDN) centralizes control of protection mechanisms, dynamically reallocating resources in real-time.

Advantages	**Disadvantages**
Real-time adaptability to network conditions.	Dependence on SDN controller reliability.
Optimized resource allocation.	Requires full network-wide SDN implementation.

Applications:

- Dynamic traffic engineering.
- Flexible restoration in complex mesh networks.

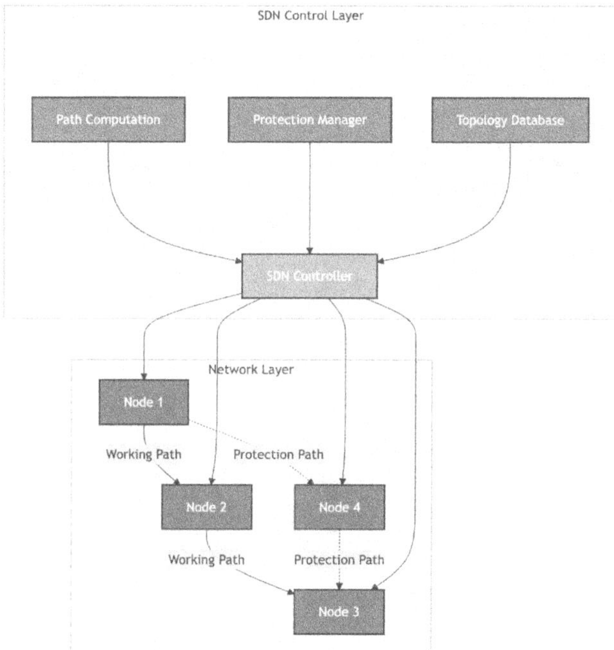

Disjoint Path Protection

Disjoint path protection ensures the working and protection paths are physically or geographically diverse to minimize risks of simultaneous failures.

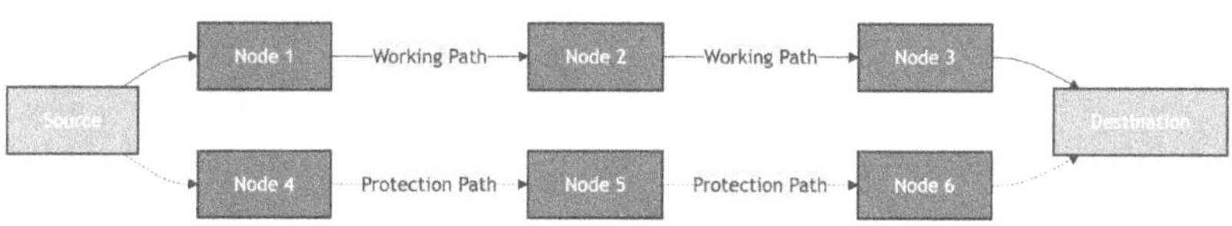

Advantages	Disadvantages
High resilience to localized disasters.	Higher cost due to diverse routing requirements.

Applications:

- Submarine cable systems.
- Networks in disaster-prone regions.

Shared Risk Group (SRG) Protection

This approach identifies components or links with shared risks (e.g., routes in the same duct) and ensures backup paths avoid those risks.

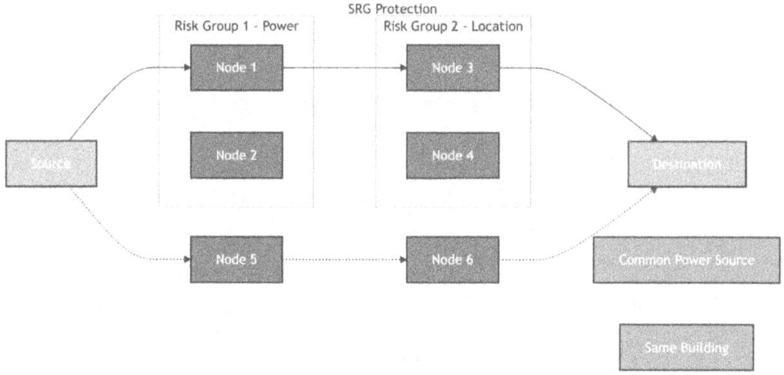

Advantages	Disadvantages
Enhanced resilience to correlated failures.	Complex implementation and management.

Applications:

- Submarine cables.
- Large-scale carrier networks.

Comparison and Selection Criteria

Protection Type	Switching Time	Resource Utilization	Extra Traffic	Implementation Complexity	Cost
OLP 1+1	<50ms	High	No	Low	High
OLP 1:1	<100ms	Medium	Yes	Medium	Medium
Y-Cable	<50ms	Medium	No	Low	Low
Client 1+1	<50ms	High	No	Low	High
LAG/LACP	Variable	Medium	Yes	Medium	Medium

DWDM Protection Comparison

Protection Type	Switching Time	Resource Usage	Scalability	Cost	Application
OCh 1+1	<50ms	High	Good	High	Critical wavelengths
OMS 1+1	<50ms	Medium	Excellent	Medium	Multi-wavelength protection
OUPSR	<50ms	Medium	Good	Medium	Ring networks
OBLSR	<50ms	Low	Excellent	Low	Metro rings

OTN Protection Comparison

Protection Type	Switching Time	Resource Usage	Management Complexity	Cost	Application
ODU SNC/N	<50ms	High	Low	High	Client protection
ODU SNC/S	<50ms	Medium	Medium	Medium	Enhanced monitoring
OTU 1+1	<50ms	High	Low	High	Line protection
Multi-layer	Variable	Very High	High	Very High	Critical services

Performance Parameters

Parameter	1+1	1:1	1:N
Switching Time	<50ms	<100ms	<100ms
Insertion Loss	3-4dB	1-2dB	2-3dB
Return Loss	>45dB	>45dB	>45dB
PDL	<0.3dB	<0.3dB	<0.3dB
Protection Capacity	100%	100%	1/N
Extra Traffic	No	Yes	Yes

Protection Features and Capabilities

Feature	1+1	1:1	1:N	Ring	Mesh
Automatic Switching	Yes	Yes	Yes	Yes	Yes
Revertive Switching	Optional	Yes	Yes	Optional	Optional
Extra Traffic	No	Yes	Yes	Depends	Yes
Hold-off Timer	Yes	Yes	Yes	Yes	Yes
Wait-to-Restore	Yes	Yes	Yes	Yes	Yes
Bidirectional Switching	Optional	Yes	Yes	Yes	Yes
APS Protocol	No	Yes	Yes	Yes	Yes
Protection Priority	No	Yes	Yes	Yes	Yes
Shared Protection	No	No	Yes	Yes	Yes
Sub-50ms Switching	Yes	No	No	Yes	Varies

Control Plane Protection Comparison

Feature	ASON	WSON	GMPLS	SDN
Control Architecture	Distributed	Distributed/Centralized	Distributed	Centralized
Protection Setup Time	Medium	Fast	Medium	Very Fast
Resource Optimization	Good	Excellent	Good	Excellent
Multi-domain Support	Limited	Good	Good	Excellent
Scalability	Medium	High	Medium	Very High
Implementation Complexity	High	Medium	High	Medium
Protection Types Supported	Multiple	Wavelength-based	LSP-based	Flow-based
Recovery Time	<100ms	<100ms	<100ms	Variable
Protection Path Computation	Distributed	Centralized/Distributed	Distributed	Centralized

Enterprise Applications

Application Type	Protection Recommendation	Alternative	Recovery Time	Remarks
Financial Trading	OLP 1+1 + Client 1+1	ASON/WSON with Fast Restoration	<50ms	Ultra-low latency requirement
Data Center Interconnect	OMS 1+1 or OBLSR	Mesh Protection	<50ms	High bandwidth, multiple wavelengths
Enterprise WAN	UPSR/SNCP	OLP 1:1	<50ms	Cost-effective, simple operation
Disaster Recovery	Multi-layer (ODU+OCh)	Mesh Protection	<100ms	Geographic diversity critical
Cloud Connectivity	OLP 1:1 or Y-Cable	OUPSR	<100ms	Balance of cost and protection

Service Provider Applications

Network Segment	Primary Protection	Alternative	Recovery Time	Key Considerations
Metro Access	UPSR or OLP 1:N	Y-Cable	<50ms	Cost-sensitive
Metro Core	BLSR/MS-SPRING	ASON with Dynamic Protection	<50ms	Ring efficiency
Regional Network	OMS + ODU	Mesh Protection	<100ms	Multiple services
Long-haul	OLP 1+1 + OTU	WSON with Path Protection	<50ms	High reliability
Submarine	1+1 with Geographic Diversity	Mesh Protection	<100ms	

Industry-Specific Requirements

Industry	Protection Type	Features	SLA Requirements	Notes
Healthcare	OLP 1+1	Dedicated paths, No traffic loss	99.999%	Critical data protection
Government	Multi-layer Protection	Physical separation, Encryption	99.999%	Security critical
Media/Broadcast	UPSR or 1+1	Low latency, Jitter control	99.99%	Quality sensitive
Manufacturing	Industrial OLP	Environmental hardening	99.99%	Harsh environments
Retail	OLP 1:1 or 1:N	Cost-effective	99.9%	Branch

Traffic Type Protection Requirements

Traffic Type	Recommended Protection	Backup Options	Requirements	Priority
Voice/VoIP	UPSR/SNCP	OLP 1+1	<50ms, Low jitter	High
Video Streaming	OLP 1:1	BLSR	<100ms, QoS maintain	Medium
Critical Data	OLP 1+1 + Client	Multi-layer	<50ms, No loss	Very High
Best Effort	OLP 1:N	Mesh Restoration	<300ms	Low
IoT/Sensors	Ring Protection	Path Protection	<200ms	Medium

Network Size and Topology

Network Scale	Protection Scheme	Topology	Cost Efficiency	Scalability
Small (<10 nodes)	UPSR/OUPSR	Ring	High	Limited
Medium (10-30 nodes)	BLSR/OBLSR	Ring/Mesh	Medium	Good
Large (30+ nodes)	Mesh + GMPLS	Mesh	Medium	Excellent
Multi-domain	ASON/WSON	Hybrid	Low	Excellent
Global	Multi-layer SDN	Mesh	Low	Excellent

Service Level Protection

Service Level	Protection Type	Recovery Time	Availability	Cost Level
Premium	1+1 at all layers	<50ms	99.999%	Very High
Gold	OLP 1+1 or BLSR	<50ms	99.99%	High
Silver	OLP 1:1	<100ms	99.9%	Medium
Bronze	OLP 1:N or Restoration	<300ms	99.5%	Low
Best Effort	Mesh Restoration	<1s	99%	Very Low

Special Requirements

Requirement	Protection Solution	Technology	Benefits	Considerations
Ultra-low Latency	1+1 with Path Selection	DWDM	Minimal delay	High cost
High Security	Diverse Path 1+1	OTN/DWDM	Physical separation	Complex
High Capacity	OMS + ODU mesh	ROADM	Efficient	Medium cost
Multi-tenant	Virtual Protection	SDN/ASON	Flexible	Shared resources
Mixed Services	Multi-layer	OTN over DWDM	Comprehensive	Complex management

Environmental Conditions

Environment	Protection Type	Features	Special Requirements	Example Use
Underground	Hardened OLP	Environmental protection	Moisture resistant	Subway systems
Aerial	Ring Protection	Wind load protection	Temperature hardened	Rural networks
Marine	1+1 with diversity	Corrosion resistant	Water proof	Offshore platforms
Industrial	Industrial OLP	EMI protection	Vibration resistant	Factory automation
Urban	Mesh Protection	Space efficient	Easy maintenance	Metro networks

Cost vs. Protection Level Matrix

Budget Level	Critical Traffic	Important Traffic	Regular Traffic	Best Effort
High	1+1 Multi-layer	OLP 1+1	OLP 1:1	Mesh
Medium	OLP 1+1	BLSR/OBLSR	OLP 1:N	Restoration
Low	UPSR/OUPSR	OLP 1:1	Path Protection	Best Effort
Minimal	Y-Cable	Ring Shared	Restoration	None

Best Practices for Network Protection

1. **Hybrid Protection Approaches**:
    - Combine protection and restoration mechanisms to balance speed and resource efficiency.
    - Example: Use 1+1 OLP for critical paths and SMP for less critical traffic.
2. **Path Diversity**:
    - Design redundant paths that are geographically diverse to avoid simultaneous failures.
    - Critical for disaster-prone areas and submarine cables.
3. **Proactive Monitoring**:
    - Use advanced monitoring systems to detect early signs of failures (e.g., signal degradation).
    - Example: Optical Performance Monitoring (OPM).
4. **Multi-Layer Coordination**:
    - Implement protection mechanisms across different network layers to ensure end-to-end reliability.
5. **Automation and SDN Integration**:
    - Automate protection switching and restoration processes for faster and more efficient recovery.

Emerging Trends in Network Protection

Trend	Description	Impact
AI-Driven Fault Prediction	Machine learning models predict potential failures, enabling proactive protection.	Improves reliability and response time.
Elastic Optical Networks	Dynamically adjust spectrum allocation to reconfigure protection paths.	Increases flexibility and efficiency.
Quantum-Safe Protection	Incorporates quantum cryptography to secure data during protection switching.	Future-proof against quantum attacks.
Energy-Efficient Protection	Optimizes power usage by activating protection resources only when needed.	Reduces operational costs and energy consumption.

Case Studies in Network Protection

Submarine Cable Networks

Submarine cables are crucial for global data traffic but are highly susceptible to fiber cuts due to fishing activities, ship anchors, and earthquakes. Key protection mechanisms include:

- **Disjoint Path Protection**: Ensures geographically diverse routes for primary and backup cables.
- **BLSR**: Used to create highly reliable rings for submarine landing stations.

Metro Networks

Metro networks, which connect urban centers, require low-latency and cost-efficient protection.

- **UPSR**: Provides fast restoration for critical services.
- **2-Fiber BLSR**: Balances cost and resource utilization for high-density traffic.

Data Center Interconnects

Data centers rely on ultra-reliable connections to maintain uptime.

- **1+1 OLP**: Used for high-capacity, low-latency links between data centers.
- **Y-Cable Protection**: Ensures redundancy at the transponder level.

Summary Table of Protection Mechanisms

Protection Type	Layer	Advantages	Disadvantages	Applications
1+1 OLP	Optical	Instantaneous switchover; high reliability.	High resource usage.	Long-haul critical spans.
1:1 OLP	Optical	Efficient resource utilization.	Slight switching delay.	Regional/metro networks.
Y-Cable Protection	Transponder	Simple implementation; cost-effective.	Signal splitting reduces power.	Data centers.
UPSR	Ring	Fast restoration; low latency.	Inefficient bandwidth utilization.	Metro and access networks.
2-Fiber BLSR	Ring	Efficient bandwidth usage.	Limited capacity.	Metro networks.
4-Fiber BLSR	Ring	High capacity; resilient to failures.	High cost and complexity.	Backbone networks.
Shared Mesh Protection	Mesh	Optimizes resource usage.	Higher switching times.	Large-scale carrier networks.
Dual-Homing	Client	Protects against node and network failures.	Requires additional hardware.	Data center interconnects.
OTN SNC Protection	Circuit (ODUk)	Granular protection; high reliability.	Resource-intensive for smaller networks.	Carrier-grade networks.
Ethernet Protection	Client	Layer-independent redundancy.	Potential latency during failover.	Enterprise/data center environments.

As optical networks continue to evolve, ensuring their reliability becomes ever more critical. Protection mechanisms like Optical Line Protection (OLP), ring-based approaches (UPSR, BLSR), and advanced mesh-based systems are essential for safeguarding network services against failures. Each mechanism has unique strengths and trade-offs, and their selection depends on network topology, scale, and service requirements.Emerging technologies such as SDN, AI-driven fault prediction, and elastic optical networks further enhance network protection by enabling dynamic, real-time adaptability. By combining traditional mechanisms with these innovations, network operators can build resilient, future-proof systems that ensure uninterrupted global connectivity.

This chapter provides a comprehensive understanding of the various protection techniques, their implementations, and their applications. Such knowledge is vital for designing and managing modern optical networks that meet the reliability demands of today's digital world.

Chapter 13

Optical Availability

Chapter 13
Optical Availability

"What you can measure, you can improve." - C.V. Raman

Optical availability is a critical metric in fiber optic communication systems that quantifies the probability that a component or system can perform its intended function for a specified interval under stated conditions. It is fundamental to service level agreements (SLAs) and network planning, directly impacting the reliability and quality of optical communication networks.

High optical availability is crucial for maintaining the quality of service in optical networks. It ensures that network services are consistently available to users, which is particularly important for critical applications such as financial services, healthcare, and emergency communications.

Defining Optical Availability

Optical availability refers to the probability that a network or part of a network is operational and capable of transmitting data as intended without significant loss or downtime. It is typically expressed as a percentage and calculated based on the uptime of the system over a given period.

Formula:

$$\text{Optical Availability (OA)} = \left(\frac{T_{\text{up}}}{T_{\text{up}}+T_{\text{down}}}\right) \times 100\%$$

where

- Tup is the uptime and
- Tdown is the downtime of the network.

$$\text{Optical Availability} = \left(\frac{11{,}000}{11{,}000+200}\right) \times 100\% = 98.21\%$$

Significance of Optical Availability

The significance of optical availability extends beyond just maintaining an operational network; it directly impacts business operations, customer satisfaction, and revenue. High availability is essential in sectors where real-time data transmission is critical, such as in financial services, healthcare, and government operations.

Key Points:

- **Business Continuity**: Ensures that business operations are not halted due to network issues.
- **Customer Trust and Retention**: High availability reduces service interruptions, enhancing customer trust and retention.
- **Compliance and SLAs**: Meets compliance requirements and SLAs, avoiding penalties and legal issues.

Factors Affecting Optical Availability

Several factors can affect the availability of an optical network, including:

- **Fiber Cuts**: Physical damage to fibers can cause significant downtime.
- **Component Failures**: Failures in optical amplifiers, switches, and other network components.
- **Network Design**: Poor network design can lead to single points of failure.
- **Maintenance Practices**: Inadequate maintenance can increase the likelihood of failures.

Calculating Optical Availability

Optical availability is calculated by considering both planned and unplanned downtimes. This involves detailed record-keeping of all incidents affecting the optical paths.

Example Calculation:
Suppose an optical network has an uptime of 11,000 hours and a downtime of 200 hours in a year:

Improving Optical Availability

Improving optical availability involves several strategies, including:

- **Redundant Path Design**: Implementing redundant paths to ensure continuous data flow even if one path fails.
- **Regular Maintenance**: Conducting regular preventive maintenance to reduce the risk of component failures.
- **Upgrading Components**: Upgrading to higher quality components that offer better performance and reliability.

Impact of Redundancy on Availability

Strategy	Availability without Redundancy (%)	Availability with Redundancy (%)
Single Path	99.5	N/A
Dual Path	99.5	99.999
Diverse Routing	99.5	99.9999

Availability Metrics

Mean Time Between Failures (MTBF)

The Mean Time Between Failures (MTBF) is a measure of the reliability of a system, typically used to predict the time between inherent failures during the operational phase of a system.

Formula:

$$\mathrm{MTBF} = \frac{T}{N}$$

where:
T = total operational time,
N = number of failures.

Mean Time To Repair (MTTR)

The Mean Time To Repair (MTTR) measures the average time required to repair a failed component or system and restore it to normal operations.

Formula:

$$\text{MTTR} = \frac{\text{Total downtime}}{\text{Number of repairs}}$$

Network Availability

Network availability calculates the percentage of time a network is available to users within a given period, incorporating both MTBF and MTTR.

$$\text{Network Availability} = \left(\frac{\text{MTBF}}{\text{MTBF+MTTR}}\right) \times 100\%$$

Service Availability

Service availability specifically refers to the availability of a particular service or application on the network.

$$\text{Service Availability} = \left(\frac{\text{Uptime of Service}}{\text{Total Time}}\right) \times 100\%$$

Component Reliability

Component reliability is the probability that a component will function without failure over a specified interval under stated conditions.

$$R(t) = e^{-\lambda t}$$

where:

- R(t) = reliability function,
- λ = failure rate,
- t = time.

System Availability

System availability is the probability that the entire system is operational and performing satisfactorily at any point in time, considering the reliability of individual components and system architecture.

where:

- Ri (t) = reliability of individual component *i*
- n = number of components.

$$\text{System Availability} = \prod_{i=1}^{n} R_i(t)$$

Failure Density Function

The failure density function, part of reliability engineering, helps determine the rate at which components are likely to fail at a specific time.

$$f(t) = \lambda e^{-\lambda t}$$

where:

- f(t) = failure density function,
- λ = rate of failure,
- t = time.

Example Reliability Data

Component	MTBF (hours)	MTTR (hours)	Reliability (%)
Optical Switch	30000	2	99.99
Amplifier	25000	3	99.98
Transceiver	40000	1.5	99.995

Unavailability

The percentage of time a network is not functional, usually calculated as follows:

For a system with 99.999% availability, known as "five nines," unavailability is 5.3 minutes per year.

$$\text{Unavailability} = (1 - \text{Availability}) \times 365 \times 24 \times 60$$

Availability Levels vs Downtime

Availability	Downtime/Year	Downtime/Month	Downtime/Week
99%	3.65 days	7.20 hours	1.68 hours
99.9%	8.76 hours	43.8 minutes	10.1 minutes
99.99%	52.56 minutes	4.38 minutes	1.01 minutes
99.999%	5.26 minutes	26.3 seconds	6.05 seconds
99.9999%	31.5 seconds	2.63 seconds	0.605 seconds

Achieving High Availability

Network Architecture Cost vs Availability

Single Path	99.9% Availability	Base Cost
1+1 Protection	99.99% Availability	2x Base Cost
Ring Protection	99.999% Availability	2.5x Base Cost
Mesh Network	99.9999% Availability	3-4x Base Cost

Strategies for improving optical availability include:

- **Redundant configurations:** Using multiple pathways to ensure reliability.
- **Component quality:** High-quality components can significantly decrease failure rates.
- **Network monitoring:** Continuous monitoring can quickly identify and rectify issues.
- **Disaster recovery plans:** Preparedness for quick recovery from major failures.

Real-World Applications

Case Study: Submarine Network Design

Submarine cables require exceptionally high availability due to their critical role in global communications and challenging repair conditions. Redundant paths and regular maintenance are essential strategies.

Advanced Considerations

- **Automated monitoring systems:** Using AI and machine learning can predict and mitigate failures before they occur.
- **Quantitative Models:** Advanced statistical models that predict failures based on historical data.

Typical Failure Rates and Repair Times

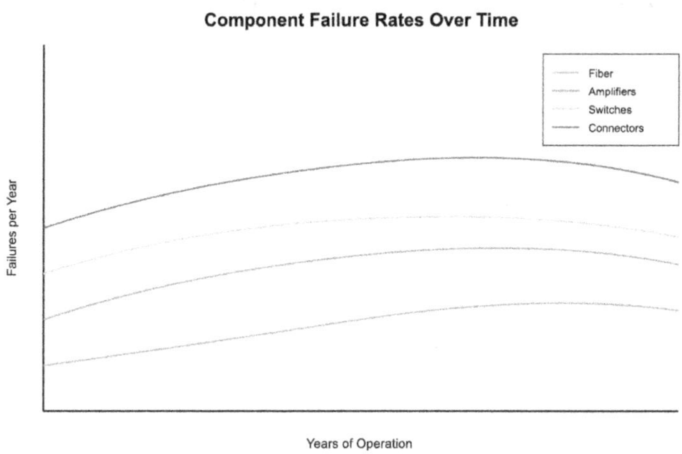

Component	Failure Rate (FITs)	MTBF (years)	MTTR (hours)	Notes
Fiber Cable	2 per 1,000 km/year	25	18	Depends on location (metro/long-haul)
Optical Amplifiers	500	15	4	High variability depending on type
Transceivers	300	20	2	Critical for network operations
Switches/Routers	1,000	10	3	Central to network reliability

This table below provides a quick reference for network designers to understand the expected lifetime and maintenance requirements of critical components.

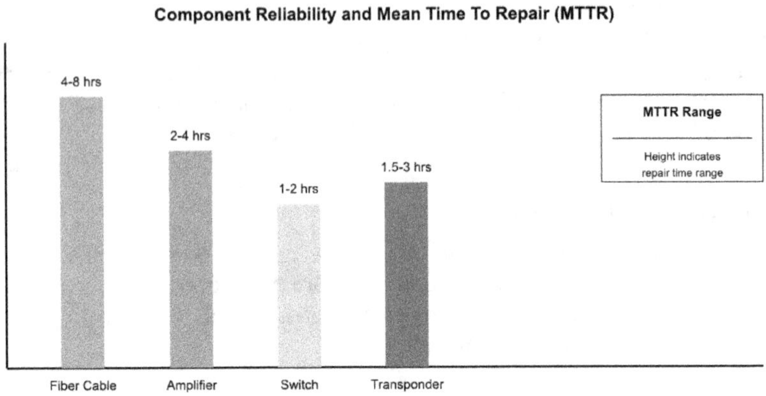

Availability Calculations for a Hypothetical Network

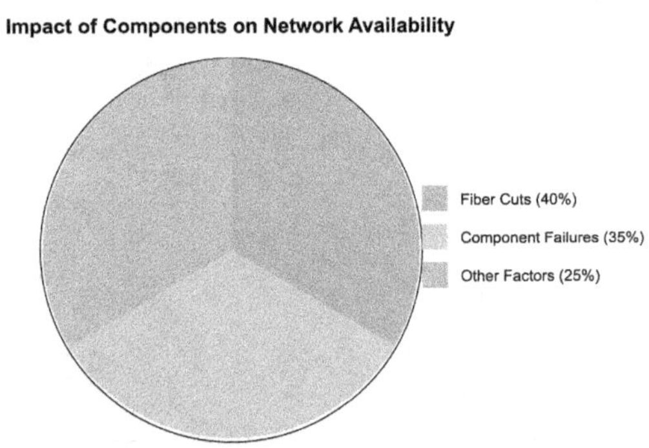

System Component	MTBF (hours)	MTTR (hours)	Availability (%)
Entire Network	30,000	4	99.987
Critical Path (Fiber)	50,000	18	99.963
Support Systems	20,000	8	99.920

Implications of Network Design on Availability

Network topology and design choices significantly affect system availability. Strategies like redundant pathways, diverse routing, and the deployment of backup systems can mitigate downtime and ensure higher availability.

In the context of optical network availability, "nines" are commonly used to describe the reliability of a network in terms of its uptime percentage over a year. Below are two essential tables that elucidate this concept. The first table details the "Five Nines" standard, while the second table expands on various "Nines" levels and their corresponding implications for downtime.

"Five Nines" Availability Calculation

Availability (%)	Unavailability (minutes/year)	Description
99.999%	5.26	Carrier-grade availability often required for critical telecommunications infrastructure, ensuring minimal downtime and service disruption.

Availability Levels and Their Implications

Availability (%)	Downtime Per Year	Description
99%	87.6 hours	Basic level, generally unacceptable in critical networks
99.9%	8.76 hours	Good for less critical applications
99.99%	52.56 minutes	Enhanced reliability suitable for most commercial operations
99.999%	5.26 minutes	"Five Nines" - Industry standard for critical telecom systems
99.9999%	31.5 seconds	"Six Nines" - Extremely high availability, used for mission-critical environments like financial transactions
99.99999%	3.15 seconds	"Seven Nines" - Extremely rare, used for highly critical applications

This above table showcases the increasing reliability and corresponding decrease in permissible downtime as the number of nines increases. It is essential for network architects and engineers to understand these levels to design and assure network services aligned with business needs and operational reliability requirements.

Interesting Graphs

Network Availability vs Annual Downtime

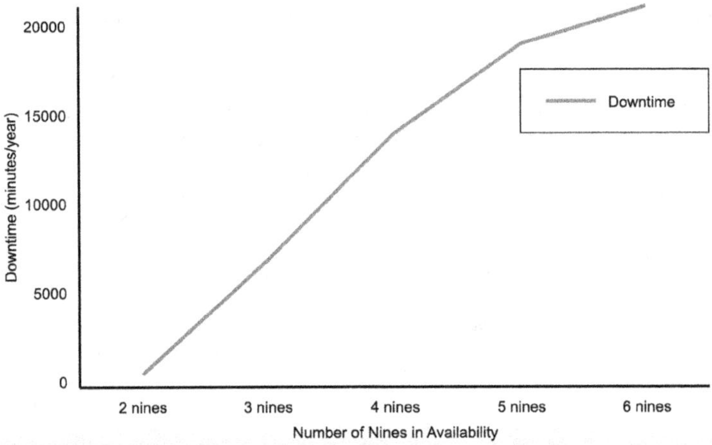

Network Architecture Availability Comparison

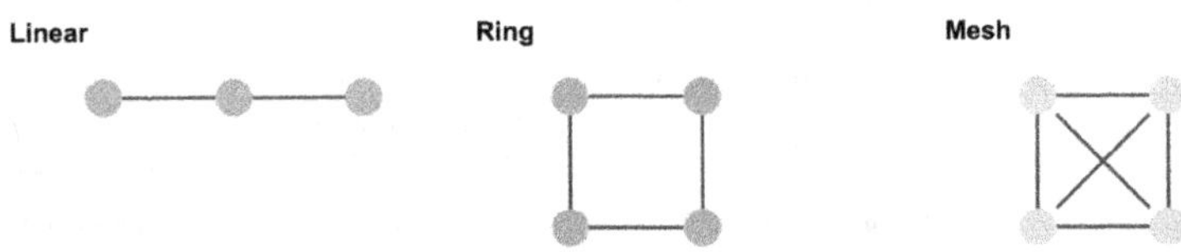

Architecture Comparison

Type	Availability	Recovery Time	Cost Factor	Complexity
Linear	99.9%	Hours	1x	Low
Ring	99.999%	50ms	2.5x	Medium
Mesh	99.9999%	10ms	3-4x	High

Chapter 14

Systems Engineering in Optical Networks

Chapter 14
Systems Engineering in Optical Networks

"Systems engineering is the bridge between possibility and reality."
- Alan Huang

Optical networks are complex systems requiring seamless integration, rigorous testing, comprehensive documentation, and continuous maintenance. Systems engineering in optical networks addresses these needs, focusing on holistic planning, integration, and validation to ensure robust and scalable network

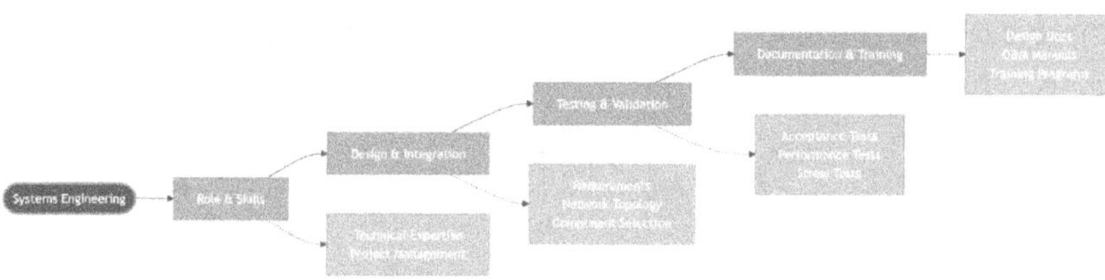

deployments. This chapter delves into the role of systems engineers in optical networks, their key responsibilities, and the practices that support high-quality network performance.

Role of Systems Engineers

Systems engineers in optical networks serve as the bridge between design, implementation, and operational teams. They are responsible for ensuring that all network components—hardware, software, and protocols—work harmoniously to meet network performance and reliability standards. Systems engineers must have a strong technical foundation in optical networking technologies, combined with expertise in project management, troubleshooting, and communication.

Primary Objectives:

- To design and integrate systems that meet customer and operational requirements.

- To ensure systems are validated and tested rigorously before deployment.
- To develop comprehensive documentation and training programs to support operations teams.

Skills Required:

- **Technical Expertise**: Knowledge of DWDM, SDH, OTN, and other optical technologies.
- **Analytical Skills**: Proficiency in analyzing system requirements and evaluating network performance metrics.
- **Project Management**: Managing timelines, budgets, and resources to ensure project milestones are met.

Key Responsibilities of Systems Engineers

Systems engineers in optical networks have multifaceted responsibilities, from design and integration to testing, validation, documentation, and training. Each area plays a crucial role in delivering a reliable, scalable, and maintainable optical network.All that you see below is part of system engineering.

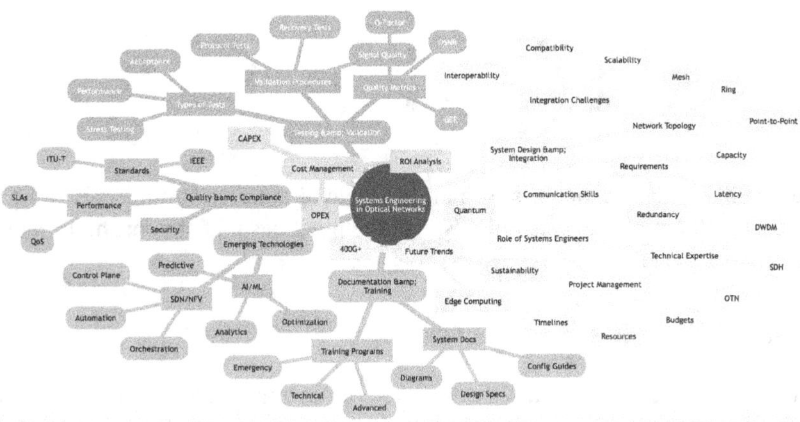

System Design and Integration

System design and integration form the foundation of an optical network. Systems engineers must translate high-level requirements into detailed designs that account for every aspect of the network, including topology, equipment, and protocols.

Design Process:

- **Requirements Gathering**: Collecting detailed specifications from stakeholders to understand capacity, redundancy, latency, and other performance criteria.
- **Network Topology Selection**: Choosing appropriate network topologies (e.g., point-to-point, ring, mesh) based on application requirements.
- **Hardware and Software Selection**: Specifying transponders, multiplexers, amplifiers, and network management systems that meet the network's requirements.

Integration Challenges:

- **Compatibility Issues**: Ensuring that components from different vendors (e.g., transponders, routers, switches) work seamlessly together.
- **Protocol Interoperability**: Aligning different communication protocols such as IP, Ethernet, and MPLS with optical technologies.
- **Scalability**: Designing systems that can scale to meet future demand without requiring significant re-engineering.

Example of System Integration in DWDM Network:

Design Objective: Implement a DWDM network with 100 Gbps channels and redundancy for metro transport.

Integration Steps:

- **Component Selection**: Choose DWDM transponders, EDFAs, and ROADMs.
- **Topology Planning**: Implement a dual-ring topology for redundancy.
- **Protocol Configuration**: Set up OTN for transport, ensuring smooth integration with IP/MPLS at network boundaries.

Testing and Validation

Testing and validation are essential in systems engineering to ensure that optical networks meet performance standards and function reliably under real-world conditions.

Types of Tests:

- **Acceptance Testing**: Confirms that equipment and network configurations meet predefined performance standards.
- **Performance Testing**: Assesses metrics such as bit error rate (BER), optical signal-to-noise ratio (OSNR), and latency.
- **Stress Testing**: Evaluates network resilience under high-traffic loads and adverse conditions.

Validation Procedures:

- **Optical Signal Quality Checks**: Testing for parameters like OSNR, Q-factor, and chromatic dispersion to ensure signal integrity across all channels.
- **Protocol Compatibility Tests**: Verifying that different network layers (e.g., OTN, DWDM, IP) work together seamlessly.
- **Failure Recovery Simulation**: Testing failover mechanisms (e.g., 1+1, 1:1 protection) to ensure rapid recovery during outages.

Documentation and Training

Documentation and training are critical for the successful deployment and ongoing management of optical networks. Systems engineers are responsible for creating comprehensive documentation that captures the network design, configuration, and operational procedures.

Documentation Requirements:

- **System Design Documentation**: Detailed diagrams, network configurations, and equipment specifications.
- **Operation and Maintenance Manuals**: Step-by-step guides for routine maintenance, troubleshooting, and emergency procedures.
- **Configuration and Firmware Documentation**: Details of software versions, firmware, and configurations used in the network to support consistent maintenance practices.

Training Programs:

- **Technical Training for Operators**: Training network operators on system configuration, monitoring, and troubleshooting techniques.

- **Emergency Response Training**: Preparing operators to handle critical scenarios, such as link failures, equipment faults, and traffic rerouting.
- **Advanced Technical Training**: Providing in-depth sessions on specific technologies (e.g., DWDM, OTN) and tools (e.g., network management systems, APS).

Emerging Technologies and Future Considerations

The landscape of optical networks is continuously evolving with new technologies and methodologies that systems engineers must incorporate into their practices.

Artificial Intelligence and Machine Learning Integration Network Optimization

AI algorithms for dynamic routing and wavelength assignment Predictive Maintenance: ML models for identifying potential failures before they occur Performance Analytics: Advanced analytics for network behavior and capacity planning.

Software-Defined Networking (SDN) and Network Function Virtualization (NFV) Control Plane Architecture

Implementation of centralized network control and management Network Programmability: Development of APIs and automation frameworks Service Orchestration: Dynamic service provisioning and resource allocation

Quality Assurance and Compliance

Systems engineers must ensure that optical networks meet industry standards and regulatory requirements while maintaining high-quality service delivery.

Standards and Certifications: Industry Compliance: Meeting ITU-T, IEEE, and other relevant standards Security Requirements: Implementing network security protocols and encryption Environmental Standards: Ensuring equipment meets power and environmental regulations

Performance Metrics and Monitoring:

Service Level Agreements (SLAs): Establishing and monitoring performance guarantees Quality of Service (QoS): Implementing mechanisms for traffic prioritization Network Health Monitoring: Continuous assessment of network performance indicators

Case Studies in Systems Engineering Real-world examples demonstrate the practical application of systems engineering principles in optical networks.

Metro Network Upgrade:

Challenge: Upgrading a legacy SONET/SDH network to modern DWDM infrastructure Solution: Phased migration approach with minimal service disruption Results: Increased capacity and improved network reliability

Multi-vendor Integration:

Challenge: Integrating equipment from different vendors in a national backbone **Solution**: Detailed interoperability testing and protocol standardization **Results**: Successful deployment with seamless inter-vendor operation

Cost Management and Resource Optimization Effective systems engineering requires careful consideration of financial and resource constraints.

Total Cost of Ownership (TCO) Analysis:

Capital Expenditure: Equipment, installation, and infrastructure costs
Operational Expenditure: Maintenance, power, and personnel costs
Lifecycle Management: Equipment refresh cycles and upgrade planning

Resource Allocation:

Personnel Management: Organizing teams for design, implementation, and operations
Equipment Planning: Managing spare parts and maintenance resources
Training Investment: Developing and maintaining technical expertise

The Future of Systems Engineering in Optical Networks As optical networks continue to evolve, systems engineering practices must adapt to new challenges and opportunities.

Technology Trends:

Quantum Communications: Preparing for quantum-safe encryption and quantum key distribution
400G and Beyond: Planning for higher-speed optical interfaces
Edge Computing Integration: Designing networks to support edge computing requirements

Sustainability Considerations:

Energy Efficiency: Implementing green networking technologies
Environmental Impact: Reducing carbon footprint through optimal design
Resource Conservation: Maximizing equipment lifecycle and minimizing waste

Example of Documentation Process:

Objective: Document a newly installed DWDM network for a regional transport provider.

Steps:

- **Design Documentation**: Create detailed diagrams showing channel allocations, protection schemes, and path redundancies.
- **Operational Guide**: Develop a manual outlining configuration commands, routine checks, and maintenance schedules.
- **Training Module**: Set up a training session covering network monitoring and emergency response.

Systems engineering is pivotal for the success of optical networks, ensuring their ability to meet modern communication demands. By adopting a structured approach to design, integration, and management, systems engineers can build networks that are efficient, reliable, and future-ready. The integration of emerging technologies, coupled with robust quality assurance and cost management practices, positions optical networks to meet the growing demands of digital transformation while maintaining high standards of performance and reliability.

Part IV

Network Operations and Management

Chapter 15

Operations in Optical Networks

Chapter 15
Operations in Optical Networks

"Operations is where theory meets practice." - Patrick Iannone

---

Operations in optical networks play a critical role in ensuring that the network runs smoothly, efficiently, and reliably. This chapter explores the various aspects of operations in optical networks, including their roles, responsibilities, and the tools and technologies they use to maintain and optimize network performance.

Role of Operations Teams

Operations teams are responsible for the day-to-day management, monitoring, and maintenance of optical networks. Their key roles include:

- **Network Monitoring**: Continuously monitoring network performance and health using various tools and systems.
- **Fault Management**: Detecting, diagnosing, and resolving network faults to minimize downtime.
- **Performance Management**: Ensuring the network meets performance standards and optimizing its efficiency.
- **Configuration Management**: Managing network configurations to ensure consistency and security.
- **Provisioning**: Setting up new services and connections in the network.
- **Capacity Planning**: Analyzing and planning for future network capacity needs to ensure scalability.

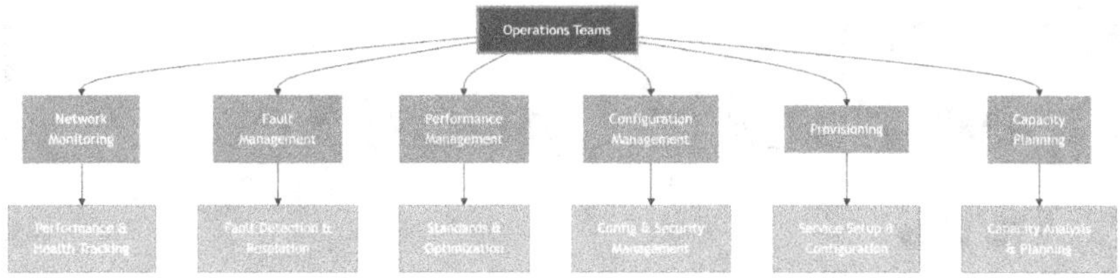

Network Monitoring

Network monitoring involves the continuous observation of network parameters to ensure optimal performance and early detection of issues. Key aspects include:

- **Performance Metrics**: Monitoring metrics such as bandwidth utilization, latency, packet loss, and error rates.
- **Alarms and Alerts**: Setting up thresholds for various parameters and generating alarms when thresholds are exceeded.
- **Monitoring Tools**: Using network management systems (NMS), performance monitoring tools, and optical performance monitors (OPMs).

Example: A network operations center (NOC) uses a combination of SNMP (Simple Network Management Protocol) and specialized software to monitor the health of a DWDM network. If the bit error rate (BER) on a specific channel exceeds a predefined threshold, an alarm is triggered, and the operations team investigates the issue.

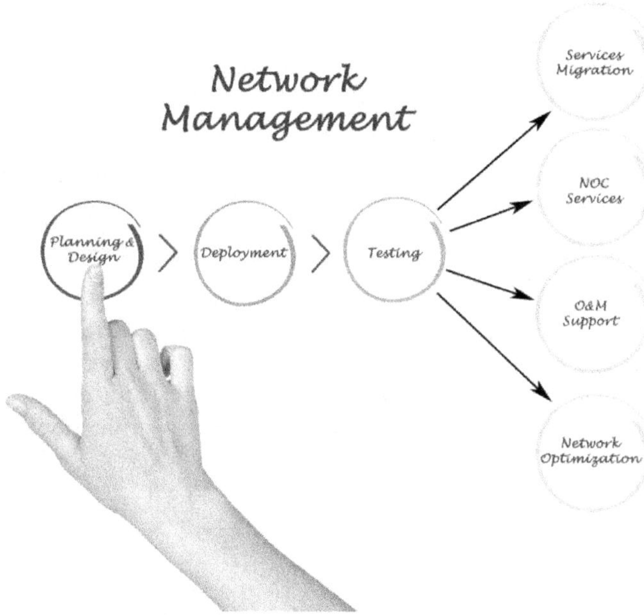
Network Management
Planning & Design
Deployment
Testing
Services Migration
NOC Services
O&M Support
Network Optimization

Fault Management

Fault management involves detecting, isolating, and resolving faults in the network to minimize downtime and service disruption. Key steps include:

- **Fault Detection**: Using monitoring tools and alarms to detect faults.
- **Fault Diagnosis**: Analyzing the cause of the fault using diagnostic tools and techniques.
- **Fault Resolution**: Implementing corrective actions to resolve the fault and restore normal operation.

Example: If a fiber cut is detected in the network, the operations team uses an optical time-domain reflectometer (OTDR) to locate the exact point of the cut. The team then dispatches field technicians to repair the fiber and restore service.

Performance Management

Performance management involves monitoring and optimizing the network to ensure it meets performance standards. Key activities include:

- **Performance Analysis**: Analyzing performance data to identify trends and areas for improvement.
- **Optimization**: Implementing changes to optimize network performance, such as adjusting configurations or upgrading hardware.
- **Reporting**: Generating performance reports to provide insights into network health and efficiency.

Example: The operations team analyzes network utilization reports and identifies a bottleneck in a specific segment. They optimize the network by reconfiguring traffic flows and upgrading the capacity of that segment.

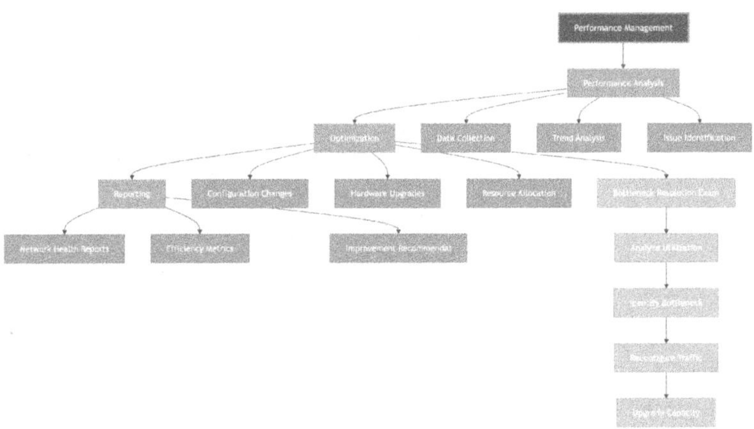

Configuration Management

Configuration management involves maintaining accurate records of network configurations and ensuring consistency across the network. Key aspects include:

- **Configuration Tracking**: Keeping track of all network configurations and changes.
- **Configuration Auditing**: Regularly auditing configurations to ensure compliance with standards and policies.
- **Change Management**: Managing changes to configurations in a controlled and systematic manner.

Example: The operations team uses a configuration management database (CMDB) to track all network devices and their configurations. Before making any changes, they perform a risk assessment and follow a change management process to ensure minimal disruption.

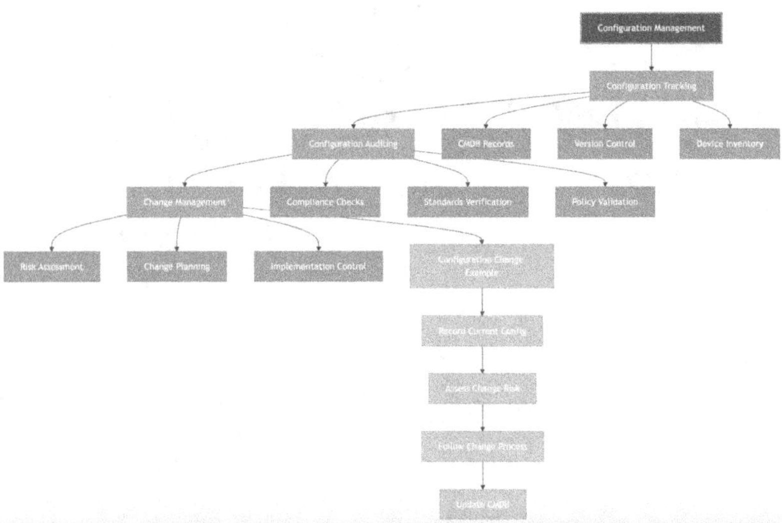

Provisioning

Provisioning involves setting up new services and connections in the network. Key activities include:

- **Service Activation**: Activating new services and ensuring they are correctly configured.
- **Resource Allocation**: Allocating network resources, such as bandwidth and wavelengths, to new services.
- **Testing and Validation**: Testing new services to ensure they meet performance standards before going live.

Example: A new customer requests a high-speed connection. The operations team provisions the service by configuring the necessary DWDM channels, allocating bandwidth, and testing the connection to ensure it meets the required performance criteria.

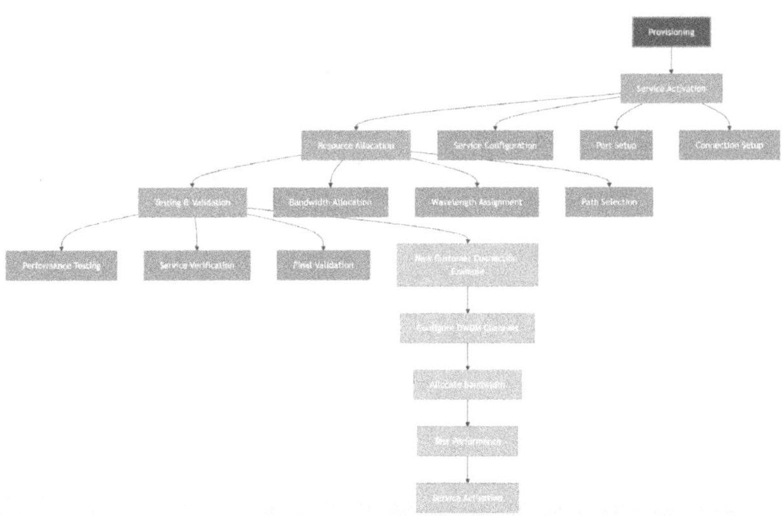

Capacity Planning

Capacity planning involves analyzing current network usage and planning for future growth to ensure the network can scale to meet increasing demand. Key steps include:

- **Usage Analysis**: Analyzing current and historical network usage data.
- **Forecasting**: Predicting future usage trends based on growth patterns and market demands.
- **Planning**: Developing plans to expand network capacity, such as adding new fibers, wavelengths, or upgrading equipment.

Example: The operations team analyzes usage data and forecasts that the network will need to support an additional 10 Tbps of traffic in the next year. They develop a plan to upgrade the DWDM system by adding more channels and installing new optical amplifiers.

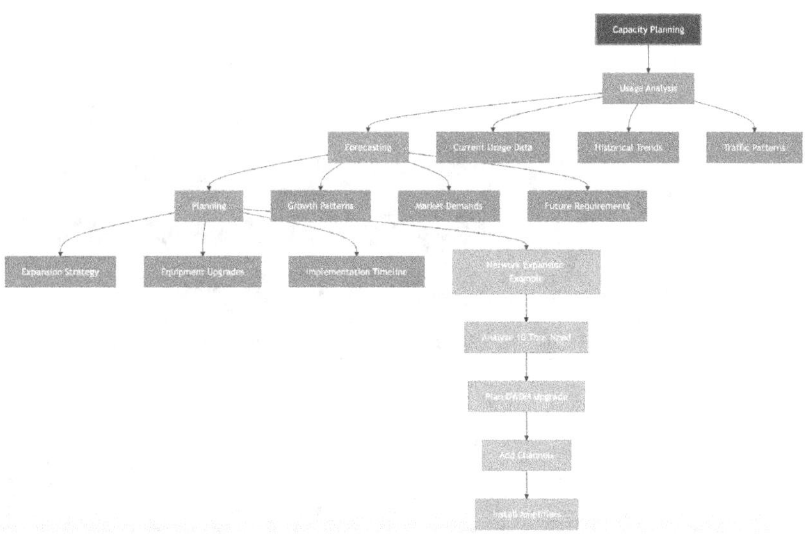

Tools and Technologies

Operations teams use a variety of tools and technologies to manage optical networks effectively:

- **Network Management Systems (NMS)**: Centralized systems that provide a comprehensive view of network health and performance.
- **Optical Performance Monitors (OPMs)**: Devices that monitor the performance of optical signals in real-time.
- **Optical Time-Domain Reflectometers (OTDRs)**: Tools used for diagnosing and locating faults in optical fibers.
- **Configuration Management Databases (CMDBs)**: Databases that store and track network configurations.
- **Performance Monitoring Tools**: Software tools that monitor and analyze network performance metrics.

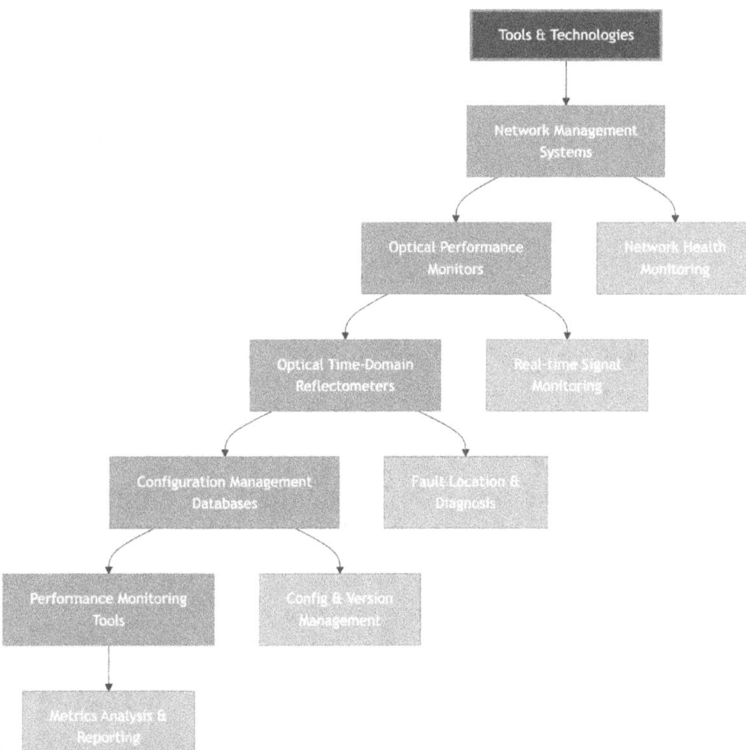

Data and Statistics

Recent data and statistics highlight the importance and effectiveness of network operations:

- **Network Downtime Costs**: According to Gartner, the average cost of network downtime is $5,600 per minute, emphasizing the importance of efficient fault management and rapid resolution.
- **Performance Improvement**: Studies show that effective performance management can improve network efficiency by up to 30%, resulting in significant cost savings and better user experiences.
- **Automation Impact**: The adoption of automation in network operations has reduced manual errors by 70% and improved provisioning times by 50%.

Chapter 16

Alarm and Performance Management

Chapter 16
Alarm and Performance Management

"Performance management is about preventing problems, not just solving them." - Ivan Kaminow

---

Alarm and performance management are critical aspects of maintaining and optimizing optical networks. Effective management ensures network reliability, performance, and rapid fault resolution. This chapter explores the principles, methodologies, and practical considerations for implementing robust alarm and performance management systems in optical networks.

Principles of Alarm and Performance Management

Alarm and performance management involve monitoring network health, detecting and responding to issues, and ensuring that the network meets performance standards.

- **Monitoring**: Continuously tracking network performance and health metrics.
- **Alarm Generation**: Setting thresholds for various parameters and generating alarms when thresholds are exceeded.
- **Fault Detection and Isolation**: Quickly identifying and isolating faults to minimize impact.
- **Performance Analysis**: Analyzing performance data to identify trends and areas for improvement.
- **Reporting**: Providing detailed reports on network performance and health.

TMN Architecture

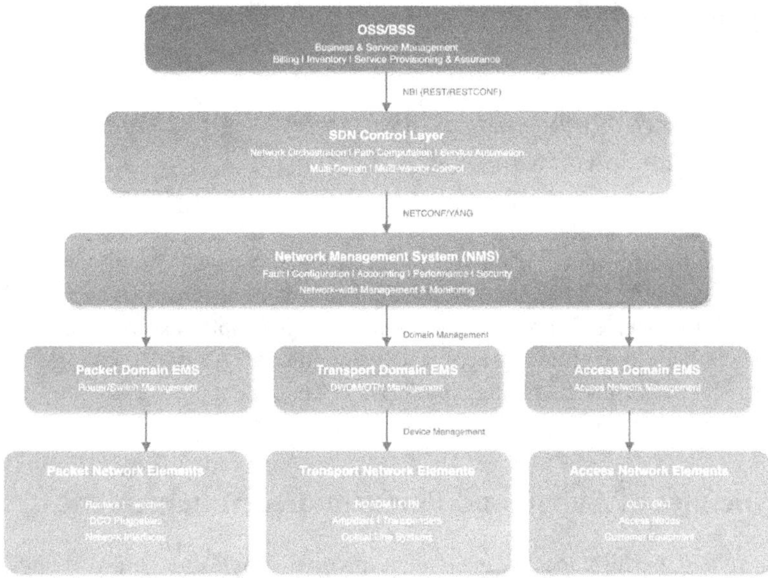

Overview of Modern Telecommunications Network Architecture and Management

- **OSS/BSS:** The OSS (Operational Support Systems) and BSS (Business Support Systems) layer serves as the backbone for business and service management within a telecommunications network. This layer handles essential functions such as billing, inventory management, service provisioning, and assurance. It ensures that the customer and service information is managed effectively to support other network operations and service delivery.
- **SDN Control Layer:** The Software Defined Networking (SDN) Control Layer modernizes the management of network services through network orchestration, path computation, and service automation. It provides a centralized control point that can communicate across multiple domains and with various vendor equipment, streamlining operations and enhancing the network's responsiveness to changing conditions and demands.
- **Network Management System (NMS):** The Network Management System is crucial for overseeing the network's day-to-day operations.

It addresses comprehensive needs such as fault management, configuration, accounting, performance monitoring, and security. This system plays a pivotal role in ensuring the network's overall health and efficiency, providing network-wide management and monitoring capabilities.

- **EMS (Element Management System):** The EMS is divided into different domains to handle specific types of network elements:
    - **Packet Domain EMS** focuses on the management of routers and switches, integral for directing data in network infrastructures.
    - **Transport Domain EMS** is responsible for managing dense wavelength division multiplexing (DWDM) and optical transport network (OTN) systems, crucial for the backbone of high-capacity network communications.
    - **Access Domain EMS** manages access network elements like optical line terminals (OLTs) and network termination (ONTs), essential for the final delivery of services to the end-users.
- **Network Elements Layer:** This layer includes all physical devices and technologies deployed in the network:
    - **Packet Network Elements** like routers, switches, and direct client optics (DCO pluggables) facilitate data transportation and interface connectivity.
    - **Transport Network Elements** such as reconfigurable optical add-drop multiplexers (ROADMs), optical transport networks (OTN), amplifiers, and transponders form the core of the optical transmission system, managing the signal distribution and integrity.
    - **Access Network Elements** handle the distribution of services to end-users through components like optical line terminals (OLTs), optical network terminals (ONTs), access nodes, and customer equipment, establishing the link between the network and its users.

Each of these layers and elements plays a distinct role in the architecture and management of a modern telecommunications network, ensuring efficient operation, service delivery, and maintenance across various parts of the system.

Key Components of Alarm and Performance Management

- **Network Monitoring Systems (NMS)**
    - Centralized systems that provide a comprehensive view of network health and performance.

    - Collect data from various network elements and present it in a unified interface.
- **Performance Metrics**
    - Bandwidth utilization, latency, jitter, packet loss, error rates, and optical signal-to-noise ratio (OSNR).
    - Key Performance Indicators (KPIs) to assess network health.
- **Alarm Systems**
    - Real-time alarm generation based on predefined thresholds.
    - Categorization of alarms based on severity (e.g., critical, major, minor).
- **Fault Management Systems**
    - Tools and processes to detect, diagnose, and resolve network faults.
    - Integration with monitoring systems for automated fault detection and resolution.
- **Performance Management Tools**
    - Software tools that analyze performance data and provide insights for optimization.
    - Predictive analytics to forecast potential issues and recommend preventive measures.

Implementing Alarm and Performance Management

- **Defining Monitoring Objectives**
    - Identify key metrics and KPIs to be monitored.
    - Establish performance standards and acceptable thresholds for each metric.
- **Setting Up Monitoring Infrastructure**
    - Deploy network monitoring systems (NMS) to collect data from network elements.
    - Integrate monitoring tools with existing network management systems.
- **Alarm Configuration**
    - Define thresholds for various performance metrics.
    - Configure alarm systems to generate alerts when thresholds are exceeded.
    - Categorize alarms based on severity and set up escalation procedures.
- **Fault Detection and Isolation**

    - Implement automated fault detection systems that use performance data to identify issues.
    - Use diagnostic tools to isolate faults and determine their root cause.
- **Performance Analysis and Optimization**
    - Regularly analyze performance data to identify trends and areas for improvement.
    - Implement optimization strategies based on analysis, such as traffic engineering, load balancing, and configuration adjustments.
- **Reporting and Documentation**
    - Generate regular reports on network performance and health.
    - Document all incidents, resolutions, and performance optimization measures.

Practical Examples

- **Real-Time OSNR Monitoring**

  Scenario: An optical network operator needs to monitor OSNR in real-time to ensure signal quality.

  Implementation:

    - **Tools Used**: Optical performance monitors (OPMs) integrated with the NMS.
    - **Process**:
        - OPMs continuously measure OSNR across various network segments.
        - The NMS collects OSNR data and generates alarms if OSNR falls below the acceptable threshold (e.g., 20 dB for 100G channels).
        - Alarms trigger automated diagnostic routines to identify and isolate the cause of degradation.
    - **Outcome**: Proactive detection of OSNR issues, leading to faster resolution and minimized impact on network performance.
- **Latency and Jitter Management**

  Scenario: A financial institution requires low latency and minimal jitter for high-frequency trading applications.

  Implementation:

    - **Tools Used**: Network performance monitoring tools and low-latency routing protocols.

- **Process**:
    - Performance monitoring tools continuously measure latency and jitter across the network.
    - Alarms are generated if latency or jitter exceeds predefined thresholds (e.g., 1 ms for latency, 0.1 ms for jitter).
    - Network paths are dynamically adjusted using low-latency routing protocols to optimize performance.
- **Outcome**: Ensured low latency and minimal jitter, meeting the stringent performance requirements of high-frequency trading applications.

- **Bandwidth Utilization Analysis**

  Scenario: An ISP needs to optimize bandwidth utilization to prevent congestion and ensure quality of service.

  Implementation:

    - **Tools Used**: Bandwidth monitoring tools integrated with the NMS.
    - **Process**:
        - Bandwidth monitoring tools track utilization across various network segments.
        - Alarms are generated if utilization exceeds a certain threshold (e.g., 80%).
        - Performance analysis identifies traffic patterns and congestion points.
        - Traffic engineering and load balancing techniques are applied to redistribute traffic and alleviate congestion.
    - **Outcome**: Improved bandwidth utilization, reduced congestion, and enhanced quality of service for customers.

Advanced Troubleshooting Techniques

Fault Classification Matrix

Fault Type	Indicators	Root Causes	Resolution Time
Signal Degradation	OSNR drop	Component aging, misalignment	2-4 hours
Hard Failure	LOS/LOL	Fiber cut, equipment failure	4-8 hours
Intermittent Issues	BER spikes	Environmental factors	24-48 hours

System Performance	Capacity reduction	Configuration drift	1-2 hours

Diagnostic Flowchart example

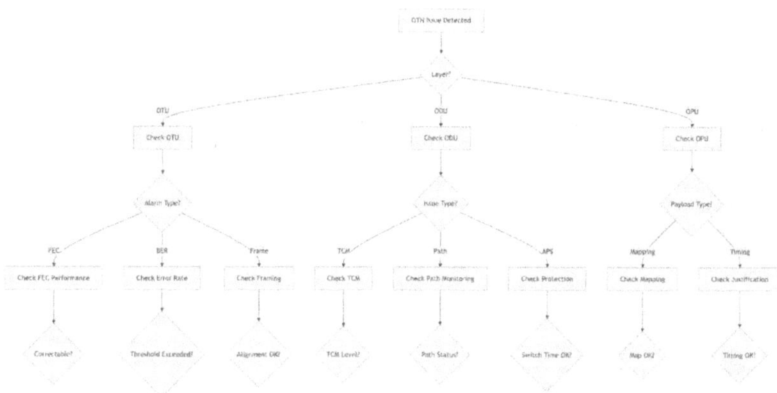

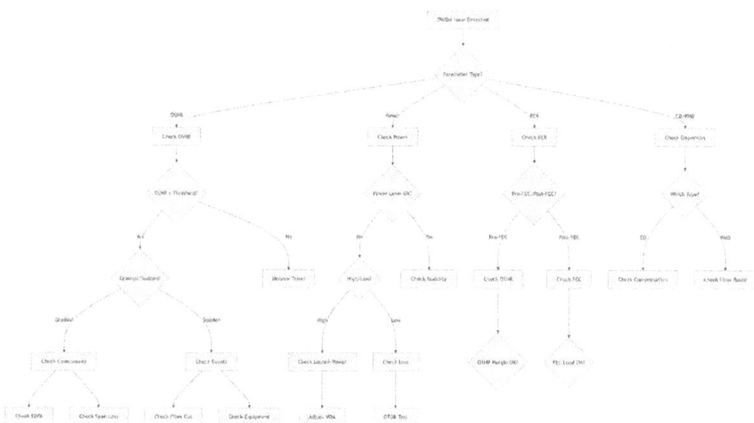

Test Equipment Specifications

Instrument	Measurement	Accuracy	Use Case

OTDR	Distance/Loss	±0.01 dB/km	Fiber fault location
OSA	Spectrum	±0.1 nm	Channel analysis
BERT	BER	10^-15	System performance
PMD Analyzer	PMD	±0.1 ps	Fiber qualification

Key Performance Indicators

KPI	Normal Range	Warning	Critical	Action
OSNR	> 23 dB	20-23 dB	< 20 dB	Optimize power
Q-Factor	> 7	6-7	< 6	Check FEC
Power	-5 to +5 dBm	±7 dBm	±10 dBm	Adjust VOA
BER	< 10^-12	10^-9	10^-6	Troubleshoot

Root Cause Analysis

Stage	Activities	Tools	Output
Data Collection	Gather alarms, logs	NMS, OSA	Raw data
Analysis	Correlation, trending	AI/ML tools	Fault patterns
Verification	Testing hypotheses	Test equipment	Confirmed cause
Resolution	Implement fix	Maintenance tools	Service restoration

RCA Process Flow

Ethernet Issue example

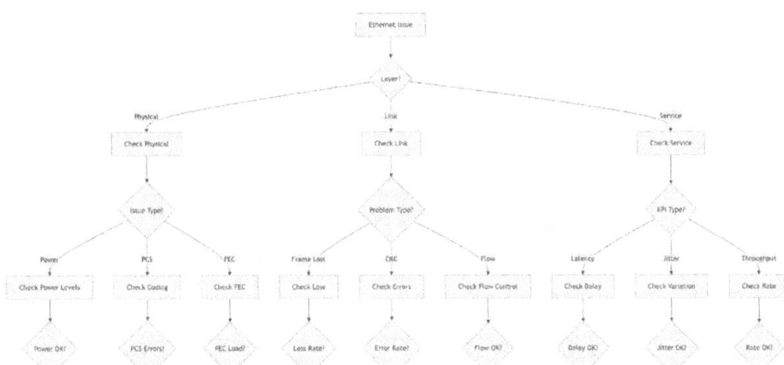

Alarm Detection

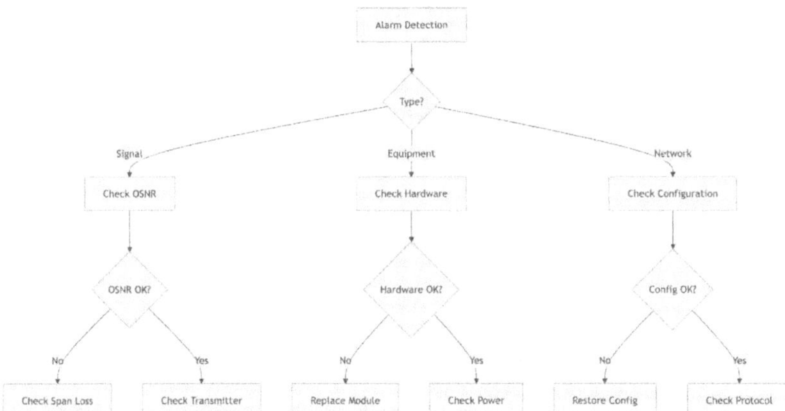

Optical Network Performance Parameters Guide

Physical Layer (Optical) Parameters

Analog Parameters

Optical Signal-to-Noise Ratio (OSNR)

Ratio of signal power to noise power in optical domain

- Typical values: >20 dB for optimal performance
- Measured at various points along the optical path
- Critical for determining system margin

Q-Factor

Quality factor indicating signal quality in terms of BER

- Typically >6 for acceptable performance
- Direct correlation with Bit Error Rate (BER)

- Q = 6 corresponds to BER of 10^-9

Chromatic Dispersion (CD)

Wavelength-dependent signal spreading

- Measured in ps/nm/km
- Accumulates linearly with distance
- Compensation required for long-haul systems

Polarization Mode Dispersion (PMD)

Signal spreading due to polarization effects

- Measured in ps/√km
- Random nature, varies with time
- Critical for high-speed systems (>10G)

Other Analog Parameters

- Received Power Level (dBm)
- Launch Power (dBm)
- Extinction Ratio (dB)
- Cross-Talk (dB)
- Optical Return Loss (dB)
- Dispersion Power Penalty (dB)

Digital Layer Parameters

OTN Layer (G.709)

OTU (Optical Transport Unit)

- BER (Bit Error Rate): Typically 10^-12 to 10^-15
- FEC Performance: Pre-FEC BER, Post-FEC BER
- OTU Frame Errors
- OTU Background Block Errors (BBE)

ODU (Optical Data Unit)

- Path Monitoring:
- Errored Seconds (ES)
- Severely Errored Seconds (SES)
- Background Block Errors (BBE)
- Unavailable Seconds (UAS)

OPU (Optical Payload Unit)

- Payload Type Mismatch
- Payload Structure Mismatch
- Client Signal Fail (CSF)

Ethernet Layer Parameters

Frame Level Metrics

- Frame Error Rate (FER)
- Frame Loss Ratio (FLR)
- Frame Delay (FD)
- Frame Delay Variation (FDV)
- Frame Out of Order Ratio

Error Detection

- CRC Errors
- Jabber Frames
- Runt Frames
- Collision Rate
- Late Collisions

DWDM System Parameters

Channel Parameters

- Channel Power (dBm)
- Channel Spacing (GHz)
- Channel Drift (GHz)
- Channel Cross-talk (dB)
- Channel OSNR

System Level Parameters

- Total System Power
- Power Tilt
- Gain Flatness
- System Margin
- Link Budget

Service Level Parameters

Availability Metrics

- Network Availability (%)
- Mean Time Between Failures (MTBF)
- Mean Time To Repair (MTTR)
- Protection Switching Time

Quality of Service Metrics

- End-to-End Delay
- Jitter
- Packet Loss Rate
- Throughput

Comprehensive Optical Network Alarms Guide

1. Physical Layer Alarms

Optical Power Alarms

Alarm	Severity	Description	Typical Causes
LOS (Loss of Signal)	Critical	No optical power detected	Fiber break, disconnected fiber, transmitter failure
LOL (Loss of Light)	Critical	Optical power below sensitivity threshold	Bent fiber, dirty connector, degraded transmitter
High Rx Power	Major	Received power above maximum threshold	Short link, incorrect attenuation settings
Low Rx Power	Major	Received power below minimum threshold	High link loss, degraded components

Laser and Temperature Alarms

- Laser Bias Current High/Low **Major**
- Laser Temperature High/Low **Major**
- TEC (Thermoelectric Cooler) Failure **Major**
- Module Temperature High/Low **Warning**

2. DWDM Layer Alarms

Channel Alarms

Alarm	Severity	Description
Channel Power Fail	Critical	Individual channel power loss
Channel Power High/Low	Major	Channel power outside operat-ing range
OSNR Degradation	Major	Channel OSNR below thresh-old
Wavelength Drift	Warning	Channel wavelength outside specification

Amplifier Alarms

- EDFA Pump Failure **Critical**
- Gain Out of Range **Major**
- ASE Noise High **Warning**
- Output Power Deviation **Major**

3. OTN Layer Alarms

OTU (Optical Transport Unit) Alarms

Alarm	Severity	Description
LOF (Loss of Frame)	Critical	OTU framing loss
OTU-AIS	Major	Alarm Indication Signal received
OTU-BDI	Major	Backward Defect Indication

FEC Excessive Errors	Major	High FEC correction rate

ODU (Optical Data Unit) Alarms

- ODU-AIS (Alarm Indication Signal) **Major**
- ODU-OCI (Open Connection Indication) **Major**
- ODU-LCK (Locked) **Major**
- ODU-BDI (Backward Defect Indication) **Major**
- ODU-CSF (Client Signal Fail) **Major**
- ODU-TIM (Trace Identifier Mismatch) **Minor**

OPU (Optical Payload Unit) Alarms

- OPU-PLM (Payload Mismatch) **Major**
- OPU-CSF (Client Signal Fail) **Major**
- OPU-AIS (Alarm Indication Signal) **Major**

4. Ethernet Layer Alarms

Physical Layer Alarms

- Loss of Signal **Critical**
- Local Fault **Major**
- Remote Fault **Major**
- Link Down **Major**

MAC Layer Alarms

Alarm	**Severity**	**Description**
Excessive Collisions	Minor	High collision rate detected
FCS Error Rate High	Warning	Frame Check Sequence errors exceed threshold
Broadcast Storm	Major	Excessive broadcast traffic

MAC Address Flapping	Warning	MAC address moving between ports

5. Protection and Equipment Alarms

Protection Switching Alarms

- Protection Switch (Automatic) Minor
- Protection Switch (Forced) **Warning**
- Protection Path Failure Critical
- Working Path Failure **Major**

Equipment Alarms

Alarm	**Severity**	**Description**
Fan Failure	Major	Cooling fan malfunction
Power Supply Failure	Critical	Power supply unit failure
High Temperature	Major	Equipment temperature exceeds threshold
Module Communication Failure	Major	Internal communication loss with module

6. Management System Alarms

System Level Alarms

- Database Backup Failure Minor
- NTP Sync Loss Warning
- Memory Usage High Warning
- CPU Usage High Warning
- Disk Space Low Warning

OTN and DWDM Alarm Reference Guide

1. OTN Layer Alarms

1.1 OTU (Optical Transport Unit) Alarms

Alarm/Defect	Severity	Description	Typical Causes
LOS (Loss of Signal)	Critical	No optical power detected at receiver	Fiber cut, disconnected fiber, equipment failure
LOF (Loss of Frame)	Critical	OTU framing lost for 3ms or more	Signal degradation, mismatched configuration
OOF (Out of Frame)	Major	Frame alignment errors detected	Signal corruption, equipment issues
LOM (Loss of Multiframe)	Major	Multiframe alignment lost	Synchronization issues
OOM (Out of Multiframe)	Major	Multiframe errors detected	Frame synchronization problems

Alarm/Defect	Severity	Description	Typical Causes

FEC-EXC (FEC Excessive)	Major	FEC correction rate exceeds threshold	Signal degradation, high BER
FEC-DEG (FEC Degraded)	Minor	FEC correction near threshold	Signal quality issues
IAE (Incoming Alignment Error)	Major	OTU alignment errors detected	Synchronization problems
BIAE (Backward Incoming Alignment Error)	Major	Backward direction alignment errors	Remote end synchronization issues

1.2 ODU (Optical Data Unit) Alarms

Alarm/Defect	**Severity**	**Description**	**Action**
AIS (Alarm Indication Signal)	Major	All-1's signal replacing normal traffic	Check upstream equipment
OCI (Open Connection Indication)	Major	Path not connected to client signal	Verify connection configuration
LCK (Locked)	Major	Administrative lock condition	Check management configuration
BDI (Backward Defect Indication)	Major	Remote end detecting problems	Check far end equipment

Alarm/Defect	**Severity**	**Description**	**Action**
TIM (Trace Identifier Mismatch)	Major	Expected SAPI/DAPI mismatch	Verify path configuration

DEG (Signal Degrade)	Minor	Signal quality degradation	Monitor performance metrics
SSF (Server Signal Fail)	Critical	Lower layer signal failure	Check physical layer
CSF (Client Signal Fail)	Major	Client signal failure indication	Check client equipment

1.3 OPU (Optical Payload Unit) Alarms

Alarm/Defect	Severity	Description	Action
PLM (Payload Type Mismatch)	Major	Incorrect payload type detected	Verify mapping configuration
PRDI (Payload Running Disparity Indicator)	Minor	Payload adaptation issues	Check mapping parameters
AIS (OPU-AIS)	Major	Payload replaced with AIS	Check upstream client signal

2. DWDM Layer Alarms

2.1 Optical Channel Alarms

Alarm/Defect	Severity	Description	Action

OCH-LOS (Loss of Signal)	Critical	Channel power loss detected	Check transponder, mux/demux
OCH-LOF (Loss of Frame)	Critical	Channel framing lost	Verify optical channel path
OCH-PF (Power Fail)	Major	Channel power outside range	Check power levels, attenuation

2.2 Multiplexer Section Alarms

Alarm/Defect	**Severity**	**Description**	**Action**
OMS-LOS	Critical	Loss of all optical channels	Check fiber span, amplifiers
OMS-AIS	Major	Multiplexer section failure	Check upstream equipment
OMS-BDI	Major	Backward defect in mux section	Check downstream equipment

2.3 Amplifier Alarms

Alarm/Defect	Severity	Description	Action
AMP-FAIL	Critical	Amplifier failure	Check power, pump lasers
GAIN-LOW	Major	Gain below threshold	Check input power, settings
ASE-HIGH	Minor	Excessive ASE noise	Check gain settings

OTN Alarm Troubleshooting Guide

1. OTU (Optical Transport Unit) Layer

Alarm	Severity	Consequences	Root Causes	Recommended Actions
LOS (Loss of Signal)	Critical	- Complete traffic loss - Protection switching - Service disruption	- Fiber break - Disconnected fiber - Faulty transceiver - Dirty connectors	1. Check physical fiber connections 2. Verify optical power levels 3. Clean fiber connectors 4. Test fiber continuity 5. Replace transceiver if needed

LOF (Loss of Frame)	Critical	- Frame synchronization lost - Service interruption - Data errors	- Signal degradation - FEC failures - Clock synchronization issues - Configuration mismatch	1. Check FEC status 2. Verify clock source 3. Check configuration matching 4. Monitor BER statistics 5. Check optical power levels
FEC-EXC (FEC Excessive)	Major	- High bit error rate - Potential traffic loss - Degraded performance	- Signal degradation - Optical path issues - Aging components - Power level issues	1. Monitor pre-FEC BER 2. Check optical power levels 3. Verify OSNR 4. Check chromatic dispersion 5. Verify optical path quality
BDI (Backward Defect Indication)	Major	- Remote end issues - Potential traffic impact - Bidirectional issues	- Far-end signal problems - Path issues - Equipment failures	1. Check far-end alarms 2. Verify bidirectional path 3. Test remote equipment 4. Check protection status 5. Verify configurations

2. ODU (Optical Data Unit) Layer

Alarm	Severity	Consequences	Root Causes	Recommended Actions
AIS (Alarm Indication Signal)	Major	- Traffic interruption - Path failure indication - Service degradation	- Upstream failures - Equipment issues - Path failures	1. Check upstream equipment 2. Verify path continuity 3. Check cross-connects 4. Monitor tributary signals 5. Check protection status
OCI (Open Connection Indication)	Major	- No client signal - Service unavailable - Configuration issues	- Misconfiguration - Client signal missing - Cross-connect issues	1. Verify cross-connects 2. Check client signal 3. Review configuration 4. Check tributary mapping 5. Verify client interface
LCK (Locked)	Major	- Administrative lockout - Planned maintenance - Service interruption	- Administrative action - Maintenance activity - Protection switching	1. Check maintenance schedule 2. Verify administrative state 3. Review change records 4. Check protection status 5. Coordinate unlocking

TIM (Trace Identifier Mismatch)	Major	- Path mismatch - Misrouted traffic - Service issues	- Incorrect configuration - Wrong connections - Database errors	1. Verify SAPI/DAPI settings 2. Check path routing 3. Review configurations 4. Update trail trace 5. Document changes

3. OPU (Optical Payload Unit) Layer

Alarm	Severity	Consequences	Root Causes	Recommended Actions
PLM (Payload Type Mismatch)	Major	- Payload processing failure - Service interruption - Client signal issues	- Wrong mapping configuration - Client signal mismatch - Equipment incompatibility	1. Verify payload type settings 2. Check client signal type 3. Review mapping configuration 4. Check equipment compatibility 5. Update configuration

CSF (Client Signal Fail)	Major	- Client signal problems - Service disruption - End-to-end issues	- Client equipment failure - Interface issues - Signal quality problems	1. Check client equipment 2. Verify interface status 3. Test client signal 4. Check signal quality 5. Coordinate with client
PRDI (Payload Running Disparity)	Minor	- Adaptation issues - Potential data errors - Performance impact	- Clock synchronization - Mapping issues - Payload adaptation problems	1. Check clock sources 2. Verify mapping parameters 3. Monitor performance 4. Check buffer status 5. Adjust timing settings

Data and Statistics

Recent data and statistics highlight the importance of effective alarm and performance management:

- **Network Downtime Impact**: Network downtime can cost enterprises up to $5,600 per minute, emphasizing the need for rapid fault detection and resolution.
- **Performance Optimization**: Studies show that effective performance management can improve network efficiency by up to 30%, resulting in significant cost savings and better user experiences.
- **Alarm Generation**: Modern network management systems can reduce the number of false alarms by up to 70%, ensuring that operators focus on critical issues.

Alarm and performance management are essential for maintaining and optimizing optical networks. By implementing robust monitoring systems, setting appropriate thresholds, and using advanced tools for fault detection and performance analysis, network engineers and professionals can ensure high network reliability and performance. As networks continue to grow and evolve, the role of effective alarm and performance management will become increasingly important in ensuring seamless and efficient network operations.

Chapter 17

Automation in Optical Networks

Chapter 17
Automation in Optical Networks

"Automation is not about replacing humans; it's about empowering them." - David Payne

---

Automation is reshaping the landscape of optical networking, driving efficiencies across every stage of the network lifecycle—from development to operations. The complexity of managing high-speed, high-capacity optical networks demands tools and processes that can minimize human intervention, reduce errors, and improve overall performance. Automation covers multiple areas, including network design, provisioning, testing, monitoring, maintenance, and management, with a special emphasis on real-time data analysis, predictive maintenance, and dashboarding for service metrics and availability.

This chapter will explore the scope of automation in optical networking, broken down into its key phases:

- Development
- Testing and Validation
- Deployment
- Operations and Maintenance
- Management and Dashboarding
- Availability and Service Metrics

Automation in Optical Network Development

Software-Defined Networking (SDN) and Programmable Optical Networks

SDN Overview: SDN is a foundational technology for automating optical networks. By decoupling the control plane from the data plane, SDN enables centralized, software-driven control of network elements. This allows operators to programmatically configure and manage their networks.

Benefits for Development:

- **Reduced Complexity**: SDN abstracts the underlying hardware, allowing developers to focus on service logic rather than hardware configurations.
- **Faster Innovation**: New services can be developed and deployed rapidly without the need for manual network reconfigurations.
- **Programmability**: With programmable optical networks, developers can implement APIs that allow external applications to dynamically configure wavelength routing, service provisioning, and bandwidth allocation.
- **Example**: A service provider implements an SDN-based automation platform for metro networks, allowing new 400G services to be provisioned dynamically through APIs without requiring manual intervention.

Automated Design and Simulation Tools

Role of Automation in Design: Optical network design traditionally involved significant manual effort, with engineers calculating link budgets, planning amplifier placements, and configuring protection schemes. Automated design tools now allow engineers to simulate and optimize network architectures based on real-world constraints, such as fiber loss, dispersion, and latency requirements.

Key Tools and Features:

- **Network Simulators**: Tools like OptSim and VPIphotonics enable developers to simulate the performance of complex optical systems, testing for factors like chromatic dispersion and nonlinearity before deployment.
- **AI-Driven Design**: Machine learning algorithms are being integrated into design tools to optimize network layouts, reducing fiber costs while maximizing capacity and resilience.
- **Practical Case**: A national operator uses an AI-powered design tool to optimize its DWDM long-haul network, cutting costs by reducing unnecessary amplifiers while maintaining service quality.

Automation in Optical Network Testing and Validation

Automated Testing for Optical Components

- **Optical Transceivers and Amplifiers**: The testing of optical transceivers (e.g., 100G, 400G, 800G coherent optics) and amplifiers is critical to ensure they meet performance specifications. Automated test suites enable continuous testing of parameters like OSNR, BER (bit error rate), and eye diagrams without human intervention.

- **Test Automation Platforms**: Tools like IXIA, Spirent, and EXFO provide automated testing solutions that can simulate network conditions, run stress tests on transceivers, and validate the performance of complex network topologies.
- **Use Case**: A large service provider automates the testing of its 400G coherent transceivers before deployment by using a test platform that measures BER and latency under different power levels and signal degradation conditions.

Validation in Virtualized Environments

- **Network Function Virtualization (NFV)**: NFV enables the virtualization of network functions, allowing operators to simulate real-world scenarios in virtual environments before actual deployment. Automated testing in NFV environments provides engineers with the ability to detect issues early, reducing risks during the deployment phase.
- **End-to-End Testing**: With automation, it's possible to run continuous tests across both the physical and virtual layers of the network, ensuring that hardware and software components are integrated seamlessly. This ensures the network can meet stringent performance and reliability targets.
- **Practical Example**: An enterprise automates end-to-end testing of its hybrid fiber-radio network using an NFV environment, detecting and resolving interoperability issues between physical transceivers and virtualized control systems.

Automation in Optical Network Deployment

Automated Provisioning and Service Activation

- **Zero-Touch Provisioning**: With automation, new network services can be provisioned automatically based on predefined templates. This eliminates the need for manual configurations, reducing time-to-market for new services.
- **Dynamic Resource Allocation**: As demand fluctuates, automated systems can dynamically allocate bandwidth, adjust wavelengths, and optimize optical paths based on traffic patterns. This is particularly useful for data center interconnects (DCIs) where traffic spikes can occur unpredictably.
- **Example**: A data center provider uses an automated SDN controller to dynamically allocate 400G optical wavelengths based on traffic demand between two cities. This allows the provider to handle peak traffic without over-provisioning resources.

Automated Fiber Deployment and Monitoring

- **Automated Splicing and Testing**: In large-scale optical network deployments, especially in long-haul and metro areas, fiber splicing and testing can be automated. Advanced optical test units can automatically detect fiber issues, perform OTDR tests, and report back to a central system.

- **Geospatial Fiber Mapping**: Automation tools equipped with GPS and GIS capabilities can map fiber routes in real-time, ensuring accurate network documentation and reducing the risk of misconfigured fiber connections during future expansions.
- **Use Case**: A national telecom operator automates the deployment of a new fiber network using robotic splicing tools and OTDR testing units that detect and repair fiber defects without human intervention.

Automation in Optical Network Operations and Maintenance

Predictive Maintenance with AI and Machine Learning

- **AI-Powered Maintenance**: Automation tools powered by AI analyze historical data and real-time network conditions to predict when network components, such as transceivers or amplifiers, are likely to fail. Predictive maintenance allows operators to replace failing components before they impact service, reducing downtime.
- **Proactive Fault Detection**: Machine learning models can detect patterns in network behavior, flagging potential failures before they occur. Automated alerts are sent to technicians, enabling them to take action before service is disrupted.
- **Example**: A Tier-1 telecom operator uses AI to monitor its long-haul optical links. The system predicts amplifier degradation based on OSNR trends, allowing technicians to schedule proactive replacements before the amplifiers fail.

Self-Healing Optical Networks

- **Real-Time Fault Recovery**: Self-healing networks can automatically detect and resolve faults without human intervention. This is achieved through real-time monitoring of network performance and automated rerouting of traffic in the event of a failure.
- **Fast Reroute (FRR)**: When a fiber cut or equipment failure occurs, automation enables fast reroute (FRR) mechanisms, redirecting traffic over alternative paths within milliseconds, ensuring minimal service disruption.
- **Use Case**: A submarine cable operator automates fault recovery in its global network. When a fiber cut is detected, the system automatically reroutes traffic across a redundant path, ensuring continuous service for critical financial transactions.

Automated Network Diagnostics and Root Cause Analysis

- **Real-Time Diagnostics**: Automation tools continuously monitor optical performance metrics, such as OSNR, power levels, and error rates. When an anomaly is detected, the system runs diagnostics to identify the root cause, enabling faster resolution.
- **Automated Ticketing and Escalation**: Once a fault is detected and diagnosed, automated systems can generate trouble tickets, assign them to the appropriate teams, and escalate them based on predefined severity levels.
- **Example**: An enterprise optical network automatically detects a drop in OSNR on a critical link. The system runs a diagnostic test and identifies the cause as a faulty transponder. A ticket is automatically generated and assigned to the field team for immediate repair.

Automation in Network Management, Dashboarding, and Analytics

Centralized Network Management

- **Unified Control with SDN**: SDN controllers enable centralized management of the entire optical network, providing real-time visibility into network performance and allowing operators to configure and control network elements from a single platform.
- **Multi-Layer Network Management**: Advanced automation tools enable multi-layer management, where both the optical layer (Layer 1) and higher layers (Layer 2/3) are managed simultaneously. This enables more efficient service delivery and better coordination between transport and IP networks.
- **Practical Example**: A global service provider uses an SDN-based network management platform to monitor both optical and IP networks from a single dashboard. This integration allows the operator to optimize traffic across both layers, improving overall service performance.

Real-Time Dashboarding for Optical Networks

- **Overview**: Real-time dashboards provide operators with an instant view of network health, performance, and traffic conditions. Automation platforms feed live data into centralized dashboards, giving operators access to critical metrics such as bandwidth utilization, latency, jitter, packet loss, OSNR, and link availability.
- **Advanced Visualization Tools**: Dashboards today often integrate AI-powered analytics, predictive models, and multi-layer visualizations, enabling engineers to drill down into network layers (e.g., physical, optical, IP) for deeper insights. Tools such as Grafana, Kibana, and proprietary platforms from vendors like Cisco and Juniper offer sophisticated dashboarding capabilities.

- **Dynamic Network Heatmaps**: Visualizing network performance through heatmaps can help detect congestion points, monitor resource utilization, and visualize where issues are likely to occur. Operators can automate threshold-based alerts, triggering real-time notifications when certain performance metrics are breached.
- **Practical Example**: A data center interconnect (DCI) network uses a real-time dashboard to monitor 400G optical links between two locations. The dashboard displays metrics such as OSNR, BER (bit error rate), and power levels for each wavelength. Engineers are alerted via automated email or SMS when the OSNR drops below the threshold, allowing them to take preemptive action before the link degrades further.

Predictive Analytics and Capacity Forecasting

- **Capacity Management with Automation**: Predictive analytics enable operators to forecast traffic growth, anticipate bottlenecks, and automate bandwidth provisioning. By analyzing historical traffic data and applying machine learning models, the network can dynamically adjust its resources to meet future demands.
- **Automated Bandwidth Optimization**: As network traffic patterns shift, automation systems can intelligently reallocate bandwidth between services and routes. This ensures optimal resource utilization without manual intervention.
- **Use Case**: A Tier-1 service provider uses predictive analytics to manage bandwidth in its metro network. The system predicts a traffic surge in a particular region due to a major event and automatically provisions additional wavelengths in the affected routes, ensuring seamless service delivery.

Automation for Network Availability and Service Metrics

Automated Availability Management

- **Maintaining "Five Nines" (99.999%) Availability**: Automation tools are key to achieving and maintaining high availability targets. By integrating fault-tolerant designs, redundancy, and real-time monitoring, automated systems can detect and resolve network issues before they impact service. Systems like self-healing networks and Fast Reroute (FRR) mechanisms ensure that traffic is dynamically rerouted in the event of a failure.
- **Automated Fiber Protection**: Fiber cuts are one of the most common causes of network outages, particularly in long-haul and submarine systems. Automation in protection schemes, such as 1+1 or 1:1 protection switching, ensures traffic is immediately shifted to a redundant path with minimal impact on service.
- **Example**: A global cloud provider runs a 400G backbone network with 1+1 protection in place. When a primary fiber link between two data cen-

ters experiences a cut, the network instantly switches traffic to a backup path, ensuring continuous service for critical applications. The automated system also triggers a repair team to investigate the fiber fault, which is identified through real-time OTDR testing.

Service-Level Agreements (SLAs) and Real-Time Monitoring

- **Automated SLA Tracking**: Automation tools enable continuous monitoring of key performance indicators (KPIs) that are critical for meeting Service-Level Agreements (SLAs), such as latency, jitter, uptime, and packet loss. These tools generate real-time reports and provide alerts when SLA thresholds are breached.
- **Customizable SLA Dashboards**: Service providers can create customizable dashboards to monitor SLA compliance across different customers or services. The dashboards provide detailed metrics and historical data, allowing operators to track performance over time and make necessary adjustments to maintain service quality.
- **Use Case**: An enterprise provider uses an automated SLA monitoring tool to track the performance of its high-capacity 100G connections for financial clients. The system monitors latency and packet loss in real-time and sends automated reports to clients at the end of each month. When latency exceeds 1 ms, the system generates an alert, prompting immediate investigation.

Automation for Operations and Maintenance

Automated Alarm Correlation and Root Cause Analysis

- **Alarm Correlation Tools**: Automated systems in optical networks often generate a high volume of alarms when an issue occurs. Alarm correlation tools use AI to sift through thousands of alarms, identifying the root cause of the problem. This reduces noise in the system and helps engineers focus on resolving the critical issue.
- **Root Cause Automation**: Once the root cause is identified, automation systems can trigger predefined workflows to resolve the issue. These workflows could include running diagnostic tests, reconfiguring network elements, or initiating traffic rerouting.
- **Example**: A telecom operator experiences a drop in OSNR across multiple optical links in its long-haul network. The automated alarm correlation system identifies a faulty amplifier as the root cause and triggers a series of automated tests. Once confirmed, the system escalates the issue to the maintenance team and suggests rerouting options to minimize service impact.

Self-Healing Networks with SDN and AI

- **Real-Time Self-Healing**: Optical networks integrated with SDN and AI can respond to failures in real-time, automatically reconfiguring routes and wavelengths to maintain service. By analyzing network traffic patterns and optical performance metrics, the system can reroute traffic around failures or congested links without manual intervention.
- **Dynamic Resource Reallocation**: SDN controllers, combined with AI, enable networks to self-optimize. For example, if a link starts to degrade, the network can dynamically reallocate resources (e.g., additional wavelengths) to mitigate the issue.
- **Use Case**: A submarine cable system uses a self-healing architecture based on SDN and AI. When an optical transponder starts to experience BER degradation, the system automatically reroutes traffic through an alternate transponder. It also notifies the operations team to investigate the degrading transponder, minimizing service impact.

Service Metrics and Continuous Performance Monitoring

Key Service Metrics for Optical Networks

- **Optical Signal-to-Noise Ratio (OSNR)**: OSNR is a critical metric in optical networks that directly affects the quality of signal transmission. Automation platforms continuously monitor OSNR across network segments and alert operators if it drops below the required threshold for error-free transmission.
- **Bit Error Rate (BER)**: Monitoring BER is essential in high-capacity optical networks. Automated systems regularly test optical paths and provide insights into the bit error rate for each wavelength. This helps operators detect issues before they affect customer services.
- **Latency and Jitter**: For real-time applications such as video conferencing and gaming, low latency and jitter are critical. Automated systems monitor these metrics and dynamically adjust routing paths to maintain optimal performance.
- **Example**: A service provider offers real-time video streaming services. An automated monitoring platform continuously tracks latency and jitter metrics across the optical network, ensuring they stay within SLA targets. When jitter increases, the system reroutes traffic to a less congested path to maintain service quality.

Automated Performance Reporting

- **Real-Time and Historical Reports**: Automated systems generate both real-time and historical performance reports. These reports can be customized for specific customers or services, providing detailed insights into network performance over time.

- **On-Demand Analytics**: Operators can access performance data on-demand through the dashboard, which offers a comprehensive view of the network's health. Automated systems can also generate reports at regular intervals (e.g., daily, weekly, or monthly) and distribute them to relevant stakeholders.
- **Use Case**: A national carrier automates its performance reporting, generating detailed OSNR and BER reports for its 100G and 400G optical backbone. These reports are shared with internal teams and enterprise customers, ensuring transparency and SLA compliance.

Future Trends in Automation for Optical Networks

AI-Driven Closed-Loop Automation

- **What is Closed-Loop Automation?**: Closed-loop automation refers to the ability of the network to not only detect issues but also to automatically correct them without human intervention. AI and machine learning models continuously analyze network performance data, identify anomalies, and trigger automated workflows for resolution.
- **Self-Learning Systems**: Future optical networks will integrate self-learning systems that adapt to changing network conditions. These systems will be capable of making real-time adjustments based on historical data, optimizing network performance and improving resilience.
- **Example**: A global service provider uses closed-loop automation to manage its optical backbone. When a high-traffic event is detected, the system dynamically provisions additional wavelengths, balances traffic loads, and reroutes critical services to avoid congestion.

Intent-Based Networking (IBN)

- **Overview**: Intent-based networking (IBN) allows operators to define their network goals (or intent) in high-level language, and the automation platform translates this intent into network configurations. IBN eliminates the need for manual configurations, enabling a fully automated and self-optimizing network.
- **Benefits of IBN**: By leveraging AI and SDN, IBN automates complex configurations, ensures compliance with SLA requirements, and continuously monitors network conditions to align with the operator's goals.
- **Use Case**: An enterprise network uses IBN to maintain optimal network performance. The operator defines an intent for low-latency service for real-time video applications. The IBN system automatically configures the necessary optical paths and reroutes traffic as needed to maintain low latency.

Automation is transforming every aspect of optical networking, from development and deployment to operations and maintenance. By integrating AI, SDN, machine learning, and real-time monitoring, optical networks are becoming more efficient, resilient, and capable of handling the ever-increasing demand for bandwidth. Automation tools not only reduce human error but also provide operators with deeper insights into network performance, allowing them to meet stringent SLA targets and optimize network resources dynamically.

Optical Network Automation Case study

Understanding the Challenge

1. Current Operational Challenges

Challenge Area	Impact	Manual Effort	Error Risk
Configuration	Time-consuming	30min/device	High
Performance	Delayed response	Hours/incident	Medium
Fault handling	Service impact	Variable	Very High
Optimization	Resource intensive	Days/network	Medium
Documentation	Inconsistent	Hours/change	High

2. Business Impact

Impact Area	Cost Factor	Time Loss	Risk Level
Service delivery	$1000s/delay	Days	High
Network changes	$500/change	Hours	Medium
Troubleshooting	$2000/incident	4-8 hours	Critical
Optimization	$5000/month	Continuous	Medium
Compliance	$10000/violation	Periodic	High

3. Automation Layers

Layer	Function	Tools	Complexity
Physical	Hardware control	Direct APIs	High
Transport	Circuit management	NETCONF/YANG	Medium
Service	End-to-end	SDN Controllers	High
Management	Operations	Custom scripts	Medium
Orchestration	Full workflow	Frameworks	Very High

4. Automation Framework Design

Component	Purpose	Implementation	Integration
Data Model	Structure	YANG models	All layers
Protocol	Communication	NETCONF/REST	Transport
Templates	Configuration	Jinja2	Management
Scripts	Execution	Python	Operations
Validation	Verification	PyTest	Quality

5. System Components

Component	Function	Technology	Integration Point
Config Manager	Template management	Jinja2/YAML	Configuration
Device Interface	Network communication	NETCONF/SSH	Devices
Data Store	State information	Database/Files	Persistence
Workflow Engine	Process automation	Python/Framework	Orchestration
UI/API	User interface	Web/REST	Users/Systems

6. Data Flow

Stage	Process	Input	Output

Collection	Gather requirements	User input	Parameters
Validation	Check parameters	Parameters	Verified data
Template	Apply templates	Verified data	Configs
Deployment	Push to devices	Configs	Status
Verification	Check implementation	Status	Results

7. Phased Approach

Phase	**Focus**	**Duration**	**Deliverables**
1 - Foundation	Basic automation	1 month	Scripts
2 - Integration	System connection	2 months	Framework
3 - Advanced	Full automation	3 months	Platform
4 - Optimization	Enhancement	Ongoing	Improvements

8. Technology Stack Selection

Component	**Technology Choice**	**Alternative**	**Reason**
Language	Python	Go	Ecosystem
Config Mgmt	YAML + Jinja2	XML	Readability
Protocol	NETCONF	REST	Transaction
Framework	Custom + Libraries	Vendor	Flexibility

Testing	PyTest	UnitTest	Features

9. Development Tools Matrix

Tool Category	**Windows**	**MacOS**	**Purpose**
IDE	VSCode/PyCharm	VSCode/PyCharm	Development
Version Control	Git/GitHub Desktop	Git/Terminal	Source Control
Virtual Env	venv/conda	venv/conda	Isolation
Package Mgmt	pip/requirements.txt	pip/brew	Dependencies
Testing	PyTest/Debugger	PyTest/Debugger	Validation

10. Module Responsibilities

Module	**Responsibility**	**Dependencies**	**Interface**
device_manager	Device communication	netconf/ssh	DeviceAPI
config_manager	Config handling	yaml/jinja2	ConfigAPI
workflow_engine	Process automation	core modules	WorkflowAPI
models	Data structures	database	ModelAPI
utils	Helper functions	standard lib	UtilsAPI

interfaces	External comm	protocols	CommAPI

Large-Scale Card Reset Process Flow

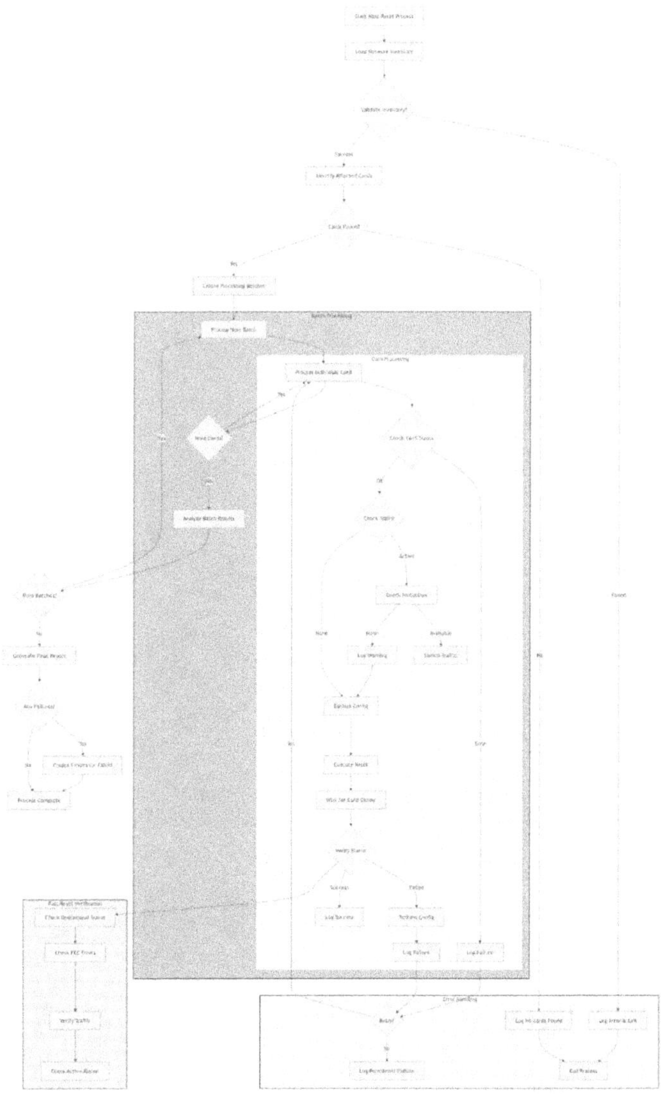

Workflow

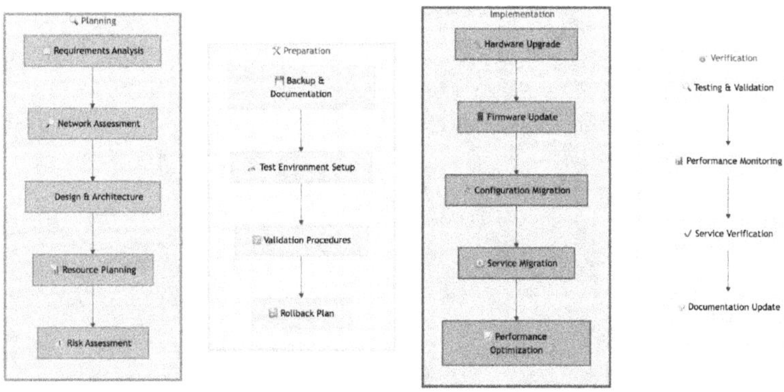

Planning
Requirements Analysis
Network Assessment
Design & Architecture
Resource Planning
Risk Assessment
Preparation
Backup & Documentation
Test Environment Setup
Validation Procedures
Rollback Plan
Implementation
Hardware Upgrade
Firmware Update
Configuration Migration
Service Migration
Performance Optimization
Verification
Testing & Validation
Performance Monitoring
Service Verification
Documentation Update

Chapter 18

Network Upgrades and Maintenance

Chapter 18
Network Upgrades and Maintenance

"Maintenance is not a cost, it's an investment." - Donald Keck

---

Upgrading an optical network involves several critical considerations to ensure a smooth transition and minimal disruption to existing services.

- **Capacity Requirements**: Assessing current and future bandwidth needs to determine the required upgrade capacity.
- **Technology Advancements**: Incorporating the latest technologies to enhance network performance and efficiency.
- **Cost-Benefit Analysis**: Evaluating the costs and benefits of different upgrade options to ensure cost-effectiveness.
- **Compatibility and Interoperability**: Ensuring new components are compatible with existing infrastructure.
- **Downtime and Disruption**: Minimizing network downtime and service disruption during the upgrade process.
- **Scalability and Future-Proofing**: Designing the upgrade to accommodate future growth and technological advancements.

Planning an Upgrade

Effective planning is crucial for a successful network upgrade. Key steps include:

1. **Assessment and Analysis**: Conducting a thorough assessment of the current network, including performance metrics, capacity usage, and existing infrastructure.
2. **Requirement Definition**: Defining the requirements for the upgrade based on current needs and future projections.
3. **Technology Selection**: Selecting the appropriate technologies and components for the upgrade, such as new transponders, amplifiers, or DWDM systems.
4. **Design and Engineering**: Creating detailed upgrade plans and engineering designs, including network diagrams and configuration changes.

5. **Testing and Validation**: Testing the new components and configurations in a controlled environment to validate performance and compatibility.
6. **Implementation Planning**: Developing a detailed implementation plan, including timelines, resource allocation, and risk management strategies.
7. **Execution and Monitoring**: Executing the upgrade plan and continuously monitoring the network to identify and address any issues.

Practical Upgrade Scenarios

1. Capacity Upgrade Example

Scenario: A telecommunications provider needs to upgrade their metro optical network to support increasing data traffic due to the rise of streaming services and cloud computing.

Steps:

- **Assessment**: Analyze current traffic patterns and forecast future demand. Current usage is at 80% capacity, and traffic is expected to grow by 50% over the next two years.
- **Requirement Definition**: Determine that the network needs to support an additional 10 Tbps of capacity.
- **Technology Selection**: Choose to upgrade the existing DWDM system to support 400 Gbps per channel, up from 100 Gbps.
- **Design and Engineering**: Create a design that includes new high-capacity transponders and optical amplifiers to support the increased bandwidth.
- **Testing and Validation**: Test the new equipment in a lab environment to ensure it meets performance standards.
- **Implementation Planning**: Develop a phased implementation plan to upgrade one segment at a time, minimizing downtime.
- **Execution and Monitoring**: Upgrade the network in phases, starting with core links, and monitor performance to ensure smooth operation.

2. Technology Integration Example

Scenario: A financial institution needs to integrate a new photonic switch into their existing optical network to improve latency and reliability for high-frequency trading.

Steps:

- **Assessment**: Evaluate the current network architecture and identify the optimal points for integrating the new switch.
- **Requirement Definition**: Define the performance requirements, including latency reduction targets and reliability standards.
- **Technology Selection**: Select a photonic switch that meets the performance requirements and is compatible with the existing network components.
- **Design and Engineering**: Design the integration plan, including network reconfigurations and interface adjustments.
- **Testing and Validation**: Test the photonic switch in conjunction with existing components to ensure compatibility and performance.
- **Implementation Planning**: Develop an implementation plan that includes a detailed schedule and contingency plans for potential issues.
- **Execution and Monitoring**: Implement the integration during off-peak hours to minimize disruption and continuously monitor the network for any performance issues.

Mathematical Formulas and Examples

1. Link Budget Calculation

Upgrading a network often involves recalculating the link budget to ensure the new components maintain signal integrity. The link budget formula is:

$$P_{RX}=P_{TX}-\alpha\times L-M+G$$

Where:

- P_{RX} = Received power
- P_{TX} = Transmitted power
- α = Fiber attenuation (dB/km)
- L = Fiber length (km)
- M = Margin for safety and additional losses (dB)
- G = Gain from optical amplifiers (dB)

Example: If P_{TX}=0 dBm, α=0.25 dB/km, L=100 km, M=3 dB, and G=20 dB: PRX=0 dBm−(0.25 dB/km×100 km)−3 dB+20 dB P_{RX}=0 dBm−25 dB−3 dB+20 dB=−8 dBm

2. Capacity Calculation Using Shannon Capacity Limit

When upgrading to new technologies, it's important to understand the theoretical maximum capacity using the Shannon Capacity Limit:

$$C=B\log_2(1+SNR)$$

Where:

- C = Channel capacity (bps)

- B = Bandwidth (Hz)
- SNR = Signal-to-noise ratio (linear scale)

Example: For an upgraded DWDM channel with a bandwidth of 50 GHz and an SNR of 25 dB (which corresponds to an SNR linear value of 316): $C=50\times109\log_2(1+316)$ $C=50\times109\log_2(317)$ $C\approx50\times109\times8.303$ $C\approx415.15$ Gbps

Data and Statistics

Recent data and statistics highlight the importance of network upgrades:

- **Global Bandwidth Demand**: Global IP traffic is expected to reach 396 exabytes per month by 2025, necessitating frequent network upgrades.
- **Market Growth**: The optical networking market is projected to grow from $14.9 billion in 2020 to $24.4 billion by 2026, driven by the need for network upgrades and new technologies.
- **Downtime Costs**: Network downtime can cost enterprises up to $5,600 per minute, underscoring the importance of minimizing disruption during upgrades.

Pre-Upgrade Safety Checklist for Optical Device Software Upgrade

1. Initial Assessment and Documentation

- Document current software version and configuration
- Verify device serial numbers and hardware compatibility
- Take screenshots of current performance metrics and power levels
- Document all configured services and client connections
- Create network topology diagram showing device connections
- Record all protection groups and their current states
- Verify optical power levels and record baseline measurements

2. Pre-Upgrade Preparation

- Download and verify software package MD5/SHA checksums
- Confirm device has sufficient memory for upgrade
- Check battery backup and power supply redundancy
- Verify management network stability
- Create full database backup
- Export current configuration files
- Schedule maintenance window with all stakeholders
- Prepare rollback software package
- Test upgrade procedure in lab environment (if possible)

3. Service Impact Assessment

- Identify all affected customers and services
- Document protection switching capabilities
- Verify redundant paths for critical services
- Prepare customer notification with accurate timing
- Calculate estimated downtime
- Identify service restoration priority list
- Verify monitoring systems are functional

4. Safety Measures

- Ensure physical access to device
- Verify console access is working
- Test backup management connection
- Prepare emergency contact list
- Verify UPS/power systems
- Check environmental conditions (temperature/humidity)
- Ensure adequate lighting in work area

5. Upgrade Execution

- Perform final pre-upgrade health check
- Take final backup before starting
- Verify no active alarms
- Follow vendor-specific upgrade procedure
- Monitor optical power levels during upgrade
- Document each step as executed
- Record any unexpected behavior
- Monitor CPU and memory usage

6. Post-Upgrade Verification

- Verify software version is correct
- Check system uptime and stability
- Verify all modules are online
- Compare optical power levels with baseline
- Test all protection groups
- Verify client services are restored
- Check system logs for errors
- Perform end-to-end service testing
- Verify management system connectivity
- Check performance metrics match pre-upgrade levels

7. Documentation and Closure

- Update system documentation with new version
- Record any issues encountered and solutions
- Document any configuration changes made
- Update network management systems
- Create upgrade report
- Archive all backups and logs
- Update maintenance records

- Notify stakeholders of completion

8. Emergency Response Plan

- Documented rollback procedure
- Emergency contact numbers available
- Backup files readily accessible
- Recovery time objectives defined
- Alternative access methods prepared
- Spare parts location identified
- Escalation procedures documented

9. Critical Warnings

1. Never upgrade multiple devices simultaneously
2. Always maintain console access during upgrade
3. Never interrupt the upgrade process once started
4. Keep original software version readily available
5. Monitor optical power levels continuously
6. Maintain backup management connectivity
7. Follow vendor-specific procedures exactly

10. Required Tools

- Console cable and adapter
- Laptop with terminal software
- Optical power meter
- Network cable tester
- Backup storage device
- Vendor documentation
- Emergency procedures manual

Post-Upgrade Safety Checklist for Optical Device Software Upgrade

1. Immediate Post-Upgrade Verification

- Verify successful completion of upgrade process and system boot
- Confirm new software version is correctly installed and active
- Check all hardware modules are recognized and operational
- Verify no critical alarms are present in the system
- Confirm management interface accessibility
- Check CPU, memory, and disk utilization are within normal ranges
- Verify system time and NTP synchronization
- Monitor power consumption and temperature readings

2. Service Verification

- Verify all configured services are running
- Check status of all client interfaces and connections

- Confirm protection groups are in expected states
- Test automatic protection switching functionality
- Verify optical power levels match pre-upgrade baseline
- Check OSNR (Optical Signal-to-Noise Ratio) measurements
- Test end-to-end connectivity for all critical paths
- Verify QoS settings and traffic prioritization

3. Performance Assessment

- Compare current performance metrics with pre-upgrade baseline
- Check system response times and latency
- Verify bandwidth utilization patterns
- Monitor error counters on all interfaces
- Test system stability under normal load
- Verify proper functioning of all management systems
- Check synchronization status of all timing interfaces
- Monitor BER (Bit Error Rate) on all active channels

4. Configuration Validation

- Compare current configuration with pre-upgrade backup
- Verify all customer-specific configurations are preserved
- Check routing protocol operations and neighbor relationships
- Confirm security settings and access controls
- Verify SNMP configurations and trap destinations
- Test all configured alerts and notifications
- Check backup configurations are properly saved
- Verify database integrity and synchronization

5. Security Assessment

- Verify all security features are operational
- Check user access levels and permissions
- Test authentication mechanisms
- Verify encryption settings
- Check firewall rules and access lists
- Confirm secure management access
- Test security alarm functions
- Verify audit logging is operational

6. Network Integration

- Test integration with network management systems
- Verify proper reporting to monitoring platforms
- Check all network protocols are functioning
- Test interoperability with adjacent systems
- Verify proper handling of maintenance signals
- Check proper operation of network discovery protocols
- Test all configured backup paths
- Verify proper operation of network services

7. Documentation and Records

- Document all post-upgrade test results
- Record any deviations from expected behavior
- Update system documentation with new features
- Document any workarounds or special procedures
- Update network diagrams if needed
- Record optical power readings and performance metrics
- Document any configuration changes made
- Update maintenance records and databases

8. Customer Service Verification

- Verify all customer services are restored
- Test customer-facing interfaces
- Confirm service quality meets SLA requirements
- Document service restoration times
- Verify customer monitoring and reporting
- Test customer-specific features and configurations
- Check customer notification systems
- Verify billing and service tracking systems

9. Long-term Monitoring Plan

- Define extended monitoring period
- Establish performance baseline metrics
- Set up trending analysis
- Configure additional logging if needed
- Schedule follow-up health checks
- Plan periodic protection switching tests
- Set up automated monitoring alerts
- Define escalation thresholds

10. Close-out Procedures

- Obtain stakeholder sign-off
- Archive all upgrade documentation
- Update asset management systems
- Clear any temporary files or configurations
- Remove any temporary access provisions
- Update software inventory systems
- Schedule next maintenance window
- Distribute final upgrade report

Critical Post-Upgrade Checks

1. Verify no traffic loss or errors on any interface
2. Confirm all protection mechanisms are functional
3. Verify all management and monitoring systems are operational
4. Check all customer services are meeting SLA requirements
5. Confirm system stability under full load
6. Verify all security measures are in place
7. Ensure proper backup and recovery systems are operational

Required Monitoring Tools

- Optical power meter
- Protocol analyzer
- Network monitoring system
- Performance measurement tools
- Configuration management system
- Log analysis tools
- Traffic generators (if needed)
- Test equipment for specific services

Documentation Requirements

- Post-upgrade test results
- Performance measurements
- Configuration changes
- Issue logs and resolutions
- Service restoration records
- Customer sign-off documents
- Updated system documentation
- Final upgrade report

Upgrading optical networks is essential to meet growing demand, incorporate new technologies, and improve performance and reliability. By understanding the key considerations, planning steps, and practical examples, network engineers and professionals can effectively manage the upgrade process. As data demands continue to rise, regular network upgrades will remain crucial to maintaining high-capacity, efficient, and reliable optical networks.I will recommend readers to think and make a plan to semi automate process to speed up and avoid manual errors while pre and post checks.

Part V

Integration and Future Trends

Chapter 19

Collaboration with Other Networking Technologies

Chapter 19 Collaboration with Other Networking Technologies

"Integration is not just connecting systems; it's making them work as one." - Tingye Li

---

In the rapidly evolving landscape of communications, optical networks are increasingly integrated with other networking technologies to enhance performance, scalability, and flexibility. This chapter explores how optical networks collaborate with various networking technologies, the benefits of such integration, and practical examples.

Importance of Collaboration in Networking

Collaborating with other networking technologies allows optical networks to leverage the strengths of each technology, creating a more robust and versatile network infrastructure. This integration is crucial for meeting the diverse needs of modern applications, from high-speed data transfer to real-time communication and cloud services.

Key Networking Technologies Collaborating with Optical Networks

1. **Ethernet**
    - **Integration**: Optical networks often use Ethernet protocols for high-speed data transfer over fiber optics.
    - **Benefits**: Provides a cost-effective and widely adopted standard for local and wide area networks (LANs and WANs).
    - **Example**: 10GbE, 40GbE, and 100GbE Ethernet standards are commonly used in data centers to achieve high-speed connectivity over optical fiber.
2. **MPLS (Multiprotocol Label Switching)**
    - **Integration**: MPLS is used to direct data from one network node to the next based on short path labels rather than long network addresses.

- **Benefits**: Enhances traffic engineering, improves quality of service (QoS), and supports the creation of virtual private networks (VPNs).
- **Example**: An enterprise network uses MPLS over an optical backbone to ensure efficient routing and high QoS for critical applications.

3. **IP (Internet Protocol)**
    - **Integration**: Optical networks form the backbone for IP networks, carrying vast amounts of data across long distances.
    - **Benefits**: Provides a scalable and interoperable platform for a wide range of internet services and applications.
    - **Example**: Tier-1 ISPs use optical fiber to connect major cities and international hubs, supporting global internet traffic with high bandwidth and low latency.
4. **SDN (Software-Defined Networking)**
    - **Integration**: SDN separates the control plane from the data plane, allowing centralized control of network resources.
    - **Benefits**: Enhances network programmability, simplifies management, and enables dynamic adjustment of network configurations.
    - **Example**: A data center uses SDN to manage optical switches and routers, dynamically allocating bandwidth based on real-time traffic demands.
5. **NFV (Network Function Virtualization)**
    - **Integration**: NFV virtualizes network functions such as firewalls, load balancers, and routers, running them on standard servers.
    - **Benefits**: Reduces the need for specialized hardware, increases network agility, and lowers operational costs.
    - **Example**: A telecom operator deploys virtualized network functions over an optical network to offer flexible and scalable services to customers.
6. **Wireless Technologies (5G)**
    - **Integration**: Optical networks provide the high-speed backbone for wireless networks, especially for 5G deployments.
    - **Benefits**: Ensures high-capacity and low-latency backhaul for wireless access networks.

- **Example**: 5G base stations connect to the core network via high-capacity optical links, supporting high-speed mobile broadband and IoT applications.

Practical Examples of Collaboration

1. **Optical and Ethernet Integration**

Scenario: A data center needs to upgrade its network to support higher data rates and lower latency.

Implementation:

- **Technology**: Deploy 100GbE over single-mode fiber to connect servers and storage devices.
- **Benefits**: Achieves high-speed, low-latency connectivity, improving data center performance and efficiency.
- **Outcome**: Enhanced data transfer rates and reduced latency, supporting demanding applications like real-time analytics and large-scale data processing.

2. **Optical and MPLS Integration**

Scenario: An enterprise requires a reliable and efficient way to manage its WAN traffic across multiple locations.

Implementation:

- **Technology**: Use MPLS over an optical backbone to ensure efficient routing and high QoS.
- **Benefits**: Optimizes network performance, ensures reliable data delivery, and supports VPNs for secure communication.
- **Outcome**: Improved network efficiency and reliability, supporting seamless communication between branch offices and the central data center.

3. **Optical and SDN Integration**

Scenario: A service provider aims to optimize network resources and automate network management.

Implementation:

- **Technology**: Implement SDN controllers to manage optical switches and dynamically allocate bandwidth.
- **Benefits**: Enhances network flexibility, reduces manual configuration, and allows real-time network adjustments.
- **Outcome**: Increased network agility and efficiency, enabling the provider to quickly adapt to changing traffic patterns and customer demands.

4. **Optical and 5G Integration**

Scenario: A telecom operator is deploying a 5G network and needs a high-capacity, low-latency backhaul solution.

Implementation:

- **Technology**: Use optical fiber to connect 5G base stations to the core network.
- **Benefits**: Provides the necessary bandwidth and low latency to support high-speed mobile broadband and IoT applications.
- **Outcome**: Enhanced mobile network performance, supporting applications such as autonomous vehicles, smart cities, and augmented reality.

Benefits of Collaboration

1. **Enhanced Performance**
    - Combining optical networks with other technologies leverages the strengths of each, resulting in higher data rates, lower latency, and improved reliability.
2. **Scalability**
    - Integrated networks can scale more easily to accommodate growing data demands and evolving application requirements.
3. **Cost Efficiency**
    - Using standardized technologies and virtualization reduces the need for specialized hardware, lowering capital and operational expenses.
4. **Flexibility**
    - Collaborative networks are more adaptable to changing traffic patterns, new applications, and technological advancements.
5. **Simplified Management**
    - Centralized control and automation streamline network management, reducing complexity and the potential for human error.

Following visualization demonstrates four major interconnected domains in optical networking, shown by distinct color groups:

1. **Optical Core Network (Red Section):**
    - This is the backbone infrastructure containing OTN, DWDM, and ROADM technologies
    - DWDM multiplies network capacity by transmitting multiple wavelengths
    - ROADMs provide flexible routing by dynamically managing optical paths
    - All components connect to ensure high-capacity, flexible data transmission
2. **Access Networks (Blue Section):**
    - Shows last-mile technologies connecting to end-users
    - PON distributes optical signals to multiple locations
    - FTTH provides direct fiber connections to homes
    - Metro Ethernet serves business and enterprise customers
3. **Wireless Technologies (Green Section):**
    - Demonstrates how optical networks support wireless services
    - 5G relies on optical backhaul for high-speed connectivity
    - WiFi-6 provides local high-speed wireless access
    - IoT networks connect numerous devices and sensors
4. **Cloud & Data Center (Yellow/Beige Section):**
    - Shows how optical networks support cloud infrastructure
    - Data centers require high-bandwidth interconnects
    - Cloud IaaS needs reliable, high-speed connectivity
    - Edge computing brings processing closer to users

The connecting lines between components show critical integration points, such as:

- "High Capacity" links between OTN and DWDM
- "Backhaul" connections from ROADM to 5G
- "DC Interconnect" between DWDM and Data Centers
- "Last Mile" connections from PON to FTTH

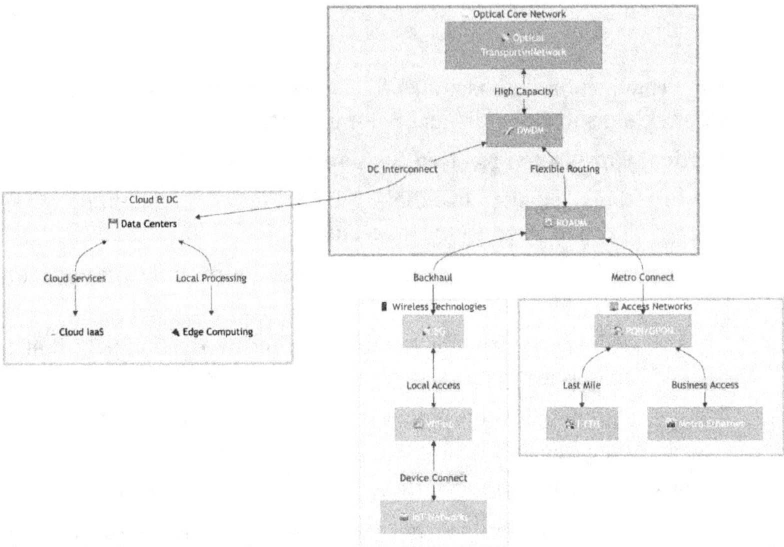
Optical Core Network
DWDM
ROADM
High Capacity
DC Interconnect
Flexible Routing
Cloud & DC
Data Centers
Cloud Services
Local Processing
Cloud IaaS
Edge Computing
Backhaul
Metro Connect
Wireless Technologies
Access Networks
Local Access
Device Connect
Last Mile
Business Access

Chapter 20

Future of Optical Networking

Chapter 20
Future of Optical Networking

"Tomorrow's networks are built on today's innovations."
- Charles Kao

The future of optical networking is being shaped by the exponential growth in data traffic, driven by technologies such as 5G, artificial intelligence (AI), cloud computing, and the Internet of Things (IoT). To meet the demands of these new technologies, optical networks must evolve to deliver higher capacity, lower latency, and greater flexibility. This chapter explores emerging technologies such as space-division multiplexing (SDM), 800G and 1T transceivers, the rise of integrated photonics, and the development of quantum communication systems. The chapter also discusses the growing importance of automation, machine learning, and energy efficiency in next-generation optical networks.

Key Trends Driving the Future of Optical Networks

1. **Increasing Demand for Bandwidth**
    - The global demand for bandwidth is growing rapidly, driven by data-intensive applications like video streaming, cloud computing, and AI. To accommodate this growth, optical networks must evolve to support higher-capacity links, greater spectral efficiency, and more flexible network architectures.
    - **Projected Growth**: Global internet traffic is expected to exceed 400 exabytes per month by 2025, with mobile and IoT devices generating significant portions of this data.

2. **Low-Latency Requirements for 5G and Beyond**
    - Next-generation applications such as autonomous vehicles, remote surgery, and virtual reality require ultra-low-latency networks. Optical networks will need to support latency in the range of milliseconds to microseconds, with 5G networks placing particular emphasis on low-latency backhaul.

- **Latency Target**: 5G networks aim for end-to-end latencies of under 1 millisecond in certain applications, such as vehicle-to-vehicle communication or augmented reality gaming.

Emerging Technologies in Optical Networking

1. **Space-Division Multiplexing (SDM)**
   - **What is SDM?**: Space-Division Multiplexing (SDM) is an emerging technology that increases the capacity of fiber networks by using multiple spatial channels within a single fiber. These channels can take the form of multiple cores (multi-core fiber) or multiple modes (multi-mode fiber), allowing multiple independent data streams to be transmitted simultaneously.
   - **Benefits**:
     - **Higher Capacity**: SDM significantly increases the capacity of fiber by transmitting multiple spatial channels, without increasing the fiber's physical footprint.
     - **Energy Efficiency**: By consolidating multiple channels into a single fiber, SDM reduces the energy consumption and hardware required to manage multiple fibers.
   - **Example: A research project successfully demonstrated the transmission of 10 spatial channels over a multi-core fiber, achieving a total capacity of 1 petabit per second. This breakthrough has the potential to revolutionize long-haul and submarine networks, where the need for higher capacity is critical.**
2. **800G and 1T Optical Transceivers**
   - **Advancements in Optical Transceivers**: To meet the growing demand for bandwidth, optical transceiver technology is advancing toward 800G and 1T data rates. These transceivers enable high-capacity links in data centers, metro networks, and long-haul networks, reducing the need for parallel fiber deployments and improving overall network efficiency.
   - **Technology Overview**:
     - **Modulation Formats**: 800G and 1T transceivers utilize advanced modulation formats such as

64QAM and higher, combined with coherent detection and digital signal processing (DSP).

- **Baud Rate**: Increasing the baud rate (symbol rate) is a key factor in achieving higher data rates. For example, 800G transceivers may use 64 Gbaud symbols, while 1T systems could use even higher baud rates, such as 128 Gbaud.

- **Use Case: A cloud service provider deploys 800G transceivers in its data center interconnects (DCI) to handle massive data transfers between facilities. By using high-baud-rate transceivers, the provider reduces the number of fiber pairs required for the same capacity, lowering operational costs and energy consumption.**

3. **Integrated Photonics**
   - **What is Integrated Photonics?**: Integrated photonics refers to the integration of multiple optical functions onto a single chip, similar to how electronic integrated circuits (ICs) revolutionized computing. Photonic integrated circuits (PICs) combine components such as lasers, modulators, waveguides, and detectors onto a single substrate, offering significant benefits in terms of size, power consumption, and cost.
   - **Benefits**:
     - **Miniaturization**: Integrated photonics dramatically reduces the size of optical components, making them ideal for space-constrained environments like data centers.
     - **Power Efficiency**: By integrating multiple components onto a single chip, integrated photonics reduces power consumption, making it more energy-efficient than traditional discrete optical components.
     - **Cost Savings**: The ability to mass-produce photonic chips using existing semiconductor fabrication techniques lowers the cost of optical components, driving down the cost of high-capacity networking.
   - **Example: A telecom operator deploys PIC-based transceivers in its metro network, enabling the transition to 400G and 800G services while reducing power consumption by 30% compared to traditional optical components.**
4. **Quantum Communication**

- **The Role of Quantum in Optical Networks**: Quantum communication is an emerging field that leverages the principles of quantum mechanics to enable ultra-secure communication. Quantum key distribution (QKD) is one of the most promising applications of quantum communication, providing theoretically unbreakable encryption by using quantum entanglement and superposition.
- **Quantum Networks**: In the future, optical networks could be integrated with quantum networks, where quantum bits (qubits) are transmitted over optical fibers using single photons. This has potential applications in secure government and military communications, as well as in financial services and healthcare.
- **Example**: China's Micius satellite demonstrated the first successful quantum key distribution (QKD) link between space and ground, marking a significant milestone in quantum-secure communication over optical networks.

The Impact of AI and Machine Learning on Optical Networks

1. **AI-Driven Network Management**
    - **Automation and Optimization**: Artificial intelligence (AI) and machine learning (ML) are becoming critical tools in managing complex optical networks. By analyzing traffic patterns, predicting failures, and optimizing routing decisions in real-time, AI can dramatically improve the performance and reliability of optical networks.
    - **Traffic Management**: AI algorithms can dynamically adjust network configurations based on real-time traffic patterns, ensuring optimal resource allocation and reducing congestion.
    - **Predictive Maintenance**: AI-based predictive maintenance can analyze historical performance data and environmental conditions to predict when components are likely to fail. This allows operators to replace or repair equipment before it causes network downtime.
    - **Example**: A major cloud provider uses AI-based traffic engineering to manage its 400G optical backbone. By analyzing real-time traffic data and predicting future demand, the system automatically adjusts wavelength allocations and

reroutes traffic to avoid congestion, improving network efficiency by 20%.

2. **Machine Learning in Coherent Optics**
   - **Signal Optimization**: Machine learning algorithms are increasingly being integrated into coherent optical systems to optimize signal recovery and compensate for impairments such as chromatic dispersion, polarization mode dispersion, and nonlinearities. These algorithms enable coherent transceivers to adapt to changing network conditions and maintain optimal performance.
   - **Dynamic Modulation and Power Control**: ML algorithms can dynamically adjust the modulation format and launch power of coherent transceivers to maximize spectral efficiency and reduce power consumption, based on real-time network conditions.
   - **Example**: In a long-haul optical network, ML algorithms optimize the performance of 800G coherent transceivers by adjusting the modulation format and power settings in response to changes in OSNR, chromatic dispersion, and fiber nonlinearity.

Sustainability and Energy Efficiency in Optical Networks

1. **The Need for Sustainable Networks**
   - As global energy consumption continues to rise, the ICT industry, including optical networks, faces increasing pressure to reduce its carbon footprint. Future optical networks must be designed with energy efficiency and sustainability in mind, reducing the overall power consumption of network infrastructure while still meeting the growing demand for bandwidth.
2. **Energy-Efficient Optical Components**
   - **Low-Power Transceivers**: Advances in optical transceiver design, such as integrated photonics and pluggable coherent optics, are reducing the power consumption of high-capacity links. These low-power transceivers are essential for achieving energy-efficient data centers and long-haul networks.
   - **Optical Amplifiers**: Newer designs of erbium-doped fiber amplifiers (EDFAs) and Raman amplifiers are more energy-

efficient, providing higher gain with lower power input, which reduces overall network energy consumption.

- **Example**: A data center operator reduces its energy consumption by 30% by replacing legacy 100G transceivers with integrated 400G coherent optics that use half the power per bit.

3. **Green Optical Networks**
   - **Renewable Energy for Optical Infrastructure**: Optical networks are increasingly being powered by renewable energy sources such as solar and wind. This reduces the environmental impact of network infrastructure while ensuring that the networks remain operational even in areas where the electrical grid is unstable.
   - **AI for Energy Optimization**: AI-based energy management systems can dynamically adjust power consumption across the network based on current traffic demands, reducing energy waste during periods of low utilization.
   - **Example**: A telecom operator deploys a green optical network powered by solar energy in a rural area, reducing its reliance on traditional power sources and lowering its carbon footprint.

Real-World Case Studies in Future Optical Technologies

1. **Space-Division Multiplexing for Long-Haul Networks**
   - **Scenario**: A submarine cable operator is facing capacity constraints in its transoceanic links. To increase capacity without laying additional cables, the operator implements space-division multiplexing (SDM) using multi-core fiber.
   - **Outcome**: SDM increases the capacity of the cable by a factor of 10, allowing the operator to meet growing demand for international bandwidth while avoiding the high costs of new cable installations.
2. **800G Coherent Optics in Data Center Interconnects (DCI)**
   - **Scenario**: A hyperscale cloud provider needs to upgrade its data center interconnects to handle increasing traffic driven by AI workloads and cloud-based services. The provider deploys 800G coherent optics with flex-grid ROADMs to support dynamic bandwidth allocation.

- **Outcome**: The provider achieves a 2x increase in data center capacity while reducing the power consumption of its optical links by 25%.

3. **Quantum Key Distribution for Secure Communication**
   - **Scenario**: A government agency requires ultra-secure communication links for transmitting sensitive data. The agency deploys a quantum communication network using quantum key distribution (QKD) over its existing optical fiber infrastructure.
   - **Outcome**: The quantum communication network provides theoretically unbreakable encryption, ensuring that the agency's communications are secure even in the face of future quantum computing threats.

Part VI

Professional Development

Chapter 21

Engineering Roles in Optical Networking

Chapter 21
Engineering Roles in Optical Networking

"In engineering, wisdom comes from experience, and experience comes from mistakes." - Alan Willner

---

The optical networking industry encompasses a wide range of engineering roles, each contributing to the design, implementation, operation, and optimization of optical networks. This chapter explores the different types of engineers in the optical industry, their roles and responsibilities, and the skills required for each position.

Types of Engineers in the Optical Industry

1. **Optical Network Design Engineers**
   - **Role**: Design and plan optical network infrastructures, including fiber layouts, equipment selection, and network topology.
   - **Responsibilities**:
     - Analyze network requirements and design solutions that meet performance, scalability, and cost objectives.
     - Select appropriate optical components such as transceivers, amplifiers, and multiplexers.
     - Develop detailed network diagrams and documentation.
     - Collaborate with other engineering teams to ensure seamless integration.
   - **Skills**:
     - Proficiency in network design tools (e.g., CAD software, simulation tools).
     - Strong understanding of optical transmission principles and technologies.
     - Analytical skills and attention to detail.

- Knowledge of industry standards and best practices.

Example: An optical network design engineer plans a new metro network using DWDM technology to support high-capacity data transmission across a city, ensuring redundancy and scalability.

2. **Systems Engineers**
    - **Role**: Oversee the end-to-end implementation and integration of optical network systems.
    - **Responsibilities**:
        - Integrate optical components and systems into the existing network infrastructure.
        - Conduct testing and validation to ensure system performance and reliability.
        - Optimize network configurations to enhance efficiency and performance.
        - Provide technical support and troubleshooting for network issues.
    - **Skills**:
        - Expertise in system integration and network protocols.
        - Problem-solving and diagnostic skills.
        - Familiarity with testing and measurement equipment.
        - Ability to work collaboratively with cross-functional teams.

    Example: A systems engineer integrates new 400G transponders into a data center network, conducting extensive testing to validate performance and ensure seamless operation with existing equipment.

3. **Field Engineers**
    - **Role**: Perform on-site installation, maintenance, and repair of optical network components.
    - **Responsibilities**:
        - Install and configure optical equipment such as fiber optic cables, connectors, and network devices.
        - Conduct field testing and troubleshooting to identify and resolve issues.

        - Perform routine maintenance and upgrades to ensure network reliability.
        - Document installation and maintenance activities.
    - **Skills**:
        - Hands-on experience with fiber optic installation and splicing.
        - Proficiency in using testing and measurement tools (e.g., OTDR, power meters).
        - Technical knowledge of optical networking equipment.
        - Strong problem-solving skills and attention to detail.

    Example: A field engineer installs new fiber optic cables for a regional ISP, performing splicing and testing to ensure optimal signal quality and minimal attenuation.

4. **Optical Network Operations Engineers**
    - **Role**: Monitor and manage the day-to-day operations of optical networks.
    - **Responsibilities**:
        - Monitor network performance and health using network management systems (NMS).
        - Respond to and resolve network alarms and incidents.
        - Perform network maintenance and optimization tasks.
        - Collaborate with design and field engineers to implement network changes and upgrades.
    - **Skills**:
        - Proficiency in network management tools and software.
        - Strong understanding of network monitoring and troubleshooting techniques.
        - Analytical skills to interpret performance data and identify issues.
        - Ability to work under pressure and respond to critical incidents.

    Example: An optical network operations engineer uses a NMS to monitor a national backbone network, responding to alarms and coordinating with field teams to resolve fiber cuts and equipment failures.

5. **Research and Development (R&D) Engineers**
   - **Role**: Innovate and develop new optical networking technologies and solutions.
   - **Responsibilities**:
     - Conduct research on emerging optical technologies and applications.
     - Design and prototype new optical components and systems.
     - Test and validate new technologies in lab environments.
     - Collaborate with product development teams to bring new solutions to market.
   - **Skills**:
     - Advanced knowledge of optical physics and engineering principles.
     - Experience with simulation and modeling tools.
     - Creativity and innovation in problem-solving.
     - Strong analytical and experimental skills.

   Example: An R&D engineer develops a new silicon photonics transceiver, conducting extensive lab testing to validate performance and reliability before commercialization.

6. **Project Engineers**
   - **Role**: Manage and coordinate optical network projects from inception to completion.
   - **Responsibilities**:
     - Define project scope, objectives, and deliverables.
     - Develop project plans and timelines.
     - Coordinate with various engineering teams and stakeholders.
     - Monitor project progress and ensure timely completion.
   - **Skills**:
     - Strong project management and organizational skills.
     - Ability to manage multiple tasks and priorities.

- Excellent communication and coordination abilities.
- Knowledge of optical networking technologies and project management tools.

Example: A project engineer oversees the deployment of a new international submarine cable, coordinating with design, field, and operations teams to ensure successful project execution.

7. **Technical Support Engineers**
    - **Role**: Provide technical assistance and support for optical network products and solutions.
    - **Responsibilities**:
        - Assist customers with installation, configuration, and troubleshooting of optical equipment.
        - Diagnose and resolve technical issues remotely or on-site.
        - Provide training and documentation to customers and internal teams.
        - Collaborate with R&D and engineering teams to address complex issues.
    - **Skills**:
        - Strong problem-solving and diagnostic skills.
        - Excellent communication and customer service abilities.
        - Technical knowledge of optical networking products.
        - Ability to work independently and as part of a team.

    Example: A technical support engineer helps a telecom operator troubleshoot and resolve issues with a recently deployed DWDM system, ensuring minimal downtime and optimal performance.

8. **Pre-Sales Engineer**
    - **Role**: Bridge technical and commercial aspects, supporting sales teams with technical expertise in optical networking solutions.
    - **Responsibilities**:
        - Analyze customer requirements and propose suitable optical networking solutions

        - Create technical proposals and presentations for potential clients
        - Conduct product demonstrations and proof of concept implementations
        - Provide technical consulting during the sales process
    - **Skills**:
        - Deep technical knowledge of optical networking products
        - Strong communication and presentation abilities
        - Solution architecting capabilities
        - Business acumen and cost analysis skills
    - **Example**: A pre-sales engineer designs a custom ROADM solution for a telecom provider, demonstrating cost savings and performance improvements over their existing infrastructure.

9. **Post-Sales Engineer**
    - **Role**: Ensure successful implementation and customer satisfaction after the sale of optical networking solutions.
    - **Responsibilities**:
        - Oversee installation and deployment of optical networking equipment
        - Provide technical support and troubleshooting
        - Conduct customer training and knowledge transfer
        - Manage technical documentation and project handover
    - **Skills**:
        - Hands-on experience with optical networking equipment
        - Problem-solving and troubleshooting expertise
        - Project management capabilities
        - Customer relationship management
    - **Example**: A post-sales engineer guides a customer through the deployment of a new optical transport network, providing training and resolving implementation challenges.

10. **Testing Engineer**
    - **Role**: Verify and validate optical networking equipment and solutions through comprehensive testing.

- **Responsibilities**:
  - Develop and execute test plans for optical equipment
  - Perform interoperability testing between different vendors
  - Conduct performance and stress testing
  - Document test results and report issues
- **Skills**:
  - Expertise in optical test equipment and procedures
  - Knowledge of testing methodologies and standards
  - Analytical and debugging skills
  - Quality assurance principles
- **Example**: A testing engineer validates a new 400G optical transceiver's performance across different environmental conditions and network scenarios.

Skills and Qualifications

1. **Educational Background**
   - Bachelor's or master's degree in electrical engineering, telecommunications, physics, or a related field.
   - Specialized training or certifications in optical networking technologies.
2. **Technical Skills**
   - Proficiency in optical networking concepts and technologies.
   - Experience with testing and measurement tools.
   - Knowledge of network design, integration, and management tools.
   - Hands-on experience with fiber optic installation and maintenance.
3. **Soft Skills**
   - Strong problem-solving and analytical abilities.
   - Excellent communication and teamwork skills.
   - Attention to detail and a commitment to quality.
   - Ability to adapt to new technologies and rapidly changing environments.

Chapter 22

Interview Guidelines for Engineers

Chapter 22
Interview Guidelines for Engineers

"Your interview answers should reflect not just what you know, but how you think." - Nick Holonyak Jr.

Preparing for an interview in the optical networking industry requires a comprehensive understanding of technical concepts, industry trends, and the specific requirements of the role. This chapter provides guidelines for engineers preparing for interviews, including common questions, key topics to study, and tips for success.Also navigating a job interview successfully is crucial for any job seeker looking to make a positive impression. This often intimidating process can be transformed into an empowering opportunity to showcase your strengths and fit for the role. Here are refined strategies and insights to help you excel in your next job interview.

Startegies to excel in Interviews

1. Focus on Positive Self-Representation

When asked to "tell me about yourself," this is your chance to control the narrative. This question is a golden opportunity to succinctly present yourself by focusing on attributes that align closely with the job requirements and the company's culture. Begin by identifying your key personality traits and how they enhance your professional capabilities. Consider what the company values and how your experiences and strengths play into these areas. Practicing your delivery can boost your confidence, enabling you to articulate a clear and focused response that demonstrates your suitability for the role. For example, explaining how your collaborative nature and creativity in problem-solving match the company's emphasis on teamwork and innovation can set a strong tone for the interview.

2. Utilize the Power of Storytelling

Personal stories are not just engaging; they are a compelling way to illustrate your skills and character to the interviewer. Think about your past professional experiences and select stories that reflect the qualities the employer is seeking. These narratives should go beyond simply stating facts; they should convey your personal values, decision-making processes, and the impact of your actions. Reflect on challenges you've faced and how you've overcome them, focusing on the insights gained and the results driven. This method helps the interviewer see beyond your resume to the person behind the accomplishments.

3. Demonstrate Vulnerability and Growth

It's important to be seen as approachable and self-aware, which means acknowledging not just successes but also vulnerabilities. Discussing a past failure or challenge and detailing what you learned from it can significantly enhance your credibility. This openness shows that you are capable of self-reflection and willing to grow from your experiences. Employers value candidates who are not only skilled but are also resilient and ready to adapt based on past lessons.

4. Showcase Your Authentic Self

Authenticity is key in interviews. It's essential to present yourself truthfully in terms of your values, preferences, and style. This could relate to your cultural background, lifestyle choices, or personal philosophies. A company that respects and values diversity will appreciate this honesty and is more likely to be a good fit for you in the long term. Displaying your true self can also help you feel more at ease during the interview process, as it reduces the pressure to conform to an idealized image.

5. Engage with Thoughtful Questions

Asking insightful questions during an interview can set you apart from other candidates. It shows that you are thoughtful and have a genuine interest in the role and the company. Inquire about the team dynamics, the company's approach to feedback and growth, and the challenges currently facing the department. These questions can reveal a lot about the internal workings of the company and help you determine if the environment aligns with your professional goals and values.

The Ultimate Guide to Common Interview Questions and Strategic Answers

This comprehensive guide will help you prepare for common interview questions with strategic, authentic responses that highlight your value while maintaining professionalism. Remember that the key to interview success is preparation combined with authenticity.

Core Interview Questions

1. Tell Me About Yourself

Strategy: Structure your response using the Present-Past-Future formula

- **Present:** Brief overview of your current role and key responsibilities
- **Past:** Relevant experiences and achievements that led you here
- **Future:** Why you're excited about this opportunity

]**Example Response:** "I'm currently a senior project manager at Tech Solutions, leading a team of 12 developers across multiple high-impact projects. I began my career as a software developer, which gives me strong technical insight, and progressively moved into project management where I discovered my passion for leading teams and delivering complex projects. I'm now looking to bring my technical background and leadership experience to a larger organization like yours, where I can contribute to more ambitious initiatives."

2. Why Are You Looking to Leave Your Current Position?

Strategy: Focus on growth opportunities while remaining positive

- Emphasize pull factors (what attracts you to the new role)
- Avoid negative comments about current employer
- Frame the change as a strategic career move

Example Response: "While I've learned tremendously in my current role and am grateful for the opportunities I've had, I'm looking to expand my expertise in cloud architecture, which aligns perfectly with your organization's focus on cloud-native solutions."

3. What Do You Know About Our Organization?

Strategy: Demonstrate thorough research and genuine interest

- Recent company achievements
- Company culture and values
- Industry position and market trends
- Future direction and strategic initiatives

Example Response: "I've followed your company's journey closely, particularly your recent expansion into sustainable technology solutions. Your commitment to reducing carbon footprints through innovative software solutions aligns with my personal values. I was especially impressed by your recent partnership with GreenTech and the impact it's had on reducing energy consumption in data centers."

Behavioral Questions

4. Describe a Challenging Situation and How You Handled It

Strategy: Use the STAR method (Situation, Task, Action, Result)

- Choose a relevant example
- Focus on your problem-solving process
- Highlight collaborative aspects
- Emphasize positive outcomes and lessons learned

Example Response: "In my current role, we faced a critical system outage during our peak season. As the lead developer:

- **Situation**: The payment processing system went down during Black Friday
- **Task**: Needed to restore service while minimizing revenue loss
- **Action**: Led a cross-functional team, implemented emergency protocols, and established hourly stakeholder communications
- **Result**: Restored service within 2 hours and implemented new monitoring systems to prevent future incidents"

5. How Do You Handle Conflict in the Workplace?

Strategy: Focus on:

- Professional communication
- Active listening
- Solution-oriented approach
- Learning and growth from experience

Example Response: "I believe in addressing conflicts early through open communication. Recently, when there was a disagreement about project priorities between teams, I organized a workshop to map out dependencies and impact. This helped everyone understand the bigger picture and led to a collaborative solution that actually improved our workflow."

Career Development Questions

6. Where Do You See Yourself in Five Years?

Strategy: Balance ambition with realism

- Show alignment with company growth
- Demonstrate commitment to professional development
- Express realistic aspirations

Example Response: "I aim to grow into a technical leadership role where I can mentor others while continuing to contribute to strategic initiatives. I'm particularly interested in developing expertise in emerging technologies and helping organizations navigate digital transformation."

Salary and Negotiation

7. What Are Your Salary Expectations?

Strategy: Research-based approach

- Know industry standards
- Consider total compensation package
- Maintain flexibility while knowing your worth

Example Response: "Based on my research of similar roles in this market and my experience level, I'm looking for a total compensation package in the range of [X-Y]. However, I'm open to discussion as I consider other factors like growth opportunities and overall benefits package."

Questions to Ask the Interviewer

Strategic Questions That Show Interest and Intelligence

1. "What does success look like in this role after the first 90 days?"
2. "How does this role contribute to the company's long-term goals?"
3. "Can you tell me about the team's biggest challenges and opportunities?"
4. "What opportunities exist for professional development and growth?"
5. "How would you describe the company culture and team dynamics?"

Best Practices

Do:

- Research thoroughly before the interview
- Prepare specific examples and stories
- Focus on relevant achievements
- Show enthusiasm and genuine interest
- Ask thoughtful questions
- Follow up with a thank-you note

Don't:

- Speak negatively about previous employers
- Give memorized, robotic answers
- Lie or exaggerate
- Focus solely on salary and benefits
- Forget to show your personality

Remote Interview Tips

- Test your technology beforehand
- Ensure a professional background
- Maintain eye contact through the camera
- Dress professionally
- Have backup communication methods ready

Final Notes

Remember that interviews are a two-way conversation. While you're being evaluated, you're also assessing if the role and company are right for you. Stay authentic while putting your best foot forward, and approach each interview as an opportunity to learn and grow professionally.

Common Optical Interview Questions

1. **Technical Questions**
    - **Fiber Optics Basics**: Explain the principle of total internal reflection in optical fibers.
    - **Attenuation and Dispersion**: How do attenuation and dispersion affect signal transmission in optical fibers?
    - **Optical Components**: Describe the functions of components such as DWDM, EDFAs, and transceivers.
    - **Network Design**: How would you design a high-capacity metro optical network?
    - **Troubleshooting**: How would you diagnose and fix a high bit error rate in an optical link?
2. **Behavioral Questions**
    - **Problem-Solving**: Describe a challenging technical problem you faced and how you resolved it.
    - **Teamwork**: Give an example of a successful project you worked on as part of a team.
    - **Adaptability**: How do you stay updated with the latest advancements in optical networking?
3. **Scenario-Based Questions**
    - **Network Optimization**: Given a network with increasing data traffic, how would you optimize the existing infrastructure?
    - **Failure Response**: How would you respond to a major network outage affecting multiple customers?

Key Topics to Study

1. **Fundamentals of Optical Networking**
    - Principles of light transmission in optical fibers.
    - Types of optical fibers: single-mode and multi-mode.
    - Optical signal characteristics: wavelength, frequency, and bandwidth.
2. **Optical Components and Devices**
    - Transceivers: SFP, QSFP, and coherent transceivers.
    - Multiplexers: CWDM and DWDM.
    - Amplifiers: EDFA, Raman amplifiers.
    - Switches and routers used in optical networks.
3. **Network Design and Planning**
    - Designing high-capacity networks with redundancy and scalability.
    - Fiber layout planning and link budget calculations.
    - Dispersion management and compensation techniques.
    - Protection mechanisms: 1+1, 1:1, ring protection.
4. **Testing and Troubleshooting**
    - Use of OTDRs, optical power meters, and spectrum analyzers.
    - Identifying and resolving common network issues: attenuation, dispersion, reflections.
    - Techniques for optimizing network performance.
5. **Emerging Technologies**
    - Trends in optical networking: 400G/800G, silicon photonics, SDN, and NFV.
    - Applications of machine learning and AI in network optimization.
    - Future directions: quantum networking, space-division multiplexing.

Tips for Success

1. **Research the Company**
    - Understand the company's products, services, and market position.
    - Familiarize yourself with recent news, projects, and technological innovations related to the company.

2. **Prepare Your Resume**
   - Highlight relevant experience, skills, and certifications.
   - Include specific examples of projects and accomplishments in optical networking.
3. **Practice Technical Questions**
   - Review key concepts and practice explaining them clearly and concisely.
   - Use online resources, textbooks, and professional networks to prepare for technical questions.
4. **Develop Behavioral Responses**
   - Reflect on your past experiences and prepare responses to common behavioral questions.
   - Use the STAR (Situation, Task, Action, Result) method to structure your answers.
5. **Engage in Mock Interviews**
   - Practice with peers, mentors, or professional coaches.
   - Focus on both technical and behavioral questions to build confidence.
6. **Stay Updated**
   - Follow industry news, publications, and conferences to stay informed about the latest trends and advancements.
   - Join professional organizations and online communities related to optical networking.

Practical Examples and Case Studies

1. Designing a Metro Optical Network

Scenario: You are asked to design a high-capacity metro network for a growing city.

Preparation:

- **Understand Requirements**: Gather information on expected traffic load, redundancy needs, and future scalability.
- **Design**: Plan a DWDM-based network with redundant fiber paths and use of EDFAs for amplification.
- **Documentation**: Prepare detailed network diagrams, equipment lists, and a link budget.

Interview Focus:

- Explain the design choices and their benefits.
- Discuss potential challenges and how to address them.

2. Troubleshooting a High Bit Error Rate

Scenario: A client reports a high bit error rate in their optical network.

Preparation:

- **Identify Possible Causes**: Consider factors like fiber attenuation, dispersion, and equipment faults.
- **Testing Plan**: Plan to use an OTDR to check fiber integrity, an optical power meter to measure signal strength, and a spectrum analyzer to identify noise and interference.
- **Solution**: Propose corrective actions based on the test results.

Interview Focus:

- Detail the step-by-step troubleshooting process.
- Highlight the importance of accurate testing and timely resolution.

Chapter 23

Facts and Statistics in Optical Networking

Chapter 23
Facts and Statistics in Optical Networking

"Statistics tell stories that shape our industry's future." - David Miller

---

Understanding key facts and statistics about optical networks helps in appreciating their significance, growth trends, and technological advancements. This chapter provides a comprehensive overview of essential facts, statistics, and trends in the optical networking industry.

Market Overview

1. **Global Market Size**
    - The global optical networking market is projected to grow from approximately $14.9 billion in 2020 to $24.4 billion by 2026.
    - This growth is driven by increasing data traffic, the proliferation of data centers, and the expansion of high-speed internet services.
2. **Regional Growth**
    - North America holds a significant market share due to advanced infrastructure and high demand for high-speed networks.
    - Asia-Pacific is expected to witness the highest growth rate, fueled by rapid urbanization, increasing internet penetration, and investments in 5G and broadband infrastructure.
3. **Example**: In 2023, the Asia-Pacific region accounted for 35% of the global optical networking market, with China and India being the major contributors.

Technology Adoption

1. **High-Speed Optical Transceivers**

- The adoption of 100G, 200G, and 400G transceivers is increasing, driven by the need for higher bandwidth in data centers and metro networks.
- 800G transceivers are emerging, promising to further enhance network capacity and efficiency.

2. **DWDM and Coherent Optics**
   - Dense Wavelength Division Multiplexing (DWDM) technology is widely adopted for long-haul and metro networks, enabling high-capacity data transmission over a single fiber.
   - Coherent optical technology, using advanced modulation formats and digital signal processing (DSP), is crucial for achieving high data rates and long transmission distances.

Example: By 2025, it is estimated that over 50% of data center interconnects will use 400G coherent optics, up from 20% in 2021.

Network Traffic and Capacity

1. **Global IP Traffic**
   - Global IP traffic is expected to reach 396 exabytes per month by 2025, up from 230 exabytes per month in 2020.
   - Video streaming, cloud computing, and IoT applications are the primary drivers of this growth.
2. **Data Center Growth**
   - The number of hyperscale data centers is projected to increase from 500 in 2020 to over 700 by 2025.
   - These data centers require high-capacity optical networks to handle massive amounts of data transfer and storage.

Example: In 2022, hyperscale data centers accounted for 50% of all data center traffic, highlighting the need for robust optical networking solutions.

https://www.ibisworld.com/us/bed/internet-traffic-volume/88089/

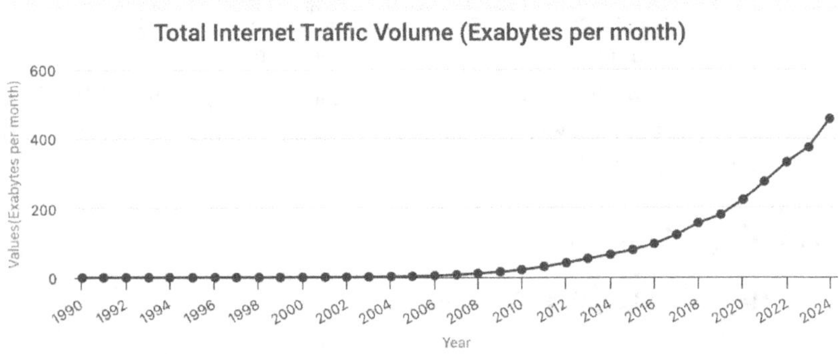

Performance and Reliability

1. **Fiber Optic Performance**
    - Single-mode fibers typically exhibit attenuation rates of 0.2-0.35 dB/km at 1550 nm, making them suitable for long-distance transmission.
    - Advanced fiber types, such as ultra-low loss fibers, offer even lower attenuation rates, enhancing long-haul network performance.
2. **Network Availability**
    - Achieving "five nines" (99.999%) availability is a common goal for critical optical networks, equating to a maximum downtime of approximately 5.26 minutes per year.
    - This high level of availability is crucial for applications in finance, healthcare, and emergency services.

Example: A telecom operator achieving five nines availability ensures that their network is down for no more than 5.26 minutes in a year, providing high reliability for their customers.

Emerging Trends

1. **5G and Optical Networks**
    - The deployment of 5G networks is driving significant investment in optical backhaul infrastructure to support high-speed, low-latency communication.
    - Optical networks are essential for connecting 5G base stations to the core network, handling increased data traffic and providing the necessary bandwidth.
2. **Quantum Networking**
    - Quantum networking is an emerging field that leverages quantum mechanics for ultra-secure communication.
    - While still in the research phase, quantum key distribution (QKD) and other quantum technologies hold promise for enhancing network security.

Example: Research institutions and telecom operators are collaborating on quantum networking projects, with pilot deployments of QKD systems already underway in several countries.

Practical Examples and Case Studies

1. **5G Backhaul Deployment**

   Scenario: A telecom operator is deploying a 5G network in a major city and needs robust optical backhaul.

   Implementation:

   - **Technology**: Deploy high-capacity DWDM systems to connect 5G base stations to the core network.
   - **Outcome**: Achieved high-speed, low-latency backhaul, supporting the high data rates and reliability required for 5G services.

2. **Hyperscale Data Center Interconnect**

   Scenario: A cloud service provider is expanding its data center infrastructure and requires efficient interconnect solutions.

   Implementation:

   - **Technology**: Use 400G coherent optics to interconnect data centers, enabling high-capacity, low-latency data transfer.
   - **Outcome**: Enhanced data center performance, supporting rapid data growth and ensuring seamless service delivery.

Key Statistics

1. **Fiber Deployment**
   - Over 1 billion kilometers of optical fiber have been deployed globally.
   - China leads in fiber deployment, accounting for over 60% of the world's fiber optic cable production.
2. **Internet Users**
   - As of 2023, there are over 5 billion internet users worldwide, with significant growth in developing regions.
   - High-speed broadband penetration is increasing, with fiber-to-the-home (FTTH) connections surpassing 500 million globally.
3. **Investment in Optical Networks**
   - Global investment in optical networking infrastructure is projected to exceed $100 billion by 2025.
   - Major investments are focused on upgrading existing networks to support higher data rates and expanding fiber coverage in underserved areas.

Example: Governments and private companies in the United States and Europe are investing heavily in broadband infrastructure, with initiatives aimed at bridging the digital divide and ensuring universal high-speed internet access.

Additional Data and Trends

1. **Bandwidth Demand Growth**
    - Annual global IP traffic is growing at a compound annual growth rate (CAGR) of 26%.
    - This growth is driven by the increasing number of connected devices, video consumption, and the proliferation of cloud services.
2. **Optical Fiber Innovations**
    - Developments in fiber optics, such as bend-insensitive fibers and multi-core fibers, are enhancing network performance and flexibility.
    - These innovations help reduce signal loss and support higher data rates over longer distances.
    - **Example**: Bend-insensitive fibers are increasingly used in FTTH deployments to facilitate easier installation in tight spaces without compromising performance.
3. **Environmental Impact**
    - Optical networks are becoming more energy-efficient, with advancements in low-power components and systems.
    - The shift towards greener technologies is driven by the need to reduce operational costs and environmental impact.

Example: Data centers are adopting energy-efficient optical transceivers and implementing innovative cooling solutions to reduce energy consumption and carbon footprint.

4. **Security Enhancements**
    - With growing concerns about data security, optical networks are incorporating advanced encryption techniques and secure transmission methods.
    - Quantum encryption and other cutting-edge technologies are being explored to enhance data protection.

Example: Quantum key distribution (QKD) trials are being conducted to secure sensitive communications, leveraging the principles of quantum mechanics to prevent eavesdropping.

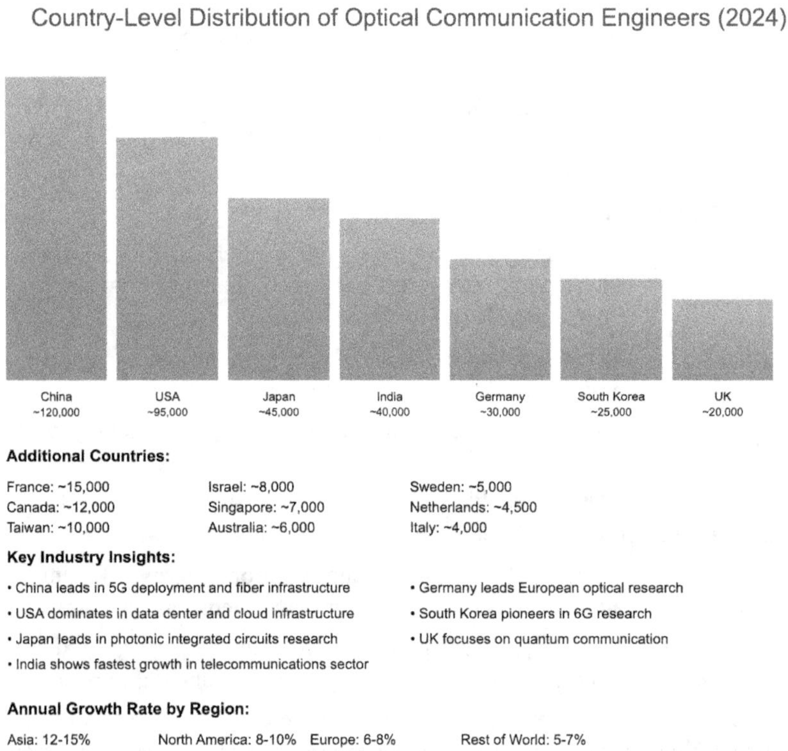

The optical networking industry is characterized by rapid growth, technological innovation, and increasing demand for high-speed, reliable communication. By understanding key facts and statistics, engineers and professionals can better appreciate the significance of optical networks and their impact on modern communications.

Chapter 24

Interview Questions and Answers

Chapter 24
Interview Questions and Answers

"Statistics tell stories that shape our industry's future." - David Miller

---

At this very end chapter ,I would like you to provide some of the common technical questions and their answers which will act as a refresher and get you ready for next course of career.These questions are either asked in an interview or I have asked interviewing someone or common questions asked in industry.I have already shared few on my website (https://mapyourtech.-com/) too for my readers.

Optical Engineers Interview Questions and Answers

1. Explain the basic principle of DWDM.

DWDM works by combining multiple wavelengths (or channels) of light onto a single optical fiber, each carrying a different data stream. This is achieved using multiplexers at the transmitting end and demultiplexers at the receiving end. The primary advantage is the ability to increase the bandwidth of a fiber network significantly by utilizing different wavelengths for different channels, enabling efficient use of the available fiber infrastructure.

2. How does DWDM differ from CWDM (Coarse Wavelength Division Multiplexing)?

The key difference lies in channel spacing and the number of wavelengths. DWDM has closely spaced channels (typically 0.8 nm or 100 GHz apart), allowing for more channels on a single fiber, which results in higher data transmission rates. CWDM, on the other hand, has wider channel spacing (typically 20 nm), making it less expensive but with lower capacity compared to DWDM.

3. What are the advantages of using DWDM in optical networks?

DWDM provides several advantages, including increased bandwidth capacity, efficient use of existing fiber infrastructure, support for multiple data rates and protocols on the same fiber, scalability for future upgrades, and the ability to transmit data over long distances with minimal signal degradation using amplification technologies like EDFAs.

4. Describe the function of an optical add-drop multiplexer (OADM) in a DWDM system.

An OADM selectively adds or drops specific wavelengths of light from a multi-wavelength DWDM signal, allowing for more flexible and dynamic routing of channels in a network. This enables intermediate access points without the need to demultiplex the entire signal, enhancing network efficiency and reducing costs.

5. What is the role of an erbium-doped fiber amplifier (EDFA) in DWDM networks?

EDFAs are used to amplify optical signals in DWDM networks without converting them to electrical signals. They boost the strength of the signal across a range of wavelengths (C-band), compensating for losses incurred over long distances and through various optical components, thus enabling long-haul transmission.

6. How do you manage channel spacing in a DWDM system?

Channel spacing in DWDM is managed using precise wavelength allocation and stabilization techniques. This involves the use of wavelength lockers, temperature-controlled lasers, and accurate wavelength calibration to ensure that each channel stays within its designated spacing, minimizing crosstalk and interference.

7. Explain the concept of wavelength conversion in DWDM networks.

Wavelength conversion is the process of changing the wavelength of an optical signal without altering its data content. This is useful in DWDM networks for routing flexibility, wavelength reuse, and managing wavelength contention. It is typically achieved using optical-electrical-optical (OEO) converters or all-optical converters.

8. What are the common challenges associated with DWDM deployment?

Common challenges include managing signal attenuation and dispersion, ensuring precise wavelength stabilization, dealing with non-linear effects like four-wave mixing, cross-phase modulation, and self-phase modulation, maintaining signal integrity over long distances, and the complexity of network design and management.

9. How do you measure and mitigate crosstalk in DWDM systems?

Crosstalk is measured using instruments like optical spectrum analyzers to detect unwanted signal interference between channels. Mitigation techniques include optimizing channel spacing, using high-quality optical components, ensuring proper alignment and isolation of wavelengths, and maintaining strict power levels.

10. What is the function of a transponder in a DWDM network?

A transponder converts incoming electrical signals into optical signals and vice versa. It typically includes a transmitter and a receiver, with the transmitter converting electrical signals into specific wavelengths for transmission, and the receiver converting incoming optical signals back into electrical form for further processing.

11. Explain the importance of dispersion management in DWDM systems.

Dispersion management is crucial for maintaining signal integrity over long distances. Chromatic dispersion can cause pulse broadening, leading to intersymbol interference. Techniques like dispersion-compensating fibers, fiber Bragg gratings, and electronic dispersion compensation are used to counteract these effects and ensure clear signal transmission.

12. How do you handle non-linear effects in DWDM networks?

Non-linear effects, such as self-phase modulation, cross-phase modulation, and four-wave mixing, can distort signals. Handling these effects involves optimizing power levels, using advanced modulation formats, deploying dispersion management techniques, and designing network topologies that minimize non-linear interactions.

13. What is the purpose of OTN in modern optical networks?

OTN provides a standardized framework for transporting, multiplexing, switching, and managing different types of digital traffic over an optical network. It enhances the capacity, scalability, and reliability of optical networks, supporting high-speed data transmission and efficient network management.

14. Explain the structure of an OTN frame.

An OTN frame consists of three main parts: the Optical Payload Unit (OPU), which carries the client data; the Optical Data Unit (ODU), which adds overhead for performance monitoring and error detection; and the Optical Transport Unit (OTU), which provides additional overhead for frame alignment, FEC, and optical layer management.

15. What are the key differences between OTN and SONET/SDH?

OTN supports higher data rates and more efficient bandwidth utilization than SONET/SDH. It includes advanced FEC for improved error correction, better support for data-centric services, and enhanced scalability. OTN also simplifies network management and interoperability across different vendor equipment compared to SONET/SDH.

16. Describe the function of ODU (Optical Data Unit) in OTN.

The ODU is responsible for encapsulating client data with additional overhead for performance monitoring, fault management, and error detection. It ensures data integrity and enables efficient multiplexing of lower-rate signals into higher-rate signals for transport over the optical network.

17. How is forward error correction (FEC) implemented in OTN?

FEC in OTN is implemented at the OTU layer, where additional redundant bits are added to the data stream to detect and correct errors during transmission. Common FEC schemes used in OTN include Reed-Solomon and BCH codes, which improve signal quality and extend transmission distances.

18. What is the role of an OTS (Optical Transport Section) in OTN?

The OTS layer handles the physical aspects of optical transmission, including signal propagation, amplification, and multiplexing. It provides the optical path for the OTU and ensures reliable transport of optical signals across the network, managing aspects like optical power levels and signal quality.

19. Explain the concept of multiplexing in OTN.

Multiplexing in OTN involves combining multiple lower-rate ODU signals into a higher-rate OTU signal for efficient transport over a single optical fiber. This is achieved using techniques like time-division multiplexing (TDM) and wavelength-division multiplexing (WDM), optimizing the use of available bandwidth and network resources.

20. What are the benefits of using OTN for network management and monitoring?

OTN provides comprehensive network management and monitoring capabilities, including in-band performance monitoring, fault detection, and automatic protection switching. It enables real-time visibility into network performance, simplifies fault localization, and enhances overall network reliability and service quality.

21. How does OTN support different client signals (e.g., Ethernet, SONET/SDH, Fibre Channel)?

OTN supports different client signals by encapsulating them into the ODU, which includes client-specific overhead for mapping and adaptation. This allows for seamless transport of various data types over a unified optical network, enabling interoperability and efficient bandwidth utilization.

22. What is the difference between single-mode and multi-mode fiber?

Single-mode fiber has a smaller core diameter (typically 9 microns) and supports long-distance transmission with higher bandwidth and lower attenuation. Multi-mode fiber has a larger core diameter (typically 50 or 62.5 microns) and is used for shorter distances due to higher modal dispersion and attenuation.

23. Explain the concept of optical signal-to-noise ratio (OSNR) and its importance in optical networks.

OSNR is the ratio of the signal power to the noise power within a specific bandwidth. It is a critical parameter in optical networks, indicating the quality of the optical signal. High OSNR values correspond to better signal quality and lower bit error rates, essential for reliable data transmission.

24. Describe the process of link budget analysis in optical communication.

Link budget analysis involves calculating the total optical power losses and gains along a transmission path to ensure the received signal is above the receiver sensitivity threshold. It includes factors like fiber attenuation, connector losses, splice losses, and amplifier gains, helping design robust and reliable optical links.

25. What are the common types of optical connectors and their applications?

Common optical connectors include SC (Subscriber Connector), LC (Lucent Connector), ST (Straight Tip), and MPO (Multi-fiber Push On). They are used to join optical fibers with minimal loss and reflection, facilitating easy connection and disconnection in fiber optic networks for applications like telecommunications, data centers, and enterprise networks.

26. How do you perform optical time-domain reflectometry (OTDR) testing?

OTDR testing involves sending a series of optical pulses into a fiber and measuring the backscattered light as a function of time. This helps identify faults, splices, bends, and the overall length of the fiber. OTDR provides a graphical trace representing the fiber's characteristics, aiding in troubleshooting and maintenance.

27. What are the main causes of signal loss in optical fibers?

Signal loss in optical fibers can be attributed to intrinsic factors like absorption and scattering, as well as extrinsic factors like bending, splices, connectors, and manufacturing defects. Proper installation and maintenance practices can help minimize these losses and maintain optimal signal integrity.

28. Explain the concept of chromatic dispersion and its impact on optical communication.

Chromatic dispersion occurs when different wavelengths of light travel at different speeds in a fiber, causing pulse broadening and intersymbol interference. It impacts high-speed optical communication by limiting the maximum transmission distance and data rate. Dispersion compensation techniques are used to mitigate its effects.

29. What is the significance of polarization mode dispersion (PMD) in optical networks?

PMD arises from the birefringence in optical fibers, causing different polarization modes to travel at different speeds. This leads to pulse broadening and degradation of signal quality, particularly in high-speed networks. Managing PMD involves using low-PMD fibers, proper cable installation, and electronic compensation techniques.

30. How do you ensure network reliability and fault tolerance in optical communication systems?

Network reliability and fault tolerance are ensured through redundancy (e.g., using ring or mesh topologies), automatic protection switching, real-time monitoring, and maintenance practices. Techniques like 1+1 and 1:1 protection schemes, as well as proactive fault management systems, help maintain uninterrupted service and quick recovery from failures.

31. What is the primary function of a transponder in optical communication?

A transponder converts an incoming optical signal to an electrical signal, processes it, and then retransmits it as an optical signal at a different wavelength. This conversion is essential for signal regeneration and wavelength conversion. For example, a transponder might receive a 1550 nm signal, convert it to an electrical signal, and retransmit it at 1310 nm.

32. How do transponders contribute to signal regeneration in optical networks?

Transponders regenerate signals by converting optical signals to electrical, cleaning up the signal (removing noise and jitter), and then converting it back to optical. This process eliminates noise and distortion accumulated over long distances, ensuring signal integrity. Typical regeneration distances can vary but are often around 80-100 km in standard fiber without additional amplification.

33. What is the typical range of wavelengths a transponder can handle?

Modern transponders typically handle wavelengths in the range of 1260 nm to 1625 nm, covering both the C-band (1530-1565 nm) and L-band (1565-1625 nm), with some support for the S-band (1460-1530 nm).

34. Explain the role of Forward Error Correction (FEC) in transponders.

FEC in transponders improves data integrity by detecting and correcting errors in the transmitted data. It adds redundant data bits to the signal, which are used to identify and correct errors at the receiver end. Common FEC schemes include Reed-Solomon and BCH codes, improving the BER (bit error rate) from 10^-3 to 10^-15 or better.

35. What are the differences between a transponder and a transceiver?

A transponder converts signals between optical and electrical forms and can change wavelengths, often including FEC and other processing. A transceiver, however, is a simpler device that only converts electrical signals to optical and vice versa, without wavelength conversion or additional processing.

36. Describe how a coherent transponder works.

A coherent transponder uses advanced modulation techniques (such as QPSK or QAM) and coherent detection to achieve higher data rates and longer transmission distances. It processes both the amplitude and phase of the signal, allowing for more efficient use of bandwidth and improved resistance to impairments like chromatic dispersion and PMD (polarization mode dispersion).

37. What are the common applications of transponders in optical networks?

Transponders are used in DWDM systems, for signal regeneration, wavelength conversion, and as interfaces between different types of networks or equipment. They are critical in long-haul and metro networks, data centers, and submarine cable systems.

38. How does a transponder facilitate wavelength conversion?

A transponder facilitates wavelength conversion by converting the incoming optical signal to an electrical signal, then re-encoding it onto a different optical wavelength for transmission. This process allows for flexible wavelength management and routing in DWDM systems, enabling efficient use of the optical spectrum.

39. What is the typical power consumption of a modern optical transponder?

The power consumption of a modern optical transponder ranges from 10 to 30 watts, depending on its capabilities and the data rates it supports. High-performance coherent transponders might consume closer to 30 watts.

40. Explain the term 'bit error rate' (BER) in the context of transponders.

BER measures the number of bit errors divided by the total number of bits transmitted over a communication channel. In transponders, a low BER (e.g., 10^-15) indicates a high-quality signal with fewer errors, essential for reliable data transmission.

41. What is the importance of wavelength stability in transponders?

Wavelength stability ensures that the signal remains within its designated channel without drifting, which is crucial to prevent crosstalk and interference in DWDM systems. Wavelength drift can be controlled within ±0.01 nm.

42. How do you monitor and manage transponders in an optical network?

Transponders are monitored and managed using network management systems (NMS) that provide real-time data on performance metrics, signal quality, and fault conditions. Remote configuration and diagnostics are also possible, typically through SNMP (Simple Network Management Protocol) or proprietary management interfaces.

43. What advancements have been made in transponder technology recently?

Recent advancements include the development of coherent transponders, higher data rate support (up to 800 Gbps), improved FEC algorithms, and integration with software-defined networking (SDN) for enhanced control and flexibility.

44. Describe the concept of tunable transponders.

Tunable transponders can adjust their transmission wavelength over a range of channels, providing flexibility in network planning and management by allowing dynamic wavelength allocation. They typically support tuning across the entire C-band (1530-1565 nm).

45. What is the impact of temperature variations on transponder performance?

Temperature variations can affect the wavelength stability and signal integrity of transponders. Modern transponders include temperature control mechanisms, such as thermoelectric coolers, to maintain performance within specified limits (typically -5 to 70 degrees Celsius).

46. How do transponders support network scalability?

Transponders support network scalability by enabling the addition of new wavelengths or channels without significant changes to the existing infrastructure, allowing for incremental capacity upgrades. This modularity is key for future-proofing networks.

47. Explain the term 'Optical Reach' concerning transponders.

Optical reach refers to the maximum distance an optical signal can travel without requiring regeneration. Advanced transponders with coherent detection and FEC can achieve optical reaches of up to 4000 km or more in submarine cable systems.

48. What role do transponders play in network protection schemes?

Transponders can be part of protection schemes like 1+1 or 1:1, where they provide backup paths for data transmission. In case of a failure, the transponder switches to the backup path to maintain service continuity, ensuring high network reliability.

49. How do transponders handle different modulation formats?

Transponders support various modulation formats (e.g., NRZ, QPSK, 16-QAM) by adjusting their transmission and reception capabilities, allowing for flexible adaptation to different network requirements and data rates. For example, QPSK might be used for 100 Gbps channels, while 16-QAM might be used for 400 Gbps.

50. What is the future outlook for transponder technology?

The future outlook includes higher data rates (beyond 800 Gbps), integration with artificial intelligence for smarter network management, increased energy efficiency, and further miniaturization for deployment in various environments, including data centers and metropolitan networks.

51. What is the primary function of a multiplexer (MUX) in optical communication?

A multiplexer combines multiple optical signals of different wavelengths into a single optical fiber, allowing for efficient utilization of the fiber's bandwidth. For example, a DWDM multiplexer can combine up to 96 channels, each carrying 100 Gbps, into a single fiber.

52. How does a demultiplexer (DEMUX) differ from a multiplexer?

A demultiplexer separates a composite optical signal into its component wavelengths, directing each wavelength to a different output fiber. It performs the reverse function of a multiplexer, enabling the separation of signals for further processing or delivery.

53. Explain the working principle of an Arrayed Waveguide Grating (AWG) multiplexer/demultiplexer.

An AWG uses an array of waveguides with different path lengths to create constructive and destructive interference patterns, allowing it to multiplex or demultiplex different wavelengths accurately. AWGs are commonly used in DWDM systems due to their high channel count and precise wavelength handling.

54. What are the key differences between passive and active MUX/DEMUX devices?

Passive MUX/DEMUX devices do not require external power and rely on optical filters or gratings, while active devices use electronic components and require power, offering features like signal amplification and wavelength conversion. Passive devices typically have lower insertion loss and are more cost-effective for many applications.

55. How does Wavelength Selective Switching (WSS) enhance the functionality of MUX/DEMUX devices?

WSS allows dynamic reconfiguration of wavelengths in real-time, enabling flexible routing and efficient use of network resources by switching individual wavelengths as needed. This capability is essential for reconfigurable optical add-drop multiplexers (ROADMs) in agile optical networks.

56. What is the typical insertion loss for a MUX/DEMUX device?

The typical insertion loss for a MUX/DEMUX device ranges from 1 to 5 dB, depending on the design and number of channels. Lower insertion loss is preferable to minimize signal degradation.

57. How do you measure the isolation performance of a MUX/DEMUX device?

Isolation performance is measured by the ability of the device to prevent crosstalk between adjacent channels. It is typically quantified in dB, with values above 30 dB indicating high isolation, ensuring minimal interference between channels.

58. Describe the role of optical add-drop multiplexers (OADM) in DWDM networks.

OADMs allow specific wavelengths to be added or dropped at intermediate points without affecting the remaining wavelengths, enabling flexible and scalable network architectures. For instance, in a metro network, an OADM can add/drop specific channels for local access while passing through other channels.

59. What are the advantages of using thin-film filters in MUX/DEMUX devices?

Thin-film filters provide precise wavelength selection, low insertion loss, high isolation, and compact design, making them ideal for dense wavelength division multiplexing (DWDM) applications. They typically offer channel spacing of 100 GHz or 50 GHz.

60. Explain the concept of channel spacing in MUX/DEMUX devices.

Channel spacing refers to the wavelength separation between adjacent channels in a MUX/DEMUX device. In DWDM systems, typical channel spacing is 50 GHz (0.4 nm) or 100 GHz (0.8 nm). Narrower spacing allows for more channels but requires more precise filtering.

61. How do you manage thermal stability in MUX/DEMUX devices?

Thermal stability is managed through temperature-compensated designs, including materials with low thermal expansion coefficients and integrated temperature control mechanisms. This ensures consistent performance across varying environmental conditions.

62. What are the common applications of MUX/DEMUX devices in optical networks?

Common applications include DWDM systems, metropolitan area networks (MANs), long-haul networks, and data centers, where efficient bandwidth utilization and flexibility are crucial. For example, a DWDM system might use a MUX to combine 80 channels of 100 Gbps each into a single fiber.

63. How do you perform wavelength calibration for MUX/DEMUX devices?

Wavelength calibration involves using a known light source and measuring the output wavelengths to ensure they match the design specifications. Calibration is critical for maintaining accurate wavelength separation and minimal crosstalk.

64. Describe the impact of non-linear effects on MUX/DEMUX performance.

Non-linear effects, such as four-wave mixing and cross-phase modulation, can cause signal distortion and crosstalk. MUX/DEMUX devices must be designed to minimize these effects through optimal channel spacing and power management.

65. What are the challenges associated with scaling MUX/DEMUX devices for higher channel counts?

Challenges include maintaining low insertion loss, high isolation, and thermal stability, as well as managing increased complexity and cost. Advanced materials and manufacturing techniques are required to overcome these challenges, especially for devices with 80 or more channels.

66. Explain the concept of 'flattened passband' in MUX/DEMUX devices.

A flattened passband refers to the wavelength range where the insertion loss is relatively constant. It ensures consistent performance across the channel, reducing signal degradation and improving overall system performance. Typically, a flattened passband can be around ±0.1 nm from the center wavelength.

67. How do you test and verify the performance of a MUX/DEMUX device?

Testing involves measuring key parameters like insertion loss, isolation, crosstalk, return loss, and wavelength accuracy using optical spectrum analyzers and other test equipment. Ensuring these parameters meet specifications is crucial for reliable operation.

68. What is the significance of return loss in MUX/DEMUX devices?

Return loss measures the amount of reflected light at the input and output ports. High return loss (e.g., >45 dB) is desirable to prevent signal degradation and interference in the network, ensuring efficient signal transmission.

69. Describe the future trends in MUX/DEMUX technology.

Future trends include higher channel counts, integration with photonic integrated circuits (PICs), enhanced thermal stability, lower insertion loss, and improved flexibility through reconfigurable devices. Developments in materials and manufacturing processes will drive these advancements.

70. How do hybrid MUX/DEMUX devices differ from traditional ones?

Hybrid MUX/DEMUX devices combine multiple technologies (e.g., thin-film filters and AWGs) to achieve better performance, flexibility, and scalability. They offer optimized characteristics by leveraging the strengths of different approaches, enabling higher channel counts and lower losses.

71. What is the primary function of an optical amplifier in a communication system?

An optical amplifier boosts the power of an optical signal without converting it to an electrical signal, enabling long-distance transmission with minimal signal degradation. For example, an EDFA can amplify a 1550 nm signal by 20-30 dB.

72. Describe the working principle of an Erbium-Doped Fiber Amplifier (EDFA).

An EDFA uses a length of fiber doped with erbium ions. When pumped with a laser at 980 nm or 1480 nm, the erbium ions amplify the incoming signal through stimulated emission, boosting the signal power across a range of wavelengths (typically C-band, 1530-1565 nm).

73. How does a Raman amplifier differ from an EDFA?

A Raman amplifier uses the Raman scattering effect to amplify signals directly within the transmission fiber, providing distributed amplification and allowing for broader wavelength operation compared to EDFAs. Raman amplifiers can operate in both the C-band and L-band (1565-1625 nm).

74. What are the advantages of using semiconductor optical amplifiers (SOAs)?

SOAs offer compact size, integration with other semiconductor devices, fast response times, and the ability to amplify a wide range of wavelengths. They are useful in applications like optical switching, modulation, and access networks.

75. Explain the concept of gain in optical amplifiers.

Gain refers to the amplification factor of an optical amplifier, measured in dB. It indicates how much the amplifier boosts the signal power, with typical values ranging from 20 to 30 dB for EDFAs. For example, if an EDFA amplifies a 1 mW signal to 100 mW, the gain is 20 dB.

76. What is the role of gain flattening in optical amplifiers?

Gain flattening ensures consistent amplification across different wavelengths, preventing some channels from being amplified more than others. This is critical in DWDM systems to maintain uniform signal strength and avoid channel imbalance.

77. How do you manage noise figure in optical amplifiers?

The noise figure measures the added noise by the amplifier, with lower values being desirable. It is managed by optimizing the design, using high-quality components, and minimizing pump power fluctuations. Typical noise figures for EDFAs are around 4-6 dB.

78. What is the significance of pump lasers in optical amplifiers?

Pump lasers provide the energy required for amplification. In EDFAs, they typically operate at wavelengths of 980 nm or 1480 nm, exciting the erbium ions to amplify the signal. The quality and stability of the pump lasers directly affect the amplifier's performance.

79. Describe the impact of gain saturation in optical amplifiers.

Gain saturation occurs when the input signal power exceeds the amplifier's capability to provide further gain, leading to a reduction in amplification efficiency. It can cause signal distortion and reduced performance. Managing input power levels is crucial to avoid saturation.

80. How do you prevent non-linear effects in optical amplifiers?

Non-linear effects like self-phase modulation and four-wave mixing are prevented by managing the input power levels, optimizing the amplifier design, and using dispersion management techniques. Keeping power levels within specified limits helps mitigate these effects.

81. What are the typical applications of optical amplifiers in communication networks?

Applications include long-haul transmission, metropolitan area networks, data centers, and submarine cables, where signal amplification is needed to maintain signal quality over extended distances. For example, EDFAs are commonly used in DWDM systems to amplify multiple wavelengths simultaneously.

82. Explain the term 'gain bandwidth' in the context of optical amplifiers.

Gain bandwidth refers to the range of wavelengths over which the amplifier provides sufficient gain. For EDFAs, the typical gain bandwidth is around 1530 to 1565 nm (C-band). A broader gain bandwidth allows for more channels to be amplified simultaneously.

83. How do hybrid amplifiers enhance network performance?

Hybrid amplifiers combine different amplification technologies (e.g., EDFA and Raman) to achieve broader gain bandwidth, improved noise performance, and better overall signal quality. They are particularly useful in high-capacity and long-distance networks.

84. What are the challenges associated with deploying optical amplifiers in networks?

Challenges include managing non-linear effects, ensuring consistent gain across channels, dealing with temperature variations, and integrating amplifiers with existing network infrastructure. Careful design and deployment strategies are needed to address these challenges.

85. How do optical amplifiers support high-capacity DWDM systems?

Optical amplifiers boost the signal power of multiple wavelengths simultaneously, enabling long-distance transmission and higher data rates in DWDM systems by maintaining signal integrity. For example, EDFAs can amplify signals across 40 or more channels, each carrying 100 Gbps.

86. Describe the importance of gain equalization in optical amplifiers.

Gain equalization ensures that all channels in a DWDM system receive uniform amplification, preventing some channels from being over-amplified while others are under-amplified. This maintains signal quality and system performance across the entire wavelength range.

87. What is the role of mid-span amplifiers in optical networks?

Mid-span amplifiers are placed at intermediate points along a transmission path to boost the signal power, compensating for losses and extending the reach of the optical link. They are essential in long-haul and submarine cable systems to maintain signal integrity.

88. How do you monitor and manage the performance of optical amplifiers?

Performance is monitored using network management systems (NMS) that provide real-time data on gain, noise figure, input/output power levels, and operational status, allowing for proactive maintenance and optimization. Remote monitoring and control are often implemented through SNMP or proprietary protocols.

89. What advancements have been made in optical amplifier technology?

Recent advancements include higher gain and lower noise figure EDFAs, broadband Raman amplifiers, integration with photonic integrated circuits (PICs), and the development of more energy-efficient designs. These advancements improve performance and reduce operational costs.

90. What is the future outlook for optical amplifier technology?

The future outlook includes further integration with other optical components, increased bandwidth and data rates, improved energy efficiency, and enhanced capabilities for dynamic and flexible network management. Continued research and development will drive these innovations.

91. What is the primary function of an Erbium-Doped Fiber Amplifier (EDFA)?

An EDFA amplifies optical signals by using a length of fiber doped with erbium ions, which are excited by a pump laser, causing them to amplify the signal through stimulated emission. This process boosts the signal power without converting it to electrical form.

92. Explain the working principle of Raman amplifiers.

Raman amplifiers use the Raman scattering effect, where the pump laser interacts with the transmission fiber to transfer energy to the signal, providing distributed amplification along the fiber length. This method can amplify signals over a wide range of wavelengths.

93. What are the advantages of using EDFAs in optical networks?

EDFAs offer high gain (20-30 dB), low noise figure (4-6 dB), wide gain bandwidth (typically C-band, 1530-1565 nm), and the ability to amplify multiple wavelengths simultaneously. These characteristics make them ideal for DWDM systems and long-distance transmission.

94. How do Raman amplifiers differ from EDFAs in terms of application?

Raman amplifiers provide distributed amplification and can operate over a broader range of wavelengths. They are used to extend the reach of the optical link and improve signal quality in conjunction with EDFAs, particularly in long-haul and submarine cable systems.

95. Describe the typical gain and noise figure of an EDFA.

The typical gain of an EDFA ranges from 20 to 30 dB, with a noise figure of around 4 to 6 dB. These values indicate the amplifier's ability to boost signal power while maintaining low levels of added noise.

96. What are the key components of an EDFA?

Key components include the erbium-doped fiber, pump lasers (operating at 980 nm or 1480 nm), wavelength-division multiplexers (WDM) to combine pump and signal light, and optical isolators to prevent feedback. These components work together to achieve efficient signal amplification.

97. How do you optimize the performance of Raman amplifiers?

Performance is optimized by carefully managing the pump power, pump wavelength, and fiber type, as well as using advanced techniques like distributed Raman amplification and hybrid amplification with EDFAs. Proper design and deployment ensure optimal signal quality and reach.

98. Explain the significance of the gain spectrum in EDFAs.

The gain spectrum indicates the range of wavelengths over which the EDFA provides amplification. A flat gain spectrum ensures uniform amplification across all channels in a DWDM system, maintaining signal quality and minimizing channel imbalance.

99. How do temperature variations affect EDFA performance?

Temperature variations can impact the gain and noise figure of an EDFA. Modern EDFAs include temperature control mechanisms, such as thermoelectric coolers, to maintain stable performance across a range of operating conditions (-5 to 70 degrees Celsius).

100. What are the typical applications of Raman amplifiers in optical networks?

Applications include long-haul transmission, submarine cables, and high-capacity DWDM systems, where distributed amplification and extended reach are crucial. Raman amplifiers are often used in combination with EDFAs for optimal performance.

101. Describe the process of gain flattening in EDFAs.

Gain flattening involves using specially designed filters or additional dopants to ensure that the gain is uniform across the entire amplification bandwidth. This prevents some channels from being over-amplified while others are under-amplified, maintaining signal quality.

102. What are the challenges associated with deploying Raman amplifiers?

Challenges include managing non-linear effects, optimizing pump power and wavelength, ensuring compatibility with existing fiber infrastructure, and handling the increased complexity of distributed amplification. Proper design and deployment strategies are essential to address these challenges.

103. How do hybrid EDFA/Raman amplifiers enhance network performance?

Hybrid amplifiers combine the benefits of both EDFAs and Raman amplifiers, providing broader gain bandwidth, improved noise performance, and extended reach. They are particularly useful in high-capacity and long-distance networks, where enhanced signal quality is essential.

104. What is the impact of pump laser power on EDFA performance?

Pump laser power directly affects the gain and noise figure of an EDFA. Higher pump power generally results in higher gain, but excessive power can cause non-linear effects and signal distortion. Managing pump power is crucial for optimal performance.

105. Explain the term 'double-pumped EDFA'.

A double-pumped EDFA uses two pump lasers at different wavelengths (e.g., 980 nm and 1480 nm) to achieve higher gain and improved noise performance, allowing for more efficient and flexible amplification. This configuration enhances the overall performance and versatility of the amplifier.

106. How do you manage non-linear effects in Raman amplifiers?

Non-linear effects are managed by optimizing the pump power, using dispersion management techniques, and selecting appropriate fiber types to minimize interactions between the pump and signal light. Proper system design and deployment help mitigate these effects.

107. Describe the role of optical isolators in EDFAs.

Optical isolators prevent back reflections and feedback into the EDFA, which can cause instability and degradation of the amplified signal. They ensure unidirectional flow of light through the amplifier, maintaining signal quality and amplifier performance.

108. What advancements have been made in EDFA technology recently?

Advancements include higher gain and lower noise figure designs, integration with photonic integrated circuits (PICs), improved thermal management, and development of more energy-efficient pump lasers. These improvements enhance performance and reduce operational costs.

109. What is the future outlook for EDFA and Raman amplifier technology?

The future outlook includes further integration with other optical components, increased bandwidth and data rates, improved energy efficiency, and continued improvements in gain and noise performance for more demanding applications. Research and development will drive these innovations.

110. How do you test and verify the performance of EDFA and Raman amplifiers?

Testing involves measuring key parameters like gain, noise figure, input/output power levels, and operational stability using optical spectrum analyzers, power meters, and other test equipment. Ensuring these parameters meet specifications is crucial for reliable operation.

111. What are the main types of optical fibers used in communication?

The main types are single-mode fiber (SMF) and multi-mode fiber (MMF). SMF has a small core diameter (around 9 microns) and supports long-distance, high-bandwidth communication, while MMF has a larger core diameter (50 or 62.5 microns) and is used for shorter distances due to higher modal dispersion.

112. Explain the differences between single-mode and multi-mode fibers.

Single-mode fibers have a core diameter of about 9 microns and support one propagation mode, making them suitable for long-distance transmission with low attenuation (around 0.2 dB/km). Multi-mode fibers have core diameters of 50 or 62.5 microns, supporting multiple propagation modes and are used for shorter distances (up to 2 km) due to higher attenuation (around 3 dB/km) and modal dispersion.

113. What is the typical core diameter of a single-mode fiber?

The typical core diameter of a single-mode fiber is approximately 9 microns, which allows for single-mode propagation and minimizes modal dispersion, enabling long-distance and high-bandwidth communication.

114. Describe the concept of numerical aperture (NA) in optical fibers.

Numerical aperture (NA) is a measure of the light-gathering ability of an optical fiber, defined as the sine of the maximum angle at which light can enter the fiber and still be guided. It determines the fiber's acceptance cone and affects the coupling efficiency. Typical NA values are 0.1 for single-mode fibers and 0.2-0.3 for multi-mode fibers.

115. What are the attenuation characteristics of single-mode and multi-mode fibers?

Single-mode fibers have lower attenuation (around 0.2 dB/km at 1550 nm) compared to multi-mode fibers (around 3 dB/km at 850 nm), making them more suitable for long-distance communication. Attenuation increases with wavelength for both fiber types.

116. How does chromatic dispersion affect optical fibers?

Chromatic dispersion causes different wavelengths of light to travel at different speeds, leading to pulse broadening and potential signal distortion. It impacts the maximum transmission distance and data rate of the fiber. For example, single-mode fibers typically have chromatic dispersion values of 17 ps/nm·km at 1550 nm.

117. What is the significance of polarization mode dispersion (PMD) in single-mode fibers?

PMD occurs due to birefringence in single-mode fibers, causing different polarization modes to travel at different speeds. It can limit the performance of high-speed optical communication systems by introducing pulse broadening. Typical PMD values are around 0.1 ps/√km for modern fibers.

118. Explain the term 'mode field diameter' in single-mode fibers.

Mode field diameter (MFD) refers to the effective diameter of the light-carrying region in a single-mode fiber, which is slightly larger than the core diameter. It is crucial for splicing and connector compatibility. Typical MFD values are around 10.4 microns at 1550 nm.

119. What are the common types of multi-mode fibers?

The common types are OM1, OM2, OM3, OM4, and OM5, classified based on their core diameter, bandwidth capacity, and intended application. OM4 and OM5 support higher data rates (up to 100 Gbps) and longer distances (up to 550 meters) compared to OM1 and OM2.

120. How do you measure the attenuation of an optical fiber?

Attenuation is measured using an optical power meter and light source or an optical time-domain reflectometer (OTDR). It determines the signal loss per unit length (dB/km). OTDR provides a detailed trace of the fiber, showing loss events along the length.

121. What are the typical applications of single-mode fibers?

Applications include long-haul telecommunication, metropolitan area networks (MANs), submarine cables, and high-speed data centers, where long-distance and high-bandwidth capabilities are essential. Single-mode fibers are preferred for distances exceeding 10 km.

122. Describe the impact of bending loss on optical fibers.

Bending loss occurs when the fiber is bent beyond a certain radius, causing light to escape from the core. It leads to increased attenuation and signal loss, particularly in single-mode fibers. Bend-insensitive fibers have been developed to mitigate this effect, with bending losses of less than 0.1 dB/turn at a 10 mm radius.

123. What are the benefits of using graded-index multi-mode fibers?

Graded-index multi-mode fibers have a refractive index that gradually decreases from the core center to the cladding, reducing modal dispersion and enabling higher bandwidth over longer distances compared to step-index fibers. For example, OM4 fibers can support 10 Gbps up to 550 meters.

124. How do you perform an OTDR test on optical fibers?

An OTDR sends optical pulses into the fiber and measures the backscattered light as a function of time, providing a graphical representation of the fiber's characteristics, including splice losses, bends, and overall length. It helps identify faults and measure attenuation along the fiber.

125. What is the typical bandwidth-distance product for multi-mode fibers?

The bandwidth-distance product varies by fiber type, with OM1 offering 200 MHz·km, OM2 500 MHz·km, OM3 2000 MHz·km, OM4 4700 MHz·km, and OM5 similar to OM4 but optimized for wideband applications. This product indicates the fiber's ability to support high data rates over distance.

126. Explain the concept of 'zero-dispersion wavelength' in single-mode fibers.

The zero-dispersion wavelength is the wavelength at which chromatic dispersion in a single-mode fiber is zero. It typically occurs around 1310 nm, minimizing pulse broadening and enabling high-speed transmission. Dispersion-shifted fibers are designed to have zero dispersion around 1550 nm.

127. What are the differences between standard single-mode fiber (SSMF) and non-zero dispersion-shifted fiber (NZ-DSF)?

SSMF has its zero-dispersion wavelength around 1310 nm, while NZ-DSF is designed to have low but non-zero dispersion around the 1550 nm wavelength range, reducing non-linear effects in DWDM systems. NZ-DSF balances the trade-off between dispersion and non-linearities.

128. How do you splice optical fibers, and what are the key considerations?

Splicing involves aligning and joining two fibers end-to-end, either through fusion splicing (melting the fibers together) or mechanical splicing (aligning and holding fibers with a fixture). Key considerations include cleanliness, alignment precision, and minimizing splice loss (typically less than 0.1 dB for fusion splices).

129. Describe the role of cladding in optical fibers.

The cladding surrounds the core and has a lower refractive index, ensuring total internal reflection of light within the core, guiding the light along the fiber, and protecting the core from external damage and contamination. The cladding diameter is typically 125 microns.

130. What advancements have been made in optical fiber technology recently?

Advancements include the development of bend-insensitive fibers, which reduce bending losses, higher bandwidth multi-mode fibers for data centers, and low-loss single-mode fibers for long-haul and submarine applications. Additionally, the integration of optical fibers with photonic integrated circuits (PICs) for enhanced performance and scalability has been a significant advancement. For example, new single-mode fibers have attenuation as low as 0.15 dB/km at 1550 nm.

131. What is the primary function of a Raman amplifier in optical communication?

Raman amplifiers boost the power of an optical signal by transferring energy from a pump laser to the signal through the Raman scattering effect. This process amplifies the signal along the fiber length, enhancing long-distance transmission.

132. Explain the working principle of Raman amplifiers.

Raman amplifiers use the Raman scattering effect, where a high-power pump laser interacts with the transmission fiber, causing energy transfer to the signal light. This interaction amplifies the signal over a range of wavelengths.

133. What are the typical pump wavelengths used in Raman amplifiers?

Typical pump wavelengths used in Raman amplifiers range from 1420 nm to 1480 nm for C-band amplification, and around 1360 nm for L-band amplification. These wavelengths are chosen to optimize the Raman gain efficiency.

134. How does the Raman gain spectrum affect amplifier performance?

The Raman gain spectrum is broad, allowing for amplification over a wide range of wavelengths. The peak gain occurs when the pump wavelength is approximately 100 nm shorter than the signal wavelength, providing a gain bandwidth of about 5 THz.

135. What is the typical gain provided by a Raman amplifier?

Raman amplifiers typically provide a gain of 10-15 dB, depending on the pump power and fiber length. Higher gains can be achieved with increased pump power and optimized fiber properties.

136. How does distributed Raman amplification differ from lumped Raman amplification?

Distributed Raman amplification occurs along the entire length of the transmission fiber, while lumped Raman amplification occurs at discrete points. Distributed amplification offers better noise performance and extended reach.

137. What are the advantages of using Raman amplifiers in long-haul optical networks?

Raman amplifiers provide benefits such as extended reach, improved noise performance, and the ability to amplify signals across a broader wavelength range. They are particularly useful in long-haul and submarine optical networks.

138. Describe the impact of non-linear effects on Raman amplifier performance.

Non-linear effects like stimulated Brillouin scattering (SBS) and four-wave mixing (FWM) can degrade Raman amplifier performance. Managing these effects involves optimizing pump power and using dispersion management techniques.

139. How do you manage the noise figure in Raman amplifiers?

The noise figure of Raman amplifiers is managed by optimizing the pump power and wavelength, as well as the fiber properties. Typical noise figures range from 4 to 6 dB, depending on the amplifier design and operating conditions.

140. What is the significance of pump power in Raman amplifiers?

Pump power is critical in Raman amplifiers as it directly affects the gain and noise figure. Higher pump power generally increases gain but can also introduce non-linear effects. Optimal pump power balances gain and noise performance.

141. How do temperature variations affect Raman amplifier performance?

Temperature variations can impact the Raman gain efficiency and wavelength stability. Modern Raman amplifiers include temperature control mechanisms to maintain stable performance across varying environmental conditions.

142. What are the typical applications of Raman amplifiers in optical networks?

Raman amplifiers are used in long-haul transmission, submarine cables, and high-capacity DWDM systems, where distributed amplification and extended reach are crucial. They are often combined with EDFAs for optimal performance.

143. How do hybrid Raman/EDFA amplifiers enhance network performance?

Hybrid Raman/EDFA amplifiers combine the benefits of both technologies, providing broader gain bandwidth, improved noise performance, and extended reach. This combination enhances signal quality and network performance.

144. What is the role of gain flattening filters in Raman amplifiers?

Gain flattening filters are used in Raman amplifiers to ensure uniform gain across all channels in a DWDM system. These filters prevent some channels from being over-amplified while others are under-amplified.

145. Describe the future trends in Raman amplifier technology.

Future trends in Raman amplifier technology include further integration with photonic integrated circuits (PICs), improved energy efficiency, broader wavelength coverage, and enhanced capabilities for dynamic and flexible network management.

146. What is the primary function of an EDFA in optical communication?

An EDFA amplifies optical signals by using a length of fiber doped with erbium ions. When pumped with a laser, the erbium ions amplify the incoming signal through stimulated emission, boosting the signal power without converting it to electrical form.

147. Explain the working principle of an EDFA.

An EDFA works by doping a length of optical fiber with erbium ions. When this fiber is pumped with a laser at wavelengths of 980 nm or 1480 nm, the erbium ions are excited to a higher energy state. As the signal light passes through the doped fiber, it stimulates the excited erbium ions to drop to a lower energy state, emitting photons that amplify the signal light.

148. What are the typical pump wavelengths used in EDFAs?

The typical pump wavelengths used in EDFAs are 980 nm and 1480 nm. The 980 nm pump wavelength is more efficient in terms of excitation, while the 1480 nm pump wavelength provides a higher pump absorption and is more effective in longer fibers.

149. What is the typical gain provided by an EDFA?

EDFAs typically provide a gain of 20-30 dB, depending on the pump power and the length of the doped fiber. The exact gain can be adjusted by varying the pump power and fiber length to meet specific network requirements.

150. What is the noise figure of an EDFA and how is it managed?

The noise figure of an EDFA typically ranges from 4 to 6 dB. It is managed by optimizing the design of the amplifier, including the choice of pump wavelength, pump power, and erbium-doped fiber length. Proper management of these parameters ensures minimal additional noise in the amplified signal.

151. How does the gain spectrum of an EDFA affect its performance?

The gain spectrum of an EDFA is typically centered around the C-band (1530-1565 nm) and provides amplification across this wavelength range.

The shape of the gain spectrum can affect the uniformity of signal amplification across different channels, which is crucial in DWDM systems to ensure consistent performance.

152. What is gain flattening in EDFAs and why is it important?

Gain flattening in EDFAs is the process of ensuring uniform gain across all wavelengths in a DWDM system. This is achieved using gain flattening filters. It is important to prevent some channels from being over-amplified while others are under-amplified, which maintains signal quality and system performance.

153. Describe the impact of temperature variations on EDFA performance.

Temperature variations can affect the gain and noise figure of an EDFA. Erbium-doped fibers and pump lasers are sensitive to temperature changes, which can lead to fluctuations in performance. Modern EDFAs include temperature control mechanisms, such as thermoelectric coolers, to maintain stable performance over a range of operating conditions (-5 to 70 degrees Celsius).

154. What are the advantages of using EDFAs in long-haul optical networks?

EDFAs offer several advantages in long-haul optical networks, including high gain, low noise figure, and the ability to amplify multiple wavelengths simultaneously. This makes them ideal for extending the reach of optical signals in DWDM systems, where they can amplify signals over long distances without the need for electrical regeneration.

155. How do EDFAs handle high input power levels?

EDFAs are designed to handle high input power levels by using advanced pump control and gain management techniques. These include the use of automatic gain control (AGC) and automatic power control (APC) to ensure consistent output power and prevent saturation, which can degrade signal quality.

156. What is the typical insertion loss of an EDFA?

The typical insertion loss of an EDFA is around 0.5 to 1.0 dB. This loss occurs due to the components used in the amplifier, such as the erbium-doped fiber, pump couplers, and isolators. Minimizing insertion loss is crucial to maintain the overall signal quality in the network.

157. Explain the concept of double-pass EDFAs and their benefits.

Double-pass EDFAs use a configuration where the signal passes through the erbium-doped fiber twice, either by reflecting it back through the fiber or using a loop. This design increases the effective gain and improves the noise figure, making the amplifier more efficient for applications requiring high gain.

158. How do you optimize the performance of an EDFA in a DWDM system?

Optimizing the performance of an EDFA in a DWDM system involves adjusting the pump power, selecting the appropriate erbium-doped fiber length, and using gain flattening filters. Additionally, managing the input power levels and ensuring proper temperature control are essential for consistent performance.

159. What are the typical applications of EDFAs in optical networks?

EDFAs are widely used in long-haul telecommunication networks, metropolitan area networks (MANs), submarine cables, and data centers. They are essential for amplifying signals in DWDM systems, where multiple wavelengths are transmitted simultaneously over long distances.

160. Describe the future trends in EDFA technology.

Future trends in EDFA technology include the integration with photonic integrated circuits (PICs) for more compact and efficient designs, improved energy efficiency, broader wavelength coverage, and enhanced capabilities for dynamic and flexible network management. Continued advancements in materials and manufacturing processes will drive these innovations.

161. What are the main types of optical fibers used in communication?

The main types of optical fibers used in communication are single-mode fiber (SMF) and multi-mode fiber (MMF). SMF has a small core diameter of about 9 microns and supports long-distance, high-bandwidth communication with low attenuation. MMF has a larger core diameter, typically 50 or 62.5 microns, and is used for shorter distances due to higher modal dispersion.

162. Explain the differences between single-mode and multi-mode fibers.

Single-mode fibers have a small core diameter (~9 microns) and support a single propagation mode, which allows for long-distance transmission with low attenuation (around 0.2 dB/km). Multi-mode fibers have larger core diameters (50 or 62.5 microns) and support multiple propagation modes, resulting in higher attenuation (around 3 dB/km at 850 nm) and modal dispersion, limiting their effective distance to about 2 km.

163. What is the typical core diameter of a single-mode fiber?

The typical core diameter of a single-mode fiber is approximately 9 microns. This small core size allows only one mode of light to propagate, minimizing dispersion and allowing for longer transmission distances.

164. Describe the concept of numerical aperture (NA) in optical fibers.

Numerical aperture (NA) is a measure of the light-gathering ability of an optical fiber, defined as the sine of the maximum angle at which light can enter the fiber and still be guided. NA determines the fiber's acceptance cone and affects the coupling efficiency. For single-mode fibers, the NA is typically around 0.1, while for multi-mode fibers, it ranges from 0.2 to 0.3.

165. What are the attenuation characteristics of single-mode and multi-mode fibers?

Single-mode fibers have lower attenuation, typically around 0.2 dB/km at 1550 nm, making them suitable for long-distance communication. Multi-mode fibers have higher attenuation, around 3 dB/km at 850 nm, limiting their use to shorter distances.

166. How does chromatic dispersion affect optical fibers?

Chromatic dispersion occurs when different wavelengths of light travel at different speeds in a fiber, causing pulse broadening and potential signal distortion. It impacts the maximum transmission distance and data rate. For single-mode fibers, typical chromatic dispersion values are around 17 ps/nm·km at 1550 nm.

167. What is the significance of polarization mode dispersion (PMD) in single-mode fibers?

PMD arises from birefringence in single-mode fibers, causing different polarization modes to travel at different speeds. It can limit the performance of high-speed optical communication systems by introducing pulse broadening. Typical PMD values for modern fibers are around 0.1 ps/√km.

168. Explain the term 'mode field diameter' in single-mode fibers.

Mode field diameter (MFD) refers to the effective diameter of the light-carrying region in a single-mode fiber, which is slightly larger than the core diameter. It is crucial for splicing and connector compatibility. Typical MFD values are around 10.4 microns at 1550 nm.

169. What are the common types of multi-mode fibers?

Common types of multi-mode fibers include OM1, OM2, OM3, OM4, and OM5. They are classified based on core diameter, bandwidth capacity, and intended application. OM3 and OM4 are designed for high-speed applications, supporting 10 Gbps over 300 and 550 meters, respectively. OM5 is optimized for wideband multimode fiber (WBMMF) applications.

170. How do you measure the attenuation of an optical fiber?

Attenuation is measured using an optical power meter and light source or an optical time-domain reflectometer (OTDR). It determines the signal loss per unit length (dB/km). OTDR provides a detailed trace of the fiber, showing loss events along the length.

171. What are the typical applications of single-mode fibers?

Single-mode fibers are used in long-haul telecommunication, metropolitan area networks (MANs), submarine cables, and high-speed data centers. They are preferred for distances exceeding 10 km due to their low attenuation and high bandwidth capabilities.

172. Describe the impact of bending loss on optical fibers.

Bending loss occurs when the fiber is bent beyond a certain radius, causing light to escape from the core. It leads to increased attenuation and signal loss, particularly in single-mode fibers. Bend-insensitive fibers have been developed to mitigate this effect, with bending losses of less than 0.1 dB/turn at a 10 mm radius.

173. What are the benefits of using graded-index multi-mode fibers?

Graded-index multi-mode fibers have a refractive index that gradually decreases from the core center to the cladding, reducing modal dispersion and enabling higher bandwidth over longer distances compared to step-index fibers. OM3 and OM4 fibers, for example, can support 10 Gbps over 300 and 550 meters, respectively.

174. How do you perform an OTDR test on optical fibers?

An OTDR sends optical pulses into the fiber and measures the backscattered light as a function of time, providing a graphical representation of the fiber's characteristics, including splice losses, bends, and overall length. It helps identify faults and measure attenuation along the fiber.

175. What is the typical bandwidth-distance product for multi-mode fibers?

The bandwidth-distance product varies by fiber type, with OM1 offering 200 MHz·km, OM2 500 MHz·km, OM3 2000 MHz·km, OM4 4700 MHz·km, and OM5 similar to OM4 but optimized for wideband applications. This product indicates the fiber's ability to support high data rates over distance.

176. What are non-linearities in optical fibers, and why are they significant?

Non-linearities in optical fibers are phenomena where the response of the fiber to light is not directly proportional to the input power. They become significant at high optical power levels and can impact signal quality and system performance by causing effects such as distortion, crosstalk, and signal degradation.

177. Explain the phenomenon of self-phase modulation (SPM) in optical fibers.

SPM occurs when the intensity of the optical signal itself causes a change in the refractive index of the fiber, leading to a phase shift that varies with the signal's power. This effect broadens the signal spectrum and can distort the transmitted signal, especially in high-power, long-haul transmissions.

178. What is cross-phase modulation (XPM), and how does it affect multi-channel systems?

XPM occurs in multi-channel systems when the intensity variations of one wavelength channel cause phase shifts in other co-propagating channels. This leads to crosstalk and signal distortion, particularly in DWDM systems where many channels are closely spaced. The extent of XPM depends on the channel spacing, power levels, and fiber properties.

179. Describe the process of four-wave mixing (FWM) in optical fibers.

FWM is a non-linear optical process where three different wavelengths interact within the fiber to generate a fourth wavelength. This effect is more pronounced in DWDM systems with closely spaced channels, leading to crosstalk and interference. FWM efficiency increases with higher channel power and lower dispersion.

180. How does stimulated Brillouin scattering (SBS) impact optical communication?

SBS is a non-linear effect where the optical signal interacts with acoustic waves in the fiber, leading to the backward scattering of light and potential signal loss. It becomes significant at high power levels and can limit the maximum transmit power in long-haul systems. Typical SBS thresholds are around 10-20 mW.

181. Explain the role of stimulated Raman scattering (SRS) in optical fibers.

SRS occurs when high-power optical signals cause energy transfer from one wavelength to another, typically from shorter to longer wavelengths. This results in signal depletion and crosstalk between channels. SRS can impact DWDM systems by reducing the power of shorter wavelength channels and amplifying longer ones.

182. What are the practical techniques to mitigate self-phase modulation (SPM) in optical systems?

To mitigate SPM, techniques include reducing the launch power, using dispersion management to broaden the pulse and reduce peak power, and employing advanced modulation formats that are less susceptible to SPM effects, such as differential phase-shift keying (DPSK) or coherent detection schemes.

183. How can cross-phase modulation (XPM) be minimized in DWDM systems?

XPM can be minimized by optimizing channel spacing to reduce inter-channel interactions, using dispersion management to reduce the overlap of signal spectra, and balancing power levels across channels to prevent high-power signals from disproportionately affecting others.

184. What strategies are used to reduce the impact of four-wave mixing (FWM) in optical networks?

Strategies to reduce FWM include using fibers with higher chromatic dispersion to reduce phase matching, optimizing channel spacing to avoid closely spaced wavelengths, reducing signal power levels, and employing hybrid modulation formats that are less prone to non-linear interactions.

185. Describe the effect of chromatic dispersion on non-linearities in optical fibers.

Chromatic dispersion can help mitigate non-linear effects by broadening the pulse width, reducing peak power, and thereby lowering the intensity-dependent non-linear interactions. However, too much dispersion can lead to pulse broadening and inter-symbol interference. Proper dispersion management balances these effects to optimize performance.

186. What is the impact of polarization mode dispersion (PMD) on non-linear effects in optical fibers?

PMD causes different polarization modes to travel at different speeds, leading to pulse broadening and potential distortion. This can interact with non-linear effects, such as SPM and XPM, to further degrade signal quality. Managing PMD is crucial in high-speed systems to maintain signal integrity.

187. How does fiber type influence non-linear effects in optical communication?

Different fiber types have varying levels of susceptibility to non-linear effects. For example, dispersion-shifted fibers (DSF) are more prone to FWM due to low dispersion at 1550 nm, while non-zero dispersion-shifted fibers (NZ-DSF) balance dispersion and non-linearities. Standard single-mode fibers (SSMF) offer a good compromise with moderate dispersion and reduced non-linearities.

188. What role does optical power play in the generation of non-linear effects?

Optical power is a critical factor in the generation of non-linear effects. Higher power levels increase the intensity of light within the fiber, which amplifies non-linear interactions such as SPM, XPM, FWM, SBS, and SRS. Managing input power levels is essential to minimize these effects.

189. Explain how advanced modulation formats can mitigate non-linearities in optical fibers.

Advanced modulation formats, such as differential phase-shift keying (DPSK), quadrature phase-shift keying (QPSK), and coherent detection, can mitigate non-linearities by reducing peak power, spreading the signal energy more evenly, and improving signal resilience to distortions. These formats also enable more efficient use of the optical spectrum.

190. Discuss the future trends in managing non-linearities in optical fiber systems.

Future trends in managing non-linearities include the development of new fiber types with optimized dispersion and non-linear properties, the use of digital signal processing (DSP) to compensate for non-linear distortions, the integration of photonic integrated circuits (PICs) for better control over non-linear effects, and the adoption of machine learning algorithms to dynamically adjust system parameters for optimal performance.

191. What are linear attenuation losses in optical fibers, and how do they impact performance?

Linear attenuation losses occur due to absorption and scattering within the fiber. Absorption is caused by impurities and intrinsic material properties, while scattering, primarily Rayleigh scattering, is due to microscopic variations in the fiber. These losses reduce signal power over distance, impacting performance by limiting transmission distance. Typical attenuation is around 0.2 dB/km for single-mode fibers at 1550 nm.

192. How does chromatic dispersion affect optical signal transmission?

Chromatic dispersion causes different wavelengths to travel at different speeds, leading to pulse broadening and intersymbol interference. This limits the maximum data rate and transmission distance. For example, in single-mode fibers, chromatic dispersion is around 17 ps/nm·km at 1550 nm, which can be managed using dispersion compensation techniques.

193. What is polarization mode dispersion (PMD), and why is it significant in high-speed networks?

PMD occurs due to birefringence in the fiber, causing different polarization modes to travel at different speeds, leading to pulse broadening and signal distortion. PMD is significant in high-speed networks because it can limit data rates and degrade signal quality. Typical PMD values are around 0.1 ps/√km.

194. Describe the effects of reflection and refraction at fiber connections and splices.

Reflection and refraction at fiber connections and splices cause signal loss and backscattering. This can lead to increased attenuation and signal distortion. High-quality connectors and splicing techniques are essential to minimize these effects, with typical insertion losses of 0.1 to 0.5 dB per connection or splice.

195. What is the role of return loss in optical fibers, and how is it measured?

Return loss measures the amount of light reflected back toward the source, indicating the quality of fiber connections and splices. It is measured in dB, with higher values indicating better performance. Typical return loss values should be greater than 45 dB to ensure minimal signal reflection.

196. What is self-phase modulation (SPM), and how does it affect optical signals?

SPM occurs when the intensity of the optical signal itself causes a change in the refractive index of the fiber, leading to a phase shift that varies with the signal's power. This effect broadens the signal spectrum and can distort the transmitted signal, especially in high-power, long-haul transmissions.

197. Explain cross-phase modulation (XPM) and its impact on DWDM systems.

XPM occurs in multi-channel systems when the intensity variations of one wavelength channel cause phase shifts in other co-propagating channels. This leads to crosstalk and signal distortion, particularly in DWDM systems where many channels are closely spaced. The extent of XPM depends on the channel spacing, power levels, and fiber properties.

198. Describe the process of four-wave mixing (FWM) and its effect on signal integrity.

FWM is a non-linear optical process where three different wavelengths interact within the fiber to generate a fourth wavelength. This effect is more pronounced in DWDM systems with closely spaced channels, leading to crosstalk and interference. FWM efficiency increases with higher channel power and lower dispersion.

199. What is stimulated Brillouin scattering (SBS), and how does it impact long-haul transmission?

SBS is a non-linear effect where the optical signal interacts with acoustic waves in the fiber, leading to the backward scattering of light and potential signal loss. It becomes significant at high power levels and can limit the maximum transmit power in long-haul systems. Typical SBS thresholds are around 10-20 mW.

200. How does stimulated Raman scattering (SRS) affect multi-channel systems?

SRS occurs when high-power optical signals cause energy transfer from one wavelength to another, typically from shorter to longer wavelengths. This results in signal depletion and crosstalk between channels. SRS can impact DWDM systems by reducing the power of shorter wavelength channels and amplifying longer ones.

201. What are the challenges of deploying optical fiber in urban environments?

Challenges include physical obstacles, such as buildings and underground infrastructure, regulatory and permitting issues, and the high cost of installation. Managing these challenges requires careful planning, coordination with local authorities, and sometimes using alternative deployment methods like aerial fiber.

202. How do environmental factors, such as temperature and humidity, affect fiber performance?

Environmental factors can affect the physical properties of the fiber and its components. Temperature variations can cause expansion and contraction, leading to increased attenuation and signal distortion. Humidity can affect splice and connector performance by causing corrosion. Proper environmental controls and protective enclosures are essential for maintaining performance.

203. What are the maintenance requirements for an optical fiber network?

Maintenance requirements include regular inspection and cleaning of connectors, monitoring signal performance, and promptly addressing any identified issues such as attenuation spikes or fiber breaks. Network management systems (NMS) and OTDRs are used for monitoring and diagnostics.

204. How do you manage fiber bends and minimize bending losses?

Fiber bends should be managed by adhering to the minimum bend radius specifications provided by the manufacturer. Using bend-insensitive fibers, appropriate routing and securing techniques, and protective conduits can help minimize bending losses, which typically increase attenuation significantly if the bend radius is too small.

205. What is the impact of fiber aging and degradation on network performance?

Fiber aging and degradation can lead to increased attenuation, signal distortion, and higher error rates. Over time, physical and chemical changes in the fiber material can cause these effects. Regular testing and monitoring are essential to identify aging fibers and replace them as needed to maintain network performance.

206. How do you handle fiber splicing in the field, and what are the key considerations?

Fiber splicing in the field is typically done using fusion splicing, which involves aligning and melting the fiber ends together. Key considerations include ensuring cleanliness, precise alignment, and minimal splice loss (typically less than 0.1 dB). Proper training and high-quality splicing equipment are essential for successful splices.

207. What are the best practices for installing and managing fiber optic connectors?

Best practices include cleaning connectors before mating, ensuring proper alignment, using connectors with low insertion and return loss, and protecting connectors from dust and moisture. Regular inspection and maintenance help maintain connector performance.

208. Explain the importance of fiber testing and certification during installation.

Fiber testing and certification ensure that the installed fiber meets performance specifications and is free of defects. Tests include measuring attenuation, return loss, and verifying proper splicing and connectorization. Certification provides documentation that the fiber installation meets industry standards, reducing the risk of future issues.

209. What are the common methods for fiber fault detection and localization?

Common methods include using OTDRs, which send light pulses through the fiber and measure backscattered light to identify faults such as breaks, bends, and splices. Visual fault locators (VFLs) can also be used to identify breaks and bends in short-distance fibers by injecting visible light into the fiber.

210. How do you manage and document fiber network infrastructure?

Managing and documenting fiber network infrastructure involves maintaining detailed records of fiber routes, splice points, and connector locations. Using geographic information systems (GIS) and network management software helps track infrastructure and plan for maintenance and expansion. Accurate documentation ensures efficient troubleshooting and network management.

211. How do linear and non-linear effects interact in high-power optical transmission?

In high-power optical transmission, linear effects like attenuation and dispersion interact with non-linear effects such as SPM, XPM, and FWM. High power levels can exacerbate non-linearities, while dispersion can spread out pulses and reduce peak power, mitigating some non-linear effects. Balancing power levels and managing dispersion are critical to optimize performance.

212. What are the challenges of integrating new technologies, such as coherent detection, with existing fiber infrastructure?

Integrating new technologies like coherent detection involves ensuring compatibility with existing fiber infrastructure, managing higher data rates and signal processing requirements, and addressing potential non-linear effects. Upgrading equipment and fiber management systems, as well as providing additional training for personnel, are necessary to successfully implement new technologies.

213. How do you ensure network reliability and fault tolerance in fiber optic systems?

Ensuring network reliability and fault tolerance involves using redundant paths, automatic protection switching (APS), and real-time monitoring systems. Designing networks with ring or mesh topologies and implementing rigorous testing and maintenance protocols also help maintain high reliability.

214. What operational issues arise from using different fiber types (e.g., SMF vs. MMF) in the same network?

Using different fiber types in the same network can lead to compatibility issues, such as mode mismatch and increased attenuation at junction points. Proper connectors and mode conditioning patches are required to transition between fiber types. Additionally, careful planning and network design are necessary to ensure seamless integration.

215. How do you address the impact of fiber cuts and physical damage on network performance?

Addressing fiber cuts and physical damage involves rapid detection and localization using OTDRs and other diagnostic tools, followed by prompt repair or replacement of the damaged fiber. Implementing redundant paths and automatic rerouting protocols can minimize service disruption during repairs.

216. What are the considerations for deploying fiber optic networks in harsh environments?

Deploying fiber optic networks in harsh environments requires selecting fibers with enhanced durability, such as armored cables, and ensuring proper protective enclosures. Environmental factors like temperature extremes, moisture, and physical stress must be considered. Regular inspections and maintenance are essential to ensure long-term performance.

217. How do you manage power budgets in long-haul optical networks?

Managing power budgets involves calculating the total optical power loss over the transmission path and ensuring that the received power is above the sensitivity threshold of the receivers. This includes accounting for losses from attenuation, splices, connectors, and non-linear effects. Amplifiers like EDFAs and Raman amplifiers are used to boost signal power and extend transmission distances.

218. Explain the role of dispersion compensation in maintaining signal integrity.

Dispersion compensation is essential to counteract chromatic dispersion, which causes pulse broadening and signal distortion. Dispersion-compensating fibers (DCFs) or modules (DCMs) are used to introduce negative dispersion, balancing the positive dispersion of the transmission fiber. This maintains signal integrity and allows for higher data rates over longer distances.

219. What are the practical challenges of implementing high-capacity DWDM systems?

Implementing high-capacity DWDM systems involves managing channel spacing to avoid crosstalk, ensuring precise wavelength control, and handling increased power levels that can exacerbate non-linear effects. Advanced modulation formats and coherent detection are often used to maximize capacity. Proper planning, high-quality components, and rigorous testing are essential to address these challenges.

220. How do you ensure proper fiber optic cable management in large installations?

Proper fiber optic cable management in large installations involves using structured cabling systems, organizing cables with trays, racks, and patch panels, and labeling all connections and routes clearly. Ensuring adequate bend radius control and protecting cables from physical damage are also crucial. Regular audits and documentation updates help maintain an organized and efficient network.

221. What is the primary function of a transponder in optical communication?

A transponder converts an incoming optical signal to an electrical signal, processes it, and then retransmits it as an optical signal at a different wavelength. This conversion is essential for signal regeneration, wavelength conversion, and modulation format adaptation, enabling efficient and flexible optical networks.

222. How does a coherent transponder differ from a non-coherent transponder?

A coherent transponder uses advanced modulation techniques and coherent detection, which involves mixing the received signal with a local oscillator laser to extract amplitude, phase, and polarization information. Non-coherent transponders use simpler direct detection methods that only detect the signal intensity. Coherent transponders provide higher data rates, better spectral efficiency, and improved performance over longer distances.

223. Explain the concept of modulation in transponders.

Modulation in transponders refers to the process of encoding information onto an optical carrier signal. Common modulation formats include NRZ (Non-Return-to-Zero), RZ (Return-to-Zero), DPSK (Differential Phase Shift Keying), QPSK (Quadrature Phase Shift Keying), and higher-order QAM (Quadrature Amplitude Modulation) formats like 16-QAM and 64-QAM. Each format offers different trade-offs in terms of spectral efficiency, sensitivity, and robustness to noise and non-linearities.

224. What are the advantages of using coherent detection in transponders?

Coherent detection offers several advantages, including higher data rates (up to 400 Gbps and beyond), improved spectral efficiency, better tolerance to chromatic dispersion and PMD (Polarization Mode Dispersion), and the ability to use advanced modulation formats. Coherent transponders can also leverage digital signal processing (DSP) for enhanced performance and signal recovery.

225. How does digital signal processing (DSP) enhance the performance of coherent transponders?

DSP in coherent transponders is used to compensate for various impairments such as chromatic dispersion, PMD, and non-linear effects. It also enables advanced modulation formats and coherent detection techniques. DSP algorithms process the received signal to recover the transmitted data accurately, improving overall link performance and enabling higher data rates.

226. Describe the typical channel power levels used in transponders.

Typical channel power levels in transponders range from -10 dBm to 0 dBm per channel, depending on the system design and fiber characteristics. Higher power levels can improve signal-to-noise ratio (SNR) but may also increase the likelihood of non-linear effects such as four-wave mixing and cross-phase modulation.

227. What is the maximum power handling capability of a transponder?

The maximum power handling capability of a transponder depends on the design and components used. For coherent transponders, typical maximum input power levels range from 0 dBm to +10 dBm. Exceeding these levels can cause signal distortion and damage to the optical components.

228. How do transponders handle wavelength conversion?

Transponders handle wavelength conversion by converting the incoming optical signal to an electrical signal and then retransmitting it at a different optical wavelength. This process allows for flexible wavelength routing and management in DWDM systems, facilitating efficient use of the optical spectrum.

229. Explain the role of forward error correction (FEC) in transponders.

FEC in transponders improves data integrity by detecting and correcting errors in the transmitted data. It adds redundant data bits to the signal, which are used to identify and correct errors at the receiver end. Common FEC schemes include Reed-Solomon and BCH codes, which can significantly improve the bit error rate (BER) and overall link performance.

230. What are the common applications of transponders in optical networks?

Transponders are used in DWDM systems for signal regeneration, wavelength conversion, and modulation format adaptation. They are critical in long-haul and metro networks, data centers, and submarine cable systems. Coherent transponders are particularly valuable for high-capacity, long-distance links due to their advanced performance capabilities.

231. How do tunable transponders enhance network flexibility?

Tunable transponders can adjust their transmission wavelength over a range of channels, providing flexibility in network planning and management by allowing dynamic wavelength allocation. This capability is essential for optimizing spectral efficiency and accommodating changing traffic patterns without requiring physical reconfiguration of the network.

232. Describe the impact of chromatic dispersion on transponder performance and how it is managed.

Chromatic dispersion causes different wavelengths to travel at different speeds, leading to pulse broadening and signal distortion. Coherent transponders with DSP can effectively compensate for chromatic dispersion, maintaining signal integrity over long distances. Non-coherent transponders may require external dispersion compensation modules (DCMs) to manage dispersion effects.

233. What is polarization multiplexing, and how is it used in coherent transponders?

Polarization multiplexing is a technique used in coherent transponders to double the data rate by transmitting two separate data streams on orthogonal polarization states of the same wavelength. This technique, combined with coherent detection and DSP, enhances spectral efficiency and increases the capacity of optical links.

234. Explain the importance of wavelength stability in transponders.

Wavelength stability ensures that the signal remains within its designated channel without drifting, preventing crosstalk and interference in DWDM systems. Transponders use temperature control, wavelength lockers, and feedback mechanisms to maintain precise wavelength stability, typically within ±0.01 nm.

235. What are the challenges of implementing high-order modulation formats in transponders?

High-order modulation formats, such as 16-QAM and 64-QAM, offer higher spectral efficiency but require higher SNR and are more susceptible to noise and non-linear effects. Implementing these formats in transponders requires advanced DSP, precise power management, and high-quality components to maintain performance and minimize signal degradation.

236. How does power consumption vary between coherent and non-coherent transponders?

Coherent transponders typically consume more power than non-coherent transponders due to the additional DSP and complex modulation techniques. Power consumption for coherent transponders can range from 10 to 30 watts, whereas non-coherent transponders may consume 5 to 15 watts.

237. Describe the role of optical amplifiers in conjunction with transponders.

Optical amplifiers, such as EDFAs and Raman amplifiers, are used in conjunction with transponders to boost signal power and extend transmission distances. Amplifiers compensate for losses incurred along the fiber path, ensuring that the signal remains above the receiver sensitivity threshold. They are essential for long-haul and high-capacity networks.

238. What is the significance of bit error rate (BER) in transponder performance?

BER measures the number of bit errors divided by the total number of bits transmitted over a communication channel. A low BER (e.g., 10^-15) indicates a high-quality signal with fewer errors, essential for reliable data transmission. FEC and DSP in transponders help achieve low BER by correcting errors and compensating for impairments.

239. How do transponders support different data rates and protocols?

Transponders support various data rates and protocols, such as Ethernet, SONET/SDH, and Fibre Channel, by using flexible modulation formats and DSP algorithms. Coherent transponders can adapt to different data rates (e.g., 100 Gbps, 200 Gbps, 400 Gbps) and provide seamless interoperability between different network equipment and standards.

240. Explain the concept of optical reach concerning transponders.

Optical reach refers to the maximum distance an optical signal can travel without requiring regeneration. Advanced transponders with coherent detection and DSP can achieve optical reaches of up to 4000 km or more in submarine cable systems, reducing the need for intermediate regenerators and enhancing network efficiency.

241. What role do transponders play in network protection and restoration schemes?

Transponders play a crucial role in network protection and restoration schemes, such as 1+1 or 1:1 protection, where they provide backup paths for data transmission. In case of a failure, the transponder switches to the backup path to maintain service continuity, ensuring high network reliability.

242. How do transponders handle varying signal conditions and impairments?

Transponders handle varying signal conditions and impairments using DSP algorithms to compensate for chromatic dispersion, PMD, non-linear effects, and noise. They continuously monitor signal quality and adjust parameters to optimize performance, maintaining robust and reliable communication links.

243. Describe the importance of return loss and insertion loss in transponders.

Return loss measures the amount of reflected light at the input and output ports, while insertion loss measures the signal loss due to the transponder itself. High return loss (e.g., >45 dB) and low insertion loss (e.g., <1 dB) are desirable to prevent signal degradation and ensure efficient signal transmission through the transponder.

244. What advancements have been made in transponder technology recently?

Recent advancements in transponder technology include higher data rate support (up to 800 Gbps and beyond), improved FEC algorithms, integration with SDN (Software-Defined Networking) for enhanced control and flexibility, and the development of photonic integrated circuits (PICs) for more compact and energy-efficient designs.

245. How do transponders support network scalability and future upgrades?

Transponders support network scalability and future upgrades by offering tunable wavelengths, flexible modulation formats, and adaptable data rates.

This allows network operators to incrementally increase capacity and adapt to evolving traffic demands without significant changes to the existing infrastructure.

246. Explain the concept of forward error correction (FEC) gain in transponders.

FEC gain refers to the improvement in signal quality and error performance achieved through the use of FEC. It is measured as the difference in required SNR between a system with and without FEC to achieve the same BER. Typical FEC gain can range from 6 to 9 dB, significantly enhancing link performance.

247. What are the operational considerations for deploying transponders in a DWDM system?

Operational considerations for deploying transponders in a DWDM system include managing channel spacing to avoid crosstalk, ensuring wavelength stability, balancing power levels to prevent non-linear effects, and using amplifiers to extend reach. Proper network planning and monitoring are essential to maintain performance and reliability.

248. How do transponders contribute to the overall cost-effectiveness of optical networks?

Transponders contribute to the cost-effectiveness of optical networks by enabling efficient use of the optical spectrum, supporting high data rates, and reducing the need for frequent regeneration. Tunable and coherent transponders also provide flexibility and scalability, allowing network operators to optimize capacity and performance while minimizing capital and operational expenses.

249. What are the future trends in transponder technology?

Future trends in transponder technology include the development of higher data rates (beyond 1 Tbps), integration with artificial intelligence for smarter network management, increased energy efficiency, and further miniaturization for deployment in various environments, including data centers and metropolitan networks.

250. How do you test and verify the performance of transponders in a live network?

Testing and verifying the performance of transponders in a live network involves measuring key parameters such as BER, SNR, wavelength stability, and channel power levels. Tools like optical spectrum analyzers, power meters, and BER testers are used to ensure transponders meet performance specifications and operate reliably. Regular monitoring and diagnostics help maintain network health and address issues promptly.

251. How do you perform an optical link budget analysis, and what factors do you consider?

Optical link budget analysis involves calculating the total loss and gain in an optical link to ensure that the received signal power is above the receiver sensitivity threshold. Factors considered include fiber attenuation, connector and splice losses, dispersion, non-linear effects, and the gain provided by amplifiers. The analysis ensures reliable signal transmission over the desired distance.

252. Describe the process of installing and splicing fiber optic cables in the field.

Installing and splicing fiber optic cables involves laying the fiber along the designated route, securing it in place, and splicing the fibers at joint locations. Fusion splicing is commonly used, where the fiber ends are aligned and fused together using an electric arc. Key considerations include maintaining cleanliness, precise alignment, and minimizing splice loss (typically <0.1 dB).

253. How do you test the integrity of fiber optic cables after installation?

Testing the integrity of fiber optic cables involves using an OTDR to measure the backscatter and reflections along the fiber. This helps identify faults such as breaks, bends, and splice losses. Additional tests include end-to-end attenuation measurements using an optical power meter and light source, and inspecting connectors for cleanliness and proper mating.

254. What are the common causes of signal loss in optical fibers, and how do you mitigate them?

Common causes of signal loss include fiber attenuation, connector and splice losses, bending losses, and contamination. Mitigation strategies involve using high-quality components, maintaining cleanliness, adhering to minimum bend radius specifications, and performing regular inspections and maintenance.

255. Explain the importance of proper cable management in an optical network installation.

Proper cable management ensures that fibers are organized, protected from physical damage, and easily accessible for maintenance and troubleshooting. It involves using cable trays, racks, and patch panels, maintaining proper bend radius, labeling cables, and avoiding excessive tension. Good cable management improves network reliability and simplifies future upgrades.

255. How do you handle fiber optic connectors to ensure low insertion loss and high return loss?

Handling fiber optic connectors involves cleaning the connector end faces before mating, ensuring proper alignment, and using high-quality connectors with low insertion loss (<0.3 dB) and high return loss (>45 dB). Regular inspection and maintenance of connectors help maintain performance.

256. What are the steps for performing a polarization mode dispersion (PMD) test, and why is it important?

PMD testing involves using a PMD analyzer to measure the differential group delay (DGD) between the principal states of polarization in a fiber. It is important because high PMD can cause pulse broadening and signal degradation, especially in high-speed networks. The test helps identify fibers with excessive PMD and ensures compliance with network specifications.

257. Describe the impact of environmental factors on fiber optic network performance and how you address them.

Environmental factors such as temperature, humidity, and physical stress can affect fiber performance. Temperature variations can cause expansion and contraction, leading to increased attenuation. Humidity can cause corrosion in connectors. Protective enclosures, environmental controls, and selecting appropriate fiber types help mitigate these impacts.

258. How do you perform a dispersion compensation calculation for a long-haul optical link?

Dispersion compensation calculation involves determining the total chromatic dispersion accumulated over the transmission distance and selecting appropriate dispersion-compensating modules (DCMs) or fibers to counteract it. The goal is to minimize pulse broadening and maintain signal integrity. The calculation considers the dispersion coefficient (ps/nm·km) and the length of the fiber.

259. What techniques do you use to ensure the accuracy of OTDR measurements?

Ensuring OTDR measurement accuracy involves calibrating the OTDR, using appropriate launch and receive fibers to avoid dead zones, setting correct measurement parameters (e.g., pulse width, averaging time), and interpreting the OTDR trace correctly. Regular maintenance and software updates also help maintain accuracy.

260. Explain the process of troubleshooting a fiber optic network when experiencing high attenuation.

Troubleshooting high attenuation involves identifying the location and cause of the loss using tools like OTDRs, visual fault locators (VFLs), and power meters. Steps include checking for dirty or damaged connectors, inspecting splices, testing for bends or breaks in the fiber, and verifying the performance of optical amplifiers. Each issue is addressed accordingly to restore optimal performance.

261. What are the best practices for maintaining fiber optic splicing equipment?

Best practices include regular cleaning of splicing electrodes, aligning and calibrating the splicer, replacing worn or damaged components, and following the manufacturer's maintenance schedule. Proper storage and handling of the splicer also prevent damage and ensure reliable operation.

262. How do you ensure network redundancy and reliability in an optical fiber network?

Ensuring network redundancy involves designing the network with multiple paths (e.g., ring or mesh topologies) and implementing automatic protection switching (APS) to reroute traffic in case of a failure. Regular testing, monitoring, and maintenance help maintain reliability and quickly address any issues that arise.

263. Describe the process of cleaning and inspecting fiber optic connectors before installation.

Cleaning and inspecting fiber optic connectors involve using specialized cleaning tools (e.g., lint-free wipes, cleaning fluid, one-click cleaners) to remove dust and debris from the connector end faces. Inspection is done using a fiber microscope to ensure the connectors are clean and free from scratches or other defects. Proper cleaning and inspection help achieve low insertion loss and high return loss.

264. What considerations do you take into account when designing a DWDM system?

Designing a DWDM system involves considering factors such as channel spacing, wavelength allocation, power levels, dispersion management, and non-linear effects. It also includes selecting appropriate transponders, amplifiers, and filters to ensure optimal performance and scalability. Network planning tools and simulations help optimize the design.

265. How do you manage power levels in a multi-channel DWDM system to avoid non-linear effects?

Managing power levels involves ensuring that the total input power is within the fiber's non-linear threshold to avoid effects like four-wave mixing and cross-phase modulation. This can be achieved by using variable optical attenuators (VOAs) to balance power levels, employing power management algorithms, and regularly monitoring the power levels of each channel.

266. What are the steps for performing an end-to-end optical link test?

An end-to-end optical link test involves measuring the optical power loss across the entire link using an optical power meter and light source. Steps include connecting the light source at the transmitter end, measuring the received power at the receiver end, and comparing the results to the calculated link budget. Any discrepancies indicate potential issues that need to be addressed.

267. Explain the importance of wavelength stability in DWDM transponders and how it is maintained.

Wavelength stability ensures that each channel stays within its designated wavelength range, preventing crosstalk and interference. It is maintained using temperature-controlled lasers, wavelength lockers, and feedback control systems. Regular monitoring and calibration also help maintain stability.

268. How do you handle the integration of new technologies, such as coherent transponders, into existing fiber networks?

Integrating new technologies involves assessing compatibility with existing infrastructure, ensuring sufficient power and dispersion management, and upgrading network management systems. Training personnel on the new technology and performing extensive testing and validation are also crucial for successful integration.

269. What are the operational challenges of managing a large-scale fiber optic network, and how do you address them?

Operational challenges include maintaining accurate documentation, managing network upgrades and expansions, ensuring consistent performance, and quickly addressing faults. Solutions involve using comprehensive network management systems (NMS), implementing robust maintenance protocols, and having a well-trained team to handle issues efficiently.

270. Describe the steps for performing a visual fault location test on a fiber optic link.

A visual fault location test involves using a visual fault locator (VFL) that emits visible red light into the fiber. The steps include connecting the VFL to the fiber, observing the fiber for any visible breaks or bends where the light escapes, and marking the fault locations for repair. This test is useful for identifying faults in short-distance fibers.

271. How do you ensure proper synchronization and timing in optical transport networks (OTN)?

Ensuring proper synchronization involves using precise timing sources such as GPS or IEEE 1588 Precision Time Protocol (PTP) to synchronize network elements. Timing signals are distributed using Synchronous Ethernet (SyncE) or dedicated timing channels in the OTN. Regular monitoring and maintenance ensure synchronization accuracy.

272. What are the best practices for documenting fiber optic network installations?

Best practices include maintaining detailed records of fiber routes, splice points, connector locations, and equipment specifications. Using geographic information systems (GIS) and network management software helps organize and update documentation. Accurate records facilitate efficient troubleshooting and future network expansions.

273. How do you perform a fiber characterization test, and what parameters are measured?

Fiber characterization involves a series of tests to measure parameters such as attenuation, chromatic dispersion, PMD, and non-linear effects. The tests are performed using specialized equipment like OTDRs, dispersion analyzers, and PMD analyzers. The results provide a comprehensive assessment of the fiber's performance and suitability for high-speed transmission.

274. Describe the process of upgrading an optical network to support higher data rates.

Upgrading an optical network involves assessing the current infrastructure, ensuring that fiber quality and dispersion management can support higher data rates, and selecting appropriate transponders and amplifiers. The process includes planning and scheduling upgrades, performing tests and validations, and minimizing downtime during the transition.

275. What are the considerations for deploying optical fibers in data centers?

Considerations include ensuring high-density cabling to maximize space utilization, using bend-insensitive fibers to accommodate tight bends, managing thermal environments to prevent overheating, and implementing structured cabling systems for efficient cable management. Reliability, scalability, and ease of maintenance are also critical factors.

276. How do you address the issue of optical power loss due to fiber aging and degradation?

Addressing optical power loss involves regular testing and monitoring to identify aging fibers, performing preventive maintenance, and replacing degraded fiber segments. Using higher-quality fibers with better resistance to environmental factors and implementing protective measures can also extend the lifespan of the fibers.

277. What are the steps for configuring and calibrating an optical transponder?

Configuring and calibrating an optical transponder involves setting the correct wavelength, modulation format, and power levels, and ensuring proper synchronization with the network. Calibration includes verifying wavelength accuracy, adjusting power levels, and testing for signal quality metrics like BER. Regular calibration ensures optimal performance.

278. Explain the role of automatic protection switching (APS) in optical networks.

APS provides redundancy by automatically switching to a backup path in case of a failure in the primary path. It ensures continuous service by detecting faults and rerouting traffic within milliseconds. APS is critical for maintaining high network reliability and minimizing downtime.

279. What are the operational challenges of managing high-capacity DWDM systems, and how do you overcome them?

Operational challenges include managing power levels, avoiding non-linear effects, ensuring wavelength stability, and maintaining performance over long distances. Overcoming these challenges involves using advanced transponders with DSP, implementing power management algorithms, regularly monitoring network performance, and using high-quality components.

280. What are the key steps involved in testing a new optical transponder?

Testing a new optical transponder involves several steps: initial setup and configuration, wavelength and power level verification, BER testing, signal quality assessment, and stress testing under various conditions. The process includes interoperability tests with other network components, environmental tests to ensure performance under different temperatures and humidity levels, and compliance with industry standards.

282. How do you perform a bit error rate (BER) test on an optical link?

A BER test involves sending a known pattern of bits through the optical link and comparing the received pattern with the transmitted one. The BER is calculated as the ratio of erroneous bits to the total transmitted bits. This test helps assess the link's error performance and the impact of impairments like noise and dispersion.

283. What is the importance of optical return loss (ORL) testing, and how is it conducted?

ORL testing measures the amount of light reflected back toward the source, indicating the quality of fiber connections and splices. High ORL values (e.g., >45 dB) are desirable to prevent signal degradation. The test is conducted using an optical return loss meter, which measures the reflected light at each connection point.

284. Explain the process of optical time-domain reflectometer (OTDR) testing.

OTDR testing involves sending a series of optical pulses into the fiber and measuring the backscattered light as a function of time. The OTDR generates a trace that shows the fiber's characteristics, including loss events, splices, bends, and overall length. It helps identify faults and measure the attenuation profile of the fiber link.

285. How do you validate the wavelength stability of a DWDM transponder?

Validating wavelength stability involves monitoring the transponder's output wavelength over time and under varying environmental conditions. This can be done using an optical spectrum analyzer (OSA) to ensure the wavelength remains within the specified tolerance (typically ±0.01 nm). Temperature cycling tests help verify stability across a range of operating temperatures.

286. What are the best practices for cleaning and inspecting fiber optic connectors before testing?

Best practices include using specialized cleaning tools like lint-free wipes, cleaning fluid, and one-click cleaners to remove dust and debris from connector end faces. Inspection with a fiber microscope ensures the connectors are clean and free from scratches or other defects, ensuring accurate test results and low insertion loss.

287. Describe the steps for performing a polarization mode dispersion (PMD) test.

PMD testing involves using a PMD analyzer to measure the differential group delay (DGD) between the principal states of polarization in a fiber. The test setup includes a polarized light source and a receiver that analyzes the time delay between polarization modes. The results indicate the fiber's PMD value, which should be within acceptable limits for high-speed transmission.

288. How do you conduct an end-to-end attenuation test on an optical link?

An end-to-end attenuation test involves connecting a light source to one end of the fiber and an optical power meter to the other end. The light source emits a known power level, and the power meter measures the received power. The difference between the transmitted and received power levels represents the total attenuation of the link, typically measured in dB.

289. What is chromatic dispersion testing, and why is it important?

Chromatic dispersion testing measures the spread of different wavelengths traveling through the fiber, which can cause pulse broadening and signal distortion. It is important for high-speed links where dispersion can limit performance. The test uses a dispersion analyzer to measure the delay difference between wavelengths and calculates the dispersion coefficient (ps/nm·km).

290. How do you validate the performance of an optical amplifier in a link?

Validating the performance of an optical amplifier involves measuring its gain, noise figure, and output power levels. The test setup includes an optical spectrum analyzer (OSA) to measure the amplified signal's spectrum and a power meter to verify the output power. Gain flatness and stability tests ensure consistent performance across the amplifier's operating range.

291. Explain the significance of return loss testing for fiber optic connectors.

Return loss testing measures the amount of light reflected back from a connector or splice, indicating the quality of the connection. High return loss values (e.g., >45 dB) are desirable as they indicate low reflection and minimal signal degradation. The test is conducted using a return loss meter or an OTDR with a specialized return loss feature.

292. How do you perform an environmental stress test on optical products?

Environmental stress testing involves subjecting optical products to extreme temperature, humidity, and mechanical stress conditions to assess their durability and performance. The tests include temperature cycling, humidity chambers, vibration and shock testing, and thermal shock tests. The products are monitored for any performance degradation or failure.

293. What are the key parameters measured during optical power testing?

Key parameters measured during optical power testing include the output power level, input power level, and the power loss across different components (e.g., connectors, splices, amplifiers). These measurements ensure that the power levels are within the specified range for optimal performance and help identify any excessive losses or power mismatches.

294. Describe the process of validating the modulation format of an optical transponder.

Validating the modulation format involves verifying that the transponder correctly implements the desired modulation scheme (e.g., QPSK, 16-QAM). The process includes measuring the signal's constellation diagram using a coherent receiver and DSP to analyze the modulation accuracy, error vector magnitude (EVM), and symbol error rate (SER).

295. How do you ensure compliance with industry standards during optical product testing?

Ensuring compliance involves testing the optical product against relevant industry standards (e.g., ITU-T, IEEE, Telcordia). This includes verifying parameters such as wavelength accuracy, power levels, dispersion, and non-linear effects. Certification from accredited testing laboratories and adherence to standard test procedures are essential for compliance.

296. Explain the importance of eye diagram analysis in optical signal testing.

Eye diagram analysis provides a visual representation of the signal quality and timing characteristics. It helps identify issues such as jitter, noise, and signal distortion. A clean, open eye diagram indicates good signal integrity, while a closed or distorted eye suggests potential problems. The analysis is performed using an oscilloscope with an eye diagram feature.

297. What are the steps for performing a visual inspection of fiber optic components?

Visual inspection involves using a fiber microscope to examine the end faces of connectors and splices for cleanliness and damage. The steps include cleaning the components, inspecting for scratches, cracks, or debris, and ensuring proper alignment and mating. This inspection helps prevent signal loss and reflection issues.

298. How do you validate the performance of a DWDM system under varying load conditions?

Validating a DWDM system under varying load conditions involves testing the system with different channel counts and data rates to assess performance. This includes measuring BER, signal-to-noise ratio (SNR), and power levels across all channels. Stress testing with maximum channel loads ensures the system can handle peak traffic without degradation.

299. Describe the process of optical spectrum analysis and its significance.

Optical spectrum analysis involves using an optical spectrum analyzer (OSA) to measure the power distribution of an optical signal across different wavelengths. It is significant for identifying channel spacing, power levels, and signal integrity in DWDM systems. The analysis helps detect issues such as crosstalk, wavelength drift, and amplifier gain flatness.

300. How do you ensure the reliability of fiber optic splices during testing?

Ensuring splice reliability involves performing mechanical and environmental tests, such as tensile strength testing, temperature cycling, and moisture resistance tests. OTDR measurements verify splice loss, and visual inspections ensure proper alignment and cleanliness. Consistent results across multiple tests confirm splice reliability.

301. Explain the importance of measuring the differential group delay (DGD) in optical fibers.

Measuring DGD is important for assessing PMD, which causes pulse broadening and signal distortion. High DGD values can limit the performance of high-speed optical links. The measurement involves using a PMD analyzer to determine the delay difference between the principal states of polarization, ensuring the fiber meets the required PMD specifications.

302. How do you perform a link validation test for a new optical network deployment?

Link validation involves testing the optical link for key parameters such as attenuation, dispersion, PMD, and BER. The process includes setting up test equipment (e.g., OTDR, power meters, dispersion analyzers), conducting end-to-end measurements, and comparing results against design specifications. Successful validation ensures the link is ready for service.

303. What are the steps for conducting a dispersion penalty test on an optical link?

Dispersion penalty testing involves measuring the impact of chromatic dispersion on signal quality. The steps include transmitting a known signal through the fiber, measuring the received signal quality (e.g., Q-factor, BER), and comparing it to a baseline measurement without dispersion. The difference indicates the dispersion penalty, which should be within acceptable limits.

304. Describe the importance of measuring the optical signal-to-noise ratio (OSNR) in DWDM systems.

OSNR measures the ratio of signal power to noise power and is critical for assessing signal quality in DWDM systems. High OSNR indicates good signal integrity, while low OSNR suggests potential issues such as amplifier noise or crosstalk. OSNR is measured using an OSA and helps ensure reliable communication at high data rates.

305. How do you validate the performance of optical switches in a network?

Validating optical switches involves testing their switching speed, insertion loss, crosstalk, and repeatability. The tests include measuring the time it takes for the switch to change states, the signal loss through the switch, and the level of unwanted signal coupling between ports. Ensuring consistent performance under various conditions is essential for reliable operation.

306. What are the steps for performing a polarization-dependent loss (PDL) test on optical components?

PDL testing involves measuring the variation in signal loss due to changes in the state of polarization. The steps include using a tunable laser source, a polarization controller, and a power meter to measure the loss at different polarization states. The maximum variation in loss indicates the PDL, which should be minimized for high-performance components.

307. Explain the significance of temperature cycling tests for optical transponders.

Temperature cycling tests assess the transponder's performance under varying temperature conditions. The tests involve subjecting the transponder to extreme temperature changes (e.g., -40°C to +85°C) and monitoring key parameters such as wavelength stability, output power, and BER. Successful temperature cycling tests ensure the transponder can operate reliably in different environments.

308. How do you perform a forward error correction (FEC) gain test on an optical link?

FEC gain testing involves comparing the BER before and after applying FEC. The test setup includes transmitting a known signal through the link, measuring the BER without FEC, enabling FEC, and re-measuring the BER. The difference in BER indicates the FEC gain, which demonstrates the effectiveness of error correction in improving link performance.

309. Describe the process of validating the dynamic range of an optical amplifier.

Validating the dynamic range involves measuring the amplifier's gain and noise figure across a range of input power levels. The test includes setting up a variable optical attenuator to adjust the input power, measuring the output power and noise figure with an OSA and power meter, and ensuring the amplifier maintains performance within the specified range.

310. What are the considerations for conducting a long-term reliability test on optical products?

Long-term reliability testing involves subjecting optical products to extended periods of operation under normal and accelerated stress conditions (e.g., temperature, humidity, mechanical stress). The tests include continuous performance monitoring, periodic measurements of key parameters, and failure analysis. Ensuring consistent performance over time confirms the product's reliability and durability.

311. What are the key considerations when planning an optical link?

Key considerations include determining the link distance, required data rate, type of fiber (single-mode or multi-mode), budget for power loss (link budget), chromatic dispersion, polarization mode dispersion (PMD), non-linear effects, and environmental factors. Proper planning ensures that the link meets performance requirements and reliability standards.

312. How do you calculate the optical link budget?

The optical link budget is calculated by accounting for the total losses and gains in the optical path. It includes the transmitter output power, receiver sensitivity, fiber attenuation (typically 0.2 dB/km for single-mode fiber at 1550 nm), connector and splice losses (around 0.1 to 0.5 dB per connection/splice), and the gain from optical amplifiers. The link budget ensures that the received power is above the receiver's sensitivity threshold.

313. What is the significance of receiver sensitivity in optical link design?

Receiver sensitivity is the minimum optical power level required for the receiver to correctly decode the incoming signal with an acceptable bit error rate (BER). It typically ranges from -28 dBm to -8 dBm, depending on the data rate and modulation format. Ensuring the received power exceeds the receiver sensitivity threshold is crucial for reliable communication.

314. How do you account for chromatic dispersion in optical link design?

Chromatic dispersion is managed by calculating the dispersion accumulation over the link distance and compensating for it using dispersion-compensating modules (DCMs) or fibers (DCFs). For single-mode fibers, the chromatic dispersion coefficient is around 17 ps/nm·km at 1550 nm. Proper compensation prevents pulse broadening and maintains signal integrity.

315. What is the impact of polarization mode dispersion (PMD) on high-speed optical links?

PMD causes differential delays between different polarization modes, leading to pulse broadening and signal distortion. It is particularly critical in high-speed links (>10 Gbps). The PMD coefficient is typically around 0.1 ps/√km. Managing PMD involves using fibers with low PMD values and compensating devices if necessary.

316. How do you design a link to minimize non-linear effects like self-phase modulation (SPM) and four-wave mixing (FWM)?

Minimizing non-linear effects involves optimizing the power levels, choosing fibers with appropriate dispersion characteristics, and spacing channels to reduce interaction. Keeping the launch power below the non-linear threshold (typically around 10-20 dBm) and using dispersion management techniques help mitigate these effects.

317. What are the typical loss values for connectors and splices in an optical link?

Typical loss values are around 0.1 to 0.5 dB per connector and splice. High-quality connectors and precise splicing techniques are essential to minimize these losses. Proper documentation and testing ensure that the cumulative losses remain within the designed link budget.

318. Describe the role of optical amplifiers in extending the reach of an optical link.

Optical amplifiers, such as EDFAs and Raman amplifiers, boost the optical signal power to compensate for losses incurred over long distances. They are placed at regular intervals (typically every 80-100 km) to maintain signal strength above the receiver sensitivity threshold, enabling long-haul communication.

319. How do you determine the placement of optical amplifiers in a long-haul link?

The placement is determined by the link budget calculation, considering fiber attenuation, connector and splice losses, and the gain of the amplifiers. Amplifiers are typically placed every 80-100 km, ensuring the signal power remains above the receiver sensitivity threshold. The exact placement depends on the specific link conditions and amplifier characteristics.

320. What is the significance of return loss in optical link design, and what are typical values?

Return loss measures the amount of light reflected back toward the source, indicating the quality of fiber connections and splices. High return loss values (e.g., >45 dB) are desirable to prevent signal degradation and ensure efficient signal transmission. It is measured using an optical return loss meter.

321. How do you design a DWDM system to ensure channel spacing and avoid crosstalk?

Designing a DWDM system involves selecting appropriate channel spacing (e.g., 50 GHz, 100 GHz) to prevent crosstalk. The choice of spacing depends on the number of channels and the system's spectral efficiency. Using high-quality filters and precise wavelength control ensures minimal crosstalk and optimal channel performance.

322. What are the key factors in selecting the type of fiber for an optical link?

Factors include the required data rate, link distance, dispersion characteristics, and environmental conditions. Single-mode fibers (SMF) are preferred for long-haul and high-speed links due to their low attenuation and dispersion. Multi-mode fibers (MMF) are suitable for short-distance and lower-speed applications due to their higher core diameter.

323. How do you perform a risk assessment for an optical link deployment?

A risk assessment involves identifying potential risks, such as physical damage, environmental factors, and operational issues. Mitigation strategies include selecting robust fibers, using protective enclosures, implementing redundancy, and conducting thorough testing. Regular monitoring and maintenance also help manage risks.

324. What are the considerations for deploying optical fibers in harsh environments?

Considerations include selecting fibers with enhanced durability (e.g., armored cables), using protective enclosures, ensuring proper environmental controls (e.g., temperature, humidity), and planning for physical stress factors. Regular inspections and maintenance ensure long-term performance in harsh environments.

325. Describe the process of validating an optical link design before deployment.

Validating an optical link design involves performing simulations, conducting lab tests, and creating a detailed link budget analysis. It includes verifying that all components meet the required specifications, testing for signal quality metrics (e.g., BER, SNR), and ensuring compliance with industry standards.

326. How do you calculate the maximum allowable attenuation for an optical link?

The maximum allowable attenuation is calculated by subtracting the receiver sensitivity from the transmitter output power, accounting for the total loss budget, including fiber attenuation, connector and splice losses, and any additional margins. The result ensures the received power remains above the receiver sensitivity threshold.

327. What are the key parameters to monitor during the operation of an optical link?

Key parameters include optical power levels, BER, SNR, chromatic dispersion, PMD, and non-linear effects. Monitoring these parameters helps ensure optimal performance and quickly identify any issues that may arise. Network management systems (NMS) provide real-time monitoring and diagnostics.

328. How do you design an optical link to ensure scalability for future upgrades?

Ensuring scalability involves designing with extra capacity, using flexible and tunable components, planning for future bandwidth needs, and selecting modular equipment. Scalable designs allow for easy upgrades and expansions, accommodating evolving network requirements without significant reconfiguration.

329. What are the best practices for documenting an optical link design?

Best practices include maintaining detailed records of the link budget calculations, component specifications, fiber routes, splice points, and testing results. Using standardized templates and software tools ensures consistent documentation. Accurate records facilitate troubleshooting, maintenance, and future upgrades.

330. Describe the process of designing a fiber optic network with ring topology.

Designing a ring topology involves connecting network nodes in a circular configuration, providing redundancy and fault tolerance. The design includes calculating link budgets for each segment, selecting appropriate fibers and components, and ensuring efficient signal routing. Ring topologies offer high reliability and resilience to single points of failure.

331. How do you ensure compliance with industry standards in optical link design?

Ensuring compliance involves adhering to standards set by organizations like ITU-T, IEEE, and Telcordia. This includes following guidelines for optical power levels, dispersion management, non-linear effects, and environmental requirements. Certification from accredited testing laboratories confirms compliance.

332. What are the considerations for designing an optical link in a metropolitan area network (MAN)?

Considerations include selecting fibers suitable for shorter distances and higher traffic density, planning for multiple access points, ensuring low latency, and managing dispersion and non-linear effects. Scalability, reliability, and cost-effectiveness are also crucial factors in MAN design.

333. How do you address the challenge of fiber aging and degradation in optical link design?

Addressing fiber aging and degradation involves selecting high-quality fibers with low attenuation and robust construction, planning for regular maintenance and testing, and implementing protective measures to prevent physical damage. Proactive replacement of aging fibers ensures long-term performance.

334. What are the key factors in designing a high-capacity DWDM system?

Key factors include optimizing channel spacing, managing power levels, ensuring wavelength stability, compensating for dispersion, and minimizing non-linear effects. Advanced modulation formats and coherent detection techniques enhance capacity and performance. Proper planning and monitoring ensure reliable operation.

335. How do you perform a dispersion penalty analysis for an optical link?

Dispersion penalty analysis involves calculating the impact of chromatic dispersion on signal quality, typically measured as the increase in BER or reduction in SNR. The analysis includes simulating different dispersion values, measuring signal performance metrics, and determining the maximum allowable dispersion for the desired data rate.

336. What are the best practices for designing an optical link in a data center environment?

Best practices include using high-density cabling solutions, selecting bend-insensitive fibers, managing thermal environments, ensuring proper cable management, and planning for future scalability. Low-latency and high-reliability designs are crucial for data center performance.

337. Describe the process of designing an optical link for submarine cable systems.

Designing submarine cable systems involves selecting robust, low-attenuation fibers, using optical amplifiers at regular intervals, ensuring redundancy and fault tolerance, and planning for environmental conditions such as pressure and temperature. Detailed route surveys and extensive testing ensure long-term reliability and performance.

338. How do you calculate the dispersion budget for a long-haul optical link?

The dispersion budget is calculated by summing the chromatic dispersion values for each fiber segment, including any dispersion-compensating modules (DCMs). The total dispersion must be within the acceptable limits for the desired data rate and modulation format to prevent signal distortion.

339. What are the considerations for designing an optical link in a rural area?

Considerations include selecting fibers suitable for long distances, ensuring reliable power supply for amplifiers, planning for physical challenges such as terrain and weather, and implementing protective measures against environmental factors. Cost-effectiveness and scalability are also important.

340. Explain the role of network management systems (NMS) in optical link design and operation.

NMS play a crucial role in monitoring and managing optical links, providing real-time data on key parameters like power levels, BER, SNR, and dispersion. NMS enable proactive maintenance, fault detection, and efficient troubleshooting, ensuring optimal performance and reliability of the optical network.

341. What is OSNR, and why is it important in optical communication?

OSNR (Optical Signal-to-Noise Ratio) measures the ratio of signal power to noise power in an optical channel. It is important because a higher OSNR indicates better signal quality and lower error rates. Typical OSNR values for reliable communication are above 20 dB.

342. How is OSNR measured, and what is the typical threshold for acceptable performance?

OSNR is measured using an optical spectrum analyzer (OSA) by comparing the signal power to the noise power within a specific bandwidth. The typical threshold for acceptable OSNR is around 20 dB for standard modulation formats like NRZ, but higher data rates and advanced modulation formats may require OSNR values above 25 dB.

343. Explain the concept of ROSNR and its significance.

ROSNR (Received Optical Signal-to-Noise Ratio) measures the OSNR at the receiver end of an optical link. It is significant because it indicates the quality of the received signal, which directly affects the bit error rate (BER) and overall system performance. Maintaining a high ROSNR is crucial for error-free communication.

344. What factors can degrade OSNR in an optical link?

Factors that degrade OSNR include fiber attenuation, amplifier noise, dispersion, non-linear effects, crosstalk, and signal reflections. Proper link design, including the use of low-noise amplifiers, dispersion compensation, and high-quality components, helps maintain high OSNR.

345. Describe the impact of OSNR on BER and system performance.

A higher OSNR typically results in a lower BER, improving system performance. For example, an OSNR of 20 dB might result in a BER of 10^-12, while an OSNR of 15 dB could increase the BER to 10^-9. Ensuring sufficient OSNR is essential for maintaining low error rates and reliable communication.

346. What is GOSNR, and how does it differ from OSNR?

GOSNR (General Optical Signal-to-Noise Ratio) is a broader term that can encompass various definitions of OSNR, depending on the measurement context and equipment used. It generally refers to the overall signal-to-noise ratio in the optical domain. OSNR is a more specific term typically used in DWDM systems and measured using an OSA.

347. How do you calculate the Q-factor in optical communication?

The Q-factor is calculated using the formula Q = (S1 - S0) / (σ1 + σ0), where S1 and S0 are the signal levels for binary 1 and 0, respectively, and σ1 and σ0 are the standard deviations of the noise for binary 1 and 0. A higher Q-factor indicates better signal quality. A typical threshold for acceptable performance is a Q-factor above 6.

348. What is the relationship between the Q-factor and BER?

The Q-factor and BER are inversely related; a higher Q-factor corresponds to a lower BER. The relationship is given by the formula BER = 0.5 * erfc(Q / √2), where erfc is the complementary error function. For example, a Q-factor of 6 corresponds to a BER of approximately 10^-9.

349. Explain the significance of a high Q-factor in optical links.

A high Q-factor indicates a high-quality signal with minimal noise and distortion, leading to a lower BER and more reliable communication. It is crucial for ensuring the integrity of transmitted data, especially in high-speed and long-distance optical links.

350. How do you measure BER in an optical communication system?

BER is measured by sending a known bit pattern through the optical link and comparing the received pattern with the transmitted one. The BER is calculated as the ratio of erroneous bits to the total transmitted bits. BER testers or analyzers are used for this purpose.

351. What is the typical BER threshold for reliable optical communication?

The typical BER threshold for reliable optical communication is 10^-12 or lower for standard applications. For more demanding applications, such as high-speed data transmission, a BER of 10^-15 may be required.

352. Describe the impact of fiber non-linearities on OSNR and BER.

Fiber non-linearities, such as self-phase modulation (SPM) and four-wave mixing (FWM), can degrade OSNR by introducing additional noise and crosstalk. This degradation increases the BER, reducing the overall performance of the optical link. Managing power levels and using dispersion management techniques help mitigate these effects.

353. How does dispersion affect OSNR and Q-factor in optical links?

Dispersion causes pulse broadening, which can overlap adjacent pulses and increase noise, reducing OSNR and Q-factor. Proper dispersion compensation is essential to maintain high OSNR and Q-factor, ensuring signal integrity and low BER.

354. What are the key parameters to monitor for maintaining high OSNR in a DWDM system?

Key parameters include channel power levels, amplifier noise figure, wavelength stability, and dispersion. Regular monitoring and adjustments ensure that these parameters remain within optimal ranges, maintaining high OSNR and reliable system performance.

355. Explain the concept of eye diagram analysis and its relation to Q-factor and BER.

Eye diagram analysis provides a visual representation of signal quality, showing the overlap of multiple bits in a single time frame. A clear, open eye indicates high signal quality, corresponding to a high Q-factor and low BER. Conversely, a closed or distorted eye suggests poor signal quality and higher BER.

356. How do you optimize the design of an optical link to achieve high OSNR?

Optimizing the design involves selecting low-loss fibers, using high-quality amplifiers with low noise figures, implementing proper dispersion management, and ensuring optimal power levels. These measures help maintain high OSNR, ensuring reliable communication.

357. What are the common methods for improving OSNR in an existing optical link?

Common methods include adding optical amplifiers, using dispersion compensation, upgrading to lower-loss fibers, and optimizing power levels. Regular maintenance and monitoring help identify areas for improvement and maintain high OSNR.

358. Describe the impact of amplifier noise figure on OSNR and system performance.

The noise figure of an amplifier indicates the amount of noise added to the signal during amplification. A lower noise figure results in higher OSNR, improving system performance. Amplifiers with noise figures below 5 dB are typically preferred for high-performance optical links.

359. How does wavelength division multiplexing (WDM) affect OSNR and BER?

WDM can affect OSNR and BER by introducing crosstalk and non-linear effects between closely spaced channels. Proper channel spacing, power management, and high-quality components help minimize these effects, maintaining high OSNR and low BER.

360. What role does forward error correction (FEC) play in improving BER?

FEC adds redundant data to the transmitted signal, allowing the receiver to detect and correct errors. This improves BER by several orders of magnitude, enhancing the reliability of optical communication. Common FEC schemes include Reed-Solomon and BCH codes.

361. Explain the importance of real-time OSNR monitoring in optical networks.

Real-time OSNR monitoring helps detect and address issues promptly, maintaining optimal system performance. It allows for proactive maintenance and adjustments, preventing degradation of signal quality and ensuring reliable communication.

362. What are the typical OSNR requirements for different modulation formats (e.g., NRZ, QPSK, 16-QAM)?

Typical OSNR requirements vary by modulation format. For NRZ, OSNR requirements are around 20 dB. For QPSK, they are around 15-20 dB, and for higher-order formats like 16-QAM, OSNR requirements can be 25 dB or higher. Higher-order modulation formats require higher OSNR due to their increased sensitivity to noise.

363. How do environmental factors, such as temperature, affect OSNR and BER?

Environmental factors can cause fluctuations in fiber attenuation and component performance, affecting OSNR and BER. Temperature changes can alter the refractive index of fibers and the behavior of amplifiers, leading to variations in signal quality. Proper environmental controls and robust design mitigate these effects.

364. Describe the process of conducting an OSNR test using an optical spectrum analyzer (OSA).

Conducting an OSNR test with an OSA involves connecting the OSA to the optical link, setting the resolution bandwidth, and measuring the power levels of the signal and noise at the desired wavelength. The OSNR is calculated as the ratio of the signal power to the noise power within the same bandwidth, typically expressed in dB.

365. What are the challenges of maintaining high OSNR in long-haul optical links?

Challenges include managing fiber attenuation, amplifier noise, dispersion, and non-linear effects over long distances. Regular placement of low-noise amplifiers, effective dispersion compensation, and careful power management are essential to maintain high OSNR in long-haul links.

366. How do you assess the impact of non-linear effects on OSNR and Q-factor in high-power optical links?

Assessing the impact involves simulating and measuring the link performance under different power levels, identifying non-linear effects like SPM and FWM. Analyzing the changes in OSNR and Q-factor helps determine the optimal power levels and mitigation strategies to minimize non-linear impact.

367. What is the role of Q-factor in evaluating the performance of an optical receiver?

The Q-factor evaluates the receiver's ability to distinguish between different signal levels, indicating signal quality and noise levels. A high Q-factor means the receiver can accurately detect and decode the signal, resulting in a lower BER and better overall performance.

368. Explain the relationship between OSNR and modulation format for achieving low BER.

Different modulation formats have varying OSNR requirements for achieving low BER. Higher-order modulation formats (e.g., 16-QAM) are more sensitive to noise and require higher OSNR to maintain low BER, while simpler formats (e.g., NRZ) can achieve low BER with lower OSNR. Choosing the appropriate modulation format based on the available OSNR is crucial for reliable communication.

369. How do you use OSNR measurements to optimize the placement of optical amplifiers?

OSNR measurements help determine the optimal intervals for placing amplifiers to ensure the signal remains above the noise floor. By monitoring OSNR along the link, amplifiers can be placed at points where the signal begins to degrade, maintaining high OSNR and reliable performance throughout the link.

370. What are the industry standards and thresholds for OSNR, Q-factor, and BER in optical communication?

Industry standards and thresholds vary depending on the application and modulation format. For example, ITU-T G.694.1 specifies OSNR requirements for DWDM systems, with typical OSNR thresholds around 20-25 dB for high-speed links. Q-factor thresholds are usually above 6 for acceptable performance, and BER thresholds are typically 10^-12 or lower for reliable communication. Compliance with these standards ensures interoperability and high performance in optical networks.

371. What is the noise figure (NF) in optical amplifiers, and why is it important?

The noise figure (NF) is a measure of the noise added by an amplifier relative to an ideal noiseless amplifier. It is expressed in dB and is crucial because a lower NF indicates better amplifier performance, contributing to a higher OSNR and better overall signal quality in optical communication systems.

372. How is the noise figure of an EDFA calculated?

The noise figure of an EDFA is calculated using the formula: NF = 10 * $\log_{10}$((SNR_in / SNR_out)), where SNR_in is the signal-to-noise ratio at the input and SNR_out is the signal-to-noise ratio at the output. EDFAs typically have noise figures between 4 and 6 dB.

373. What factors affect the noise figure of an EDFA?

Factors affecting the noise figure of an EDFA include the pump wavelength, pump power, erbium ion concentration, the length of the doped fiber, and the design of the amplifier (e.g., single-stage or double-stage). Higher pump power and optimized erbium concentration can help minimize the NF.

374. Describe the impact of the noise figure on the performance of a DWDM system using EDFAs.

In a DWDM system, a lower noise figure of EDFAs results in a higher OSNR for each channel, improving the overall signal quality and reducing the BER. This is particularly important for long-haul transmission, where multiple amplifiers are used, as the noise accumulates with each amplification stage.

375. How do Raman amplifiers differ from EDFAs in terms of noise figure?

Raman amplifiers typically have a lower noise figure compared to EDFAs because the amplification occurs within the transmission fiber itself, reducing the amount of noise added. Raman amplifiers can achieve noise figures around 2-3 dB, making them suitable for applications requiring low noise and high OSNR.

376. What are the key design considerations to minimize the noise figure in Raman amplifiers?

Key design considerations include optimizing the pump wavelength and power, using backward pumping to reduce signal noise interaction, and selecting the appropriate fiber type and length for efficient Raman scattering. Careful design and optimization can help achieve a low noise figure and high performance.

377. Explain the role of noise figure in hybrid amplifiers (EDFA-Raman).

In hybrid amplifiers, combining EDFA and Raman amplification can result in a lower overall noise figure compared to using EDFAs alone. The Raman amplifier provides low-noise amplification, while the EDFA boosts the signal power further. This combination enhances OSNR and extends transmission distances with lower noise accumulation.

378. How does the noise figure of an optical pre-amplifier affect receiver sensitivity?

The noise figure of an optical pre-amplifier directly impacts receiver sensitivity. A lower noise figure improves the OSNR at the receiver, allowing the receiver to detect weaker signals with lower error rates. This enhances the overall sensitivity and performance of the optical communication system.

379. What are the typical noise figure values for semiconductor optical amplifiers (SOAs)?

Semiconductor optical amplifiers (SOAs) generally have higher noise figures compared to EDFAs and Raman amplifiers, typically ranging from 5 to 10 dB. This higher NF is due to the inherent noise generated by the semiconductor materials and the amplification process.

380. Describe the methods used to measure the noise figure of optical amplifiers.

The noise figure of optical amplifiers is measured using the optical spectrum analyzer (OSA) method or the electrical method. The OSA method involves measuring the signal and noise power levels at the input and output of the amplifier. The electrical method involves converting the optical signal to an electrical signal and measuring the SNR before and after amplification.

381. How does temperature affect the noise figure of optical amplifiers?

Temperature variations can impact the noise figure of optical amplifiers by affecting the gain medium and pump laser performance. Higher temperatures can increase the noise figure by introducing additional thermal noise and reducing the efficiency of the gain medium. Temperature stabilization techniques are essential to maintain a consistent NF.

382. What is the impact of noise figure on the OSNR in a cascaded amplifier system?

In a cascaded amplifier system, the noise figure of each amplifier stage contributes to the overall OSNR degradation. A higher NF in any stage results in a lower OSNR at the system output. Minimizing the noise figure at each stage is crucial to maintain a high OSNR and reliable performance across the entire link.

383. Explain the relationship between gain and noise figure in optical amplifiers.

There is a trade-off between gain and noise figure in optical amplifiers. While increasing the gain improves signal strength, it can also amplify the noise, potentially increasing the NF. Optimizing the gain to achieve the desired signal power without significantly increasing the noise is essential for maintaining a low NF.

384. How does the design of erbium-doped fiber affect the noise figure of an EDFA?

The design of erbium-doped fiber, including the concentration of erbium ions and the length of the doped section, affects the noise figure of an EDFA. Higher erbium concentration and optimized fiber length can improve the amplifier's efficiency and reduce the NF. However, excessive doping can lead to increased noise and reduced performance.

385. What are the advancements in optical amplifier technology aimed at reducing the noise figure?

Advancements include the development of low-noise pump lasers, optimized erbium-doped fibers, advanced Raman scattering techniques, and hybrid amplifier designs. These innovations aim to reduce the NF, enhance OSNR, and improve the overall performance and reliability of optical communication systems.

Appendices

Bibliography and References

Books

1. Keiser, G. (2010). *Optical Fiber Communications*. McGraw-Hill Education.

2. Agrawal, G. P. (2012). *Fiber-Optic Communication Systems*. Wiley.

3. Ramaswami, R., Sivarajan, K. N., & Sasaki, G. H. (2009). *Optical Networks: A Practical Perspective*. Morgan Kaufmann.

Journals and Articles

1. Winzer, P. J. (2017). "Scaling Optical Fiber Networks: Challenges and Solutions." *Optics and Photonics News*.

2. Essiambre, R.-J., & Tkach, R. W. (2012). "Capacity Trends and Limits of Optical Communication Networks." *Proceedings of the IEEE*.

Industry Reports

1. Cisco Systems. (2020). *Cisco Annual Internet Report (2018–2023)*. Retrieved from Cisco.

2. Dell'Oro Group. (2021). *Optical Transport Market 5-Year Forecast Report*.

Standards and Specifications

1. ITU-T Recommendation G.652: *Characteristics of a single-mode optical fibre and cable*. International Telecommunication Union.

2. IEEE 802.3: *Ethernet Standards*. Institute of Electrical and Electronics Engineers.

Websites and Online Resources

1. *Light Reading*. (2021). "The Future of Optical Networks: Key Trends and Technologies." Retrieved from Light Reading.

2. *Optical Society of America (OSA)*. (2020). "Optical Fiber Communication Conference (OFC) Proceedings." Retrieved from OSA Publishing.

3. MapYourTech.com https://mapyourtech.com/

Optical Networking Acronyms and Definitions

Transmission and Multiplexing

- **WDM** (Wavelength Division Multiplexing): Technology that combines multiple optical signals on a single fiber by using different wavelengths of laser light
- **DWDM** (Dense Wavelength Division Multiplexing): Advanced form of WDM that enables even more channels to be multiplexed on a single fiber
- **CWDM** (Coarse Wavelength Division Multiplexing): Form of WDM with wider channel spacing and fewer channels than DWDM
- **TDM** (Time Division Multiplexing): Method of transmitting multiple digital signals over a single channel by dividing time into discrete intervals
- **OTDM** (Optical Time Division Multiplexing): Implementation of TDM in the optical domain

Network Components and Equipment

- **OLT** (Optical Line Terminal): Equipment that serves as the service provider endpoint of a PON
- **ONU** (Optical Network Unit): Device that converts optical signals to electrical signals at the customer premises
- **ONT** (Optical Network Terminal): Similar to ONU, specifically used in FTTH applications
- **ROADM** (Reconfigurable Optical Add-Drop Multiplexer): Device that can add, block, pass or redirect wavelength channels
- **OXC** (Optical Cross Connect): Device that switches high-speed optical signals in a network
- **OA** (Optical Amplifier): Device that amplifies optical signals directly without conversion to electrical signals
- **EDFA** (Erbium Doped Fiber Amplifier): Type of optical amplifier using erbium-doped fiber

Network Architectures and Protocols

- **PON** (Passive Optical Network): Point-to-multipoint network architecture using unpowered optical splitters
- **GPON** (Gigabit Passive Optical Network): PON standard supporting higher rates, up to 2.488 Gbps downstream
- **EPON** (Ethernet Passive Optical Network): PON standard based on Ethernet protocols

- **XG-PON** (10-Gigabit Passive Optical Network): PON standard supporting 10 Gbps downstream
- **APON** (ATM Passive Optical Network): Original PON standard based on ATM technology
- **BPON** (Broadband Passive Optical Network): Enhanced version of APON
- **NG-PON2** (Next-Generation Passive Optical Network 2): Latest PON standard supporting multiple wavelengths

Fiber Types and Infrastructure

- **SMF** (Single Mode Fiber): Optical fiber that carries light only directly down the fiber axis
- **MMF** (Multi Mode Fiber): Optical fiber that carries multiple light modes
- **DCF** (Dispersion Compensating Fiber): Special fiber used to compensate for chromatic dispersion
- **DSF** (Dispersion Shifted Fiber): Fiber with modified dispersion characteristics
- **NZDSF** (Non-Zero Dispersion Shifted Fiber): Fiber with small but non-zero dispersion at 1550nm

Performance and Monitoring

- **OSNR** (Optical Signal-to-Noise Ratio): Measure of the ratio of signal power to noise power in an optical channel
- **BER** (Bit Error Rate): Ratio of bit errors to total transmitted bits
- **PMD** (Polarization Mode Dispersion): Form of modal dispersion where two different polarizations travel at different speeds
- **CD** (Chromatic Dispersion): Variation in the speed of light in a fiber based on wavelength
- **OPM** (Optical Performance Monitoring): Continuous monitoring of optical signal quality
- **OTDR** (Optical Time Domain Reflectometer): Instrument used to characterize optical fiber

Network Services and Applications

- **FTTH** (Fiber to the Home): Fiber optic cable connection directly to the home
- **FTTB** (Fiber to the Building): Fiber optic cable connection to a building
- **FTTC** (Fiber to the Curb): Fiber optic cable connection to the curb near homes
- **FTTN** (Fiber to the Node): Fiber optic cable connection to a street cabinet

- **OTN** (Optical Transport Network): Standard for encapsulating and transporting various client signals
- **SDH** (Synchronous Digital Hierarchy): International standard for high-speed telecommunications transport
- **SONET** (Synchronous Optical Network): American standard for high-speed telecommunications transport

Protection and Restoration

- **OLP** (Optical Line Protection): Mechanism to protect against fiber cuts and equipment failures
- **OSPF** (Open Shortest Path First): Routing protocol often used in optical networks
- **UPSR** (Unidirectional Path Switched Ring): SONET ring architecture providing path protection
- **BLSR** (Bidirectional Line Switched Ring): SONET ring architecture providing line protection

Signal Processing and Modulation

- **DSP** (Digital Signal Processing): Electronic processing of digital signals for improved transmission quality
- **FEC** (Forward Error Correction): Technique to control errors in data transmission
- **NRZ** (Non-Return to Zero): Basic digital modulation format
- **RZ** (Return to Zero): Modulation format where signal returns to zero between bits
- **QAM** (Quadrature Amplitude Modulation): Advanced modulation technique using both amplitude and phase
- **QPSK** (Quadrature Phase Shift Keying): Digital modulation scheme using phase variations
- **PAM4** (4-level Pulse Amplitude Modulation): Modulation scheme using four distinct amplitude levels

Testing and Measurement

- **OSA** (Optical Spectrum Analyzer): Device for measuring optical power vs wavelength
- **BMP** (Bit Error Rate Test Pattern): Specific pattern used for testing error rates
- **EVM** (Error Vector Magnitude): Measure of digital modulation quality

- **PRBS** (Pseudo-Random Bit Sequence): Test pattern for system evaluation
- **VOA** (Variable Optical Attenuator): Device for adjusting optical power levels
- **PDL** (Polarization Dependent Loss): Power variation due to polarization changes
- **WDL** (Wavelength Dependent Loss): Power variation across wavelengths

Network Management and Control

- **SDN** (Software Defined Networking): Approach to network management that enables dynamic adjustment
- **NFV** (Network Function Virtualization): Virtualization of network node functions
- **NMS** (Network Management System): System for managing network components
- **EMS** (Element Management System): System for managing individual network elements
- **API** (Application Programming Interface): Interface for controlling network elements
- **YANG** (Yet Another Next Generation): Data modeling language for network configuration
- **NETCONF** (Network Configuration Protocol): Protocol for network device configuration

Advanced Technologies

- **CDR** (Clock and Data Recovery): Circuit for extracting timing from received data
- **PIC** (Photonic Integrated Circuit): Integration of multiple photonic functions
- **SOA** (Semiconductor Optical Amplifier): Amplifier based on semiconductor gain medium
- **MEMS** (Micro-Electro-Mechanical Systems): Tiny mechanical devices in optical systems
- **WSS** (Wavelength Selective Switch): Device for routing specific wavelengths
- **PLC** (Planar Lightwave Circuit): Optical circuit fabricated on flat substrate
- **SiP** (Silicon Photonics): Integration of optical components in silicon

Quality of Service and Standards

- **QoS** (Quality of Service): Performance level of a telecommunications service

- **SLA** (Service Level Agreement): Guaranteed service performance metrics
- **ITU-T** (International Telecommunication Union - Telecommunication): Standards body
- **IEEE** (Institute of Electrical and Electronics Engineers): Professional organization setting standards
- **TIA** (Telecommunications Industry Association): Standards organization
- **MEF** (Metro Ethernet Forum): Industry alliance defining carrier ethernet standards

Emerging Technologies

- **SDM** (Space Division Multiplexing): Using multiple spatial channels for transmission
- **MCF** (Multi-Core Fiber): Fiber containing multiple cores for parallel transmission
- **FMF** (Few-Mode Fiber): Fiber supporting a small number of guided modes
- **QKD** (Quantum Key Distribution): Secure communication using quantum properties
- **AO** (All-Optical): Systems operating entirely in the optical domain
- **IoT** (Internet of Things): Network of connected devices and sensors
- **5G** (Fifth Generation): Latest mobile network technology often using optical backhaul

Network Security and Encryption

- **OPU** (Optical Payload Unit): Container for client signals in OTN
- **ODU** (Optical Data Unit): Digital container in OTN hierarchy
- **OTU** (Optical Transport Unit): Basic frame format in OTN
- **TPD** (Transponder): Device converting between different optical formats
- **OPS** (Optical Packet Switching): Switching of optical packets
- **OBS** (Optical Burst Switching): Switching of optical bursts
- **OCh** (Optical Channel): Single wavelength channel in a WDM system

Data Center Optics

- **PSM4** (Parallel Single Mode 4-lane): Four-lane parallel optical interface
- **CWDM4** (Coarse WDM 4-lane): Four-wavelength CWDM interface
- **SR4** (Short Reach 4-lane): Short-reach parallel multimode interface
- **DR4** (Data Center Reach 4-lane): Single-mode parallel interface for data centers

- **FR4** (Facility Reach 4-lane): Extended reach data center interface
- **AOC** (Active Optical Cable): Cable with integrated optical transceivers
- **DAC** (Direct Attach Cable): Copper cable for short connections

Transceiver Technology

- **SFP** (Small Form-factor Pluggable): Common transceiver form factor
- **SFP+** (Enhanced Small Form-factor Pluggable): 10G version of SFP
- **QSFP** (Quad Small Form-factor Pluggable): Four-channel transceiver
- **QSFP28** (28Gbps Quad Small Form-factor Pluggable): 100G version of QSFP
- **OSFP** (Octal Small Form-factor Pluggable): Eight-channel transceiver
- **CFP** (C Form-factor Pluggable): Larger form factor for high-speed interfaces
- **DSFP** (Dual Small Form-factor Pluggable): Dual-channel transceiver

Advanced Transmission Techniques

- **PDM** (Polarization Division Multiplexing): Multiplexing using different polarizations
- **CoWDM** (Coherent Wavelength Division Multiplexing): Advanced coherent WDM
- **OCDM** (Optical Code Division Multiplexing): Multiplexing using optical codes
- **SCM** (Subcarrier Multiplexing): Multiple signals on RF subcarriers
- **FDM** (Frequency Division Multiplexing): Multiple signals at different frequencies
- **CDM** (Code Division Multiplexing): Multiple signals using different codes
- **MDM** (Mode Division Multiplexing): Multiplexing using different fiber modes

Coherent Systems

- **CDC** (Colorless, Directionless, Contentionless): Advanced ROADM functionality
- **IQ** (In-phase and Quadrature): Components of complex modulation
- **LO** (Local Oscillator): Reference signal in coherent detection
- **ICR** (Integrated Coherent Receiver): Receiver for coherent signals
- **DSK** (Differential Shift Keying): Phase modulation technique
- **PMD** (Polarization Mode Dispersion): Dispersion due to polarization
- **DGD** (Differential Group Delay): Time delay between polarization modes

Network Synchronization

- **PTP** (Precision Time Protocol): Protocol for precise timing
- **SyncE** (Synchronous Ethernet): Ethernet with synchronization
- **PRC** (Primary Reference Clock): Master timing source
- **SSU** (Synchronization Supply Unit): Timing distribution unit
- **BITS** (Building Integrated Timing Supply): Facility timing system
- **GNSS** (Global Navigation Satellite System): Satellite-based timing
- **ToD** (Time of Day): Absolute time reference

Optical Layer Protection

- **OPS** (Optical Protection Switching): Protection at optical layer
- **OCh-P** (Optical Channel Protection): Protection of individual channels
- **OMS-P** (Optical Multiplex Section Protection): Protection of multiplexed signals
- **OTS-P** (Optical Transmission Section Protection): Protection of transmission section
- **SNCP** (SubNetwork Connection Protection): Path-level protection
- **MSP** (Multiplex Section Protection): Section-level protection
- **APS** (Automatic Protection Switching): Automated protection mechanism

Performance Monitoring and Management

- **OPM** (Optical Performance Monitor): Device monitoring optical signals
- **BDI** (Backward Defect Indication): Upstream fault indication
- **FDI** (Forward Defect Indication): Downstream fault indication
- **TCM** (Tandem Connection Monitoring): Monitoring of sub-paths
- **TTI** (Trail Trace Identifier): Path identification
- **PM** (Performance Monitoring): General performance tracking
- **OAM** (Operations, Administration, and Maintenance): Network management functions

Advanced Control Plane

- **GMPLS** (Generalized Multi-Protocol Label Switching): Control plane protocol
- **PCE** (Path Computation Element): Route calculation component
- **PCEP** (Path Computation Element Protocol): Protocol for path computation
- **BGP-LS** (Border Gateway Protocol-Link State): Topology distribution protocol
- **RSVP-TE** (Resource Reservation Protocol-Traffic Engineering): Resource reservation

- **OSPF-TE** (Open Shortest Path First-Traffic Engineering): Enhanced routing
- **UNI** (User Network Interface): Client-network interface

Quantum and Future Technologies

- **QC** (Quantum Communication): Communication using quantum effects
- **QKD** (Quantum Key Distribution): Quantum cryptography
- **QRNG** (Quantum Random Number Generator): Quantum-based randomization
- **AQC** (All-Quantum Communication): Full quantum network
- **QDL** (Quantum Dot Laser): Advanced laser technology
- **QCL** (Quantum Cascade Laser): Specialized semiconductor laser
- **QPIC** (Quantum Photonic Integrated Circuit): Quantum optical chip

Optical Amplification Technologies

- **EDFA** (Erbium-Doped Fiber Amplifier): Traditional optical amplifier
- **TDFA** (Thulium-Doped Fiber Amplifier): Amplifier for 2-micron band
- **YDFA** (Ytterbium-Doped Fiber Amplifier): Amplifier for 1-micron band
- **PDFA** (Praseodymium-Doped Fiber Amplifier): Amplifier for visible spectrum
- **RDFA** (Raman-Doped Fiber Amplifier): Distributed amplification
- **HDFA** (Hybrid-Doped Fiber Amplifier): Multiple dopant amplifier
- **PIFA** (Parametric Fiber Amplifier): Non-linear amplification

Advanced Modulation Formats

- **DP-QPSK** (Dual Polarization Quadrature Phase Shift Keying): Advanced phase modulation
- **QAM16** (16-state Quadrature Amplitude Modulation): 16-point constellation
- **QAM64** (64-state Quadrature Amplitude Modulation): 64-point constellation
- **PAM8** (8-level Pulse Amplitude Modulation): 8-level amplitude modulation
- **OFDM** (Optical Frequency Division Multiplexing): Multi-carrier modulation
- **CAP** (Carrierless Amplitude/Phase): Advanced modulation format
- **DMT** (Discrete Multi-Tone): Multi-carrier technique

Silicon Photonics Components

- **MRR** (Micro-Ring Resonator): Ring-shaped waveguide device
- **MMI** (Multi-Mode Interferometer): Beam splitter/combiner
- **AWG** (Arrayed Waveguide Grating): Wavelength multiplexer
- **MZI** (Mach-Zehnder Interferometer): Optical modulator structure
- **PDK** (Process Design Kit): Design tools for photonic chips
- **PIC** (Photonic Integrated Circuit): Integrated optical chip
- **EPIC** (Electronic-Photonic Integrated Circuit): Combined electronics and photonics

Space Division Multiplexing

- **MCF** (Multi-Core Fiber): Multiple cores in single fiber
- **FMF** (Few-Mode Fiber): Multiple modes for transmission
- **MMF** (Multi-Mode Fiber): Many modes in fiber
- **MIMO** (Multiple-Input Multiple-Output): Multiple path processing
- **MDM** (Mode Division Multiplexing): Mode-based multiplexing
- **CCM** (Core-to-Core Management): Multi-core control
- **MUX** (Modal Multiplexer): Mode combining device

Network Intelligence and Automation

- **ML** (Machine Learning): Automated learning systems
- **AI** (Artificial Intelligence): Intelligent network control
- **ANN** (Artificial Neural Network): Neural processing
- **DL** (Deep Learning): Advanced neural networks
- **RL** (Reinforcement Learning): Learning through feedback
- **CNN** (Convolutional Neural Network): Image processing network
- **RNN** (Recurrent Neural Network): Sequential data processing

Advanced Error Correction

- **SD-FEC** (Soft-Decision Forward Error Correction): Advanced error correction
- **HD-FEC** (Hard-Decision Forward Error Correction): Basic error correction
- **LDPC** (Low-Density Parity Check): Error correction code
- **BCH** (Bose-Chaudhuri-Hocquenghem): Error correction code
- **RS** (Reed-Solomon): Error correction algorithm
- **TC** (Turbo Code): Advanced error correction
- **PCC** (Polar Concatenated Code): Combined error correction

Next-Generation PON Technologies

- **25G-PON** (25 Gigabit PON): 25G symmetric PON
- **50G-PON** (50 Gigabit PON): Future PON standard
- **100G-PON** (100 Gigabit PON): Ultra-high speed PON

- **TWDM-PON** (Time Wavelength Division Multiplexed PON): Multi-wavelength PON
- **OFDM-PON** (Orthogonal Frequency Division Multiplexed PON): Advanced PON
- **UDWDM-PON** (Ultra-Dense WDM PON): Many wavelength PON
- **C-PON** (Coherent PON): Coherent detection PON

Optical Switching Technologies

- **WSS** (Wavelength Selective Switch): Wavelength routing
- **OXC** (Optical Cross Connect): Optical switching
- **MEMS** (Micro-Electro-Mechanical Systems): Mechanical switches
- **SOA** (Semiconductor Optical Amplifier): Gate switching
- **LCoS** (Liquid Crystal on Silicon): Liquid crystal switch
- **PXC** (Photonic Cross Connect): All-optical switching
- **OPS** (Optical Packet Switch): Packet-level switching

Network Telemetry and Analytics

- **INT** (In-band Network Telemetry): Network monitoring
- **TAP** (Test Access Point): Monitoring point
- **DPI** (Deep Packet Inspection): Packet analysis
- **NPB** (Network Packet Broker): Traffic management
- **APM** (Application Performance Monitoring): App monitoring
- **NTA** (Network Traffic Analytics): Traffic analysis
- **RPM** (Real-time Performance Monitoring): Live monitoring

Optical Security

- **PLS** (Physical Layer Security): Layer 1 security
- **OPE** (Optical Path Encryption): Path-level encryption
- **QPK** (Quantum Public Key): Quantum security
- **OKD** (Optical Key Distribution): Key distribution
- **PQC** (Post-Quantum Cryptography): Future-proof security
- **OTP** (One-Time Pad): Perfect encryption
- **CHE** (Chaotic Encryption): Chaos-based security

Conclusion

Optical networks form the backbone of modern communication systems, enabling high-speed data transmission over long distances. This book has aimed to provide comprehensive insights into the practical aspects of optical network communications, from fundamental principles to advanced technologies and design considerations. By leveraging the knowledge and guidelines presented, engineers and professionals can contribute to the development and optimization of robust, efficient, and scalable optical networks.All the content are meant to provide practical insights and aspects of it which is needed for engineers to excel in optical networking communications world.I have left some of theoretical information for readers to explore from my website or from great books written by great authors and focussed on the information that can provide practical insights.

About the Author

Meet Sanjay Yadav, an avid Optical Networking Professional with nearly two decades of experience across a wide range of optical networking technologies. Sanjay's expertise spans product and service development, network design and operations, automation, and tooling.

Having worked in technical support, customer service, system engineering, and software testing for various optical terrestrial, submarine, and DCI vendors, Sanjay brings a wealth of knowledge to the field. He specializes in software development and creating automation tools to solve complex networking challenges.

With a passion for sharing knowledge and exploring new technology, Sanjay strongly believes in the concept of 'Share, Explore, and Inspire with the Tech Inside You!' He has been sharing his industry learnings since 2011, having written multiple technical articles and blogs for major industry leaders in both terrestrial and submarine optical fiber space.

You can check out Sanjay's work at www.mapyourtech.com. For feedback or to connect with him directly, email feedback@mapyourtech.com or visit his LinkedIn profile at https://www.linkedin.com/in/mapyourtech/.

www.ingramcontent.com/pod-product-compliance
Lightning Source LLC
LaVergne TN
LVHW052209200926
848481LV00001B/64

* 9 7 9 8 2 3 0 6 3 6 4 3 4 *